PARIS

La Patrie, *The Motherland, dominates François Rude's stirring relief on the Arc de Triomphe*

PARIS

Vivienne Menkes-Ivry

Photographs by Joe Cornish

PASSPORT BOOKS
a division of *NTC Publishing Group*

PASSPORT'S REGIONAL GUIDES OF FRANCE

Series Editor: Arthur Eperon

Auvergne and the Massif Central
Rex Grizell

Brittany
Frank Dawes

The Dordogne and Lot
Arthur and Barbara Eperon

Languedoc and Roussillon
Andrew Sanger

The Loire Valley
Arthur and Barbara Eperon

Normandy, Picardy and Pas de Calais
Barbara Eperon

Paris
Vivienne Menkes-Ivry

Provence and the Côte d'Azur
Roger Macdonald

The Rhône Valley and Savoy
Rex Grizell

South West France
Andrew Sanger

In memory of my husband Jean Ivry,
a seven-generations Parisian

This edition first published in 1991 by Passport Books,
a division of NTC Publishing Group, 4255 West
Touhy Avenue, Lincolnwood (Chicago), Illinois
60646-1975 U.S.A. Originally published by
Christopher Helm (Publishers) Ltd., a subsidiary of
A & C Black (Publishers) Ltd., 35 Bedford Row,
London, England.
Copyright © Vivienne Menkes-Ivry.
Photographs by Joe Cornish.
Métro map reproduced courtesy of RATP.

Although great care was taken in the preparation of
this book, it is impossible, in an era of rapid change,
to ensure that the information in it remains up to
date. The author and publishers cannot accept
responsibility for inaccuracies, but they welcome
suggestions from readers for amendments.

Printed and bound in Singapore

Contents

Acknowledgements

With thanks for their help and encouragement to Marie-Françoise Cachin, Claude Combet, Nathalie Corbasson and Danièle Denis in Paris, my mother and sister and my agent Barbara Levy in London; to Yves, Georgette and Laurence Poupon for their hospitality; to Alison Starling and Darina Williams at Christopher Helm for their interest.

Introduction

Much of Paris has changed out of all recognition in recent years. A whole series of major new museums have opened since the mid-eighties: the Musée Picasso in a superbly restored mansion in the Marais; the Musée d'Orsay, focusing on late 19th-century and early 20th-century art, in a converted railway station; the Cité des Sciences et de l'Industrie, a science museum with a difference, on the site of the old slaughterhouses; a whole new wing for the Musée Carnavalet. A gleaming glass pyramid has been erected, in a fanfare of publicity, in the Cour Napoléon of the Louvre – 85 per cent of whose exhibits will have been moved and redisplayed by 1995. A gigantic arch has appeared at the end of the 'Triumphal Way' on the city's western outskirts, big enough for the cathedral of Notre Dame to fit snugly inside it. A multi-purpose sports and cultural centre, the Palais Omnisports de Bercy, has sprung up beside the Seine. On the other side of the river the wine market built by Napoleon has given way to a centre for Arab art and culture. And futuristic plans have been approved for a new national library on a site further down the river.

The bicentenary of the storming of the Bastille in July 1789 was celebrated with the official opening of a new 'people's opera house' close to where the infamous prison stood. The colourful 'belly of Paris', Zola's term for Les Halles, the centuries-old food market in the centre of the city, has been replaced by well-tended gardens, a sleek glass and concrete shopping and leisure centre, an aquarium, various cinemas and much else besides. The slaughterhouses in the south are now a large park. And all these schemes are displayed and explained in the Pavillon de l'Arsenal, a new town-planning and environment centre open to the public.

Millions of francs have been poured into these and other *grands projets*, as they are known. And what is perhaps the most ambitious scheme of all is already under way: a righting of the east–west imbalance, which has traditionally seen the better-off living in the centre or the west of Paris, while the eastern districts have been mostly working-class and in recent years have absorbed most of the influx of immigrants from North Africa, Black Africa and the Caribbean.

More impressive than any of this, perhaps, is the way the quality of life has been improved. Everywhere dusty little squares have been smartened up, decked with statues and trees, neatly fenced-off strips of lawn, tubs overflowing with flowers, benches and lamp standards in traditional designs. Traffic has been

1

White globe lamps in decorative wrought-iron holders are a feature of many a Paris square

banished from streets and squares and underground car parks have eased some of the parking problems. Swimming pools and gyms, crèches and well-stocked libraries have sprouted in each *arrondissement*. Perhaps most important of all for the city's image, and for the pleasure of visitor and inhabitant alike, the streets are cleaned daily, by employees in smart uniforms wielding matching brooms, opening the traditional sluices to keep the gutters from clogging up and driving efficient contraptions that sprinkle and sweep simultaneously. Public transport is clean, modern and mostly fast, and prices are reasonable.

All this may sound too good to be true, but there is no doubt that whereas a couple of decades ago inefficiency and squalor – picturesque squalor, but squalor none the less – were commonplace, Paris is now manifestly a city that works, that is pleasant as well as stimulating to visit.

Paris Art Nouveau

One of the familiar sights of Paris is the elegant métro entrances designed by the art nouveau architect Hector Guimard (1867–1942). With their greyish-green paint, the sinuous lines of their decoration and the arching tulip-shaped lamps seeming to sway gently on the end of their cast-iron stems, they symbolise the confidence of the Railway Era and the Exposition Universelle of 1900 – the first métro station was opened to coincide with the fair.

Guimard soon became world-famous, though the métro entrances were unpopular with Parisians (among other things the colour was branded as 'German' only thirty years after the Franco-Prussian War) and were condemned by conformist academicians. By 1904 his various designs were already being replaced by much duller entrances, and many have been demolished. But you can still see some good examples, in the place des Ternes for instance, and on the Ile de la Cité (Ⓜ Ternes and Cité). And Guimard's glass canopies with a scalloped edge over full-scale entrance pavilions that used to adorn many stations have survived in just two places: the Porte Dauphine on the edge of the Bois de Boulogne and in the place des Abbesses in Montmartre, though this one was originally in front of the Hôtel de Ville. (Ⓜ Porte Dauphine and Abbesses)

Lovers of art nouveau (which is oddly called *modern style* in French – or *style nouille*, 'spaghetti style', by its detractors) should visit the rue La Fontaine and the surrounding streets in the 16th *arrondissement*, where Guimard built a series of houses between about 1895 and 1910. The best known is the **Castel Béranger** at 14 rue La Fontaine, for which Guimard also designed the furniture and even some of the kitchen equipment. Other examples of his work can be seen at nos 17–21 and at no. 60 (**Hôtel Mezzara**) and in the rue François-Millet, at no. 11. At 122 avenue Mozart is the house Guimard designed for himself. Guided walks round this part of Paris are organised by the Caisse Nationale des Monuments Historiques (see Practical Information). A synagogue by Guimard can be visited at 10 rue Pavée, 4e, and there are interesting examples of art nouveau design in the Musée des Arts décoratifs and the Musée d'Orsay.

But perhaps the best of Paris art nouveau is to be found in a handful of celebrated turn-of-the-century restaurants, many of them listed buildings. **Maxim's** in the rue Royale, 8e and, just round the corner in the place de la Madeleine, **Lucas-Carton**, designed by the famous cabinet-maker Louis Majorelle, are well beyond the pocket of the average visitor; so is **Le Grand Véfour*** at the northern end of the Palais Royal gardens. But **Julien***, at 16 rue du fbg Saint-Denis, 10e, the **Brasserie Bofinger*** in the place de la Bastille, 4e, and **Vagénende** at 142 blvd Saint-Germain, 6e are more affordable. And in the rue Marbeuf, 8e, just off the Champs-Elysées, you can rejoice over the chance discovery a few years ago of genuine art nouveau décor beneath later cladding in the rear dining room of the lively **Fermette Marbeuf***.

Incidentally, Guimard died in New York, having emigrated to the United States in 1938, worried for the safety of his Jewish wife, the American painter Adeline Oppenheim. He had been world-famous in his twenties, but his death, long before art nouveau became fashionable again, went completely unremarked.

The Wallace Fountains — and Other Watery Delights

The green cast-iron drinking fountains that are an immediately recognisable feature of Paris, with their elegantly draped ladies holding aloft a scaly dome topped with dolphins, were a gift to the city from Sir Richard Wallace, whose paintings and *objets d'art* form the basis of the Wallace Collection in London. He had a town house at 25 rue Taitbout near the Opéra, and lived for a while in the pretty château in the Bagatelle gardens on the edge of the Bois de Boulogne. His name is commemorated in the boulevard running to the north of the parc de Bagatelle. He was the illegitimate son of the Marquis of Hertford — from whom he inherited much of his collection — and founded the British Hertford Hospital in the Paris suburb of Levallois in his memory. He also built St George's Anglican Church in the rue Auguste-Vacquerie close to the avenue d'Iéna, much frequented by the British community.

The story goes that after being charged for a glass of water in a Paris café he decided it was quite wrong for the citizens of a major European capital not to have free access to drinking water. So he donated the fountains, which originally had a metal beaker on the end of a chain. There are only a few survivors of the original fifty (some say a hundred) but some replicas have been made to adorn the traffic-free squares that are a common feature of Paris today. The most-photographed of the originals is probably the one in the picturesque place Emile-Goudeau in Montmartre (Walk 10).

Among the most attractive of the city's many ornamental fountains are the **Fontaine de l'Observatoire** (Walk 3), with its dolphins and rearing horses, the Renaissance **Fontaine des Innocents** besides Les Halles (Walk 8), the **Fontaine Molière** near the Comédie française (Walk 6) and the romantic **Fontaine Médicis** in the Luxembourg Gardens (Walk 3).

The tradition of commissioning fountains to adorn the city's squares is still alive and well. Interesting modern examples are the curious 'Blockage' in the heart of Saint-Germain-des-Prés (Walk 3), the centrepiece of Ricardo Bofill's place de Catalogne behind the Gare Montparnasse (again Walk 3) and the fountain near the new Bercy sports and leisure centre, which looks oddly like elephants' feet.

For sparkling displays of jets of water leaping into the air you have a choice between the gardens sloping down from the Trocadéro to the Seine (Walk 5), the place de la Concorde (Walk 6), the place de l'Hôtel-de-Ville (Walk 8) and the ornamental pools round the Louvre Pyramid (Walk 6), all of which are lit up at night for most of the year, at least at weekends.

What hasn't changed though is the eternal charm of Paris — a cliché of course, but like most clichés, it has a good deal of truth in it. Charm really is the word that seems most appropriate as you stroll round pretty little squares, past stylish window displays in old shop windows, admire the traditional green Wallace fountains and the art nouveau métro entrances, eat in bistrots with lacy curtains on brass rods. All these seem to have their own special charm that cancels out the irritations of big city living. Of course Paris, like any other modern metropolis, has traffic jams and ugly slabs of buildings. But they generally seem less obtrusive here. Of course there are muggings and layabouts and tramps and the other inevitable other-sides-of-the-coin of any seemingly prosperous capital. But they too impinge less on one's consciousness.

When I moved to Paris I felt sure that the charm that had never failed to exercise its magic on me during countless short visits would dissipate — as I got caught up in the daily grind of getting around, battling my way through the bureaucracy that bedevils many aspects of life in France, doing the boring shopping for screws and paperclips, soap powder and potting compost, rather than the fun shopping in boutiques and flower markets that goes with holidays or odd hours snatched from business trips. And yet, somehow, it never happened. The charm never vanished for long, it soon bobbed up again to distract me from an irritating journey or a bad-tempered exchange with a post office clerk. And now that I no longer live there but am merely a visitor, albeit a very frequent one, I understand only too well why my husband, a Parisian with seven generations of Parisians behind him, always felt an exile when his work forced him to live elsewhere. True Parisians are deeply attached to their city in the way that citizens of other places are attached to their country.

I hope that this book will help you to experience some of the charm you might otherwise miss, that is all the better for being hidden unless you know where to look. The walks it describes take you to the main sights, but they also suggest little detours to see a pretty shop front or a graceful fountain, recommend unusual ways of approaching well-known buildings, and point out little details that might go undetected.

I am firmly convinced that the best way to visit most of Paris is on foot. The excellent public transport system is invaluable for outlying districts and nearby towns like Versailles or Saint-Denis. But in the centre, where distances are not great, you will see far more and get much more out of your visit if you are walking. A word of warning, however: the long, straight avenues and the grandiose vistas that have been characteristic of many districts since the city was extensively rebuilt in the 1850s and 1860s can be deceptive. It is only too easy to think it will take only a few minutes to walk from, say, the Comédie française to the Opéra: in fact they are quite a long way apart. And anyone who sets out to walk from the place de la Concorde to the Arc de Triomphe will soon discover that it takes a good half-hour. I say this not to discourage you from walking, but to make sure that you leave enough time as appropriate. The section called 'Practical Information' gives further hints to help you enjoy and get the most out of your visit.

V. M.-I., Spring 1990

About This Book

The section providing practical information about Paris is designed to enable you to prepare your visit and to ensure that you don't waste time when you get there on sorting out the practicalities of daily life. A short chapter on the food and drink you can expect to find in Paris and a chronological table serve as an introduction to the main body of the book: a series of ten suggested walks covering the main sights and places of interest, with brief comments on side trips to places off the main route for those intrepid visitors with time to indulge their thirst for lesser-known districts and sights. A map of the city (on pp. 8–9) shows the areas covered by the walks.

I have not attempted to suggest the length of time each walk will take. I personally find that a suggested time makes me feel guilty if I am not keeping up to schedule, discourages enjoyable dawdling, and makes the whole thing seem like an exam or endurance test rather than a pleasure. Anyway, so much depends on your own interests: on how long you spend in museums or churches, whether – as I hope you will – you stop from time to time to stand and stare or watch the world go by from a café terrace or a bench in a peaceful square (I have suggested some good vantage points), whether you want to enjoy a full meal at lunchtime or simply stop off for a sandwich or picnic (again, I have suggested places for doing all of these). For those with limited time walks can be joined in the middle at some suitable point: I have indicated métro stations (in brackets with the symbol Ⓜ or ⓜ) at intervals to enable you to do so if it is more convenient.

With the exception of Walk 10, covering Montmartre and Pigalle, each walk starts off roughly where the previous walk ended. It is therefore easy to combine two walks and to break them up into different sections if this suits you better.

After each description of the walk you will find three lists: of suggested hotels to stay in within the same area as that covered by the walk; of restaurants; and of museums and places of interest described in them.

I make no pretence of having provided exhaustive lists of hotels and restaurants at the end of each chapter. I have merely made a few suggestions for places that I believe will appeal to readers of this book. The majority of the hotels are pleasant but unelaborate places with a Parisian atmosphere where you will be made to feel welcome. A few more modest (and therefore less expensive) hotels are included, along with one or two more expensive ones for that special weekend break or celebration. The lists are not equal in length: the Left Bank is the area *par excellence* for hotels of the type I have described, so you will find longer lists for those chapters (for further details see Practical Information).

The same applies to restaurants. For instance, while you will need some lunch suggestions if you are visiting the Père-Lachaise cemetery, you are less likely to be spending the evening in this part of eastern Paris. Conversely, you may well decide to eat in the livelier Latin Quarter or Saint-Germain-des-Prés even if you have just completed a walk through another district, so the lists here are again longer. With very few exceptions, I have concentrated on restaurants serving French cuisine, since like many visitors to France you may well have come at least partly for the food. The 'Food and Drink' chapter gives some suggestions for interesting tea rooms and wine bars where you can enjoy a light lunch in pleasant surroundings.

Museums and places of interest are listed at the end of each chapter in the sequence in which they are described. Closing days are given where relevant, but I do beg of you to read the warning I have given in Practical Information about constantly changing opening times.

'Beyond the Centre' covers districts outside the scope of the central walks. Divided geographically into four sections, it describes places to visit, with suggestions for combining them where relevant. Restaurants and cafés suitable for lunch or supper stops are included in the text, and so are addresses of museums and other sites.

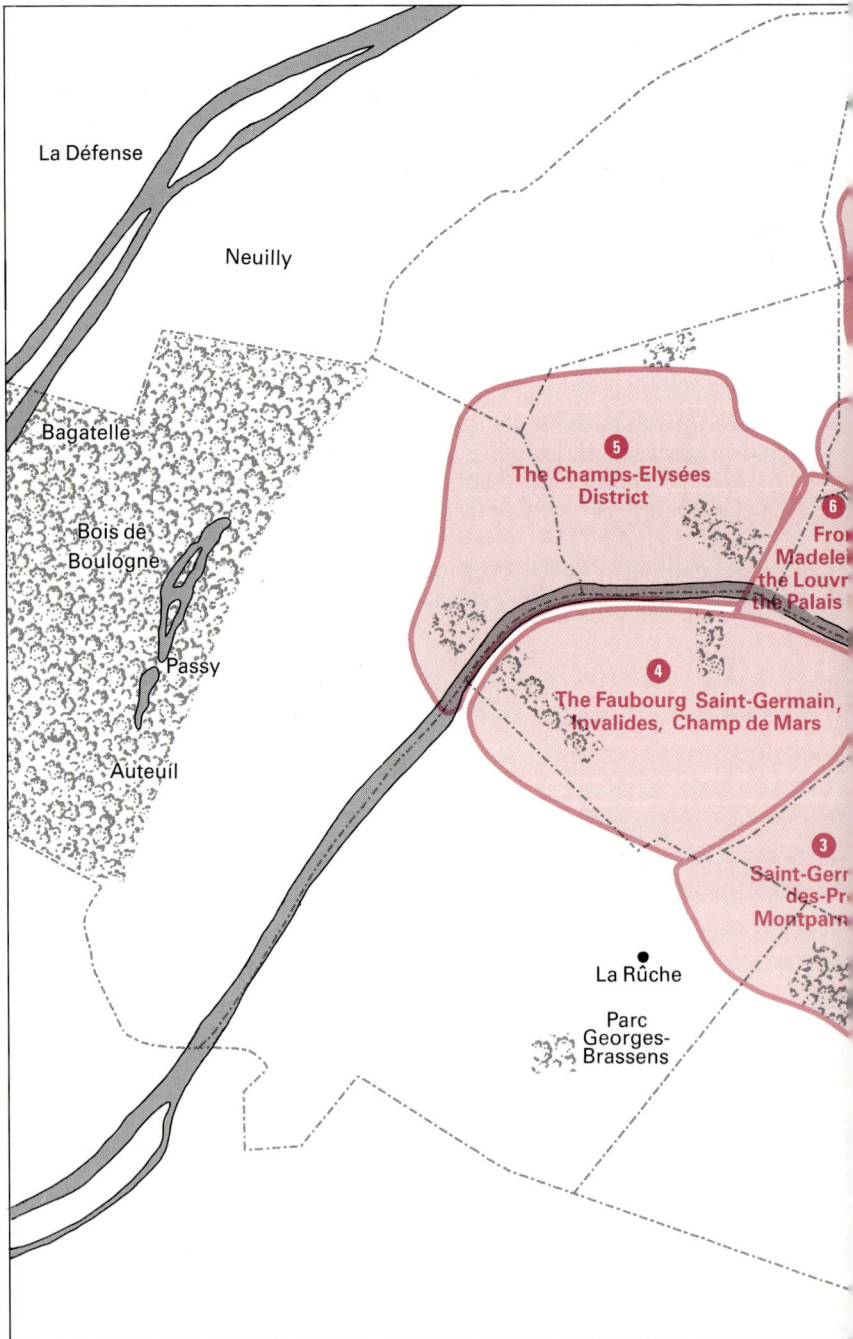

La Défense

Neuilly

Bagatelle

Bois de
Boulogne

Passy

Auteuil

⑤
**The Champs-Elysées
District**

⑥
**Fro
Madelei
the Louvr
the Palais**

④
**The Faubourg Saint-Germain,
Invalides, Champ de Mars**

③
**Saint-Gerr
des-Pr
Montparn**

● La Rûche

Parc
Georges-
Brassens

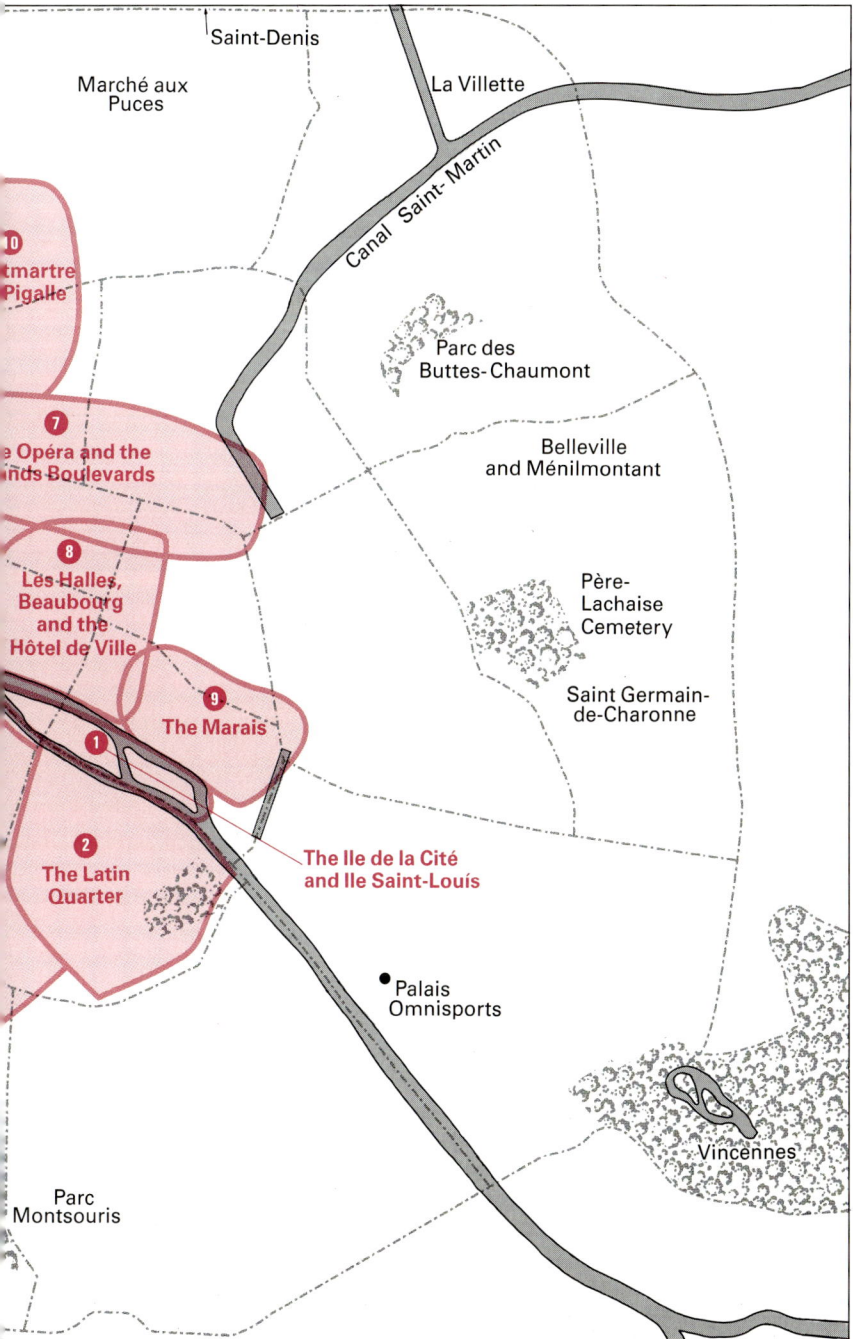

Saint-Denis

Marché aux
Puces

La Villette

Canal Saint-Martin

10
tmartre
Pigalle

Parc des
Buttes-Chaumont

7
e Opéra and the
nds Boulevards

Belleville
and Ménilmontant

8
Les Halles,
Beaubourg
and the
Hôtel de Ville

Père-
Lachaise
Cemetery

Saint Germain-
de-Charonne

9
The Marais

1

2
The Latin
Quarter

The Ile de la Cité
and Ile Saint-Louis

• Palais
Omnisports

Vincennes

Parc
Montsouris

Practical Information

Timing Your Visit

If you are free to pick a time to visit Paris, bear in mind that the city can be very sultry in summer: the whole Paris area is set in a low-lying basin, and with few green spaces in the centre and many dusty squares, it can seem oppressive. Tourist hordes also make the major sights unpleasantly crowded, with long queues to get in to museums, and as all but the poorest Parisians traditionally disappear in droves to their weekend cottages or relations in the country, or home in on seaside or mountain resorts, you'll be visiting a somewhat artificial city, empty of the people who make it live. On top of that, many restaurants, theatres and shops shut for at least a month between the *Quatorze Juillet* (Bastille Day) holiday in mid-July and early September, leaving whole districts with a dead, shuttered-up feel about them.

On the other hand, a big plus at this time of year is the relative lack of traffic. When I lived in Paris I loved spending August there: the buses, my preferred form of transport, shot to their destinations at speeds quite unattainable the rest of the year, the vistas were far lovelier without the usual endless parade of cars, and there was a friendly, conspiratorial mood as those of us left swapped tips on which baker's or shoemender's were still open − a far cry from the rough and tumble, every-man-for-himself of Parisian daily life the rest of the year.

Winter can be cold and damp, and whatever the song says, springtime in Paris rarely lives up to expectations, apart from the odd joyous day of mild sunshine and unfurling leaves and pearly evening light. The French do not go in much for spring flowers, and you'll rarely see crocuses or daffodils or tulips, except in the lovely lawns at Bagatelle in the Bois de Boulogne. The *giboulées de mars* (the French version of April showers) can be ferocious too.

Wide avenues lined with chestnut trees are an unforgettable feature of Paris, and a visit when the tall white or pink candles are in flower − usually in May − can be magical. Thanks to double summer time the long light evenings in May and June give you the maximum time for sightseeing and for leisurely walks when the daytime traffic has disappeared in all except a few streets famous for their nightlife.

But my own favourite time is the autumn, when the trees are ablaze with golden and russet tints, the heat of summer is past, yet there are still some gloriously sunny days, and you sense a general feeling of expectancy and excitement as the new season gets under way. The *rentrée* – the back-to-school (or university or work) period, after the long summer break – is a major feature of the French year, but nowhere more so than in Paris. Restaurants and shops reopen, posters appear about new theatre productions, the boutiques flaunt the new season's fashions, the little galleries on the Left Bank and the big showpiece museums start staging new exhibitions. The streets are full of people sporting glamorous tans and something of a carefree holiday aura still envelops them, before the brusqueness that is so often a Parisian characteristic re-emerges.

A final word about Christmas: in many ways it is an ideal time to be in Paris. The streets and buildings are beautifully lit – only the occasional garish display near the big department stores, elsewhere simply elegant garlands of white lights, or perhaps a few coloured fairy lights enlivening the odd tree in squares or market streets. Even the tiniest shop windows are Aladdin's caves, and the market stalls groan under the weight of terrines and pâtés in fancy shapes – miniature *foie gras* ducks are a speciality – festively hung game, superb displays of shellfish, scallop shells decoratively filled with fish in creamy sauces, slender slices of vegetable terrine in aspic, meticulously arranged pyramids of fruit and nuts. The markets are open even on Christmas morning, and the week between Christmas and New Year, far from being a dead period, is one of the busiest shopping weeks of the year, as New Year presents are as common as Christmas ones.

A Parisian Christmas is not a time for staying quietly at home with the family, but for outings to the theatre or the opera or ballet, where special performances are staged and everyone dresses up. And Christmas Eve and New Year's Eve dinners, known as *réveillons* and lasting well into the early hours (the Christmas Eve feast does not start until everyone has got back from midnight mass), are memorable occasions, with restaurants laying on champagne-laced menus – at a price, of course, but guaranteed to make you feel really festive.

Geography

Paris is divided into twenty *arrondissements* or districts, each with its own town hall. They are simply called 'the first', 'the second' and so on, written 1er, 2e, 3e, 4e (or occasionally Ier, IIe, IIIe, IVe), and pronounced *premier*, then the number with the addition of 'ième' in each case: *deuxième, troisième* down to *vingtième*. The *premier* is in the centre of the city, the other *arrondissements* following in a spiral sequence until you reach the *vingtième* on the far eastern edge. Districts north of the Seine are referred to collectively as the Right Bank (*Rive Droite*), those to the south as the Left Bank (*Rive Gauche*).

If you are writing to one of the places mentioned in the lists in this book, the post code for each *arrondissement* is 75 (for Paris) followed by one or two zeros and then the district number, to make a total of five digits. Thus an address listed as 1er should be written on the envelope as 75001 Paris, one listed as 16e as 75016 Paris. Standard hotel and restaurant guides are usually divided into *arrondissements*.

The views up and down the river Seine from the Pont des Arts are magical at any time of day

Note: If you are dialling from outside France, all the telephone numbers given in this book should be preceded by 33 (for France), then 1 (for Paris). From within France but outside the Greater Paris area, dial 16 first, wait for the second tone, then dial 1 and the number.

Getting About Paris

The first essential is to buy a small-format gazetteer (available from news stands and some café-tobacconists as well as bookshops) called *Plan de Paris par Arrondissement*. Make sure to buy one that has a separate plan for each district, as it will be much easier to use in the street than one with only a fold-out map. As well as listing all streets, squares, avenues and boulevards in inner Paris (a slightly more expensive version also includes the inner suburbs), and giving the nearest métro station(s) in each case, it offers useful information on such matters as where main post offices are to be found, and lists churches by denomination, theatres, major cinemas, night clubs and suchlike, as well as sports facilities. Route maps for each bus line are included, and a pocket inside the front or back cover contains a loose métro map and a large fold-out map of the city.

12

It is important to be aware that Paris gazetteers (though not those for other French cities, oddly enough) are invariably arranged alphabetically by the *first part* of the name. Thus the place Edith-Piaf (the two, or more, components are always hyphenated) will be found under E, not P, and the rue du Dr-Blanche under D, not B.

Transport

Whenever possible, much the pleasantest way of getting about Paris is to walk. Distances are not great (I have often been told that you can walk right across the city in 1½ hours, though I have never tried it) and you will see much more than on the métro, and be able to pause whenever the mood takes you, which is scarcely feasible on a bus, unless you are very quick off the mark.

However, there are times when you will want to take public transport. Fortunately Paris has an enviably efficient system, and one that is soon mastered even by a first-time visitor, as the various forms of transport (bus, métro or underground/ subway, and express métro) are well integrated. On top of that, it is good value and requires minimum fuss in paying for your journey: buy tickets (the same ones are valid for métro and bus) in blocks of ten (*carnets*) at métro stations, from slot machines outside major stations, or from the tobacconist counter in cafés, or go for a tourist ticket (*Formule 1*, valid for a single day, or *Paris Sésame* for various sequences of consecutive days), or a season ticket (*Carte Orange*) with a weekly or monthly coupon. On the métro a single ticket is required for any distance. On the buses, longer journeys require two tickets and occasionally (on the *Petite Ceinture* route that goes right round the city) up to four tickets. (You can buy tickets on the bus, but they will be considerably more expensive.) On the RER (*réseau express régional* or express métro) journeys within the city limits are like ordinary métro trips: use a single ticket. For journeys further afield, you must get a ticket from one of the clearly labelled slot machines.

Métro maps are posted up outside stations and on platforms. Route maps are clearly marked at bus stops and inside buses, and full bus maps for city buses and suburban lines can be consulted on métro station platforms or on free leaflets available from stations and bus termini. A recent innovation on the streets of Paris is a route-finder with push buttons which you can consult to find the quickest way to reach your destination by métro only, by bus only or a combination of both — great fun for children to use too.

The rail lines providing a shuttle service to the airports, Roissy-Rail to Roissy/ Charles-de-Gaulle airport and Orly-Rail to Orly airport, now form part of the RER network, enabling you to reach them easily from many city-centre stations without changing trains. The same is true of an increasing number of suburban lines.

The métro and RER run from about 5.30 a.m. to 12.30 a.m. but only a handful of buses operate at night (most stop between 8.30 and 9 p.m.) and on Sundays.

Taxis will rarely stop if you hail them in the street but are available at ranks at rail stations and near major tourist sights. Prices are reasonable, but drivers can rarely be persuaded to take more than three passengers at a time.

Information Sources

The main **Paris Tourist Office** is at 127 avenue des Champs-Elysées, 8e (47-23-61-72). If you go there in person, be prepared for long queues at most times of year. A wide variety of information is available from the fairly helpful hostesses or you can simply pick up leaflets about cultural events and other happenings during your stay if you have little time to spare. Hotel reservations can be made here, but usually only for that same night or the next night; a small fee is charged.

There are branch offices at the main stations, most of them open till about 10 p.m. Monday to Saturday from May to October:

Gare d'Austerlitz (45-84-91-70)
Gare de l'Est (46-07-17-73)
Gare de Lyon (43-43-33-24)
Gare du Nord (45-26-94-82)

and another at the **Eiffel Tower** (45-51-22-15) in the summer months.

By dialling 47-20-94-94 you can listen to a recorded announcement of major happenings during the week in question (plays, concerts, fairs and so on). A version in English (not always very clear) can be heard on 47-20-88-98.

Events staged by the **Mairie de Paris** (town hall) are posted up on special electronic information boards all over the city and you can obtain further information from the office just inside the rue de Rivoli entrance of the *Mairie* (just by Ⓜ Hôtel-de-Ville).

As for 'What's On' publications, you can buy *L'Officiel des Spectacles* or *Pariscope* from any news stand. They appear on Wednesdays, as that is the day all Paris cinemas change their programmes, and are an invaluable source of information on current opening times for museums, on temporary art and other exhibitions, theatre, cinema and concert programmes, and activities for children (puppet shows, Punch and Judy, circuses, amusement parks, zoos). Your hotel or one of the official tourist offices should have a copy of the free monthly *Paris-Sélection*, listing current events in various languages.

The Marais has two useful sources of information: no. 44 rue François-Miron, 4e, houses a centre designed to encourage awareness of Paris's most beautiful *hôtels* or town houses and to tell visitors about the latest state of play in the many restoration and renovation schemes; and the **Hôtel de Béthune-Sully**, 62 rue Saint-Antoine, 4e (48-87-24-14 or 42-74-22-22), contains the offices of the **Caisse Nationale des Monuments Historiques**, or Historic Buildings Commission, with a wealth of information on all state-owned historic buildings and on guided tours. The Caisse publishes a booklet every two months with full details of current exhibitions, guided tours, lectures, activities for children in museums and historic buildings in Paris and in the Ile de France region. It is available free in major sights or from the Caisse's new bookshop in the rue Saint-Antoine.

Hotels

Paris has a very large number of hotels, ranging from tiny, picturesque places with a family atmosphere to huge impersonal hotels catering mainly for business visitors. The Left Bank has the lion's share of what the French call *hôtels de charme*, delightful hotels with both charm and character, though there are also a few scattered through the Right Bank districts.

Facilities naturally vary widely, but on the whole it would be true to say that if you have not visited Paris for some time, you will be pleasantly surprised at how standards have risen: many of the Left Bank hotels that were picturesque but distinctly run down have now been modernised, and most rooms in two-star hotels and upwards now have attractive modern bathrooms, though these may be very small (perhaps with a bidet that pulls out from under the basin). Cleanliness is unlikely to be a problem nowadays, and though plumbing and wiring may still leave something to be desired, their defects will rarely represent more than a minor irritation, rather than a serious inconvenience. Efforts have also been made to reduce noise levels in rooms overlooking the street, generally by the addition of double glazing. But this does not solve the problem on hot summer nights, when you will need to leave the window open, so you should always ask for a room overlooking the courtyard at the back (most Paris buildings have one), rather than giving on to the street. A surprising number of small hotels have managed to squeeze in a lift, but it is as well to check this, as hoteliers tend to think that foreign visitors are as used to walking up a large number of floors as Parisians have traditionally needed to be.

Prices also vary considerably, not only from one hotel to another, even within the same official star category, but often in the same hotel: a poky single room at the top of the building, picturesque but spartan, may cost only half or even a third the price of a more spacious double room on a lower floor. A noticeable recent trend has been for hotels in a popular area with both tourists and French business visitors, such as Saint-Germain-des-Prés, to align their prices very closely, and, sad to say, to push them upwards so as to discourage foreign students on European tours who are increasingly haunting Saint-Germain's restaurants and cafés.

Yet it is still normal practice for hotels to charge by the room, rather than per person, which means that those travelling together will often be paying prices that seem bargains compared to other capital cities (though single visitors are inevitably penalised). A word of caution however: a recent and unwelcome development has seen a few of the new or modernised hotels on the Left Bank switching to per-person prices. Let's hope they will prove to be isolated examples.

This book cannot give anything approaching an exhaustive hotel listing. I have merely suggested a small number of places that seem to me particularly appropriate for those who wish to have a reasonably quiet and comfortable but not luxurious base, with a pleasant atmosphere and helpful staff, from which to explore Paris. Prices are moderate unless otherwise stated. Hotels are grouped at the end of each of the ten walks. I have made no attempt to list an equal number for each district. As the majority of the hotels of the type I have described are in the Latin Quarter, Saint-Germain-des-Prés and the Faubourg Saint-Germain area

15

(Walks 2, 3 and 4) the longest lists will be found there. The Champs-Elysées area is on the whole too expensive, Montparnasse and the Grands-Boulevards too noisy, the Bastille and points east still too run down, and the Marais, sadly, too residential, for there to be more than a very small choice of appropriate places to recommend in each case.

Booking well in advance is advisable at all times of year, especially for the small Left Bank hotels. Some of these small hotels now have faxes (the fax number has been included where one exists), which will ensure a rapid reply, but few like taking telephone bookings (always send a deposit and a confirmation letter if you do manage to book by telephone).

Alternatives to Hotels

Short-term lets in Paris are notoriously hard to find, but there are one or two places where you can self-cater — a tempting formula when there is so much mouth-watering food on offer in the local shops and markets.

One solution that has proved its worth is the **Résidence Charles-Dullin** in Montmartre (10 pl Charles-Dullin, 75018 Paris, 47-23-32-22) which has mostly one-room (but also a few two- and three-room) flats with small kitchens. Here you get the comforts of a hotel yet the flexibility of self-catering. You'll probably have to book for at least a week.

Shorter stays are possible at the three **Citadines**. These are not particularly atmospheric but have modern, well-planned one- and two-room flats, washing machines, car park, cafeteria; prices vary depending on the season (April, May, June is the most expensive, January and July/August the cheapest). They are fairly near the Gare d'Austerlitz and the Jardin des Plantes, the Gare Montparnasse and the Trocadéro:

Citadines Paris-Austerlitz 27 rue Esquirol, 75013 Paris (45-84-13-09)
Citadines Paris-Montparnasse 67 av du Maine, 75014 Paris (43-27-14-24)
Citadines Paris-Trocadéro 29bis rue Saint-Didier, 75016 Paris (47-04-88-02)

They don't work out cheaper than a hotel room, but you do of course have total flexibility and can save on restaurant bills.

Another solution is to stay in private accommodation on a bed-and-breakfast basis. A company called just that — **Bed & Breakfast 1** 73 rue Notre-Dame-des-Champs, 75006 Paris (43-25-43-97) — has about 250 carefully selected and inspected rooms in private homes in one of the twenty inner-city *arrondissements* and staff do their best to match up your tastes, interests and lifestyle with those of your hosts. Prices are about the same as a two-star hotel. Another company has adopted the equally alliterative French version of B&B — **Café-Couette** (*couette*, oddly enough, being the French for duvet). The formula is the same, but they grade their accommodation into two, three or four coffee-pot categories (their version of the Michelin rosette or the *gîte* ear of corn). Café-Couette is at 8 rue d'Isly, 75008 Paris (42-94-92-00).

The Paris Tourist Office (see above) can also sometimes find you a room in a private home.

Restaurants

This book can give details of only a very few of Paris's thousands of restaurants (ten thousand is the round figure usually quoted). I have aimed first to suggest a small number of places that make suitable stopping-off points during the various walks, the main criteria being pleasant and relaxing atmosphere and surroundings, good cuisine of its type and reasonably fast service. I have also included a few restaurants that would be suitable for a special and more long-drawn-out lunch on days when you are weary of too much sightseeing, and others that I recommend for an enjoyable dinner at the end of a hard day's walking and museum visiting.

I have not included the top gastronomic restaurants – they are easily found in any of the many listings guides on the market – and prices are moderate unless otherwise indicated. However, you should be aware that straying from the set-price *menu* to eat *à la carte* and/or choosing a special bottle of wine may easily transform a moderate bill into an expensive one. (See the Food and Drink chapter for general advice about eating in Paris restaurants.)

As with hotels, I have not attempted to give an equal number of suggestions for each chapter. Restaurants, tea rooms and wine bars asterisked in the text are described in greater detail either in the restaurant suggestions lists at the end of the walk or outlying district chapter, or in the tea room and wine bar box in the Food and Drink chapter. But I have also mentioned in passing a number of places where a quick meal can be enjoyed pleasantly if you do not feel like planning a meal in advance yet do not want to resort to a fast-food solution.

Museums and Places of Interest

Opening times of museums and other sights and places of interest are a problem in Paris, as they change frequently and only very rarely stay the same all year round. On the whole the days to be avoided are Monday (when all City of Paris museums shut) and Tuesday (when most state-owned museums and monuments close, as they do throughout the country). Private museums often close on Sundays. Public holidays are another difficulty, with no apparent rhyme or reason behind the choice of some to stay open, while others shut. A surprising number of even major museums observe a lunch break (though this may be lifted during the high summer months) and many places close at least an hour earlier from about October to Palm Sunday or Easter. Some châteaux on the outskirts of Paris close altogether for several months in the winter, to avoid prohibitive heating costs. And arbitrary closures are very common occurrences – caused by sudden staff shortages, or a visit by some VIP, or a film or advertising company hiring the building to shoot a couple of scenes.

I have therefore deliberately avoided giving opening times in the lists at the end of each of the ten walks, since these may well have changed by the time of your visit to Paris. I have indicated closing days and, where relevant, extended closures. But I cannot advise you strongly enough to buy the current edition of one of the local 'What's On' weeklies and check the lists given under the heading '*Musées*' or '*A travers Paris*' (see Information Sources, above).

Virtually all museums and places of interest have an admission charge, though some charge half-price or do not charge at all on Sundays (which are inevitably crowded). Wednesday afternoons in term-time (when schools have a half-holiday) may be bedevilled by boisterous school parties and are best avoided. An increasing number of museums have at least one day when visiting can be extended into the evening – a good way of avoiding the worst of the crowds. But otherwise you should expect and plan for queues virtually everywhere at the height of the summer tourist season and at Easter, and almost all year round at the most popular sights: the Eiffel Tower, the Pompidou/Beaubourg Centre, the Musée d'Orsay, the Picasso Museum, and of course the famous Pyramid entrance to the Louvre.

If you are intending to do a lot of museum visiting, consider saving yourself money and, especially, time, by buying a Museum Pass (see box).

Reductions on the price of admission are often allowed to those under eighteen (who may occasionally get in free), students, senior citizens, teachers, journalists and so on. It is always worth taking along your passport and some form of professional identification.

Churches open early in the mornings but are very often shut between about 12.30 and 4 and after 7 p.m. Visits during masses are rarely allowed.

Museum Passes

It is now possible to buy a pass (*carte musées*) valid for one, three or five days (consecutive days in the case of the longer ones), which will enable you to gain admission without queuing in sixty museums and historic buildings in Paris and the surrounding area.

The pass covers most of the major sights, including the Louvre, the Musée de Cluny, the Musée d'Orsay, the Musée Picasso, the National Museum of Modern Art in the Pompidou/Beaubourg Centre, the La Villette science and technology centre (where it becomes the equivalent of a day pass); the houses lived in by Balzac, Victor Hugo and Gustave Moreau;

the Arc de Triomphe, the Panthéon, Notre Dame's towers and Napoleon's Tomb; the château de Vincennes, the palace at Versailles and the basilica/cathedral at Saint-Denis; and many Ile de France sights.

You can buy the pass at major métro stations and at all important sights and museums and do not need to start using it the day you buy it. When you make your first visit you must fill in your name and the date and have the pass stamped. Then at each museum or sight you can go straight to the entrance without joining the queue (at the Musée d'Orsay, go to the entrance labelled '*Groupes et adhérents*' and show your pass).

Public Holidays

New Year's Day	Bastille Day (14 July)
Easter Monday (but not Good Friday)	Feast of the Assumption (15 August)
Labour Day (1 May)	All Saints (1 November)
VE Day (8 May)	Remembrance/Armistice Day
Feast of the Ascension	(11 November)
Whit Monday	Christmas Day

Entertainment

There is no space in this book to do justice to the many opportunities in Paris for entertainment, both cultural and just plain fun. Some of the city's many theatres, night clubs, discothèques and concert halls are referred to during the Walks chapters, and the Information Sources section earlier in this chapter will tell you how to find out what is going on during your visit. But the following pointers may be helpful.

Paris must surely have more **cinemas** to the square mile or kilometre than any other city. They show a huge variety of films, old and new, French and foreign (there's a Bergman and a Jean Renoir 'festival' or 'homage to' showing in one cinema or another virtually year-round). The French do not seem to mind seeing dubbed films, but foreign films with subtitles are shown too, mostly in the art cinemas on the Left Bank (look for the letters 'v.o.', meaning *version originale*, in film listings). Movie classics from all over the world feature in the very full programmes staged by the city's two *cinémathèques*, in the Palais de Chaillot, place du Trocadéro, 16e, very close to the magical Cinema Museum (Walk 5), and in the Beaubourg/Pompidou Centre, 4e.

The best-known **theatre** is of course the state-subsidised **Comédie française** (Walk 6). The commercial theatre is centred, as it has been for centuries, on the *Grands Boulevards*, near the Opéra (Walk 7), while the experimental theatres tend to be more on the fringes. Among the latter, usually showing interesting work by French and foreign playwrights, are the **Cartoucherie** in Vincennes and the **Lucernaire** in Montparnasse. The **Carré Silvia Montfort**, near the Porte de Vanves in the south, the **Amandiers** in Ménilmontant, Jean-Louis Barrault's and Madeleine Renaud's **Théâtre Renaud-Barrault** by the Rond-Point des Champs-Elysées, and the **Bouffes du Nord**, north of the Gare du Nord, where an international company presided over by Peter Brook puts on occasional and invariably excellent performances, are all well worth looking up in the current listings to see what they have on offer. The subsidised **Odéon** theatre by the Luxembourg Gardens is increasingly home to visiting foreign companies, while the **Théâtre National de Chaillot**, at the Trocadéro, often has lively versions of classics from the international repertoire.

Outside Paris the most prestigious theatre is the very pretty little opera house in the palace of Versailles, which occasionally puts on both plays and opera.

But the town of Versailles has its own theatre, and so do a number of other near-by towns and suburbs (look under *Théâtres des environs* in the various listings weeklies), the most interesting as a rule being the **Amandiers** in Nanterre and the **Gérard-Philipe** in Saint-Denis.

Café-theatres have lost much of their 'alternative' glamour but can still provide an enjoyable evening, especially if you are feeling sufficiently mellow after the good dinners some of them lay on not to notice how small and uncomfortable the actual 'theatre' is (usually just an upstairs room or a basement). The famous **chansonniers**, once very much part of the Paris scene, have dwindled to just two old favourites, the **Caveau de la République** in the boulevard Saint-Martin and the **Deux-Anes** in the boulevard de Clichy at the foot of Montmartre, but several of the well-known cabarets, such as the **Lapin Agile** in Montmartre, and the **Caveau des Oubliettes** beside the church of Saint-Julien-le-Pauvre in the Latin Quarter, still offer a nostalgically Parisian evening with old French songs and plenty of atmosphere.

Opera has naturally traditionally been performed at the glittering **Opéra** (see Walk 7), which is both very expensive and hard to get into, though **ballet** tickets are marginally easier to come by (it is also the home of the national ballet company). By the time you read this, however, the Opéra may be staging almost entirely ballet. The nearby **Opéra Comique**, also known as the **Salle Favart**, stages mostly operetta. The contentious **Opéra de la Bastille**, opened in 1989 during the bi-centenary celebrations, started showing opera in 1990, at prices allegedly designed to appeal to a more popular audience. Other more popular occasional venues for both opera and ballet are the **Palais des Congrès** at the Porte Maillot, the **Palais des Sports** at the Porte de Versailles, and the **Palais Omnisports de Paris-Bercy** on the quai de Bercy in eastern Paris, a spectacular multi-purpose sports, cultural and leisure centre opened in the late eighties. Ballet is staged all over Paris during the traditional November/December dance season and, very pleasantly, in some of the courtyards of the elegant *hôtels* in the Marais during the summer.

Concerts are also held in the Marais during the early-summer **Festival du Marais**, and during the **Festival Estival** (Summer Festival). Many of the city's churches stage concerts year-round, a good way of combining sightseeing and culture: book in plenty of time for the popular candlelit concerts in the Sainte Chapelle. The best known of the standard concert halls are the **Salle Gaveau**, 45 rue La Boétie, and the **Salle Pleyel**, 252 rue du Faubourg-Saint-Honoré, both close together in the 8e near the Champs-Elysées.

As for what the French insist on calling '**Paris by Night**', the choice is endless, ranging from trendy discos to deluxe revues known the world over — the **Lido** on the Champs-Elysées is surrounded by tourist coaches virtually every night of the year — and classy strip shows like the famous **Crazy Horse Saloon** in the avenue George-V, 8e. Full details of every conceivable type of nightlife can be found in the 'What's On' weeklies, except the private clubs — but you won't be able to get in there anyway, unless you have famous friends to pull strings for you. Paris's jazz clubs are particularly well known, including the long-standing **Caveau de la Huchette** in the Latin Quarter and the **Slow Club** in the rue de Rivoli, at both of which you can dance.

Food and Drink

There is no such thing of course as Paris cuisine. With much of its population drawn from the four corners of France and its profusion of restaurants big and small, cosy and grand, it is a melting pot in which all the country's regional cuisines can be tasted and enjoyed, along with those of other nations, with a special emphasis on her former colonies in Vietnam and North Africa. Ordinary Parisians at home eat the dishes of their native region, or that of their ancestors, or the traditional dishes of *cuisine bourgeoise*, that carefully prepared home cooking that is one of the glories of France, and far more enduring than the latest fads and fashions, *nouvelle* or otherwise.

I once read an article which claimed that the typical Paris dish is steak and chips or French fries. You can certainly find it on the menu of most Paris cafés and brasseries, though it may be a juicy *onglet* or *bavette aux échalotes*, both rather thin but tasty cuts, served with an unctuous accompaniment of shallots softened in butter, rather than the thicker piece of rump steak you are used to at home. But it obviously isn't a regional dish in the sense that a *potée auvergnate*, a Norman *canard au sang* or *poulet au cidre*, a *porc aux pruneaux* from Tours or a Provençal *daube* are regional specialities. The great joy of Paris is that you can enjoy all of these, and need never tire of any one region's dishes, as you can ring the changes between peasant fare one day, Norman richness the next, garlicky Provençal the next – and elegant *nouvelle cuisine* to follow. And the many food markets (see box) offer tempting produce from all over France to enliven your picnics.

One speciality that could perhaps be classed as Parisian, though few Parisians eat it at home, is the famous onion soup that is traditionally drunk – or rather eaten, as it is usually very thick – round the old Les Halles market area after a night on the town (Walk 8). But onion soup on a fixed-price *menu* elsewhere in Paris is often a pointer to a tourist trap, and is likely to be indigestible, with tasteless strings of melted cheese making it awkward to eat. Save it for a visit to Les Halles, where a bowl of steaming, pungently flavoured broth can be the perfect restorative. The other well-known speciality of Les Halles is pig's trotters, dipped in breadcrumbs and lightly fried – and at their best needless to say at the restaurant named after them, **Au Pied de Cochon***.

Quite a few restaurants serving regional specialities are included in the lists at the end of each walk, but it may be helpful to know that Breton restaurants are congregated near the Gare Montparnasse, Auvergnat near the Bastille – and that

The zinc-topped counter of a typical Paris café — the Vieux-Colombier near Saint-Sulpice

Above and opposite: The centuries-old food market in the rue Mouffetard in the Latin Quarter offers a feast for the eye as well as the palate

the rue Mouffetard area in the Latin Quarter is the place for Greek restaurants, while Vietnamese and Moroccan and Tunisian places are found all over the city.

The problem with Paris of course is that there are so many restaurants to choose from, it is difficult to know where to start. The lists are designed to help on this score, but you should bear in mind that there are various different types of eating places. The traditional **café**, the type with pavement tables, will generally have a limited range of basic fare – steak, omelets, perhaps *brochettes* (kebabs) or *andouillettes* (chitterling sausages), probably served with potatoes or rice, possibly a green salad; a few mixed salads in bowls; and one or two *plats du jour*, daily specials, at lunchtime. If you feel like a first course, they'll probably have pâté or soup and you can follow the main course with a fruit tart, an ice cream or a *crème caramel*. All of this will be eaten at a small, perhaps marble-topped, table covered with a fresh paper mat for each customer, the service will be deft and fast, the decibel level pretty high, your fellow diners mostly local or working in the area. Lunch in a café is a good way of soaking up the atmosphere of the area while saving precious sightseeing time. In the evenings, the menu will be even more limited and the atmosphere diluted.

A step up in comfort is the local restaurant, perhaps called a **brasserie-restaurant**, which is typically quite spacious, with large tables covered with white tablecloths and white linen napkins. The menu will be longer than in a café, with a range of meat and fish dishes, often including one or two 'house specialities', perhaps a section devoted to oysters and other seafood, and a little card attached to the top with the dishes of the day: a couple of starters, two or three main dishes, sometimes a pudding – strawberries, say, or a special tart. The quality is often surprisingly high in these unassuming places that take little notice of fashions in cuisine, and the service is usually both friendly and efficient. There may be a notice saying *restauration rapide à toute heure* ('quick eating any time of day'), but don't translate this as fast food. It merely means that meal times are not as rigid as in a full-scale restaurant and a few dishes will be available at other times, though probably not round the clock. If you don't want to spend too long on your meal, you can have just a main dish and a coffee and be out in under an hour – a feat hard to accomplish in a more fancy restaurant, where it is difficult to eat in less than two hours.

This is undoubtedly a problem for tourists trying to fit in as much sightseeing as possible. And if you decide to make do with a snack at lunchtime and eat your main meal in the evening, you will probably have to pay more. The point to remember is that even in Paris, the French still prefer to have their main meal in the middle of the day, in spite of recent changes in lifestyle. As a result, many top-class restaurants have fixed-price lunch *menus* that are remarkably good value, often half the price of an *à la carte* meal, but in the evening you will have to eat from the expensive *carte*. The plus point is that even if your budget is limited, you can treat yourself to the occasional meal in a special restaurant – but it will be a lunchtime treat rather than a gourmet dinner. Perhaps the best solution is to plan the treat on a day when you will be spending the afternoon strolling rather than museum-visiting, so you don't have to worry about opening times.

The true **brasserie** specialises in Alsatian dishes – filling *choucroutes* and

Open-air Markets

The feeling that Paris is still, in spite of modern office blocks and roaring traffic, a series of villages, is reinforced on Sunday mornings, when the inhabitants of each district flock to do their shopping and chat to their neighbours at the city's open-air food markets, some of which are centuries old. In the week they are not quite so busy, but you will still find them good places for catching a glimpse of the lives of ordinary Parisians: the concierges in their carpet slippers and aprons, the old people, both men and women with traditional string bags and *baguette* loaves tucked under their arms, the harassed young mothers frantic to finish the shopping before they have to pick up their children from school and bring them home for lunch – and also, for markets are nothing if not democratic, the chic *bourgeoises*, often with tiny lapdogs in tow, haggling over the price of meat. (It is a well-known fact that the markets in the *beaux quartiers*, the posh districts, tend to have lower prices than those in more popular areas, because the demanding ladies of leisure who inhabit them, many still with servants, have the time to bargain and insist imperiously on high standards, while the rushed working mothers in working-class districts are too busy or not sufficiently eloquent to achieve similar successes.)

The food markets are feasts for the eye as well as the palate, with their beautifully arranged pyramids of shiningly fresh vegetables, their gleaming displays of fish, their thousand-and-one varieties of *charcuterie* and glistening barrels of olives. The stallholders are often as colourful as their wares, 'crying' their merchandise in raucous voices, the men busy chatting up their female customers and slipping off at intervals to the market café for a *coup de rouge*, a quick glass of red wine, the women fussing over their elderly bachelors, wrapped up against the cold for much of the year with layer on layer of thick woollen scarves.

Among the most picturesque is the market at the Saint-Médard end of the **rue Mouffetard** (Ⓜ Censier-Daubenton) in the Latin Quarter, which has been held there since the Middle Ages. Other good ones are in the **rue de Buci** and **rue de Seine** in the heart of Saint-Germain-des-Prés (Ⓜ Mabillon, Odéon); the **place Maubert** in the Latin Quarter, held on Tuesdays, Thursdays and Saturdays only (Ⓜ Maubert-Mutualité); the **rue Cler** near the Invalides and the Eiffel Tower (Ⓜ Ecole-Militaire, Latour-Maubourg); the **place du Marché** in Neuilly, held on Wednesdays, Fridays and Sundays only, on the edge of the Bois de Boulogne (Ⓜ Les Sablons); and the **rue Lepic** in Montmartre (Ⓜ Blanche, Abbesses). But you'll find others, big and small – some consist of a mere handful of stalls – all over the city, generally open mornings only.

Most food markets have a flower stall or two, but Paris also has three large open-air markets selling nothing but flowers: on the **Ile de la Cité** close to Notre Dame (Ⓜ Cité, Châtelet); beside the **Madeleine** church (to the right when you're facing the church) (Ⓜ Madeleine); and in the **place des Ternes**, 17e, not far from the Arc de Triomphe and the Etoile (Ⓜ Ternes).

Some of the city's covered markets have recently been restored, though the famous wholesale market with its 19th-century glass and cast-iron pavilions designed by Victor Baltard, known simply as Les Halles, disappeared in 1969 and was rebuilt in the suburbs (see Walk 8). One that is back to its former splendour is the **Marché Saint-Quentin**, 85 boulevard de Magenta, 10e, near the Gare de l'Est and the Gare du Nord (Ⓜ Gare de l'Est).

The Elusive Light Lunch

Salons de Thé (Tea Rooms)

For lovers of light lunches – often an elusive commodity in Paris – the new breed of *salon de thé* or tea room is a boon and a blessing. The service can be amateurish but the décor will be attractive and the atmosphere peaceful, certainly less noisy and bustling than a café. Many are in quiet side streets away from the worst of the traffic noise.

Meal times are not as rigid as in restaurants and there is usually a good choice of savoury flans and quiches, sometimes a couple of hot *plats du jour*, a salad or two, and delicious home-made buns or cakes. A long list of different types of tea will be proffered, ranging from standard 'English breakfast' or Earl Grey (sometimes referred to as *thé à la bergamote*, flavoured with bergamot oil or essence) to exotica such as *thé aux mûres* or *thé au gingembre* (flavoured with mulberries or ginger). But wine by the glass or coffee are also available. And if you feel like a full-scale afternoon tea, home-made scones with jam and cakes of various kinds are served in pretty china.

Don't be misled by the words '*Salon de thé*' on a restaurant or café awning. They mean simply that you can order a pot or glass of tea. Instead, keep an eye out for places like those described above: as with restaurants, they will have a menu posted up outside, so you can check that it's what you are looking for. Here's a tip: many of the new-style tea rooms go in for punning titles like some of those in the list below. They rarely stay open after 6.30 or 7, so don't count on them for an evening meal. But some serve good weekend brunches.

The tea rooms listed here are all in places that make them suitable stopping-off points during one of the walks described in this book:

Angélina 226 rue de Rivoli, 1er. Once the famous Rumpelmayer (opened in 1903), now a chic tea room opposite the Tuileries Gardens, with elaborate ceiling mouldings and pillars and stylish frescoes. Over-priced but fun. Superb array of chocolates and confectionery make ideal gifts to take home. (Walk 6)

L'Arbre à Cannelle 57 passage des Panoramas, 2e. The Second Empire décor of François Marquis, once one of the country's best-known *chocolateries*, has been lovingly preserved in this 19th-century arcade leading off the boulevard Montmartre. Delicious tarts and salads, a few *plats du jour* at lunchtime, scrumptious cakes at tea or coffee time. (Walk 7)

A la Cour de Rohan passage du Commerce-Saint-André, 6e; closed Mon. Small and very pretty tea room tucked away in a little arcade off the rue Saint-André-des-Arts in Saint-Germain-des-Prés, leading into the narrow cobbled street behind the Café Procope and accessible from the carrefour de l'Odéon. (Walk 3)

L'Ebouillanté 6 rue des Barres, 4e; closed Mon. Narrow little place on two floors in a medieval street facing the lovely church of Saint-Gervais-Saint-Protais near the Hôtel de Ville. A few tables precariously perched on the sloping pavement in fine weather and service till 9 p.m. (Walk 8)

Fanny-Tea 20 pl Dauphine, 1er; closed Mon. Tiny and pretty, with a couple of spindly tables outside on this delightful triangle between the Pont Neuf and the law courts. (Walk 1)

La Fourmi Ailée 8 rue du Fouarre, 5e; closed Tue. Small literary and feminist bookshop in the front, a few tables round an open fireplace at the back, in a historic street close to the church of Saint-Julien-le-Pauvre and Notre Dame. (Walk 2)

L'Heure Gourmande 22 passage Dauphine, 6e; closed Sun. Displays of pretty china and art nouveau flower vases, a white-balustraded balcony and a tempting array of cakes and puddings on the sideboard greet you as you step in from a quiet cobbled alleyway between the rue Dauphine and the rue Mazarine in Saint-Germain-des-Prés. (Walk 3)

Marais Plus 20 rue des Francs-Bourgeois, 3e. An intellectual bookshop in the Marais with a tea room attached; conveniently open to midnight every day but Sun. (Walk 9)

Mariage Frères 30 rue du Bourg-Tibourg, 4e; closed Mon. Again in the Marais, a tea room with tall plants and colonial-style décor attached to a famous tea merchant's that has been in business since 1854. (Walk 9)

A Priori-Thé 35 galerie Vivienne, 2e. Restful place with comfortable cane chairs in a glass-roofed 19th-century shopping arcade near the Bibliothèque Nationale, leading from the rue Vivienne to the rue des Petits-Champs. (Walk 7)

Sweet et Faim 1 rue de la Bûcherie, 5e. Lovely site at a junction of several old streets in the Latin Quarter, just over the river from Notre Dame. Friendly atmosphere and a bigger choice of dishes than most tea rooms, plus luxurious champagne brunches at weekends. (Walk 2)

La Théière d'Arlequin rue Saint-André-des-Arts, 6e. Windowsills and sideboard are crammed with teapots in every shape and size (most of them for sale) in this tea room in a bustling pedestrian street leading off the place Saint-Michel. (Walk 3)

Bars à Vin (Wine Bars)

Paris has always had its traditional *bistrots à vin* and a few of these are still to be found, mostly rather shabby and frequented by hardened drinkers. Not as picturesque but certainly more stylish are the new *bars à vin* that have been springing up all over the city in recent years. They are more like what you would expect of a wine bar, with a rather fashionable clientele, a good choice of wine by the glass, and tempting platters of charcuterie and cheeses with country-style bread. They mainly cater for lunch and early evening.

Among the best known are the various **L'Ecluse** bars, which specialise in excellent (and fairly expensive) clarets. The first to open was at 15 quai des Grands-Augustins, 6e, close to the place Saint-Michel, but there are now several others, including those near the Champs-Elysées (64 rue François-1er, 8e), the Madeleine (15 pl de la Madeleine), 8e), the Bois de Boulogne (2 rue du Général-Bertier, Neuilly) and Les Halles (rue Mondétour, 1er).

—*near the Tuileries* (Walk 6): **Le Rubis** 10 rue du Marché-Saint-Honoré, 1er.
—*near the Hôtel de Ville* (Walk 9): **La Tartine** 24 rue de Rivoli, 4e.
—*in Saint-Germain-des-Prés* (Walk 3): **Le Petit Bacchus** 13 rue du Cherche-Midi, 6e.
—*in the Faubourg Saint-Germain* (Walk 4): **Au Sauvignon** 80 rue des Saints-Pères, 7e.
—*on the Ile de la Cité* (Walk 1): **Bar du Caveau** 17 pl Dauphine, 1er; **Taverne Henri-IV** 13 pl du Pont-Neuf, 1er.
—*near the Panthéon* (Walk 2): **Café de la Nouvelle Mairie** 19 rue des Fossés-Saint-Jacques, 5e.
—*near the Champs-Elysées* (Walk 5): **Le Val d'Or** 28 av Franklin-D.-Roosevelt, 8e.
—*near the Eiffel Tower* (Walk 4): **Le Sancerre** 22 av Rapp, 7e.

seafood and open fruit tarts especially, accompanied by beer or a fruity Alsace wine. It is open long hours, and is usually large, busy and noisy — a very Parisian place, in spite of the Alsace connotations. But have a good look at the menu before venturing in: some *brasseries*, like the **Brasserie Bofinger*** near the Bastille, are rather chic and therefore pricey.

A **bistrot** is more difficult to define, not least because the latest trend is for top chefs to open *'bistrot'* annexes close to their well-known restaurants. These will serve dishes that are carefully cooked and presented, but less elaborate and certainly less expensive than in the main restaurant. To a Frenchman the *bistrot du coin* is the little place on the corner, but the term may be used both for a modest local restaurant and for somewhere much trendier. As before, check the menu first.

Finally, a word on snacks. They are always expensive in France, and nowhere more so than in Paris, where an omelet and salad and a soft drink may well cost as much as a three- or even four-course fixed-price *menu* in a modest restaurant. If you want a really light meal, you'll do much better in a tea room or wine bar (see box), or in one of the new-style chains like **Oh! Poivrier!** or **Tarte Julie**, where you can get a light meal in stylish surroundings that are a vast improvement on the mediocre fast-food chains.

The History of Paris: Some Key Dates

3rd century BC	An island in the Seine is settled by a Celtic tribe called the Parisii, who live mainly by fishing and hunting wildfowl and other game (Walk 1)
52BC	Roman legions conquer the fortified island and rebuild Lutetia, the main settlement, which over the next two centuries spreads to the southern bank of the river. Some traces of this Gallo-Roman city survive in the Hôtel de Cluny and the Arènes de Lutèce (Walk 2)
1st century AD	The boatmen's corporation are an important influence in the city, becoming rich through river trading (the city's coat of arms still features a boat)
250	St Denis (or Dionysius) leads a Christian mission to the city
272	Although the city is now mostly Christian, St Denis is martyred with two companions on 'Martyrs' Mount' (now Montmartre, Walk 10)
276	A series of Barbarian raids force the Parisii to withdraw to the Ile de la Cité and build a defensive wall round it (Walk 1)
c.**300**	Lutetia is renamed Paris
360	Julian the Apostate is proclaimed emperor in the Cité
451	Attila the Hun and his hordes come close to Paris but turn back at Orléans, thus fulfilling the prediction made by Geneviève, who later becomes the city's patron saint (Walk 2)
460	The Franks lay siege to Paris; Geneviève helps to keep the starving citizens alive by organising the ferrying of supplies by river (Walk 2)

508	King Clovis of the Franks makes Paris his capital
885	The city is besieged by marauding Norman invaders, who have been terrifying the citizens with frequent raids for decades; they are eventually defeated by Count Eudes, who is elected king a few years later
1115	Abélard starts teaching in the Notre Dame cathedral school (Walk 1)
*c.***1135**	Abbot Suger has the abbey church of Saint-Denis rebuilt in the new Gothic style (Beyond the Centre)
1163	Work starts on Notre Dame cathedral (Walk 1)
1180	Philippe Auguste's city wall is started (see box); it includes the Louvre fortress (Walk 8) and the Tour de Nesle (Walk 3)
1181	A central market is built on the Right Bank (and stays there until 1969) (Walk 8)
1215	The University of Paris founded (Walk 2)
1239	Saint Louis (Louis IX) buys some sacred relics from the Emperor of Constantinople and commissions the Sainte Chapelle as a shrine to house them (Walk 1)
1253	The Sorbonne is founded (Walk 2)
1260	The boatmen's corporation takes over the running of the city, which is headed by the 'provost of the merchants'
*c.***1300**	The earliest surviving house in Paris is built (Walk 7)
1307	Philippe le Bel represses the Templars (Walk 7)
1358	Etienne Marcel leads an uprising against the monarchy and lets the English armies into Paris, but is assassinated (Walk 8)
1364	Foundation stone of the Bastille laid (Walk 9); at about this time Charles V builds a new city wall (see box)
1420	English armies under Henry V capture Paris
1429	Joan of Arc tries to win the city back but is wounded (Walk 6)

A gilded Joan of Arc in the place des Pyramides, near the spot where she was wounded in 1429

1431	Henry VI of England has himself crowned king of France in Notre Dame; seven years later Charles VII recaptures the city
c. **1475**	Hôtel de Sens built (Walk 9)
c. **1485**	Hôtel de Cluny built (Walk 2)
1530	Collège de France founded (Walk 2)
1534	Ignatius Loyola and companions take vows that lead to the founding of the Society of Jesus (Walk 10)
1546	François Ier commissions a new Renaissance palace at the Louvre (Walk 6)
1559	Henri II dies of wound received in a tournament; his widow Catherine de Médicis has the Palais des Tournelles in the Marais demolished (Walk 9) and commissions a new palace at the Tuileries (Walk 6)

1572	The Massacre of St Bartholomew, in which several thousand Protestants are slaughtered (Walk 6)
1578	Work starts on the Pont Neuf (Walk 1)
1594	Henri IV converts to Catholicism, claiming that 'Paris is well worth a mass', and settles in Paris, continuing building work at the Louvre and the Tuileries (Walk 6)
1605	Henri IV commissions the place Royale in the Marais; Louis XIII officially opens the square in 1612 after Henri's assassination and the area becomes fashionable with the aristocracy (Walk 9); five years later work starts on a new palace for Henri's widow Marie de Médicis, the Luxembourg (Walk 3)
1627	Work starts on developing the Ile Saint-Louis (Walk 1)
1632	Cardinal Richelieu commissions the Palais Cardinal (now the Palais Royal, Walk 6)
1660	Fortifications built by Charles IX and Louis XIII are pulled down; the resulting open space (the 'boulevard') is gradually transformed over the next century into a fashionable centre of entertainment (Walk 7)
1667	Le Nôtre draws up plans for extending the Tuileries and lays out what will eventually become the avenue des Champs-Elysées (Walks 5 and 6); the Cour des Miracles is demolished (Walk 7)
1670	Louis XIV founds Les Invalides (Walk 4)
1672	Louis transfers the court to Versailles
1674	Perrault's colonnade on the east front of the Louvre completed (Walk 6)
1702	First houses built round the place Vendôme (Walk 6)
c. **1710**	The Faubourg Saint-Germain becomes the centre of intellectual and aristocratic society (Walk 4)
1744	Louis XV vows to build a church dedicated to St Geneviève if he recovers from an illness; the church later becomes the Panthéon (Walk 2)

The 'Fortifs' — and Their Predecessors

The 'fortifs' — a familiar abbreviation for the fortifications built round Paris in the 1840s by prime minister (and later president) Adolphe Thiers — play an important part in the folk memory of Parisians. A decision was taken in 1841 to encircle Paris with a ring of fortifications that would draw into the city proper a number of outlying villages such as Auteuil and Passy in the west, Montmartre in the north, Belleville and Charonne in the east. The huge fortified wall, which had a wide strip of open ground on either side, was completed in 1845. By 1859 the *fortifs* had been accepted as the official boundary of Paris. But after the First World War they were no longer thought necessary and were razed to the ground in 1919. The land left empty was used to create the ring of boulevards still popularly known as the 'boulevards des Maréchaux', since they bear the names of famous French marshals (boulevard Brune, boulevard Jourdan, boulevard Kellerman, boulevard Ney and so on). Since 1973 they have been paralleled by an outer ring road, the *boulevard périphérique* (usually abbreviated to 'le périph'), which has done a great deal to relieve traffic congestion in the city centre, though it too can become congested.

Thiers's wall was only one in a long line of more or less concentric 'frontiers' round Paris. First came the Gallo-Roman wall, which marked the boundary of the Parisii's domain in the third century AD, after they had been forced by the Norman invasions to retreat from their new districts on the Left Bank of the Seine to the site of the original Lutetia on the Île de la Cité. This was followed nine hundred years later by Philippe Auguste's wall, a few fragments of which have survived (in the

southern part of the Marais, for instance, and in the Latin Quarter). This covered a much larger area, including the newly drained marshes that are now the Marais district, and stretched as far as the Montagne Sainte-Geneviève in the south. It was protected on the west by the Louvre fortress and, on the Left Bank, on a site between the Institut de France and the Monnaie (Mint), by the famous Tour de Nesle that features in a play of the same name by Alexandre Dumas *père*; on the east by huge chains slung across the Seine.

The third wall, entirely on the Right Bank and defended on the east by the infamous Bastille Prison, was put up by Charles V in the late 14th century. Its eastern portion was razed two hundred years later and the site eventually used for a wide boulevard that became ultra-fashionable in the mid-18th century, the heyday of the 'Grands Boulevards' (see Walk 7). Charles V's wall was extended westwards in the 16th century by a new rampart built under Louis XIII.

The late 18th century saw the building of the 'Tax-Collectors' Wall' (*Mur des Fermiers-Généraux*), designed to ensure that customs duties were paid on all goods that entered the city. It covered a vast area from Passy in the west to Charonne in the east and was dotted along its length with 'barriers', some of which still survive: the recently restored Rotonde de la Villette in the north-east and the Pavillon de Chartres on the edge of the Parc Monceau in the north-west are examples. This wall, the last to be built before the *fortifs*, was highly unpopular with the Parisians. Hence the punning quip: *'Le mur murant Paris rend Paris murmurant'* ('The wall ringing Paris makes Parisians grumble').

1755	Louis XV commissions a large square beside the Seine, later the place de la Concorde (Walk 6)
1784	Work starts on the 'Tax-Collectors' Wall' (see box)
1786	The Cimetière des Innocents is emptied of its dead, who are moved to the Catacombs (Walks 4 and 8); Palais Royal gardens surrounded by houses and shopping arcades (Walk 6)
1789	The fall of the Bastille signals the beginning of the French Revolution (Walk 9)
1792	The Comédie française troupe of actors moves into a new theatre at the Palais Royal (Walk 6)
1793	Louis XVI is guillotined in the place de la Concorde (Walk 6); the Louvre Museum opens (Walk 6)
1799	The city's first glass-roofed shopping arcade opens (Walk 7)
1801	The rue de Rivoli is built (Walk 6)
1804	Napoleon crowns himself emperor in Notre Dame (Walk 1); cemetery of Père-Lachaise opened (Beyond the Centre)
1806	Work starts on the Arc de Triomphe (Walk 5) and on the Arc de Triomphe du Carrousel (Walk 6); at about this time Napoleon has a wine market built on the Left Bank (Walk 2), introduces a numbering system for the city's houses, has embankments built along the Seine
1815	Under the Restoration private developers start building theatres and shopping arcades (Walk 7)
1821	The Canal Saint-Martin built (Beyond the Centre)
1830	Street fighting breaks out during the 'Trois Glorieuses' (27–9 July) and the monarchy is overthrown
1840	Napoleon's remains ceremonially transported to Les Invalides (Walk 4)
1840s	Viollet-le-Duc launches restoration programme at Notre Dame (Walk 1); elegant mansions line the Champs-Elysées (Walk 5)
1841	Work starts on the 'fortifs' (see box)

Baron Haussmann

Georges Eugène, Baron Haussmann (1809–91), undoubtedly did more to create the Paris we know today than any one person before or since. The *grands projets* embarked on in the 1980s, however impressive, pale into insignificance beside the wholesale redevelopment launched by this energetic town planner who was Prefect of the Seine (the equivalent of Mayor of Paris) under Napoleon III. It has been said that he took Paris in the space of a couple of decades from the feudal era to the modern world, and that his was the true Revolution, as far as Paris was concerned, rather than the French Revolution of 1789.

From 1853 onwards, with the enthusiastic support of the emperor, he razed whole districts to the ground, destroying virtually all the medieval houses round Notre Dame on the Ile de la Cité, for instance, cut great swathes through huddles of picturesque alleyways, moving hundreds of thousands of citizens, and laid out the spacious tree-lined boulevards that are so typical of Paris today. He was responsible for most of the city's parks, including the Bois de Boulogne, which, at the emperor's insistence, was designed to imitate London's Hyde Park. He also built the huge railway stations and the central market of Les Halles.

Haussmann is vilified by historians for his depredations, and you will often find yourself agreeing with the 19th-century writer Joris-Karl Huysmans, who deplored the 'boring symmetry' of the new thoroughfares, with their endless vistas flanked by tall, virtually identical blocks of flats, each with its first- and fourth-floor balconies. It is often a relief to come across the higgledy-piggledy streets and uneven roofscapes, the unsymmetrical squares and unexpected hillocks of the few districts that escaped the baron's pickaxe. But it has to be admitted that without his grandiose remodelling, the relative ease with which Paris traffic flows at most times of day (though not on Friday afternoons and evenings) would be inconceivable. And there is no doubt that before he changed the face of the city, much of it was squalid, unsafe and insanitary: one of his major changes was to provide efficient water and sewage systems.

The baron's schemes were by no means purely aesthetic, however. They had an underlying strategic purpose: with wide avenues and boulevards and large squares for manoeuvring it was much easier for the police and the troops to quell a riot when the effervescent Parisians, always ready to stage a revolt, took to the streets or the barricades.

The baron is immortalised in the long (his detractors would say appropriately interminable) boulevard Haussmann, which runs from the Drouot auction house east of the Opéra right through to the avenue Friedland close to the Etoile. A statue of him, rescued from the depths of the City of Paris art and furniture depository in 1988 and carefully restored, now stands on the corner of his eponymous boulevard and the rue de Laborde (Ⓜ Miromesnil, Saint-Augustin).

1842	The Madeleine is consecrated (Walk 6)
1848	Paris joins in the 'Year of Revolutions', which spells the end of the French monarchy
1850s and 1860s	Baron Haussmann transforms Paris (see box)

c. **1850**	The 'New Athens' becomes an intellectual and artistic centre (Walk 10)
1854	Haussmann lays out the Etoile (Walk 5)
1860	Outlying villages annexed to Paris, including Montmartre, which becomes a centre of bohemian and artistic life (Walk 10)
1870–1	The Franco-Prussian War brings an end to a period of prosperity; the population starves during the Siege of Paris and the Paris Commune is bloodily suppressed – the Tuileries Palace (Walk 6) and the Hôtel de Ville (Walk 8) are virtually destroyed
1875	The Opéra opens (Walk 7)
1876	A public subscription collects enough funds for work to start on the Sacré-Coeur basilica (Walk 10)
1889	The Eiffel Tower is built (Walk 4)
1900	The first underground railway (métro) line opens; the Grand Palais, the Petit Palais and the Pont Alexandre III are all built (Walk 5)
1900s	The 'Belle époque', when Paris is *the* centre of fashion and entertainment; 'modern art' first appears in Montmartre, with the birth of Cubism at the Bateau Lavoir (Walk 10)
1914	Paris is saved from a German invasion by the Battle of the Marne (Walk 4)
1919	The *fortifs* are demolished (see box)
c. **1920**	Montparnasse takes over from Montmartre as the centre of modern art (Walk 3)
1937	Palais de Chaillot built (Walk 5)
1940	The city is briefly bombed, but the Fall of France brings German occupation rather than destruction
1944	Paris is liberated; General de Gaulle leads a victory parade down the Champs-Elysées (Walk 5)

late 1940s and 1950s	The Existentialist period makes Saint-Germain-des-Prés world famous (Walk 3)
1958	Work starts on a new business and residential district at La Défense (Beyond the Centre)
1968	The 'May Events': street fighting and barricades in the Latin Quarter (Walk 2)
1969	Les Halles (central food market) moved out of Paris (Walk 8)
1973	Montparnasse Tower completed (Walk 3); *boulevard périphérique* (ring road) opens
1977	Pompidou/Beaubourg Centre opens (Walk 8); office of Mayor of Paris reinstated (Walk 8)
1985	Musée Picasso opens (Walk 9)
1986	Musée d'Orsay (Walk 4) and 'Science City' at La Villette (Beyond the Centre) open
1988	The renovated Les Halles district completed (Walk 8)
1989	Bicentenary of the Fall of the Bastille celebrated: Pyramid at the Louvre (Walk 6), new Bastille opera house (Walk 9) and *'Grande Arche'* at La Défense (Beyond the Centre) all unveiled

Walk 1
The Ile de la Cité and Ile Saint-Louis

Starting point: the northern (Right Bank) end of the Pont Neuf, 1er; Ⓜ Pont-Neuf. This first walk covers the two islands in the Seine in the centre of Paris. It starts in the first *arrondissement*, then moves on to the fourth.

This seems to me to be much the most appropriate first walk for anyone exploring Paris: it covers a small area right in the middle of the city, provides an excellent opportunity for getting your bearings, and introduces you both to the place where the history of Paris began and to two of its most important and beautiful buildings, Notre Dame cathedral and the Sainte Chapelle. It also gives you a chance to visit two places that help you to understand how the city has developed over the centuries, the archaeological 'crypt' beneath the square in front of Notre Dame, and the new Pavillon de l'Arsenal, a permanent exhibition devoted to town planning, opposite the eastern tip of the Ile Saint-Louis. And it offers glimpses of medieval Paris in the cathedral and a few surviving streets to the north of it, elegant 17th-century Paris on the Ile Saint-Louis and bombastic 19th-century architecture in the official buildings on the Ile de la Cité.

The whole walk is relatively traffic-free – a plus point if you haven't yet got used to the speed of Paris traffic – and much of it is surprisingly peaceful: even at the height of the summer tourist season, you only have to walk a few paces from the crowds in and around the great cathedral to find quiet side streets that seem to belong in some sleepy provincial town, while the Ile Saint-Louis has long been a sought-after residential area for those who can afford to pay for peace and quiet in the heart of Paris.

The walk starts at the western end of the Ile de la Cité, the boat-shaped island first inhabited in about 200BC, by the Celtic Parisii tribe who founded the primitive settlement that represents the beginning of what is now Paris, and survived mainly by fishing. Their little knot of huts gradually spread over the island and became known as Lutetia, a Celtic word for a settlement surrounded by water. In 52BC it was conquered by the Romans and rebuilt as a Gallo-Roman city whose inhabitants were chiefly boatmen plying up and down the river. By the time the old name had been abandoned in favour of Paris, in about AD350, the city had taken a boat as its symbol, and to this day the Paris coat of arms features a sailing vessel with the defiant motto *Fluctuat nec mergitur* (It is tossed by the waves but does not sink). Although the Seine is still a working river and you can often watch long barges, laden with coal or sand, slowly ploughing their way beneath the Pont Neuf, the majority of the craft on this stretch of the river are sightseeing boats of various sizes, some of which start from below the bridge. A trip on a *bateau mouche* is not to be despised: in spite of the inevitable throng of tourists, it gives you an excellent view of some of the city's most interesting buildings and even the meals on board are much better than you might expect.

In spite of its name, the **Pont Neuf** (New Bridge) is in fact the earliest surviving bridge across the Seine, dating back to 1578. In 1978 its quatercentenary was celebrated with a lively fair recreating the stalls and booths that once lined the bridge. Entertainers and showmen – dentists pulling teeth seem to have been one of the main attractions, as well as fireaters and the like – would set up shop in the semi-circular niches on either side, which now, with their stone benches, make a convenient place for unfolding your map and getting your bearings as you pick out landmarks up and down the river.

Downriver (westwards) you can see the **Monnaie** (Mint), the glittering dome of the **Institut de France**, beyond them the **Musée d'Orsay**, the splendid new museum converted from a railway station, and, in the far distance, the **Eiffel Tower**. All of these are on the Left (i.e. south) Bank. On the Right Bank you see first the **Louvre**, beyond it the treetops of the **Tuileries Gardens** and, in the background, the huge glass roof of the **Grand Palais**. Upriver you get a good view of the grim medieval towers of the **Conciergerie** on the Ile de la Cité itself, while on the Right Bank the **Tour Saint-Jacques** and the roof of the **Hôtel de Ville** are easy to pick out.

At either end of the bridge are the tall and narrow houses lining the Left Bank *quais* and the fairly downmarket department store **La Samaritaine**. This takes its name from the biblical Woman of Samaria, who was depicted drawing water for Christ on the pump house beside the bridge. This large building, surmounted by a clock tower topped by a peal of bells, was still pumping water to the Louvre and the Tuileries château and its gardens as late as 1813. There seems to be some confusion about the name: an over-enthusiastic PR person proclaims in a leaflet issued by the store that the biblical scene in question was that of the Good Samaritan, and draws a fanciful parallel with the service rendered to its customers. Don't let this inaccuracy put you off visiting La Samaritaine's famous roof terrace. If the weather is fine I recommend taking the lift up there before you start exploring the islands, to enjoy the panoramic views over the city and the bird's eye view of the Ile de la Cité as you relax with a cup of tea or coffee.

Then walk to the **place du Pont-Neuf** in the middle of the bridge to admire the equestrian statue of Henri IV, a cheerful-looking figure with a little pointed beard. 'Le bon roi Henri' – Good King Henry – was popular in his lifetime and the French still have a soft spot for him, remembering approvingly his remark about wanting to make sure that all his subjects, in the length and breadth of his kingdom, could afford to have a chicken bubbling in a pot on their hearth on

Sundays. *Poule au pot Henri IV* is a staple on many restaurant menus in Paris, and very good it is too, its steaming broth fragrant with the juices of the bird and the vegetables – usually carrots, leeks and onions – cooked with it. Henri's nickname was 'le Vert Galant', which in more innocent days used to be translated as 'a gay spark'. He enjoyed the same sort of 'merry monarch' reputation as Henry VIII, though he went in for a string of mistresses rather than a series of discarded or beheaded wives. The nickname is perpetuated in the triangular garden behind the statue that forms the prow of the island, the **square du Vert-Galant**, a favourite place for a stroll or a rest beneath the trees. This is also the starting-point for the **Bateaux-Vedettes du Pont-Neuf**, one of several types of sightseeing boats.

Now follow the king's gaze and walk across the bridge to the **place Dauphine**, a charming and peaceful square at any season, but perhaps at its most delightful in the winter, when the bare branches of the trees stand out blackly against the stern classical façade of the **Palais de Justice** (law courts) at the far end. On the left-hand corner as you reach the narrow entrance to the square is the **Taverne Henri IV***, a long-standing wine bar that has helpfully extended its opening hours to enable you to spend a convivial evening there right through to midnight. On the other side (15 place du Pont-Neuf) is a little shop selling cheap, fun jewellery that makes a good present for fashion-conscious teenagers. As the square widens out you come on the right to the island's only hotel, the very basic but atmospheric **Henri IV***. The square has another wine bar, the **Bar du Caveau** at no. 17, several restaurants, including the delightful **Paul*** at no. 15, and a pretty tea room, **Fanny-Tea***, on the left.

Turn right out of the square along the **rue Harlay**. Cross over the **quai des Orfèvres**, once the main Paris centre of the gold- and silversmiths' trade (*orfèvrerie* in French), for good views of the river and the interesting mixture of buildings lining the **quai des Grands-Augustins** on the Left Bank, some of them quite low houses, but mostly tall blocks with highly desirable penthouses at the top. Then turn left and walk past the entrance to the law courts and the headquarters of the PJ (*police judiciaire*, France's CID), generally referred to, as fans of Simenon's Maigret will know, as the Quai des Orfèvres, just as the foreign ministry is known as the Quai d'Orsay.

When you get to the **Pont Saint-Michel**, look right for a glimpse of the busy **place Saint-Michel** with its large fountain (see next walk), then turn left, cross over the *quai* and walk along the **boulevard du Palais** to the entrance to the **Sainte Chapelle** at no. 6. There is virtually certain to be a long queue and you will have to put up with airport-style bag searches and frisking, because to reach this most beautiful of chapels you have to approach the **Palais de Justice**, the city's main law courts, a favourite target for terrorist bombs – or threats to plant them. But it all seems worth it when you eventually find yourself inside the magic Gothic building with its glorious stained glass depicting hundreds of scenes from the Old Testament.

The Upper Chapel in the Gothic Sainte Chapelle, a jewel casket in stained glass, its vaulted roof daringly supported on slender columns of stone

As you climb up the narrow staircase and come out into the **Chapelle Haute**, you feel you've stepped into a casket full of brilliantly polished jewels — not an inaccurate impression really, as it was built by Louis IX as a shrine to house the most precious of relics. One of them was said to be the Crown of Thorns, acquired by Saint Louis, as he was reverently known, from Baldwin, Emperor of Constantinople, in 1239, to enable him to pay off a debt. Another was a fragment of the True Cross (both are now in Notre Dame). The chapel was designed by Pierre de Montereau or de Montreuil in the mid-1240s, when the Gothic style had reached a peak of perfection, and is a supreme example of its mixture of fragility and strength, its soaring upwards movement that makes you catch your breath in wonder. The daringly narrow piers between the tall windows, supporting the vaulted roof, make the walls seem to vanish, especially when the sun catches the stained glass and throws its brilliant reflection on the old stonework, on the decorated floor and on the sky-blue ceiling dotted with gilded stars. But the overwhelming feeling of colour is there even on dull days, making you forget the inevitable crowds.

The chapel is so narrow that the rose window seems huge. Built a century later than the rest of the windows, it is in different colours, with golds and greens predominating instead of blues and reds. To follow the sequence of the biblical scenes, buy a booklet from the lower chapel, which seems dark by comparison, though it is in fact brightly painted. Candlelit concerts are often staged in the Sainte Chapelle — book early. When you leave, pause to peer up at the stone angel perched high above the roof. He once used to rotate slowly on his axis, but sadly the mechanism is no longer working. Turn left out of the gates and walk to the corner of the boulevard, where you can admire the oldest public timepiece in Paris on the **Tour de l'Horloge**: it dates back to 1370.

The tower is one of four massive structures on the river façade of the medieval fortress of the **Conciergerie**, once part of the royal palace (Concierge was the title borne by the governor), but notorious as the grim prison where Marie-Antoinette and many thousands of others awaited their fate on the guillotine. It is an appropriately dark and gloomy contrast to the lightness and colour of the Sainte Chapelle, but worth visiting for the lovely Gothic vaulting in the guardroom and the vast Salle des Gens d'Armes, leading to the equally vast kitchens with their four monumental fireplaces. You can also visit Marie-Antoinette's cell, and see a grisly collection of mementoes in the chapel.

On the other side of the river loom the theatres in the **place du Châtelet** (Walk 8), but you should walk back to the Palais de Justice gates and cross over to the **rue de Lutèce**, now pleasantly pedestrianised, and adorned with trees and replicas of old lamps. Turn round to see the Sainte Chapelle soaring above the rooftops (but beware of cars sweeping out of the underground car park), then walk on past the splendid métro entrance with arching lamps (see Introduction) to visit the flower market in the **place Louis-Lépine**. (If it happens to be a Sunday, the banks of flowers and plants will have vanished, to be replaced by caged birds.) Turn right at the end of the square into the **rue de la Cité** and walk past the side of the **Hôtel Dieu**, a 19th-century hospital built close to the site of a much older hospice of the same name. Notice the **rue Saint-Jacques**, straight ahead beyond

A Major Archaeological Discovery

The many acts of vandalism perpetrated during the Revolution included, in 1793, hacking off the row of 13th-century statues forming the Galerie des Rois or Kings' Gallery above the portals on the west front of Notre Dame. But it was a case of mistaken identity: in their revolutionary zeal the mob had attacked the Kings of Judah, assuming they were representatives of the hated French monarchy.

The figures crashed down on the *parvis* in front of the cathedral, but the heads were somehow spirited away by an ardent royalist, who buried them beneath the courtyard of his mansion, the Hôtel Moreau, just off the boulevard Haussmann.

There they lay hidden for nearly two hundred years, until 1977, when they came to light during building work at the bank that now occupies the *hôtel*. Their recovery is generally held to be one of the twentieth century's major archaeological finds.

Restored as far as possible – most of their noses are missing – twenty-one of these still-vigorous heads now form an impressive display in the Musée de Cluny (Room VIII beside the *frigidarium*, see Walk 2). The full-length sculptures you now see on the Galerie des Rois are replicas placed there during Viollet-le-Duc's 19th-century restoration of the cathedral.

the river, climbing up the hill, and the outline of the **Panthéon** (Walk 2), then turn left for your first view of the **cathedral of Notre Dame**.

The square in front of it, known as the **Parvis** (a corruption of *paradis* or paradise), has been paved and helpfully equipped with benches, while cars and coaches have been banished to an underground car park. The building of the car park led to excavations that have resulted in the very interesting **Crypte archéologique**, reached via the steps at the western end of the square (again, be careful of the cars using the car park). This subterranean museum, opened in 1980, was built to house remains from the Gallo-Roman period onwards – seventeen centuries of history spread out *in situ*. Don't miss visiting it, as with its relief plans and its well-lit excavations it gives an excellent sense of how the city developed from a tiny Celtic settlement. It also illustrates how Baron Haussmann (see History) transformed the Ile de la Cité by demolishing the huddle of medieval buildings round the cathedral and opening up the square above your head. Until then, the cathedral was surrounded by a network of narrow streets and hemmed in by three more churches, as well as shops and houses and workshops, the Hôtel Dieu and the Foundlings' Hospital.

Whatever your view of Haussmann's *oeuvre*, you have to admit that it is a bonus to be able to admire the cathedral's façade from a distance. As you walk towards the three great portals, spare a glance to the right for the green-tinted bronze equestrian statue of Charlemagne, looking very much the medieval monarch, his hair flowing from beneath his helmet. Look out too for a star-shaped symbol in the paving marking 'Point Zéro', the place from which all distances in France are measured.

The cathedral, started in 1163, was built on the site of a whole string of earlier religious buildings, starting with a Roman temple. Twenty years later the chancel and high altar were consecrated, but the superb sculpture on the west façade

dates from 1240, the north tower is later still – and the whole cathedral, considerably altered in the 17th century, suffered badly during the Revolution. Much of what you see now is copies, but some of the original sculpture can be seen in the Musée de Cluny (see box, Walk 2). And the mighty building was in a good enough state of repair for Napoleon to crown himself emperor there in 1804, though by the middle of the 19th century it needed a campaign led by admirers of Victor Hugo's *Notre-Dame de Paris* to set in train a vast restoration programme organised by the architect Viollet-le-Duc.

After admiring the sculpture round (from left to right) the Portal of the Virgin, the Portal of the Last Judgement and the Portal of St Anne, surmounted by the Kings' Gallery, the rose window and the twin towers, make your way in through the crowds to sense the majesty of the interior, with its long nave ending in the lovely stained glass of the transept. Here you can see a beautiful 14th-century Virgin and Child always known as *Notre Dame de Paris*, and get a good view of the huge rose windows. Walk slowly round the ambulatory with its many chapels, mostly filled with elaborate tombs, and in the centre, think of Louis XIII vowing to dedicate his kingdom to the Virgin Mary if, after twenty-three years of childless marriage, he was granted an heir. The future Louis XIV was born and the vow was symbolised in a *Pietà* by Coysevox in the choir, surrounded by statues of the king and his heir.

You can visit the Treasury, once the sacristy, on the south side of the choir, but its most holy relics, transferred here from the Sainte Chapelle, are displayed only on Good Friday. And just inside the main entrance to the left are the stairs to the towers – a long climb, but worth it on a fine day for the famous views beyond the bestiary of gargoyles.

When you leave the cathedral turn left and then left again through the swing gate into the **square Jean XXIII**, the garden running along beside the river. This is the best place for enjoying the sculptures, the rose windows and the flying buttresses as you walk slowly round towards the eastern tip of the island, or pause on one of the many benches, which are surprisingly little used by tourists, though you may find locals chatting on them beneath the trees. Don't be so mesmerised by the cathedral, which is even lovelier since a major clean-up brought out the details of the stonework, that you miss the views over the river from the creeper-hung parapet. The garden continues beyond the **quai de l'Archevêché**, where it becomes the **square de l'Ile de France**, a triangular garden once housing the popular morgue – popular because coming to view the corpses was a favourite outing in the 19th century. The views of the east end of Notre Dame are quite lovely from here and you also get your first sight of the Ile Saint-Louis, linked to the Ile de la Cité by the **Pont Saint-Louis**.

At the far end of the garden is the entrance to the very moving modern memorial to the two hundred thousand French men, women and children who were deported to the Nazi concentration camps: a sobering place to reflect on

The flying buttresses of Notre Dame seem to raise up the great cathedral so that it floats above the Seine; in the foreground, a grim contrast, the bars of the Deportation Memorial

the eternal mystery of man's inhumanity to man after the splendours of the cathedral. A narrow flight of steps takes you down to a sort of crypt, right beside the river, carved with a relentless roll call of the names of the camps. Inscriptions remind you of the fate of the majority of the deportees and at the far end is the tomb of the Unknown Deportee. The feeling is one of claustrophobia – a narrow entrance between concrete slabs, bars, or wrought-iron sculpture with hard, straight lines everywhere, a series of cells leading off a circular space, an eternal flame guttering in the chilly draught from the river. But certainly an experience not to be missed.

A coffee will no doubt be welcome by this time. Strange as it may seem, the terrace of the **Esmeralda** café on the corner of the **rue du Cloître-Notre-Dame** is often peaceful, in spite of the rows of tourist coaches from all over the world lined up in front of it. The lavatories are clean too, though it hurts a bit to have to pay for them even when you're eating or drinking there. As you sip your coffee, remember that this end of the island was once covered by houses huddled together along narrow streets, before Baron Haussmann's pickaxes got to work. To get an idea of how the Ile de la Cité used to look, turn off the rue du Cloître-Notre-Dame to visit the little network of medieval streets between the cathedral and the quai aux Fleurs. Again this whole area is surprisingly quiet, almost provincial, seeming far away from the frenzied tourist hordes milling round the cathedral.

If it happens to be a Wednesday afternoon or a weekend, stop off first for a brief visit to the **Musée Notre-Dame de Paris**, opposite the superb Portail du Cloître on the north side of the cathedral, built in the mid-13th century and surmounted by the huge rose window in the north transept. The little museum has some interesting engravings of the *parvis* and of the river beside it, crammed with craft of various kinds. A plan of the Cité in 1754 shows how crowded the whole island was, with its eighteen churches or chapels (three had recently been demolished) and its huge numbers of houses. And the section devoted to Viollet-le-Duc includes sketches and a copy of his restoration scheme. It is interesting, too, to see a letter written by Victor Hugo, Alfred de Vigny, the painter Ingres and various others about the campaign to have the cathedral restored to its former splendour. A series of engravings shows how splendid it could be on great occasions – Napoleon arriving for the Easter celebration on '28 germinal An X' or Louis XVIII making a solemn entry after the fall of the Empire – and a section on the excavations beneath the *parvis* includes various Gallo-Roman and medieval objects.

Turn into the **rue Chanoinesse**, which curves round to the left. Like the surrounding streets, it has been heavily restored over the centuries, but it still gives you a good feel of the medieval structure of the area. The cathedral precinct was made up of a series of houses lived in by the canons and it was here that the

Behind Notre Dame, a crypt built beside the river as a deeply moving memorial to the two hundred thousand French citizens deported by the Nazis during the Second World War

famous schools of Notre Dame grew up round great teachers like Abélard or Bonaventure. Here too the story of Abélard and Héloïse began (see box). I always feel that the flat with the balcony at the top of no. 10, a pretty white house and probably the site of the one lived in by Héloïse's uncle Canon Fulbert, would be a perfect place to live right in the centre of Paris. Beyond here are several attractive old houses, with peaceful leafy courtyards: nos 14 and 16 on the right, for instance. No. 22 is one of only two remaining medieval canons' houses. No. 17 opposite has an old arched doorway and no. 24, the other surviving canon's house, was for many years a wine merchant's and is now an attractive but rather expensive restaurant, **La Lieutenance**, adorned with geraniums and ivy in summer. Try to see the well in the courtyard. Its menu even claims that water from the 'Samaritaine spring' is available free of charge.

Beyond here, turn right into the rather shabby **rue de la Colombe**, which slopes down to the river, becoming gradually narrower. On either side of the narrowest part are two restaurants, the elegant **L'Embellie*** in a 15th-century building and the atmospheric, if over-priced, **Colombe***, famous for its white doves cooing in cages in the window and its medieval architecture (most of the building dates from the 13th century). The doves are not just a nod to the street name – *colombe* means dove – but commemorate a touching true story that took place when the cathedral was being built. A Breton stonemason employed by Bishop Maurice de Sully lived in a rickety house in this street, right up against the Gallo-Roman rampart (the line of which is marked in the paving stones). A pair of doves had nested in the corner of the mason's only windowsill, but one day the Seine overflowed its banks and the house collapsed, trapping the female beneath the debris. The male managed to keep her alive by tossing seeds to her and feeding her drops of water through a straw until the rubble could be cleared. The story became famous throughout Paris and until recently there was a little statue of a man with a pair of doves in a niche above the building.

Continue to the **quai aux Fleurs** for views of the Seine, which burst its banks, causing legendary floods, as recently as January 1910 – a sign on the wall near here indicates the highwater mark. Slightly to the left in the distance you can catch a glimpse of the funnels projecting above the blue structure of the controversial Beaubourg Centre (Walk 8). And straight ahead, in front of the bulk of the Hôtel de Ville, is a statue of Etienne Marcel, the cloth merchant who ran Paris virtually single-handed in the 14th century. Retrace your steps and opposite the Colombe turn left into the **rue des Ursins**. The corner where it meets the **rue des Chantres** is particularly attractive, with Gothic arches on the house on the right, a tower topped by a weathercock and steps leading up to the embankment. Climb up them (this is where you can see how high the flood waters rose) and turn round for a view of the spire of Notre Dame sandwiched between the houses.

Turn right and walk along the quai aux Fleurs, pausing in front of nos 9 and 11 to pay homage to Abélard and Héloïse, whose carved portraits surmount the chastely separate doorways. This was one entrance to Canon Fulbert's house, but it was completely rebuilt in the 19th century. Notice too the attractive façade of no. 3bis, with its wrought-iron balconies. Then continue to the **Pont Saint-Louis**, which brings you to Paris's second island.

Abélard and Héloïse – a Medieval Love Story

Pierre (or Peter) Abélard, generally thought of as the most acute thinker and most original theologian of the 12th century, was a Breton born in 1079 near Nantes. At the age of 21 he came to Paris to attend lectures at the Ecole du Cloître Notre-Dame, the cathedral school, and 15 years later became a lecturer himself. He soon acquired a brilliant reputation for his 'conceptualist' teachings and exerted enormous influence over scholars and philosophers throughout Europe.

Among the canons living in the precincts of Notre Dame was Canon Fulbert, who took Abélard into his home as a lodger and as a tutor for his beautiful and highly intelligent niece Héloïse. It doesn't seem to have occurred to this miserly but naive elderly cleric that to give the handsome Abélard permission to do with his 17-year-old niece 'whatever was needed, including chastisement if necessary, to ensure that she learnt her lessons' was tantamount to encouraging a love affair, especially as Abélard was already very taken with the girl. She was no mean scholar herself and had a genuine love of learning. But, in Abélard's own words, the lessons were soon made up 'more of love and kisses than of books'.

The lovers eventually escaped from the stifling atmosphere of Notre Dame to live with Abélard's sister, where they are thought to have been married in secret. Héloïse soon gave birth to a son, for whom they chose the peculiar name of Astrolabe. They returned to Paris, but when Canon Fulbert learnt of the marriage his wrath was awful to behold. Héloïse tried to deny it, to protect her husband's career – the canon wielded considerable power – and eventually took refuge in a convent just outside Paris. But the canon sent his henchmen after Abélard, whom he ordered

to be castrated. Quite apart from the effect this butchery had on his private life, it also spelt the end of his ecclesiastical career. Abélard became a monk, but even though his teachings had been deemed heretical by a church synod, he was soon surrounded by eager disciples. The hermit's hut where he chose to live gradually expanded into a theological school, which was later taken over by a group of nuns led by Héloïse, who had taken the veil but continued to write passionate letters to Abélard.

Abélard was appointed an abbot in Brittany, but later returned to Paris, where, in open opposition to the dry and narrow scholasticism of the Ile de la Cité theologians, he started up informal open-air lecturing that eventually led, a century later, to the founding of the University of Paris. He died in 1142, on his way to Rome to defend his doctrines against charges of heresy laid by St Bernard of Clairvaux, among others. Héloïse had him buried at the monastic school she had taken over from him and 24 years later was laid to rest beside her lover. A widely believed 'miracle' is said to have taken place when Abélard's skeleton stretched out its arms to embrace his faithful mistress.

A prudish mother superior subsequently had the two separated and reburied in separate coffins. But six and a half centuries after Héloïse's death they were exhumed once again and, in an astute move designed to popularise the brand-new Père-Lachaise cemetery in eastern Paris, the lovers' remains were transferred to a single grave in the cemetery, surmounted by an elaborate tomb in appropriately Gothic style. And their touching story continues to draw more visitors to their grave than to almost any other (see Beyond the Centre).

The **Ile Saint-Louis** was originally a single island, as it is today, but in the Middle Ages was separated into two, l'Ile Notre Dame and l'Ile aux Vaches, to provide added protection for Charles V's wall. Cow Island, as the name suggests, was used for grazing cattle, but was also popular with local sportsmen and restaurant owners for the wildfowl that could be stalked in the willow- and poplar-fringed waters surrounding it. The meadows on Notre Dame Island were used by Paris's washerwomen, many of whom operated from floating wash-houses on the Seine, for spreading out their linen to dry, and on Sundays and public holidays became an informal fairground where people came from all over Paris to dance or try their skill with a bow and arrow or carouse till the early hours.

Then in the early 17th century an engineer called Christophe Marie submitted to his royal master Henri IV, and then after his assassination to his successor Louis XIII, a scheme for developing the islands as a sort of overspill for the newly fashionable Marais. His plans, which involved joining them together and linking them to both banks of the Seine, were approved and he started by building two bridges, one of which still bears his name: thus the Pont Marie has nothing to do with the Virgin Mary, as you might suppose from the original name, nor with Louis XIII's widowed mother Marie de Médicis, who watched the new king lay the foundation stone in October 1614. A new road, still called the rue des Deux-Ponts, joined the bridge to the Pont de la Tournelle, and at right angles to it, Marie built another road running right across the island from east to west, the rue Saint-Louis (now called the rue Saint-Louis-en-l'Ile). In return for these expensive operations he was granted a permit to build and run a *jeu de paume* (an indoor court for the ancestor of tennis) and a wash-house and was allowed to become one of the city's first large-scale property developers.

Over a period of about forty years, from 1620 to 1660, the meadows gave way to a series of beautiful stone mansions aligned along streets laid out on a grid pattern, many of them designed by Louis Le Vau, the architect of the Louvre and Tuileries Palaces, the lovely château of Vaux-le-Vicomte and parts of Versailles. He was also, along with the classical painter Philippe de Champaigne, one of the first residents of the new single island, which soon became a fashionable place to live. A large number of the elegant original houses are still standing, giving a pleasing all-of-a-piece impression as you stroll round the quiet streets.

After the Revolution the area suffered the same sort of decline as the nearby Marais (Walk 9), its noble mansions divided up into workshops and cheap lodgings, but during the Romantic period it became something of a centre of artistic and literary life. Baudelaire lived on the quai de Béthune and, for a few happy years, in the Hôtel Pimodan (now the Hôtel de Lauzun) on the quai d'Anjou, where with Théophile Gautier and others he experimented with the 'artificial paradises' induced by hashish. Cézanne and Daumier had studios on the island at one time and Chopin was one of many Polish writers and musicians who made their home there.

Towards the beginning of this century it gradually started to become fashionable with the wealthy once again – in the early pages of *A la recherche du temps perdu*, Proust has Marcel's great-aunt teasing Swann for deciding to live in 'an old mansion on the quai d'Orléans' rather than in the traditional haunts of the well-off bourgeoisie on the boulevard Haussmann or the avenue de l'Opéra. It is now an exclusive and self-contained residential area with a pleasantly villagey feel about it. It even has what amounts to its own village high street, with a couple of butchers, a dairy, a grocer's, a wine merchant's, florist's, a school and a church, as well as a sprinkling of art galleries, book and poster shops and a large number of restaurants. There are only two 'sights' to be visited, but this is one of the most delightful parts of Paris for a peaceful and instructive stroll.

From the **Pont Saint-Louis**, linking the island to the Ile de la Cité, you can enjoy a good view of the 17th-century buildings that make up the island and of the river – working barges often use this arm of the Seine, leaving the other side to the tourist boats. On the corner of the **rue Jean-du-Bellay** on the far side of the bridge is the lively **Brasserie de l'Ile Saint-Louis***, and on the right, a little group of cafés and restaurants with pavement tables, including the old-established **La Chaumière-en-l'Ile** and **Le Flore en l'Ile**. The island's high street starts just beyond them on the right, but before exploring it you can absorb something of the flavour of the whole area by walking round the **quai de Bourbon** to the left, raised above street level. This peaceful little oasis at the western tip of the island is lined with attractive mansions with semi-circular windows above the front doors and some interesting decorative details. It is only a few minutes' walk from the serried ranks of tourist coaches behind Notre Dame but seems like another world. Notice the medallions carved with scenes from classical mythology high up on the flat façade at the end and, at no. 45 just round the corner, the house where the Princesse Bibesco, the Romanian-born *femme de lettres* and friend of Proust and his circle, lived for many years until her death in 1973. No. 43 next door has a pretty carving over the doorway.

Turn right opposite the **Pont Louis-Philippe**, leading to the Right Bank and the Marais, and walk along the rue Jean-du-Bellay. At no. 12 **Au Pain de Sucre** is a delightful little shop specialising in sugar loaves (that's what the name means) in every colour of the rainbow – vegetable and other natural dyes only, no artificial colouring. More manageable to take home are little jars and transparent packets of multi-coloured sugar like those old-fashioned stripey jars of sand you used to buy as souvenirs in seaside resorts. Next door but one, at no. 8, the chemist still has its old apothecary's jars. Now turn left into the **rue Saint-Louis-en-l'Ile**, after pausing to admire the view of the dome and colonnade of the Panthéon straight ahead in the distance, perched high up on the Left Bank. On the right, at no. 81, a sign in the shape of a teapot swings outside a pleasant but obstinately anonymous tea room serving good flans and other light dishes. On the other side at no. 78 is a good bakery, if you prefer to start collecting ingredients for a picnic on one of the benches beneath the trees along the quai de Béthune. Further along you'll find all the other items you need in the little row of shops – a mini-supermarket selling fresh vegetables and fruit, a grocer's, a delicatessen and a dairy. At no. 69 is the first of the street's restaurants, **Le Monde des Chimères***, started many years ago by the well-known chef Jacques Manière and recently revived, and at no. 65 one of its four sought-after hotels, the **Lutèce***.

Cross over the **rue Le-Regrattier**, a peaceful side street, and continue past **Aux Anysetiers du Roy***, a lively restaurant at no. 61, and another hotel, the **Deux-**

Iles*, at no. 59. Notice the pretty carving over the doorway of no. 70, and if you're starting to fancy the idea of a pied-à-terre in this charming street, bring yourself back to earth with a bump by studying the prices in the window of the estate agent's at no. 62. (Bear in mind too that few of the tall houses have lifts and the worn stone steps of the 17th-century staircases, though very attractive, are hard to negotiate with luggage or heavy shopping!) The wine merchant's at no. 64 dates back to 1822 and at no. 51 **L'Epicerie** is not a full-scale grocer's but a narrow little shop specialising in teas packed in tins decorated with a drawing of the façade and traditional confectionery such as *Bêtises de Cambrai* – an early poster for these delicacies adorns one wall. The wonderfully elaborate façade of the other half of this building, the **Hôtel de Chenizot**, is adorned with griffons supporting a curving wrought-iron balcony. If the door is open you can peep in for a glimpse of the cornucopia carved over the far doorway. The Rococo decoration dates from 1719, about a hundred years after the mansion was built, and it originally had a large garden stretching as far as the quai d'Orléans. On the other side at no. 54 is the attractive entrance, set back behind a little courtyard/passage, to the rather expensive **Hôtel du Jeu de Paume***, whose name recalls Marie's first source of income on the island. Opposite the hotel is the jokey **Nos Ancêtres les Gaulois**, a cheerful and noisy restaurant popular with tourists and impoverished students where you can help yourself to wine from a huge barrel and where hungry children can make several journeys to the hors d'oeuvres buffet before tucking into platters of grilled meat, followed by cheese and pudding.

Beyond the **rue des Deux-Ponts** you'll probably find a queue outside no. 31: **Berthillon** draws people from all over Paris for its delicious ice cream and sorbets made with pure fruit. (Several other places on the island have a sign saying they sell Berthillon ices if your visit coincides with the shop's frequent closures.) **Au Gourmet de l'Isle*** and the chic **Orangerie** are both well-known restaurants. Notice the thick wooden beam above the first-floor windows, a forerunner of our RSJs, at no. 25, which was built in 1645 for a locksmith. Just past here the church of **Saint-Louis-en-l'Ile**, with a strange perforated spire and a clock projecting out into the street, dates from the early days of the island's development. It was designed by the resident architect Louis Le Vau in the 1660s, but not completed until over half a century later. The entrance is round the corner in the **rue Poulletier**, and if you're lucky enough to find it open (it is officially shut on Sunday afternoons and Mondays, but arbitrary closures at other times are common), you can admire the richly decorated interior, glittering with gilding and marble. No. 12 rue Poulletier is an attractive house and **Claude Aubry**, on the corner opposite the church, often has pretty tableware and other objects that make good presents.

Now walk along the other side of the rue Poulletier, past 5bis, a convent school started by St Vincent de Paul, and no. 9, where a cousin of Madame de Sévigné lived, to the **quai d'Anjou**, which has some beautiful houses and offers good views of the Right Bank beyond the roaring traffic of the riverside road commissioned by President Pompidou. Turn right and you soon come to another Le Vau building, the **Hôtel de Lauzun** at no. 17, where even the drainpipes are picked out in grey and gold and end in dolphins' heads. This beautiful and historically interesting mansion is usually open to the public at the weekends from about

Easter to the end of September and weekly guided tours take place for much of the year, generally on Tuesdays, but check locally as it has belonged to the City of Paris since the twenties and is often used for official receptions. It was commissioned from Le Vau by a wealthy arms dealer in the 1650s and the original gilded and painted ceilings and carved panelling have survived and been beautifully restored. Some of the decoration is by Charles Le Brun, who worked here at the beginning of his career, before he presided over the decorative schemes at Versailles. The mansion's original owner was the son of the people who ran the famous Pomme de Pin cabaret on the Ile de la Cité and he entertained the artists and writers of the day in style. After his death in 1681 it was briefly the property of the Duc de Lauzun, the reluctant husband of 'La Grande Mademoiselle', Louis XIV's energetic but far from beautiful cousin Anne Marie Louise d'Orléans, Duchesse de Montpensier, who supported the Fronde rebellion and took command of the Bastille, ordering its guns to be trained on the royal troops. After the Revolution it was lived in for a time by a glue manufacturer and a dyer, who turned some of the rooms into workshops and let off others.

Its most famous tenant was Baudelaire, who wrote some of the poems in *Les Fleurs du mal* in a little room up at the top of the house filled with antiques – collecting antiques was thought a most odd thing to do in those days – while his mulatto mistress Jeanne Duval, the 'Black Venus', lived in rooms he had taken for her nearby in the rue Le-Regrattier. During his three years in what was then known as the Hôtel Pimodan (one of its owners had been the Marquis de Pimodan), Baudelaire certainly attended some of the meetings of the Club des Hachichins in the lovely first-floor rooms then occupied by the painter F. Boissard de Boisdenier, along with Théophile Gautier, who later also took rooms there. But he never became a hashish addict, only an occasional user of what he refers to in *Les Paradis artificiels* as a 'yellowish-green jam'.

The decoration of the music room with its gallery dates from the early 19th century and the whole building was substantially altered at the end of that century – fireplaces were added in most of the rooms, for instance – but it still gives you a good idea of the sort of house in which a very wealthy private citizen lived in 17th-century Paris.

Turn right out of the *hôtel* and continue along the peaceful quai d'Anjou, where most of the mansions have now been restored. Daumier lived at no. 9 and the house next door, no. 7, has been the headquarters of the Corporation of Master Bakers since 1843. I have always secretly dreamed of living one day in the beautiful mansion on the corner, with its tall curving window and ivy-covered wall. But when I discovered that the **Hôtel Lambert** belonged to the Baron de Rothschild I realised that it would never be within my price range and I must continue to admire it from afar. I did once catch a glimpse of the elegant curving courtyard, when the *porte cochère* round the corner in the rue Saint-Louis-en-l'Ile swung open to let in a grand limousine, and I recommend that you should linger for a few minutes in case your luck is in, as this is probably the loveliest house on the island.

It was designed, once again, by Le Vau, who built a mansion for himself at the same time on the next-door plot (3 quai d'Anjou), neatly integrating the two façades. The commission came from Jean-Baptiste Lambert, a very wealthy financier who was an adviser to the king and the crown estates, but died young, leaving it to his brother Nicolas. Nicolas, himself a successful financier, lived in the house for fifty years and presided over the superb decoration by Charles Le Brun, Eustache Le Sueur and many other artists in the Cabinet de l'Amour, a lovely panelled room on the first floor inlaid on walls and ceiling with oval and rectangular paintings, putti and elaborately carved cornices, the Cabinet des Muses on the second floor, all paintings and mirrors, and the Galerie d'Hercule, one of the very few 17th-century painted galleries to have survived. As Nicolas Lambert had the foresight to commission a series of forty engravings of the interior decoration, it has been possible to restore them as far as possible to their original state and though of course you can't see them (a few of the paintings are now in the Louvre), it is pleasant to think that this perfect corner site still houses such splendours.

Before you complete your walk round the islands I strongly recommend a short detour to the Right Bank to visit one of Paris's newest sights, which is conveniently open until 8 p.m. every day except Monday. Cross over the **Pont de Sully**, also known as the **boulevard Henri-IV**, to the **quai Henri-IV**, which until it was joined to the Right Bank in the 19th century formed yet another island in the Seine. Continue to the **boulevard Morland** and turn right for the **Pavillon de l'Arsenal** at no. 21, opened, to surprisingly little fanfare, at the end of 1988 in a lofty converted warehouse. It is devoted to the important and topical subject of town planning and is designed both as a showcase for the work of City of Paris architects and planners and to make Parisians more aware of the many changes taking place in their city. But it is also an ideal place for visitors to get a feel of the city's layout and to take stock of both past and recent developments. A large relief model on the ground floor helps you to understand the topography and a series of computer screens offer a choice of menus on themes such as gardens or religious buildings or fountains. As the program you have selected runs through, the appropriate areas on the model light up, while the screen images are projected on a larger scale on to a slide screen at the end of the room.

You can spend many an absorbing hour playing with it and studying the panels round the walls on this floor and on the upper floor illustrating the various stages of the city's development, including bold plans currently under way to correct the centuries-old imbalance in favour of fashionable western districts and suburbs by spending large sums of money on the neglected eastern *arrondissements* — both housing and other 'social' projects and vast redevelopment schemes such as La Villette (see Beyond the Centre) or the Tolbiac site beside the river with its futuristic new National Library.

If all this has made you hungry or thirsty, **Le Sully** on the corner is a typical local café-brasserie, friendly and just right for a quick but reliable meal. (As the Pavillon de l'Arsenal is one of the very few sights in Paris not to charge an entrance fee, you might well think of breaking off your visit for refreshments — there is a lot to see — and then returning for a second look.)

Now cross back over the bridge and turn right into the **rue Saint-Louis-en-l'Ile**.

The odd little wedge-shaped house on the left-hand corner, with its countrified shutters and little garden with overhanging vine, strikes a very different note from the Hôtel Lambert opposite. And at no. 6 make sure not to miss the girls' faces beneath the balconies, with rambler roses for hair. Turn left opposite here and walk under the windowed archway of the **Hôtel de Bretonvilliers**, all that is left of a huge château-like house with elaborately carved decoration and a famous terraced garden designed by Jean Androuet du Cerceau, the youngest of a dynasty of architects and decorators, who also built the Hôtel de Sully in the Marais (Walk 9). The **Petit Hôtel de Bretonvilliers** on the left, dating from 1639, seems rather cosier than most of these great houses. Several other mansions in the **rue de Bretonvilliers** have recently been restored and converted into expensive flats. At the far end, the house on the right was built by the Princesse de Poix, the widow of the Duc de Richelieu et de Fronsac, friend of Voltaire, valiant soldier and great-nephew of the cardinal, who owned the large mansion round the corner, no. 18 quai de Béthune, for over sixty years — he died at the great age of 92, having famously acquired a string of aristocratic mistresses.

The quiet **quai de Béthune** is a good place for a rest or a picnic on one of the benches beneath the trees as you admire the elegant façades overlooking the river, almost all with balconies — quai des Balcons, they used to call it — and especially the views of Notre Dame to your right and the Latin Quarter on the far bank. Then turn right and walk along the *quai*. Baudelaire lived at no. 22, and no. 26 is particularly attractive with its blue-painted door and balconies and a roof terrace right at the top. The next two façades have some interesting carved decoration — scenes from classical mythology on no. 28 and musical instruments and garlands over the first-floor windows on no. 30. The walk ends at the **Pont de la Tournelle**, Marie's bridge leading to the Left Bank. The café opposite is a convenient stopping-off point. If none of the islands' many restaurants tempts you, it is only a short walk to the Latin Quarter (Walk 2) or the Marais (Walk 9), both of which are full of good places for leisurely meals.

Hotels and Restaurants

For general advice on choosing where to stay and where to eat, see Practical Information; prices are moderate unless otherwise stated.

Hotels

Ile de la Cité

Henri IV 25 pl Dauphine, 1er (43-54-44-53). For those who are prepared to rough it and sacrifice comfort for atmosphere (four centuries of it) and setting (one of the prettiest squares in Paris, in walking distance of many of its most interesting sights). Most rooms are very modest, and correspondingly cheap.

Ile Saint-Louis

These four hotels on the island's main street are all very pleasant, but you must book well in advance as they have only a small number of rooms and are much sought-after. As the street is narrow, it's worth trying for a room on the top floors, which are lighter and often have good views.

Deux-Iles 59 rue Saint-Louis-en-l'Ile, 4e (43-26-13-35, fax: 43-29-60-25). A 17th-century building with vaulted cellars housing a cosy *salon* with open fireplace and a bar.

Jeu de Paume 54 rue Saint-Louis-en-l'Ile, 4e (43-26-14-18). Once, as the name suggests, a set of indoor courts for the game that was a forerunner of tennis, converted in the late eighties into a charming hotel with a little garden. Some of the rather expensive rooms are on two floors.

Lutèce 65 rue Saint-Louis-en-l'Ile, 4e (43-26-23-52, fax: 43-29-60-25). Quite small but very pretty rooms, especially those tucked in under the roof.

Saint-Louis 75 rue Saint-Louis-en-l'Ile, 4e (46-34-04-80). More modest (and slightly less expensive) than the others, but still attractive, and it does now have a lift, so don't be afraid of the top floors.

Restaurants

Ile de la Cité

La Colombe 4 rue de la Colombe, 4e (46-33-37-08). A 13th-century building in a narrow street near Notre Dame; well known to tourists but still full of romantic charm with its doves cooing in cages and its tiny leafy terrace. Traditional cuisine.

L'Embellie 3 rue de la Colombe, 4e (46-33-26-29) (there's another entrance at 19 rue des Ursins); closed Sun. Almost opposite La Colombe. Medieval setting in a 15th-century building, inventive cuisine.

Paul 15 pl Dauphine, 1er (43-54-21-48); closed Mon, Tue. Overlooking the lovely place Dauphine on one side and the Seine on the other (there's another entrance on the river side at 52 quai des Orfèvres). Typical small-scale Paris restaurant, a bit over-priced but still delightful.

For light lunches see **Fanny-Tea** and **Taverne Henri IV** in box in Food and Drink.

Ile Saint-Louis

Aux Anysetiers du Roy 61 rue Saint-Louis-en-l'Ile, 4e (40-46-87-85); closed Wed. Lively atmosphere (helped by the all-the-wine-you-can-drink *menu*), friendly service and historic setting.

Brasserie de l'Ile Saint-Louis 55 quai de Bourbon, 4e (43-54-02-59); closed Wed, Thur for lunch and Aug. Unpretentious and filling Alsatian cuisine, served at long tables in this noisy but fun brasserie on the tip of the island diagonally opposite Notre Dame. Particularly popular for Sunday lunch.

Au Franc Pinot 1 quai de Bourbon, 4e (43-29-46-98); closed Sun, Mon. A 17th-century building, with interesting cuisine served in the vaulted cellars. The ground floor is a wine bar, convenient for light meals and with a good choice of wines by the glass.

Le Monde des Chimères 69 rue Saint-Louis-en-l'Ile (43-54-45-27); closed Sun, Mon. Attractive setting and traditional cuisine in the heart of the island.

Au Gourmet de l'Isle 42 rue Saint-Louis-en-l'Ile (43-26-79-27); closed Mon, Tue. Lively place specializing in *andouillettes* (chitterling sausages) and other staples from the *cuisine bourgeoise* repertoire, and at very reasonable prices.

Museums and Places of Interest

Boat trips: Bateaux-Vedettes du Pont-Neuf. Departures from sq du Vert-Galant, 1er, about every 30 min, except during lunch break (when lunch cruises can be made). Ⓜ Pont-Neuf

Sainte Chapelle blvd du Palais, 1er. Open daily but be prepared for long queues. Ⓜ Cité

Conciergerie 1 quai de l'Horloge, 1er. Open daily. Ⓜ Cité, Châtelet

Flower market pl Louis-Lépine/quai de Corse, 4e. Open Mon to Sat, starting at about 8.00 a.m. Ⓜ Cité

Bird market As above, but Sun only, from about 9.00 a.m. Ⓜ Cité

Crypte du Parvis Notre Dame (Archaeological Crypt) pl du Parvis Notre-Dame, 4e. Open daily. Ⓜ Cité

Notre Dame Cathedral *Towers* open daily; *Trésor* (collection of relics and ecclesiastical exhibits) shut Sun mornings. 10-minute video presentations in French and English. Ⓜ Cité

Mémorial de la Déportation (Crypt dedicated to deportees) sq de l'Ile-de-France, 4e (at eastern tip of island). Open daily. Ⓜ Cité, Maubert-Mutualité

Musée Notre-Dame de Paris 10 rue du Cloître-Notre-Dame, 4e. Open Wed and weekends, afternoons only. Ⓜ Cité

Hôtel de Lauzun 17 quai d'Anjou, 4e. Guided tours only. Look in the current issue of *L'Officiel des spectacles* or *Pariscope* under *conférences* for dates and get there in plenty of time, as numbers are limited and the visits are very popular. Ⓜ Pont-Marie, Sully-Morland

Pavillon de l'Arsenal (presentation of town planning and architecture in Paris) 21 blvd Morland, 4e. Closed Mon. No admission charge. Ⓜ Sully-Morland

Walk 2
The Latin Quarter

Starting point: the southern (Left Bank) end of the Pont de la Tournelle, 5e; Ⓜ Pont-Marie, Maubert-Mutualité. This Left Bank walk covers the fifth *arrondissement* and a little of the thirteenth.

The lively Quartier Latin has been the centre of Paris's university life for over seven hundred years. The term Latin Quarter is of course a misnomer nowadays: it is safe to assume that very few of the undergraduates and academics who still congregate here are capable of writing Latin, let alone conversing in it. But the name has stuck, and even though recent changes have seen the departure of many faculties to faceless modern buildings on the outskirts, and an influx of wealthy inhabitants as picturesque old streets are gentrified, the cafés on the boulevard Saint-Michel and the little restaurants in the side streets are still thronged with French students in term time and foreign students in the summer months. And although this aspect should not be exaggerated, it would take a cynical heart not to feel something of the romance of '*le vieux Paris*' in the huddle of medieval streets across the river from Notre Dame, the cluster of ancient colleges high up round the Panthéon and the crowded and colourful rue Mouffetard market area. This is also the only part of the city where you can see traces of the Romans' Lutetia – the amphitheatre and arena, and the baths that have been excavated beneath the Musée de Cluny, the very interesting medieval art and architecture museum. To the east, the district has acquired a new museum in the shape of the stylish Institut du Monde Arabe.

The walk starts at the southern end of the **Pont de la Tournelle**, which links the Ile Saint-Louis with the Left Bank. On the bridge, which offers lovely views west towards the flying buttresses of Notre Dame, seeming to raise the cathedral up so that it floats above the Seine, is a curious 1930s statue that looks distinctly like a space rocket on the verge of lift-off. It actually depicts St Geneviève, the patron saint of Paris, after whom one of the Latin Quarter's best-known streets is named: the Montagne Sainte-Geneviève leads up the hill to the Panthéon from the nearby place Maubert. Geneviève probably came from a noble family, but legend – always more romantic – has it that she was a shepherdess turned nun whose quiet confidence that divine protection would save the city from the invading Huns in 451 put some backbone into the panicking citizens. Sure enough, Attila's

Barbarians left the city alone and descended instead on Orléans. Ten years later she again earned the gratitude of Parisians by smuggling food into the Ile de la Cité during the Frankish siege. She lived on, a revered figure, to the age of nearly ninety and was buried in a basilica built by King Clovis for himself and his wife Clotilde on the site of what is now the famous Lycée Henri-IV.

If you're starting the walk in the afternoon you may like to pause for a browse in the second-hand bookstalls on the parapet beside the river (they are rarely open in the morning). Then cross over to the **quai de la Tournelle**, which has two interesting sights, one gastronomic, the other historical. The **Tour d'Argent** restaurant at no. 15 is in fact both, as it started life in the 16th century as a fairly ordinary café specialising in wild duck caught at dawn by the enterprising proprietor on what was then the Ile aux Vaches (see previous walk). Nowadays it is one of the world's most famous restaurants, celebrated for its views of Notre Dame from the dining room and its rich *haute cuisine*. Duck is still the *pièce de résistance*, especially *canard pressé* (pressed duck), first served to Edward VII when he was Prince of Wales. Each duck comes to the table numbered and the number is entered in a ledger next to the diner's name – a little touch of immortality if you can afford it. The prices are as high as its reputation, but the lunchtime *menu* might just be worth considering as a special treat, as it costs less than half an *à la carte* meal. You would have to book well in advance of course.

To tempt you further, if you patronise the restaurant you can visit the interesting little museum of gastronomy in the same building, where you'll learn among other things that forks were allegedly first introduced here into France after Henri III was intrigued by seeing two fellow-diners from Florence spearing their meat with a two-pronged instrument. The Tour d'Argent now has a small boutique on the opposite corner, so you could make do with a superior takeaway.

At no. 47 is the *quai*'s other landmark, the 17th-century **Hôtel de Miramion**, built by a rich benefactress at the end of the century to house an informal order of young women involved in visiting the local sick, who nicknamed them *miramionnes*. The connection has been maintained, as the *hôtel* is now the **Musée de l'Assistance Publique** (Museum of Health and Welfare). The subject may sound unexciting, but this is one of my favourite Paris museums, a mine of information about the way ordinary Parisians lived – and, especially, were born and died – down the centuries. It's an ideal place for picking up those miscellaneous scraps of social history that remain in the mind long after your visit. For instance Diderot, the Enlightenment philosopher who masterminded the *Encyclopédie*, was a foundling, one of many thousands of babies left on church and convent doorsteps throughout France – over 500 a year in the 17th century and many more in the 18th. The commentary posted up at intervals is revealing on attitudes to the poor and the museum is full of beautiful and interesting exhibits, including some early illuminated manuscripts, and surgeons' cases with ivory-handled instruments. I particularly like an idyllic art nouveau painting of *La Santé rendue aux malades* (*Invalids restored to health*) and a curious engraving of vaccination in an elegant drawing-room showing a morning-coated doctor holding a docile-looking calf.

Now walk along the *quai* eastwards to the point where the **boulevard Saint-Germain**, one of Haussmann's thoroughfares, meets the river. Until recently this

59

was the site of the Halle aux Vins (wine market) built under Napoleon, but it has been superseded by the glass and aluminium **Institut du Monde Arabe** (Arab Institute). It includes a museum of Arab art from the 9th century onwards and a library. The ninth-floor tea room offers light lunches and suppers, plus river views. The *quai* continues to the **Gare d'Austerlitz**, from where trains serve Orléans, Tours, south-west France and Spain. On a hot day a stroll in the gardens beside the river is doubly pleasant, as it gives you a chance to study the display of modern sculpture officially labelled the **Musée de Sculpture en Plein Air** (Open-air Sculpture Museum).

Walk up the **rue des Fossés Saint-Bernard**, which has several interesting restaurants, then cross the rue Jussieu and continue up the **rue du Cardinal-Lemoine**, originally a path running just outside Philippe-Auguste's ramparts. The *hôtel* on the left just after the crossroads, built to honour the painter Charles Le Brun, who designed much of the decorative scheme at Versailles, has been superbly restored. The rue Monge leads down to the place Maubert market, past the pretty **square Paul-Langevin** with its statue of François Villon (see box). A few steps down it will enable you to admire the caryatids on the façade of no. 25, sandwiched incongruously between ordinary little shops. (Ⓜ Cardinal-Lemoine) But you should now turn left and into the **rue des Boulangers**, an extraordinary sight in the middle of this bustling modern city – a village street that can't have changed for centuries, with its low shuttered houses and tiny front gardens. Peer into the courtyard of no. 30 and you'll find it hard to believe this isn't some sleepy provincial town. The street meanders down to the **place Jussieu**, thronged in term time with students spilling out of the cafés. The dreary modern buildings of the Pierre et Marie Curie University, now unexcitingly renamed Paris VI and Paris VII, are disfigured with graffiti, some of them a couple of decades old – a witness to more revolutionary times when student demonstrations were frequent. There is a small **Musée de Minéralogie** (Mineralogical Museum) in one of the skyscrapers that may interest specialists. (Ⓜ Jussieu).

Turn right along the rue Linné and then right again into the peaceful **rue des Arènes**. A terraced garden on the right leads to one of the few remaining traces of the Roman city of Lutetia, the amphitheatre and arena known as **Les Arènes de Lutèce**. They were virtually destroyed during the Barbarian invasions in the 3rd century and were not discovered until 1869, thanks to the ubiquitous Baron Haussmann, whose gangs of labourers were building the rue Monge. They were restored half a century later and though there isn't much to see, just rows of seats and some engraved stone slabs, this is a peaceful and very Parisian spot, popular with local children and old men playing *boules*. It's ideal for a quiet stroll, a short rest or even a picnic: the **rue Monge** has some good food shops and the **place Monge** a small open-air market.

Now walk back to the **rue de Navarre**, walk along it and turn left into the **rue Lacépède**, which brings you to the junction of the rue Linné and the rue Cuvier, adorned with the splendidly elaborate **Fontaine Cuvier** (opposite) featuring various beasts including a lion and a curiously twisting crocodile which, I was told by one of the science students who frequent the area, is anatomically incorrect (an unfortunate mistake considering that Baron Georges Cuvier, a zoologist and

François Villon

François Villon, generally thought of as France's first modern lyric poet, was born in Paris in 1431. His real name was Montcorbier (or, according to some authorities, de Logos), but he adopted that of a priest called Guillaume Villon, possibly a relative, who sent him to study at the Sorbonne University. He led by all accounts a pretty riotous life as a student, and three years after getting his master of arts degree, on a June evening in 1455, was involved in a brawl that led to his fleeing from Paris.

According to his own statement after the incident, he was idly chatting to a priest and a woman friend in the rue Saint-Jacques when another priest called Philippe Chermoye came up and lunged at him with a dagger. Chermoye's motive is unclear, but Villon drew his own dagger to counter-attack – and Chermoye died of his injuries in the Hôtel-Dieu hospital a day or so later. The first stage of Villon's life as an outlaw had begun.

He was pardoned by Charles VII the following year and returned to Paris, but was soon involved in a robbery at the Collège de Navarre in the rue Descartes. He fled from Paris once again to roam the provinces, but in 1463 was condemned to death in Paris for various crimes. Although he was eventually reprieved, the death sentence had inspired him to write his 'epitaph' in the form of the haunting La Ballade des pendus ('Oh brothers, fellow-humans, who after us shall live . . . .'), which conjures up a graphic picture of bodies swinging from a gibbet – a macabre scene that must have been familiar to the citizens of medieval Paris, which

boasted several gallows, including the infamous Montfaucon gibbet, close to what is now the Buttes-Chaumont park in the north-east.

Nothing is known of Villon after 1463, though some claim he lived to 1485. He left behind a collection of poems that still have an extraordinary immediacy 500 years later. His longest work, Le Testament, written in the early 1460s, is considered his masterpiece. It was preceded by the 300-line Le Lais (The Legacy), also known as Le Petit Testament, which is lighter in tone. His ballades, some of them larded with Parisian underworld slang, are very personal versions of a traditional French verse form developed from the work of the troubadours, and very different from English narrative ballads. The ballade has a rigid structure: three stanzas, each ending with the same line as a refrain, plus a final half stanza or envoi, and with the same three rhymes occurring throughout the poem. In the hands of the aristocratic poet Charles d'Orléans it is delicate and elegant. Villon's contribution was to create a feeling of vigour and realism, while remaining within the constraints of the form. His elegaic Ballade des dames du temps jadis, with its famous refrain 'Mais où sont les neiges d'antan?' ('Where are the snows of yesteryear?') is particularly haunting in a setting by the modern troubadour Georges Brassens.

There is a statue of Villon in the little square Paul-Langevin, where the rue des Ecoles and rue Monge meet, in the heart of the Latin Quarter with which he will always be associated.

palaeontologist, virtually invented comparative anatomy). But the creatures are an appropriate introduction to the **Jardin des Plantes** (botanical gardens), which also houses a small menagerie. The gateway opposite the fountain will bring you into the charming gardens with their statues, venerable trees, and tall greenhouses, full of tropical plants, glowing purple in the sunlight. I particularly like the statue of the naturalist Buffon, apparently sitting on a lion, a bird in his hand. But the

A Zoological Menu

The little menagerie in the Jardin des Plantes came into being during the Revolution, when a home had to be found for the exotic creatures that had been kept at the Palace of Versailles to amuse the royal court. It was France's first zoo and soon became a popular outing for Parisian families. Children loved the elephants, the bear pit and, later, the giraffes (first introduced in the 1820s), all of whom featured in a charming series of engravings depicting elegant ladies with parasols and their dandified escorts. (Reproductions in postcard format are often on sale in the good natural history bookshop in the rue Buffon beside the Jardin des Plantes.)

But when Paris was besieged during the Franco-Prussian War and the people were starving, it didn't take the practical French long to decide to eat the animals from the zoo. During the dark winter of 1870–1 the Goncourt brothers reported that they had eaten black pudding made from elephant at the Café Voisin in the rue Saint-Honoré, one of France's top restaurants at that period and a favourite of the Prince of Wales as well as a literary coterie that included Emile Zola. On Christmas Eve that year, with true Parisian panache, this enterprising restaurant offered its patrons the following menu:

Hors d'oeuvres
Butter, Radishes, Sardines,
Stuffed donkey's head

Soups
Red bean purée with *croûtons*
Elephant consommé

Entrées
Fried gudgeon, Roast camel à *l'anglaise*
Jugged kangaroo
Spare ribs of bear with pepper sauce

Roasts
Haunch of wolf with game sauce
Cat accompanied by rats
Watercress salad
Antelope terrine with truffles
Boletus mushrooms stewed in oil with garlic
Buttered *petits pois*

Dessert
Rice pudding with jam
Gruyère cheese

Nothing daunted, the diners enjoyed the finest wines as they ate their way through this exotic menu, including an 1846 Mouton-Rothschild and an 1858 Romanée-Conti.

most-photographed is the one of Henri Bernardin de Saint-Pierre, head resting pensively on his hand while his fictional lovers Paul and Virginie, who made 18th-century Europe weep for the joys of love untainted by civilisation, whisper sweet nothings in a grotto beneath his feet.

The gardens started life in the 16th century as the royal herb garden and soon became a centre for the teaching of botany and chemistry and, later, anatomy. The streets round about celebrate the scientists who made its name – Jussieu, Daubenton, Cuvier, Geoffroy Saint-Hilaire, Lamarck, Lacépède, and especially the Comte de Buffon, author of a multi-volume *Natural History* and Keeper of the King's Garden, who played a major part in the Jardin des Plantes as we see it today. During the Revolution a small menagerie was added, and a full-scale university department and museum were opened, the **Muséum d'Histoire Naturelle** (Natural History Museum). The severe buildings running beside the **rue Geoffroy-Saint-**

Hilaire and backing on to the **rue Buffon** house departments of anatomy, botany, entomology, mineralogy, palaeontology, zoology (closed for the foreseeable future) and a popular exhibition of giant crystals. The vast galleries are rather run down and plans are in hand for a major facelift by the time the museum celebrates its bicentenary in 1993, when a brand-new Evolution Gallery is scheduled to open. But they are full of interesting things and often stage good temporary exhibitions, including a famous one on fungi in October, the Salon du Champignon. Children generally love the whole place and seem to enjoy the old-fashioned menagerie more than modern zoos, perhaps because of its smaller scale. The Jardin des Plantes is also a good place for seeing ordinary Parisians. It is popular with local families and on mild summer days you'll find elderly men and women busy playing cards on little tables beneath the trees. The flower beds running down to the river are well-tended and there are various kiosks selling drinks, snacks and ice creams.

Leave by the gate in the south-east corner and cross the rue Geoffroy-Saint-Hilaire to the white and green-tiled **Mosquée** (Mosque). The entrance is on the far side, in the **place du Puits-de-l'Ermite**, but on this side you can pause for a thick sweet coffee or a refreshing mint tea in the tea room beyond the tiny garden. The guided tour includes a graceful arcaded patio garden. If you feel like an unpretentious meal surrounded by locals, cross the rue Censier and continue along the rue Geoffroy-Saint-Hilaire to the modest **Relais Saint-Hilaire** (opposite the rue Poliveau). Then follow the **rue Daubenton** to the **rue Monge** and the **place des Patriarches**, overshadowed by the church of Saint-Médard. (Ⓜ Censier-Daubenton) Until the fifties the **Marché des Patriarches**, a flea and vegetable market dating back to the 14th century, was still held in this square, which is now a good example of the more sensitive eighties town planning geared to the needs of the local inhabitants that has replaced the ruthless demolitions of earlier decades. A car park has been built beneath the square, which always seems to be full of children playing, and an attractive modern building houses a gym and low-rent housing. A friendly, neighbourly atmosphere is very apparent as you stroll through this historic district on the south-east slope of the Montagne Sainte-Geneviève, where the Roman road to Lyon once ran. Before exploring it further, have a look in **La Tuile à Loup** in the row of small shops on your left, a delightful place crammed with pottery and wooden objects and books, all connected with the various regions of France and ideal for presents. In the continuation of the rue Daubenton on the far side of the square **L'Epicerie** is another useful shop: it specialises in attractively packaged British and American goods — teas and cookies and mustards — just the thing to take, prettily gift-wrapped, to French friends who ask you for a meal.

This narrow passageway, with an excellent *charcuterie* and flower shop, is a foretaste of the **rue Mouffetard market**, which it leads into. There has been a market in the rue Mouffetard since the Middle Ages. The colourful stalls and lively stallholders, the steep and narrow street, the village-like church at the bottom of the hill make this one of the most attractive markets in Paris, open every morning except Monday and every afternoon except Sunday and Monday. The café almost opposite the rue Daubenton attracts a mixture of locals and stallholders and serves good *plats du jour* at lunchtime. Turn left down the hill, admire the hunting and shooting scenes adorning the upper storeys of the **Charcuterie Facchetti** at no. 134, then turn into the church opposite.

Saint-Médard is small and welcoming. The nave dates from the Late Gothic period, while the chancel was not completed until the mid-17th century. It became notorious in the early years of the 18th century when a curious cult grew up round the tomb of a Jansenist deacon called François Pâris. Word went round that invalids praying in the tiny cemetery had been miraculously cured and it was soon attracting huge crowds, including many young women who, presumably overcome with the excitement, promptly had fits or convulsions. The hysteria of the *convulsionnaires* eventually got out of hand and the cemetery was closed down by royal decree.

Saint-Médard was once the parish church of a largish village on the banks of the river Bièvre, which were lined with elegant villas. One of the most luxurious was built in the 14th century by Guillaume de Chanac, Bishop of Paris and Patriarch of Alexandria, and one of his relations, Bertrand de Chanac, Patriarch of Jerusalem — the two Patriarchs whose memory is perpetuated in the square. But the wealthy inhabitants were later driven out by the unpleasant smells emanating from the various industries that grew up along the river banks, many of them connected with tanning hides. (The name of the rue Mouffetard is probably a corruption of *moffettes*, an old word used to describe noxious smells.) Among the workshops was one that was to become world-famous: a dyeing works founded in the 15th century by Jean Gobelin, whose main stock-in-trade was a scarlet dye based on the cochineal beetle. His descendants diversified into weaving and handed on the business to a couple of Flemish weavers who had been brought to France by Henri IV. In 1662 the Gobelins estate was taken over by the crown at the suggestion of Louis XIV's minister Colbert, who transformed it into the Royal Weaving Establishment.

A short detour from Saint-Médard will take you, via the **rue de Bazeilles**, to the **avenue des Gobelins**, where at no. 42 you can visit the **Manufacture des Gobelins**. (Ⓜ Gobelins) The famous Gobelins tapestries are still made here, to designs by major contemporary artists, just as they were in the days when Charles Le Brun, Mignard or Poussin spread the fame of Gobelins tapestries throughout the world. The guided tour is on the long side for non-specialists, but it is interesting to see the huge old wooden looms still in use, and the cobbled courtyards adorned with statues of Colbert and Le Brun seem scarcely to have changed since the 17th century. The building itself is worth looking at from the outside, with its medallions depicting the various processes from Sheep-shearing right through to Weaving and its inscriptions of the great painters whose cartoons inspired earlier generations of weavers — Jean-Baptiste Oudry, Simon Vouet, Watteau among them. To the left of the main building the **rue Croulebarbe** takes you to the **rue Berbier-du-Mets** for a good view of the large complex of buildings. Turn right, passing the **Mobilier National**, where furniture belonging to the state is stored (the Gobelins visit includes parts of this building, used for weaving Beauvais tapestries), then right again into the **rue Gustave-Geoffroy**. The huddle of buildings on the left includes fragments of a medieval mansion called **L'Hôtel de la Reine-Blanche**, probably lived in by Charles IV's wife Blanche de Bourgogne.

Now return to the **rue Mouffetard** and climb up it, keeping an eye open for old doorways and inn signs. Beyond the market you soon come to the picturesque **passage des Patriarches** on the right and, almost opposite, the **passage des Postes**. Walk up this villagey street and turn right into the **rue Lhomond**, which brings you to the little **place Lucien-Herr**: a wall adorned with modern sculpture, a fountain in a little garden, a restaurant with lace curtains, **Chez Léna et Mimille***, and a couple of craft workshops raised up above it. From the **rue Tournefort** you get an interesting glimpse of the church of Saint-Etienne-du-Mont, high up near the Panthéon. Before visiting them, turn right off the rue Tournefort into the **rue du Pot-de-Fer**, a lively street lined with restaurants. On the corner with the rue Mouffetard is the **Fontaine du Pot-de-Fer**, which dates from the early 17th century, when Marie de Médicis had a Roman aqueduct restored to produce the necessary water for her new Luxembourg Palace with its elaborate gardens (see next walk). Almost opposite, at no. 51, a Spanish workman stumbled on an extraordinary treasure trove in 1938: over 5,000 *louis d'or*, gold coins with a portrait of Louis XV, hidden in the wall of a building due for demolition. More extraordinary still, an undated will, signed by a royal equerry, Sieur Louis Nivelle, also came to light. It took nearly fifteen years to trace Nivelle's surviving descendants – there were 84 of them – and sort out the legal tangles involved. A little higher up, set back in a courtyard to the right, the **Nouveau Théâtre Mouffetard** puts on excellent productions.

Walk on up to the **place de la Contrescarpe**, a rather self-consciously picturesque square memorably described by Ernest Hemingway, who lived nearby. It has been a centre of bohemian night life for centuries – Rabelais wrote of La Pomme de Pin, a cabaret on the corner of the **rue Blainville** (the modern sign is in the wrong place, at no. 1 in the square) – and is still a good place to sit at a café table and soak up the atmosphere, especially in the winter when locals outnumber the tourists. On the left-hand side a painted mural of a young black man smiling at a pretty servant girl bringing him a cup of steaming chocolate was once the sign of a tea room called Au Nègre Joyeux (The Jolly Negro).

The rue Blainville on the left brings you to the **rue de l'Estrapade** for a glimpse of how the narrow old streets on the top of the Montagne Sainte-Geneviève are being spruced up both by the City of Paris (which has opened a small public swimming pool on the right-hand side) and by private developers: have a look for instance at the building on the left decorated with a shop sign saying 'Brûlerie Saint-Jacques', which has been turned into highly desirable flats fronted by a courtyard with smart brass knobs on the balustrades. The tiny **L'Estrapade*** restaurant, one of my favourites, is on the corner of the **rue des Irlandais**, which still houses at the far end on the left the **Collège des Irlandais**, an Irish seminary dating from the 16th century, though it did not move here until 1769. Try to get a glimpse of the peaceful courtyard and garden, now shared with Polish seminarists. This is just one of the many colleges for young foreigners, mostly training for the priesthood, that were scattered through the Latin Quarter in the Middle Ages. The

Scots College, now a girls' hostel, is nearby at 65 rue du Cardinal-Lemoine, and the rue des Anglais, just off the boulevard Saint-Germain, perpetuates the name of the one-time Collège des Anglais.

On the other side of the rue de l'Estrapade the **rue Clotilde** is flanked on the left by the huge bulk of the **Panthéon**, on the right by the garden of the **Lycée Henri-IV**. Turn off it into the **place du Panthéon** and walk round to the top of the **rue Soufflot** for the best view of this massive building dominating the whole of the Latin Quarter, which has changed its function bewilderingly often through the centuries. (ⓂⒺⓉⓇⓄ Luxembourg) It was originally commissioned by Louis XV, who made a public vow that if he recovered from a serious illness he would build a fine new church to house St Geneviève's tomb and replace the ancient abbey church dedicated to her that then stood on top of the hill. That in turn had superseded a basilica built by King Clovis of the Franks in the early 6th century for the saint's tomb, and as a burial place for himself and his wife Queen Clotilde. Louis duly recovered and in 1755 work started under the supervision of Jacques-Germain Soufflot, who had drawn up plans for an imposing basilica in the form of a Greek cross, surmounted by a dome on a high colonnaded drum. Beneath the dome would lie the reliquary with the saint's remains. But the work was by no means plain sailing, as it turned out that the subsoil was riddled with shafts dug by the Romans some 1,600 years earlier to extract clay for pottery making. Cracks started appearing as the walls rose up, delaying matters considerably, and Soufflot died before it was completed, his death allegedly hastened by anxiety and depression over the difficulties he had encountered on this site. The church was eventually finished in 1789, only to fall victim two years later to the Revolution's love of *grandeur* and *patrie*.

The 42 large windows were blocked up, the twin belfries demolished, and the church was converted into a mausoleum for the tombs of Frenchmen the revolutionary government wished to honour, such as Mirabeau (though he was later unceremoniously ejected) and Voltaire. Napoleon promptly reversed their decision and turned it back into a church, though it wasn't officially consecrated, as the Eglise Sainte-Geneviève, until 1823, by which time Napoleon was dead and Louis XVIII was on the throne. Seven years later, it was Louis-Philippe's turn to have second thoughts: he stripped it of its church furnishings and it became a mausoleum once again. David d'Angers was commissioned to design a new pediment, which he adorned with a frieze depicting Liberty giving laurel wreaths to the Motherland, who hands them out to her Great Men — civilians on one side, military heroes on the other. Another couple of decades went by and Napoleon III had another new idea: the ex-Panthéon should become a national basilica.

So it remained for 34 years, the longest uninterrupted period in its history so far, though even then it lost its cross for a brief interlude when the *Communards*, who used it as their headquarters, replaced it with a red flag. Then at last, in 1885, an event occurred that decided the Panthéon's fate once and for all: Victor Hugo died, very much the Grand Old Man at 83. The powers that be decided that what this god-like figure deserved was a secular resting place on some grandiose site — and the ex-Panthéon was the obvious choice. So a mausoleum it once

more became, and has remained ever since, heavily overlain with symbolism as a monument to *La Patrie*.

It is important to remember all this when you visit what can otherwise seem a distinctly cold and gloomy place. (I also recommend that before venturing in you have a warming glass of wine at the **Café de la Nouvelle Mairie***, a pleasant wine bar in the rue des Fossés-Saint-Jacques just behind the building, or at one of the cafés in the rue Soufflot.) The austere interior is decorated with scenes from the life of St Geneviève by the 19th-century painter Puvis de Chavannes, in suitably cold, pale colours, along with the work of other Third Republic artists. The emptiness may seem surprising, but the tombs of the famous are all in the crypt – which is just as well, as the rest of the building is likely to be closed for restoration until the mid-1990s, though you can see the paintings from a special viewing area. Guided tours, which start from the north-east corner, take you past Gambetta's heart, concealed in an urn, and then to the tombs of Jean-Jacques Rousseau, Hugo, Emile Zola, the Socialist leader Jean Jaurès, the Resistance hero Jean Moulin and many others, including Soufflot himself.

As you walk round to the entrance, notice the two identical buildings on either side of the rue Soufflot, designed by Soufflot as a suitable setting for his mighty church, though only the one on the north, now a law faculty, was built in his lifetime. The other, a much later copy, is the town hall of the fifth *arrondissement*. For most of December and January they are lit with tiny white fairy lights picking out the classical lines of the façades – a thrilling sight with the Panthéon itself also illuminated, the sculpture on the pediment frieze standing out sharply, the dome looming behind. On the north side of the square is the **Bibliothèque Sainte-Geneviève**. It is worth climbing the stairs to peep through the doors at the iron and glass roof, very typical of 19th-century 'industrial' architecture. One rather envies the students whose passes allow them to work in this lofty, book-lined place (its collections are based on the library of the former St Geneviève Abbey), except that there is often a stale smell, compounded no doubt of too many people sweating over their studies and living in accommodation where baths are in short supply. In spite of recent reforms that have taken university departments out to less crowded suburbs, many students in Paris still have to live in poky 'maid's rooms' with no mod cons in conditions not so very different from the days when the building originally on the library's site, the Collège Montaigu, was a byword for squalor. No wonder so many of them seem to spend half their time hunched over their books at café tables in the **boulevard Saint-Michel**.

The busy roofscape of the church of **Saint-Etienne-du-Mont** straight ahead, including a spire surmounting the belfry, is a welcome relief from the severity of the Panthéon. The only blemish on the attractive **place Sainte-Geneviève** in front of it is a frozen food centre on the corner – how on earth did the owners manage to get planning permission? The church you now see, built on the site of a Romanesque one beside the abbey, was completed in stages over a period of 135

The Panthéon atop St Geneviève's Mount, seen from the statue-filled Luxembourg Gardens years ending in 1626, so its interior is largely Late Gothic while the façade is Renaissance, though the rose window is medieval. The first impression as you step inside is of a light and airy space, partly thanks to extensive cleaning and restoration at the end of the eighties. You are then struck by the rounded sweep of the spiral staircases on either side of the rood screen, the only one to have survived an 18th-century movement to remove what was once a common feature in Paris churches. In a chapel to the right-hand side is a large reliquary, glittering in the light of the forest of candles that are always lit to the memory of Paris's patron saint. Part of her tomb and a few relics lie inside it: her bones were ceremoniously burnt outside the Hôtel de Ville during the Revolution. The church is the burial place of Racine and Pascal and you can visit the rather scruffy-looking cloisters, once overlooking a cemetery and now adorned with some good 17th-century stained glass.

Walk down the narrow cobbled **rue Saint-Etienne-du-Mont** beside the church to the rue Descartes, then turn to look back and you seem to sense the presence of generations of clerics slipping past on their way to mass in the abbey of St Geneviève, parts of which have survived in the **Lycée Henri-IV**. To reach it, turn right, then right again into the **rue Clovis**. The lycée is an élite establishment, one of the best known in France — Sartre taught here. The buildings incorporate the abbey's refectory, parts of the cellars and kitchens and '**Clovis's Tower**', as the belfry is always called, though it dates from almost a thousand years after King Clovis's death.

Now walk back along the rue Clovis. Beyond the **rue Descartes**, at no. 3, you can see quite a large chunk of the medieval wall built during the reign of Philippe Auguste. To your right the rue Descartes leads back to the place de la Contrescarpe. A plaque tells you that Paul Verlaine died at no. 37, now appropriately housing a poetry club. This part of the street is lined with lively restaurants and bars with names like **The Melancholy Shark** or **The Foot Scratcher**. But as you walk down the hill in the other direction it is all very different. On your right is a well-kept public garden, with a new swimming pool and gym, still called the **Jardin de l'Ecole Polytechnique**, though the famous grande école that has been educating France's undergraduate élite since the late 18th century moved out to the suburbs at the end of the seventies. This has been the site of prestigious establishments for nearly 700 years, since Philippe le Bel's wife Jeanne de Navarre founded the Collège de Navarre, where many later monarchs studied. Like many another institution for the privileged few, it was closed down during the Revolution. The buildings are now used by the Research and Technology Ministry.

Now walk down the medieval **rue de la Montagne-Sainte-Geneviève**, once part of the Roman road to Lyon and on to Rome. Turn left into the busy **rue des Ecoles**. In the first turning on the right, the **rue des Carmes**, the police station houses the **Musée de la Préfecture de Police**, which started life in the Paris police headquarters on the Ile de la Cité and is based on the most dramatic (which often means the most macabre) items from its archives covering four centuries of crime. This is a good place to bring children, who can learn some history in the process — you can see, for instance, the statement made by Charlotte Corday after murdering Marat in his bath. (Ⓜ Maubert-Mutualité)

Further along the rue des Ecoles, on the left-hand side, you come to another élite higher-education establishment, the **Collège de France**, backing on to another famous lycée, the **Lycée Louis-le-Grand**, originally a Jesuit college, whose distinguished old boys include Molière, Voltaire, Victor Hugo and Baudelaire (who was expelled). The Collège de France was founded in 1530 by François Ier, his aim being to encourage broader and less rigid teaching than that offered by the **Sorbonne**, the best-known institution within the University of Paris, just beyond here on the far side of the rue Saint-Jacques. The lectures given at the college, many of them by major scholars, have always been open to the public free of charge. But although you can wander through the Sorbonne buildings and poke your head through the doors of the various amphitheatres, sightseeing when lectures are in progress is obviously frowned on. The **Sorbonne church**, whose entrance is in the **rue de la Sorbonne**, is also hard to visit – it is open only when special exhibitions or concerts are staged there.

The University of Paris, one of the earliest in Europe, was started on the Left Bank by Pierre Abélard and his followers as a reaction to the Establishment theology taught in the schools of dialectic on the Ile de la Cité. It was officially granted its statutes in the early 13th century and soon became famous, attracting scholars from all over the world. Classes were initially held in the open air, but in 1253 Louis IX's confessor Robert de Sorbon founded a college for needy theological students that was to develop into a powerful body that jealously guarded its autonomy. France's first printed books were produced in the original buildings, which were redesigned by Jacques Lemercier in the 17th century, on commission from Cardinal Richelieu, who also had the church built (it now houses his tomb, designed by Le Brun). But the buildings you now see were extensively rebuilt in the 19th century, when a famous ceiling was painted by Puvis de Chavannes in the *grand amphithéâtre* (main lecture hall). The Sorbonne was at the heart of the student revolts in 1968, the red flag hoisted atop its buildings, the paving stones of the surrounding streets used as missiles and barricades. None of this ferment can be sensed today, but the Sorbonne has paid the price of its key part in the 'May events': it is no longer the seat of the University of Paris but just one of its many buildings and departments, labelled Paris I, II, III and so on, that are now scattered all over Paris and its suburbs.

Opposite the main entrance to the Sorbonne, a tiny garden, the **square Paul-Painlevé**, is adorned with a statue of the 16th-century essayist Montaigne, whose feet are traditionally rubbed by students to bring them luck in their exams. After generations of vigorous rubbing the marble original was so battered that it had to be replaced by a bronze copy in 1988. On the far side of the square is the entrance to the **Musée de Cluny**, one of the earliest surviving domestic medieval buildings in Paris, commissioned by the wealthy Cluny Abbey in Burgundy on the site of the Romans' thermal baths. Parts of the baths miraculously survived even the demolitions of the Haussmann era, when the **boulevard Saint-Michel** and the **boulevard Saint-Germain** cut a swathe through this ancient district, and can still be seen both inside the museum and in the garden behind it where the two boulevards intersect. (Ⓜ Cluny-La Sorbonne)

The land and the buildings on it were bought in the 14th century as a Paris base for the abbots. Their residence was redesigned at the end of the 15th century in Renaissance style, though there is still a medieval feel about some of the decorative details. It became a Museum of the Middle Ages in the mid-19th century, based on the rich collection of medieval and Renaissance art amassed by Alexandre du Sommerard, a private collector. His son was the first curator and remained in charge for forty years, adding substantially to his father's collection. The Renaissance exhibits were moved in 1977 to a new Renaissance Museum in the Château d'Ecouen north of Paris, so what you see now is essentially medieval, plus the Roman remains excavated on the site. The labelling leaves something to be desired, but otherwise this is a very interesting museum, in a particularly pleasant setting. Most of all, it is a place for looking at details.

The oak-beamed rooms are fairly small, so you can get close to the tapestries that are its chief glory. Look for instance at the birds and flowers in the early 16th-century tapestry in the first room, depicting a concert. Then move on to the lively tapestry of a grape harvest in room II. But before you leave the room, don't miss the little strip in *millefleurs* style over the door: among the falcons and dogs is an appealing rabbit on its hind legs, nibbling at a flower. Then come a whole series of ivory objects — boxes and cases of various kinds, and intricately carved mirror backs. In Room IV a set of tapestries called *La Vie seigneuriale* is a feast of intimate and amusing details. I particularly like the homely box of wools at the feet of the lady busy at her embroidery. And in the scene depicting a lady standing in her bath in the open air, her servants grouped deferentially round holding her clothes and jewels, I always enjoy the ducks splashing merrily in the pool of dirty water pouring out of the tub.

But these early pieces are only a preparation for the museum's most famous exhibit, a beautiful set of *millefleurs* tapestries in the Rotunda on the first floor known as *La Dame à la licorne* (*The Lady with a Unicorn*). They were probably made in Bruges in the late 15th or early 16th century, for a noble family in Lyon, but much about them is mysterious, and they were not discovered until the 19th century, in a remote château in central France (the novelist George Sand played a part in bringing them to Paris). Even the subject is a matter for debate. All six tapestries feature a tall, slim lady — her maids and ladies-in-waiting are much shorter — a mild-looking lion and a rather cuddly unicorn. The scenes are staged on a dark-blue 'island' scattered, like the soft red background, with flowers, birds and animals. There is general agreement that five of the tapestries illustrate the five senses: sight and hearing on the right; touch, smell and taste on the left. Here again the details are a delight: a monkey picking a carnation out of a basket, a rabbit busy washing its face, another rabbit playfully tapping the lion with its paw, a lapdog sitting on the lady's train, or perched on a stool on an embroidered cushion. The sixth has been interpreted in various ways. I prefer the theory that the lady is not taking the necklace out of the casket held by her lady-in-waiting but putting it back, in a gesture that symbolises a refusal to succumb to the blandishments of the senses.

Beyond the Rotunda is a little chapel, low enough to give you a chance to study the Gothic tracery at close quarters. In 1515 it was the scene of a variant on the 'shotgun wedding' theme. The bride was a sister of Henry VIII of England who the previous year, at the age of sixteen, had married the recently widowed Louis XII of France. He was nearly forty years older and seemed more. Mary undoubtedly brightened up the staid widower's life with an endless round of balls and parties, but the change of pace was too much for him, and he died less than three months after the wedding. His cousin François d'Angoulême succeeded him as François Ier. But the young man's ambitions would have been shattered if Mary had turned out to be expecting an heir to the old king, so he put her in the Hôtel de Cluny for the obligatory mourning period and had her watched like a hawk. He soon discovered that she was having an affair with an Englishman, Henry Brandon, and promptly ordered them to be married that very day in the chapel. The young couple were shipped off to England, he was ennobled to become Duke of Suffolk and they lived happily ever after, soon producing a child who may or may not have been the true heir to the French throne.

There are more tapestries in the chapel, the beginning of a long sequence called *The Life of St Stephen* which continues into the next two rooms. But you should also return downstairs to visit the Roman *frigidarium* (the room for cold baths) which is as chilly as its name suggests – keep your coat with you – and, on the way, the Salle Notre Dame (Room VIII). A whole series of fragments of sculpture once on the façade of Notre Dame cathedral are gathered together here, the most important the series of 21 surviving heads from the Kings' Gallery (see box, Walk 1). In the gardens you can visit the *tepidarium* (warm bath) and *caldarium* (steam bath).

When you leave the museum, turn left into the **rue de Cluny**, and then right into the **boulevard Saint-Germain**. Walk along as far as the **place Maubert**. The name is allegedly a corruption of 'Maître Albert', alias the Scholastic philosopher Albertus Magnus, who lectured here in the mid-13th century. The square has a small street market (open on Tuesday, Thursday and Saturday mornings), a row of good food shops behind it and several lively cafés. There's also an impressive view up to the Panthéon. (Ⓜ Maubert-Mutualité)

Cross over the boulevard and take the **rue Frédéric-Sauton**, one of a network of narrow streets leading down to the Seine, all of them worth exploring. You soon come to a tiny crossroads, where it converges with the **rue de la Bûcherie** and the **rue des Grands-Degrés**. There are several good places to eat here and a lively tea room, **Sweet et Faim***, which sometimes stages jazz concerts.

A few steps further and you are on the **quai Montebello**, enjoying lovely views of Notre Dame. Two streets to the right, the **rue de Bièvre** is closed to traffic and patrolled by police day and night: President Mitterrand lives here, using the presidential palace only as an office. You can walk down this unpretentious street (but don't loiter or you'll be treated with suspicion by the police), which is typical of the area, though it has more historic associations than most: Dante had lodgings here in 1308 and is believed to have written parts of the *Divine Comedy* there.

A couple of decades ago the streets were very run down, made up mostly of rented rooms lived in by a shifting working-class population. There were plans to demolish whole streets between here and the rue Saint-Jacques and rebuild them. The gentrifiers moved in instead and the area has gone distinctly up in the world. Most of the 17th-century houses have been done up and turned into elegant flats — though the *poutres apparentes* (exposed beams) of which estate agents boast may well be bought as a job lot rather than the genuine article. The butcher, the baker and the candlestick-maker have mostly been driven out to make way for design studios and architects' offices. But, this being Paris, the restaurants are still there, and if some are chic and expensive, others are still modest: the North African restaurant in the rue de Bièvre serves cheap *couscous*, though it has sensibly added a more expensive 'presidential *couscous*' to its menu.

Walk back along the *quai* until you come to the square René-Viviani, passing on your way the **rue du Fouarre**, one of the best-known streets in Paris in the Middle Ages because of the open-air lectures held there. The students — Dante among them at one time — were expected to sit on the ground, gazing up at the lecturer at his lectern. They used to bring along bales of straw to sit on — *fouarre* in old French. The **square René-Viviani** is one of the most delightful garden-squares in Paris, famous for its views of Notre Dame and an ideal place for a rest before visiting the last two sights on this walk. But before you sit down, continue a few paces along the **rue de la Bûcherie** to **Shakespeare & Co.**, the English-language bookshop inspired by one of the same name opened in Saint-Germain-des-Prés by Sylvia Beach in the twenties and soon swarming with the expatriate writers' colony. The stock today is a pleasing jumble of new and second-hand, the atmosphere friendly — and the small ads noticeboard legendary. Just beyond here **La Bûcherie*** is probably my favourite of all Paris restaurants for a special meal — an unbeatable combination of delicious food, marvellous view and civilised and relaxed atmosphere.

Back in the square you will notice odd bits of broken statuary dotted about, a couple of sarcophagi and a tree held up by a wooden prop — a false acacia said to be the oldest in Paris, it was planted in 1601 by a botanist called Robin (hence its French name of *robinier*). Beyond it is a small, squat church, seeming even smaller by contrast with the huge cathedral. Beyond the church, a higgledy-piggledy roofscape and crooked-looking half-timbered houses. The whole effect is charming, with a random quality that speaks of centuries of haphazard development rather than the strict planning that has imposed its mark on much of Paris.

The little church of **Saint-Julien-le-Pauvre** started life in the 6th century, when a chapel dedicated to St Julian the Hospitaller, also known as 'the Poor Man', was built on to a sort of travellers' rest where pilgrims on the way to Santiago de Compostela were offered board and lodging. For this now-peaceful corner of Paris was once one of the city's busiest crossroads, where two major Roman thorough-fares met. One, leading south-west via Orléans to Spain, has survived as the **rue Saint-Jacques** (the name comes from the pilgrims who set out along it to Santiago — Saint-Jacques in French — originally using scallop shells to beg for alms, later with badges in the shape of a scallop shell in their hats: hence the *coquilles Saint-Jacques* that feature on French seafood menus). The other, leading south-east to Rome, started along today's **rue Galande**, just behind the church, well worth exploring with its medieval houses — one has one of the few surviving wooden gables in Paris – and its stone panel carved with an image of St Julian and his wife ferrying Christ across a river (above the doorway of no. 42): he is the patron saint of ferrymen and this little piece of sculpture probably came from the façade of the church.

The church you see today is one of the earliest in Paris, the only one still standing of the twenty-odd medieval places of worship that once surrounded Notre Dame. Built in the 12th and 13th centuries in the Transitional style that marked the change from Romanesque to Gothic, it was once the centre of intellectual life in Paris, transferred here from the Ile de la Cité by Abélard and his followers. For three centuries after the official founding of the University of Paris in 1208 it was the university church, and as you visit its tiny interior, you may like to imagine yourself surrounded by the exalted figures who used to worship here – Thomas Aquinas, say, or Dante or Petrarch. The church was 'sacked' in the 16th century during a particularly riotous student protest. It was subsequently more or less abandoned and the university was centred instead on the Renaissance colleges higher up St Geneviève's hill. The crumbling Gothic façade was replaced in the 17th century and since 1889 it has been a centre of Greek Catholicism (the Melchite rite), which explains why the chancel is blocked off by a screen covered with icons.

Next door to the church is a well-known tourist landmark, the **Caveau des Oubliettes**, which does still somehow manage to induce a feeling of roisterous Latin Quarter life and nostalgia for 'le vieux Paris' with its old French songs. You can even visit the dungeons (oubliettes in French because prisoners were conveniently 'forgotten' until they died of starvation, disease or despair). Walk along the rue Galande as far as the **rue Dante**, turn right and right again into the rue Saint-Jacques, then cross over and explore the **rue de la Parcheminerie**, where medieval students came for their parchment and other writing materials, and, leading off it to the right, the **rue des Prêtres-Saint-Séverin**.

This little network of streets brings you to the richly carved west front of **Saint-Séverin**, a university church well known for its concerts (often held on Sunday afternoons). The lower portions date from the 13th century, but the church was not completed for another 300 years and the tracery on the upper storeys, licking upwards like tongues of flame, is a textbook illustration of the aptness of the term 'Flamboyant' for the Late Gothic style. Inside, notice the Renaissance windows, one of them depicting the murder of ·Thomas à Becket, and especially the beautiful double ambulatory with a twisted column in the centre spreading out towards the vaulted ceiling like the fronds of a palm tree. I rather like the modern stained glass behind it, but it has many critics. The little garden, with rows of arcades which once formed part of the charnel house, is a peaceful oasis before you plunge into the teeming side streets leading to the place Saint-Michel.

Turn right into the **rue Saint-Séverin**, then left and walk down the **rue du Petit-Pont** to the **rue de la Huchette**. This lively street is crammed with cheap restaurants (most of them Greek or North African) whose proprietors compete for your custom with their elaborate window displays, their sizzling sides of meat rotating slowly on huge spits and their cheerful backchat. If you don't mind crowds you'll enjoy wandering along looking for somewhere for a snack to round off your walk,

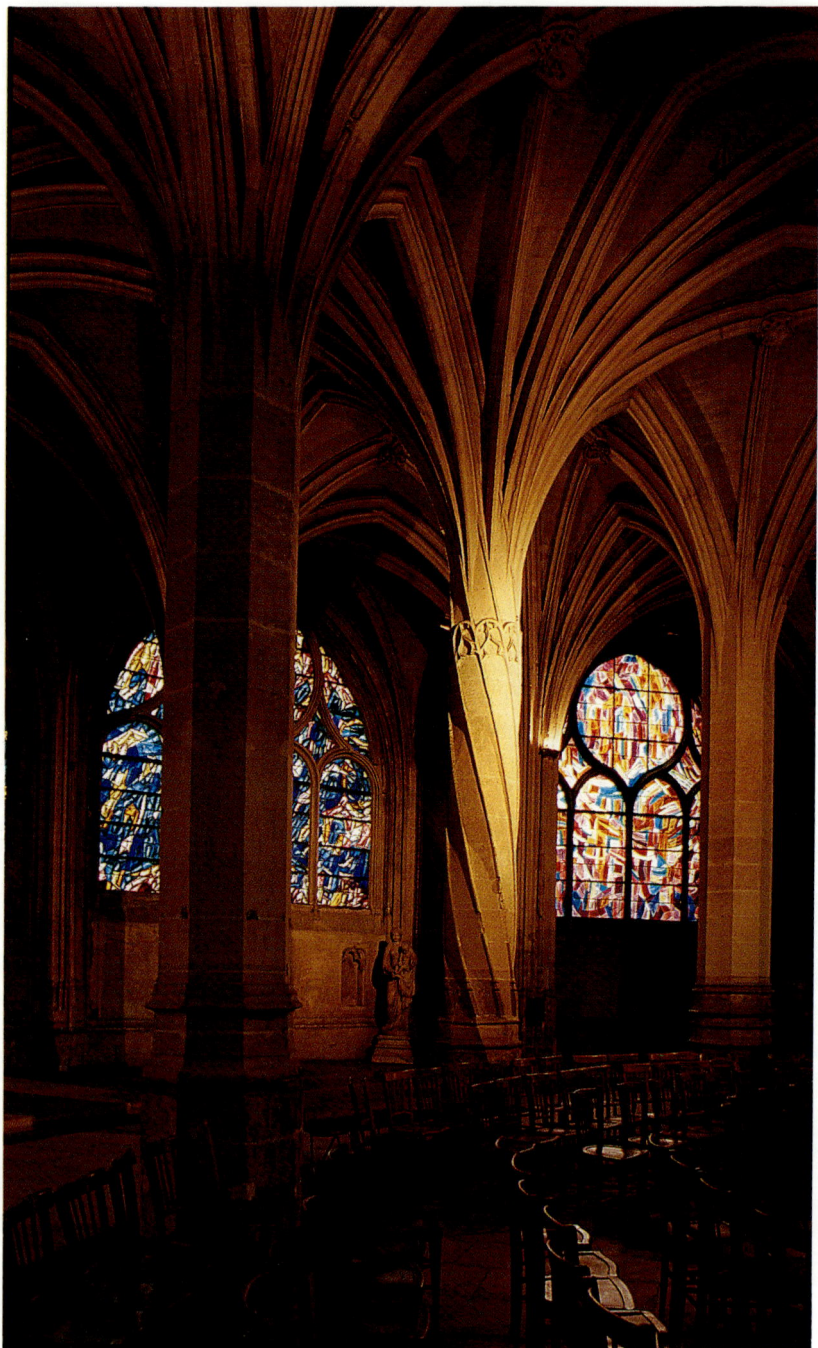

or even a full meal, though you shouldn't expect much in the way of cuisine. The atmosphere is young and relaxed and you can buy bread in fancy shapes from the popular baker's, browse in the large **Gibert Jeune** bookshop at the far end, perhaps watch a film in one of the art cinemas in the **rue de la Harpe**, or book seats for the double bill of Ionesco plays, *La Cantatrice chauve* and *La Leçon*, that have been playing at the tiny **Théâtre de la Huchette** for as long as any one can remember. The street also boasts a jazz cellar, the **Caveau de la Huchette**, and gives you a chance to see what is allegedly the narrowest street in Paris, the **rue du Chat-qui-pêche**, a distinctly unromantic alleyway leading off to the river on the right.

If you prefer an evening in less frenzied surroundings, stroll up the **boulevard Saint-Michel** (a paradise for shoe shoppers at this end), turn right into the **boulevard Saint-Germain** and head for one of the restaurants in Saint-Germain-des-Prés, which is covered in the next walk.

Hotels and Restaurants

For general advice on choosing where to stay and where to eat, see Practical Information; prices are moderate unless otherwise stated.

Hotels

Colbert 7 rue de l'Hôtel-Colbert, 5e (43-25-85-65, fax: 43-25-80-19). A 17th-century building near the Seine with a little courtyard, modernised and elegantly redecorated in 1987. Some rooms have views of Notre Dame. Fairly expensive.

Collège de France 7 rue Thénard, 5e (43-26-78-36). As the name suggests, close to the élite Collège de France, in a short street running between the rue des Ecoles and the boulevard Saint-Germain, in easy walking distance of the most interesting parts of the Latin Quarter and Saint-Germain-des-Prés.

Esméralda 4 rue Saint-Julien-le-Pauvre, 5e (43-25-78-99). Small, friendly and very popular (including a showbiz clientele) for its setting: a 17th-century building just by the church of Saint-Julien-le-Pauvre, overlooking the delightful square René-Viviani and beyond that Notre Dame.

Grandes Ecoles 75 rue Cardinal-Lemoine, 5e (43-26-79-23). It's hard to believe you're in busy, noisy Paris in this charming provincial-seeming house set well back from the street, with painted shutters and a pretty garden, yet very close to the lively place de la Contrescarpe.

Jardin des Plantes 5 rue Linné, 5e (47-07-06-20). Well sited opposite the peaceful botanical gardens and the Fontaine Cuvier. Pretty rooms with flowery decoration, a terrace on the fifth floor for summer breakfasts, a tea room for light meals, a vaulted cellar where concerts are sometimes held, even a sauna.

The double ambulatory of the church of Saint-Séverin, its twisting central column spreading out like the fronds of a palm tree against a backdrop of modern stained glass

Nations 54 rue Monge, 5e (43-26-45-24, fax: 46-34-00-13). Pleasant and well-modernised rooms, with a little patio for summer drinks. Very close to the Arènes de Lutèce (Roman theatre) and the rue Mouffetard market.

Notre Dame 19 rue Maître-Albert, 5e (43-26-79-00). Small, quiet and attractive hotel opened in the mid-eighties in a narrow street opposite Notre Dame running between the quai Montebello and the quai de la Tournelle up to the place Maubert.

Sorbonne 6 rue Victor-Cousin, 5e (43-54-58-08). Virtually opposite the Sorbonne. Small and friendly; bedrooms and bathrooms are small, but were modernised in the mid-eighties.

Restaurants

Abélard 1 rue des Grands-Degrés, 5e (43-25-16-46). Opposite Notre Dame, with good views of the cathedral from the first-floor dining room, and a few tables outside on the little square formed by the narrow streets running up from the river. Mostly seafood.

Atelier du Maître-Albert 1–5 rue Maître-Albert, 5e (46-33-13-78); open evenings only, closed Sun. Lively and fun, though the service can be a bit slow if the waiters are mesmerised by the celebrities at the next table. Convenient formula of a single *menu* (including wine) but with plenty of choice.

Balzar 49 rue des Ecoles, 5e (43-54-13-67); closed most of Aug. Authentic brasserie décor, with lots of mirrors, traditional leather-covered wall sofas and waiters in full-length aprons, and equally authentic brasserie dishes; regular clientele of academics from the Sorbonne and the various colleges nearby.

La Bûcherie 41 rue de la Bûcherie, 5e (43-54-78-06). Perfect setting almost next to the delightful square René-Viviani and Shakespeare & Co., with lovely views of Notre Dame from tables by the window, and a roaring fire in an open fireplace for cosy winter meals. Fairly expensive, but you can have tea or coffee and a quiche in the afternoons and enjoy the atmosphere without paying for a full meal.

Café de la Nouvelle Mairie See box in Food and Drink.

Chez Léna et Mimille 35 rue Tournefort, 5e (47-07-72-47); closed Sun. Perched up above a pretty square at a crossroads of historic streets between the rue Mouffetard and the Sorbonne. Unpretentious but pleasant.

Aux Délices d'Aphrodite 4 rue Candolle, 5e (43-31-40-39); closed Mon. If you feel like a break from French cuisine (even the greatest gourmets do occasionally), this is a particularly nice little Greek restaurant opposite the church of Saint-Médard. Takeaway service too.

Dodin-Bouffant 25 rue Frédéric-Sauton, 5e (43-25-25-14); closed Sun and Aug. Open late and always fashionable. The terrace just off the place Maubert is pleasant for lunch or dinner and the prices are reasonable for the quality of the mainly fish cuisine (especially the lunchtime *menu*).

L'Estrapade 15 rue de l'Estrapade, 5e (43-25-72-58). Tiny and friendly, with lacy café curtains and wall mirrors, behind the Sorbonne.

La Fourmi Ailée See box in Food and Drink.

Le Petit Navire 14 rue des Fossés-Saint-Bernard, 5e (43-54-22-52); closed Sun, Mon and about mid-July to mid-Aug. Almost opposite the Arab Institute, small, friendly and ever-popular for good-value seafood dishes.

La Saumoneraie 8 rue Descartes, 5e (43-26-39-08). Good-value annexe of an expensive and well-known fish restaurant just down the hill from the Panthéon and Saint-Etienne-du-Mont church.

La Truffière 4 rue Blainville, 5e (46-33-29-82); closed Mon. Expensive and rather chic, but with reasonable *menus*. Just off the atmospheric place de la Contrescarpe.

Le Vieux Chêne 69 rue Mouffetard, 5e (43-37-71-51); closed Sun, Mon. One of the very few French restaurants in the lively rue Mouffetard (most are Greek). Small, good-value, friendly; home-style cooking.

Au Vieux Paris 2 pl du Panthéon, 5e (43-54-79-22). Classic cuisine served in a restaurant with old beams beside Saint-Etienne-du-Mont.

Museums and Places of Interest

Musée de l'Assistance Publique (Welfare and Public Health Museum) 47 quai de la Tournelle, 5e. Closed Mon and Tue. Ⓜ Maubert-Mutualité

Institut du Monde Arabe 23 quai Saint-Bernard, 5e. Open afternoons only, but closed Mon. Ⓜ Jussieu, Sully-Morland

Musée de Minéralogie Tour 25, 4 pl Jussieu, 5e. Open Wed and Sat afternoons only. Ⓜ Jussieu

Arènes de Lutèce (Roman theatre). Entrances 49 rue Monge and rue des Arènes, 5e. Open dawn to dusk. Ⓜ Cardinal-Lemoine, Jussieu, Monge

Jardin des Plantes (botanical gardens and zoo). Entrances rue Cuvier, rue Buffon, quai Saint-Bernard and place Valhubert, all 5e. *Botanical gardens* open daily to dusk; *ménagerie-vivarium* (zoo and reptile house) open daily to 5 or 6 p.m.; *tropical greenhouses* open afternoons only. Ⓜ Austerlitz, Jussieu, Censier-Daubenton

Muséum d'Histoire Naturelle (Natural History Museum) In Jardin des Plantes (see above). Closed Tue; various departments (Anatomy, Entomology, Mineralogy, etc) have different opening times but are usually closed mornings.

Mosquée (Mosque) pl du Puits-de-l'Ermite, 5e. Closed Fri and at lunchtime. Ⓜ Censier-Daubenton, Jussieu

Manufacture Nationale des Gobelins (Tapestry Workshops) 42 av des Gobelins, 13e. Guided tours only, usually on Tue, Wed and Thur afternoons at about 2 and 3 p.m. but check locally. Ⓜ Gobelins

Panthéon pl du Panthéon, 5e. Open daily, but shuts at lunchtime except in high summer. Ⓜ Cluny-La Sorbonne, Ⓡ Luxembourg

Bibliothèque Sainte-Geneviève 10 pl du Panthéon, 5e. Ⓜ Maubert-Mutualité, Ⓡ Luxembourg

Musée de la Préfecture de Police (Police Museum) 1bis rue des Carmes, 5e. Closed weekends. Ⓜ Maubert-Mutualité

La Sorbonne Main entrance 47 rue des Ecoles, 5e. Various *amphithéâtres* (lecture halls), the main entrance hall and the library can be visited (discreetly) during the academic year. Ⓜ Cluny-La Sorbonne, Ⓡ Luxembourg

Eglise de la Sorbonne (university church) pl de la Sorbonne, 5e. Open only during special exhibitions, concerts or recitals. Ⓜ Cluny-La Sorbonne, Ⓡ Luxembourg

Musée de Cluny (Medieval Museum) 6 pl Paul-Painlevé, 5e. Closed Tue. Ⓜ Cluny-La Sorbonne

Walk 3
Saint-Germain-
des-Prés and
Montparnasse

Starting point: place Saint-Michel, 6e (the western side, on the corner of the quai des Grands-Augustins); Ⓜ Saint-Michel, Ⓡ Pont-Saint-Michel. This Left Bank walk covers most of the sixth *arrondissement*.

Though no longer a synonym for all that is up to the minute in avant-garde intellectual life – which nowadays focuses more on Les Halles and Beaubourg and, increasingly, on the up-and-coming Bastille district – Saint-Germain-des-Prés is still one of the most civilised areas of Paris and an ideal place for strolling. There are few sights to be visited, but the streets leading off the main artery, the boulevard Saint-Germain (a Haussmann creation), are full of little antique shops and smart interior decorators, of specialist bookshops and tiny art galleries. Many of the city's pleasantest informal restaurants are here, and whatever anyone tells you, it's great fun to sit at a table in – or better still, outside – the famous Deux-Magots and Flore cafés, even if they have been deserted by the intellectual giants, the heirs of Jean-Paul Sartre and Simone de Beauvoir who long ago, when existentialism was all the rage, made their reputation. The fashion boutiques are still here too, congregated mainly just south of the Saint-Germain-des-Prés crossroads. And the crowded jazz cellars and select private clubs still do a roaring trade.

Montparnasse, on the other hand, has changed dramatically since the days when, as 'Mount Parnassus', it was a lively artists' and writers' colony. The intrusive Tour Montparnasse, completed in 1974 and visible from all over Paris, has transformed the centre of the district, and even the vibrant nightlife for which it has long been famous is changing – an era came to an end recently with the closure of Bobino's music hall, where those very French entertainers Juliette Greco and Georges Brassens used to perform. Sex shops are increasingly taking over from lively, rather bohemian cabarets and restaurants.

South of the new Montparnasse station, redeveloped in preparation for the opening of the high-speed train service to Brittany and the South-west in 1990, whole districts have been razed to the ground à la Haussmann, modest housing replaced with high-rise office developments. Much of this is ugly, and unpopular in a more environment-conscious era, but more recent developments are encouraging, and considerably less faceless than their predecessors: Ricardo Bofill's work, for instance, in the rapidly changing Plaisance district.

From the **place Saint-Michel** with its elaborate fountain designed by Davioud in 1860 and adorned with a bronze figure of St Michael slaying the dragon, turn west to walk along the **quai des Grands-Augustins**. This is Paris's earliest quai or embankment, first built in the 14th century, and its name comes from the monastery of Augustinian friars set up alongside it by Saint Louis (Louis IX) a century earlier. There are a few attractive 17th-century buildings along the embankment, one of them housing the venerable **Lapérouse** (at no. 51), one of General de Gaulle's favourite restaurants. But the roar of the traffic spoils the pleasure of a stroll here, so turn left into the picturesque **rue Gît-le-Coeur**. Many of the buildings lining it date from the 15th century, including the **Vieux-Paris*** hotel at no. 9, where Ernest Hemingway and John Dos Passos, e.e. cummings and William Burroughs used to stay. Henri IV had a mistress tucked away in one of the houses, a secret that, so the story goes, gave rise to the name: 'There lies my heart' ('Ici gist mon coeur' in the French of the day) he allegedly confided to a companion as they drove along the quai.

Continue to the **rue Saint-André-des-Arts**, a pedestrians-only street usually crowded with strollers. At the Saint-Michel end it is crammed with cafés, tea rooms and sandwich places, at the other end with fashion boutiques. In between are a couple of art cinemas, card and poster shops, and at no. 40, the **Marché Saint-André**, a bookshop stocking a wide range of maps and books on Paris. The famous (and expensive) **Allard** at no. 41, often referred to as the archetypal Paris bistrot, is still in business and still very popular, even though André Allard, the son of the founder, died some time ago and his widow Fernande, a superb cook, has handed over to new owners. Racine lived in the house from 1680 to 1684.

Walk along the street to the right and turn left into the **passage du Commerce-Saint-André**, which starts as a glass-roofed arcade (with a good tea room, **A la Cour de Rohan***), then turns into a cobbled alleyway leading to the boulevard Saint-Germain. To the left a wrought-iron gate (often shut on Sundays) is the entrance to a series of leafy courtyards, the **Cour de Rohan**, one of those secret places that add greatly to the joy of exploring Paris, if you know where to look. On the right are the rear windows of the **Café Procope*** (see box), adorned with portraits of some of its habitués — Voltaire, Benjamin Franklin and Robespierre.

The passage was clearly a hive of activity during the Revolution. It also housed the printing shop (no. 8) that produced Marat's revolutionary newspaper L'Ami du peuple, and was the place where a new-fangled device allegedly invented by a doctor called Joseph-Ignace Guillotin was first tried out on sheep before being put into service as 'Madame Guillotine' during the bloody years of the Terror. The good doctor understandably tried to disclaim responsibility, and in fact he almost certainly merely championed the idea of beheading rather than inventing the actual instrument that has always been linked with his name.

The Café Procope

Le Procope, a well-known restaurant in the rue de l'Ancienne-Comédie close to the carrefour de l'Odéon, claims to have been the world's first café. It was opened in 1686 by a Sicilian called Francesco Procopio dei Coltelli, who like many of his countrymen before and since was an expert in ice-cream making as well as coffee. His café soon became one of the most fashionable places in Paris, attracting not only the actors from the Comédie française theatre, which was housed opposite at no. 14 between 1689 and 1770, but in due course all the luminaries of the Enlightenment – Voltaire and Rousseau, and the Encyclopédistes Diderot and d'Alembert. Beaumarchais, who wrote *The Barber of Seville* in the nearby rue de Condé, was an habitué, and the key figures of the Revolution, especially Danton, Robespierre and Marat, were often to be seen there, drinking punch as well as coffee. Napoleon was an occasional customer and during the Romantic era the Procope became a meeting place for Alfred de Musset and his mistress George Sand, for the poet Théophile Gautier, Hugo and Balzac. Later Verlaine and Mallarmé, and in the fifties and sixties Jean-Paul Sartre and Simone de Beauvoir, were familiar figures.

In 1988 the atmospheric but rather shabby rooms and the no more than adequate cuisine were given a facelift. The new owners decided to cash in on the revolutionary fervour brought on by the bicentenary celebrations in 1989 and have decked out the old Procope to look more or less as it must have done during the Revolution. Glass-fronted wall cabinets display tricorne hats and Phrygian bonnets and other symbolic exhibits, and upstairs patrons can study leather-bound volumes. The décor includes a portrait of Rousseau and a desk allegedly given to Voltaire by Frederick the Great. And the lunchtime *menu* certainly won't break the bank.

At the far end of the **Cour du Commerce-Saint-André**, which includes (part of no. 4) a bit of Philippe Auguste's medieval wall, the **carrefour de l'Odéon** (Odéon crossroads), has another reminder of those hectic times – a statue of Danton, which was cleaned up in 1988 in readiness for the bicentenary celebrations. He lived in a house on this very spot. South of this busy crossroads, thronged with cafés and cinemas, is the **rue de l'Ecole de Médecine**, where Charlotte Corday stabbed Marat in his bath. Beyond lie the Luxembourg Gardens, but for the moment you should head back towards the river by turning right along the **boulevard Saint-Germain** and then right again into the **rue de l'Ancienne-Comédie**. The name comes from the actors of the Comédie française, who performed at no. 14 in the late 17th and early 18th centuries, in what was once a *jeu de paume*, an indoor court where an early version of tennis was played. On the right is the entrance to the Café Procope and straight ahead, at the far end of the rue Mazarine, gleams the dome of the **Institut de France**. (Ⓜ Odéon)

You soon come to the **carrefour Buci**, with several lively cafés with pavement terraces if you feel like stopping off for a cup of coffee, and a couple of fashion boutiques (**Gudule**, on the corner of the rue Saint-André-des-Arts, is well known). There are more cafés with tables outside in the **rue de Buci** to your left, and the narrow **rue Grégoire-de-Tours** leading off it is made up almost entirely of restaurants. This is one of the district's liveliest streets at night, but many of the restaurants are tourist traps, designed to catch the unwary suburbanites who increasingly congregate here on Friday and Saturday evenings, as well as foreign visitors, so beware.

Walk past the good florist's in the rue de Buci, admire the displays in the expensive *charcuteries* on the right-hand side, but don't be tempted into taking out your purse or wallet yet. For you are now heading towards one of the best of Paris's open-air food markets, known as the **Marché Buci**, though actually most of the stalls and the little shops they front are packed tightly along the **rue de Seine**, running left towards the boulevard. Here you can choose the ingredients for a picnic, or buy a bag of cherries to eat when you next sit down to admire the view or watch the world go by. Half-hidden behind the market on the right-hand side is the modest **Hôtel Louisiane**, a landmark where both Juliette Greco and Jean-Paul Sartre once lived. Further up the rue de Buci are several good restaurants, including **Le Petit Zinc***, with a tempting display of shellfish presided over by a blue-overalled and gumbooted *écailler*, the French term for someone who earns his (or very occasionally her) living by standing out in all weathers deftly opening oysters, clams and other sought-after crustacea.

The Marché Buci, one of the city's best-known street markets

Now turn right, away from the market, and stroll down the river end of the rue de Seine, stopping off to take a look at the many art galleries. **Galerie Documenta** at no. 53 on the right-hand side specialises in early, mostly theatrical, posters. If you are looking for presents to take home, **Françoise Thibault** a few steps into the **rue de l'Echaudé** has pretty and often unusual things (there's another branch in the **rue Bourbon-le-Château** off the rue de Buci), and on the wedge-shaped corner of the rue de Seine and the rue de l'Echaudé **La Nouvelle Gravure** has a good choice of small prints and engravings. **Monsieur Renard**, just opposite, specialises in antique dolls and automata. The tiny galleries in the **rue Jacques Callot** on the right sometimes have interesting jewellery and other objects, and beyond there the rue Mazarine end of the **rue Guénégaud** is another good hunting ground. On the corner of the rue de Seine and the rue Jacques Callot is **La Palette**, a lively café-restaurant popular with a young crowd, while a few steps away in the rue Mazarine the long-time night club **L'Alacazar** is still going strong.

Walk up the rue Jacques-Callot: at the end on the left a plaque tells you that this was the site of the Jeu de Paume de la Bouteille, where Molière's company of actors performed after his death, and Molière himself started his acting career further down the rue Mazarine, at no. 12. Now turn right into the **rue Mazarine** and walk through the gate in the wrought-iron railings on the left-hand side (no. 27) into the **passage Dauphine**, another secret place. This cobbled passageway opens out into a peaceful haven of well-restored buildings, one of them housing my favourite Paris tea room, **L'Heure Gourmande***. The **rue Dauphine** at the other end is a busy street full of bookshops (including some remainder places if you feel like hunting for bargains in the way of art books), small restaurants and fashion boutiques. At no. 34 is another favourite of mine, a toy shop called **Le Monde en Marche** which eschews plastic and has only well-made wooden toys.

All the streets round here are worth exploring. In the **rue Christine** you can peer into the courtyard of the **Relais Christine** hotel, a recent conversion in what was once a 16th-century monastery. Almost opposite is a popular art cinema, **Action Christine**, mainly showing early classics. For a short detour to see some 17th-century buildings, turn left at the end of the street into the **rue des Grands-Augustins**, dating back to the Middle Ages, then left again into the **rue du Pont-de-Lodi**, which is much later but still has some traces of the huge monastery that covered the whole of this area running down to the river. When you are back in the rue Dauphine, cross over and walk down the tiny **rue de Nesle**, which again has several 17th-century buildings. The **rue de Nevers** at the far end is much older: it was built in the 13th century and originally marked the western edge of the monastery. Philippe Auguste's wall ran past here (part of it has survived at the blind end to your left) and you get a feeling of the medieval street layout as you turn right down this dark little street to the quayside.

From the **quai de Conti** you have a good view of the Ile de la Cité and the busy Pont Neuf, leading to the Right Bank (see Walk 1). Now turn left and walk past the rue Guénégaud to the **Monnaie (Mint)**. L'Hôtel des Monnaies, to give it its official name, was completed in 1777 to designs commissioned by Louis XV from Jacques-Denis Antoine, who was then unknown but later went on to design parts of the

The new Musée de la Monnaie, well displayed and offering a painless lesson in French history

Palais de Justice on the Ile de la Cité. France's coins were minted here right down to the early seventies and you can still visit the workshops where commemorative medals are made, many of them designed by well-known artists.

Walk through the handsome vestibule with its coffered ceiling, past a double staircase on the right leading to rooms now used for temporary exhibitions, into the semi-circular courtyard. Stop to admire the busts of various French monarchs, then walk across to the building on the far side, which houses the **Musée de la Monnaie (Coin and Medals Museum)**. The opening of this new museum at the end of 1988 aroused much less interest than that of more spectacular new projects. But the neglect is undeserved. The exhibits are displayed in stylish modern showcases that contrast excitingly with the arches and carved ceilings of this classical building. I can think of few better places to take children for a painless history lesson. They (and you) will enjoy spotting coins and medals with royal portraits — Henri II with an earring and a neatly trimmed beard, Henri IV's exuberantly curly hair and beard, Catherine de Médicis wearing a lace ruff and a scowl, Louis XIV as a young man with a large nose and, much later, sporting an elaborate helmet surmounted by a chariot and four. There are coins here depicting the fall of the Bastille, a set with Napoleon's many relations sitting on the thrones of Europe, and a series of medals by David d'Angers, a 'Galerie of

Contemporaries' portraying the famous figures of his age – Alfred de Musset and Goethe, Victor Hugo and George Sand, the Polish poet Adam Mickiewicz, and many others.

The machine room with its huge apparatus for checking weights, the good video presentation and the modern medals by artists like Salvador Dali all add to the pleasures of an extended visit. You might like to treat yourself to a medal by a good contemporary artist from the small boutique (displays in the windows overlooking the rue Guénégaud) – one of the Musée d'Orsay by its designer Gae Aulenti had pride of place during my last visit – but prices are high.

Turn left out of the Monnaie and walk along the quai de Conti to the **place de l'Institut**, passing the spot where the Tour de Nesle once stood. This massive structure formed the river bastion of Philippe Auguste's wall opposite the fortress of the Louvre. But it has passed into legend thanks to colourful tales of a medieval princess, Marguerite de Bourgogne, wife of Louis X, and her equally fair sister Jeanne, whose amorous adventures are recounted by François Villon and Alexandre Dumas *père* (he wrote a popular play called *La Tour de Nesle*). One of the sisters, or possibly a third who features in some versions, is said to have catapulted her lovers straight from the tower into the Seine after a frenzied night of lovemaking. Louis X did certainly have his wife executed for adultery, but the goings-on in the tower have no doubt been embroidered.

The tower and the adjoining *hôtel* have been replaced by the semi-circular façade, ending in two square pavilions, of the **Institut de France**, its central portion surmounted by the glittering dome you glimpsed earlier from the rue de l'Ancienne-Comédie. You will get a better view if you cross over to the **Pont des Arts** and walk a little way along it before turning round. The building owes its existence to a deathbed bequest by Cardinal Mazarin in 1661. Part of his vast fortune was to be used for building a college to educate sixty pupils from the four provinces he had drawn into the French kingdom. The Four Nations College, as it became known, was designed by Louis Le Vau, the architect of the Louvre and the Tuileries, and completed in the 1680s. The building still houses the **Bibliothèque Mazarine**, France's first public library, based on the cardinal's own magnificent collection of books and manuscripts. But it owes its main fame today to Napoleon's decision in 1805 to transfer to it the French Institute, which had started life in the Louvre a couple of decades earlier. The Institute is made up of five academies, one of which is known the world over as the **Académie Française** (see box).

Before continuing your walk, spend a few moments drinking in the views up and down the river from the Pont des Arts. With its benches, and even orange trees in white-painted tubs in summer, it is a pleasant place for relaxing away from the busy traffic on either side of the river. Then walk back to the *quai*, where you may like to browse in the **second-hand bookstalls** that line the central portions of both banks (see box). Then cross over the road and head for a little passage that takes you through the right-hand wing of the Institute's façade to the spot where the rue Mazarine and the rue de Seine meet in the little **square Gabriel-Pierné**. This peaceful spot, with its very French use of *trompe-l'oeil* trellising to create the effect of perspective, is a good example of the recent campaign to transform the

The Académie Française

The French Academy is only one of five prestigious academies housed in the Institut de France building on the quai de Conti. But it is the earliest: it was set up by Cardinal Richelieu in 1635 and its main function is to keep the French language pure by editing the authoritative *Dictionnaire de la Langue Française*. It is restricted to forty members, many of them writers, who are elected for life and are known ironically to the French as 'the Immortals' — though remarkably few of them have gained immortality by their work (the list of famous writers who have failed to get in is notorious, including Balzac, Proust and Zola).

The lobbying that accompanies elections on the death of a member and the solemn entry of his successor *sous la coupole* (beneath the dome) are widely reported in the press. And in 1980 the Academy hit the headlines round the world when it elected its first woman member, the Belgian-born novelist Marguerite Yourcenar. On ceremonial occasions the immortal forty wear curious bottle-green uniforms with gold-embroidered panels and knee breeches, and each carries a sword. After intense speculation it was revealed that Madame Yourcenar would simply wear a discreet outfit topped by a long black cloak designed by Yves Saint-Laurent.

The Academy issues occasional lists of 'banned' words (generally borrowed from English or examples of the hybrid language now known as *franglais*) with their 'official' French versions. 'Tour operator', for instance, was to be replaced by *voyagiste*. But these new coinings rarely catch on and are frequently ridiculed in the press and even by linguists.

The Bouquinistes

The famous green-painted book boxes perched on the parapets overlooking the Seine form part of a tradition that dates back over three centuries to the reign of Louis XIV, when second-hand booksellers used to set up temporary shop on the various bridges across the river, transporting their wares backwards and forwards on handcarts or wheelbarrows. Over the years they spread on to the quaysides, piling up their books on the parapets and on makeshift stalls.

Then in 1890 their descendants were granted official permits to keep their stock permanently in wooden boxes, fastened with a padlock. A hundred years later the green boxes are still there, somewhere near a thousand of them, covering several kilometres *in toto*, on both sides of the river. On the Left Bank they stretch right through from the Pont de Sully to the Pont Royal. On the Right Bank, from the Pont Louis-Philippe to the Pont des Arts. Most of them open at about lunchtime and stay open till 6.30 or 7 p.m., and quite a few sell prints and maps and posters as well as books.

Some have rare first editions at fancy prices, others specialise in erotica, others have a jumble of miscellaneous titles that may just include exactly what appeals to you. Browsing in them is always entertaining, though sadly an increasing number of sellers have taken to wrapping their books in Cellophane to prevent your leafing through them.

city's dusty squares into pleasant oases for local children to play in while their elders relax or sit and gossip.

The buildings now forming nos 2–10 in the rue de Seine are on the site of the entrance to a palace built by 'la reine Margot', as she is always known to Parisians. Marguerite de Valois was Henri IV's first wife and was famous both as a woman of letters (she published volumes of poetry) and for her many lovers. She was repudiated by her husband in 1599, went into exile in the Auvergne, returned to Paris six years later and lived a colourful life in the Hôtel de Sens in the Marais (Walk 9) before moving to this huge palace whose gardens, which were open to the public, stretched almost as far west as what is now the Musée d'Orsay. Part of the land was peremptorily taken from the university authorities – hence the name of the **quai Malaquais**, along which you should now walk: it is a corruption of *mal acquis* ('ill acquired').

Now turn left into the **rue Bonaparte**. Pause to pay homage to Oscar Wilde, who died (leaving the wallpaper to live on) in a seedy hotel in the **rue des Beaux-Arts** on the left. Oscar would no doubt be amused that this has now become a very chic and expensive establishment, **L'Hôtel Guy-Louis-Duboucheron** (no. 13). Other famous habitués of this little street were the poet Gérard de Nerval, the painter Corot and the novelist Prosper Mérimée. On the right is the **Ecole Nationale Supérieure des Beaux-Arts** or Academy of Art, a mainly 19th-century building (the chapel and cloisters are much earlier) with a large courtyard dotted with fragments of sculpture and architectural details and a good Renaissance archway. The gates are usually open on weekdays, but to visit the interesting temporary exhibitions you must go to the entrance on the quai Malaquais, where there is also a small art bookshop.

Opposite the courtyard runs the **rue Visconti**, where Racine lived for seven years until his death in 1669, in a building that now forms part of no. 24. Balzac lived briefly at no. 17 and ran his short-lived printing house on the ground floor. Delacroix had a studio in the same building some time before he moved to the nearby place Fürstemberg, which now houses the Delacroix Museum. To reach it turn right out of the rue Visconti into the rue de Seine, take the rue de l'Echaudé on the right and then turn right into the **rue Jacob**. This is one of the nicest streets in Saint-Germain, with many antique dealers (wonderful asparagus plates at no. 19), several pleasant hotels and some lively restaurants.

The **place Fürstemberg** leads off it to the left. One of the prettiest squares in Paris, with its tall catalpa trees, its white globe lamps and its carefully restored brick façades, it is magical at any time of year, but especially so in late spring and summer when the mauve blossoms hang down in clusters. On summer evenings concentration on its beauties may be interrupted by the strummings of youthful guitar players, who use the raised central area as an informal stage. The **Musée Delacroix** is in the north-west corner and well worth visiting for its mementoes of the artist – he died here in 1863 – and perhaps especially for the hidden garden whose trees overhang his studio, filled with paintings and drawings.

Leave the square by the southern end, facing the **Palais Abbatial** (abbot's palace) attached to the abbey of Saint-Germain-des-Prés, whose church you can reach by turning right along the **rue de l'Abbaye**. You come first to a little garden on the corner of the rue Bonaparte, dotted with fragments of sculpture from the lady chapel and a homage to the poet Guillaume Apollinaire by Picasso. On the other corner is a literary bookshop, **Le Divan**. Before visiting the church you may like to explore the streets round here. The **rue Bonaparte** has a bookshop at no. 31 specialising in the performing arts (it also sells theatre posters), various expensive interior decorators and three small boutiques called **Fabrice**. The nearest one to the church is good for stylish accessories. The **rue Guillaume-Apollinaire** has a couple of restaurants and leads to the **rue Saint-Benoît**, which on fine summer evenings, when all the restaurants have tables outside, seems more like a harbour quayside in some Mediterranean resort than a city street.

The **church of Saint-Germain-des-Prés**, the focal point of the whole district, is one of the two earliest surviving churches in Paris (Saint-Pierre in Montmartre is contemporary). It dates back to the return from Spain of the Merovingian king Childebert in the mid-6th century with St Vincent's tunic and an alleged fragment of Christ's cross. He built a monastery to house these precious relics which soon became known as Saint-Germain-des-Prés (it was surrounded by meadows or *prés*) because St Germanus, the bishop of Paris, was buried there in 576. By the 8th century it had become a large and powerful Benedictine abbey. It was destroyed several times during the Norman invasions and the existing church dates from the 11th century. The abbey did not survive the Revolution and the church required extensive restoration in the 19th century, with the result that it is an interesting mixture of styles, the mostly Romanesque nave covered by Gothic vaulting and decorated with 19th-century wall paintings, the choir almost pure Romanesque. You can see a medieval marble statue called *Notre-Dame de Consolation* and some interesting tombs and tombstones, including those of Descartes and Boileau. Concerts are held in the church, which is also a popular venue for society weddings. There is another garden on the boulevard side, and various cafés put out tables alongside the railings in summer.

But you are now close to one of the city's best-known cafés, the **Deux-Magots**, opposite the west front of the church. The name comes from the large wooden figures of Chinese sages (*magots* in French) that look down on the throngs of tourists and Parisians who people it day and night. It's expensive, but the strategic corner site makes it an ideal place for a drink or a coffee. It may no longer be the 'rendez-vous of the intellectual élite', as its menu grandly claimed until recently, but it attracts a lively crowd and is often surrounded by street entertainers. The **Café de Flore**, almost next door, doesn't have quite the same attractions, though it is also popular (the upstairs room is traditionally a gay meeting place). In between, at 170 boulevard Saint-Germain, is my favourite general bookshop in Paris, **La Hune**, helpfully open to midnight Monday to Friday (but closed on Monday morning) and a good place for browsing with its tables of new and translated fiction and its excellent art and architecture section. Almost opposite is another landmark, the **Brasserie Lipp**, which has been one of the restaurants to be seen in (in political and intellectual circles) for decades, though the cuisine is basic Alsatian brasserie food. You won't get one of the prized downstairs tables unless you're with well-known friends, but even the first-floor dining room, despised by the *cognoscenti*, does still have its share of celebrities.

But there are dozens of interesting and much cheaper restaurants in the streets running north and south of the boulevard, so if you're ready for lunch there's plenty of choice. If you prefer a picnic you can slip back to the Marché Buci. Don't be tempted by the takeaway in the **Drugstore** on the corner of the **rue de Rennes**, which is overpriced, though the basement bookshop is convenient for foreign newspapers and the late-night chemist's counter (open to 2 a.m.) is useful to know about in emergencies.

Cross from the Drugstore over the rue de Rennes, a wide and traffic-filled street leading to the **Tour Montparnasse**. Admire, or not as the case may be, the curious modern fountain in the **place du Québec** at the point where the rue de Rennes and the rue Bonaparte meet, which looks (as it is clearly supposed to) as if the paving stones have been lifted up by some subterranean plumbing disaster. Called **Embâcle** ('Obstruction' or 'Blockage'), it is by the Canadian artist Charles Daudelin. Now make for the **rue des Ciseaux** (the name comes from a medieval inn, At the Sign of the Golden Scissors) and walk down to the **rue du Four**. This street and the continuation of the rue Bonaparte are full of fashion boutiques, fun for window-shopping if not actual buying. You can also take a look at the bags and other leather accessories in **La Bagagerie** (41 rue du Four) and hunt for stylish shoes at **Tilbury**, also in the rue du Four, or in one of several shoe shops at the Saint-Germain end of the rue de Rennes.

From the bottom of the rue des Ciseaux, cross the rue du Four and turn left, then right into the **rue Princesse** for a glimpse of Paris's most exclusive private club, **Castel**. You won't get in unless you know the right people, but it's fun to know where it is. In the same street is **Village Voice**, a lively American bookshop with a tea room at the back; readings by well-known writers working in English are often staged here. The parallel **rue Mabillon** has several good restaurants, including **Aux Charpentiers*** at no. 10, once the headquarters of the carpenters' guild.

All these streets are worth exploring as you progress towards the large **place Saint-Sulpice**, rather Italianate with its imposing fountain, usually referred to as the Fontaine des Quatre Points Cardinaux, a rather complicated in-joke because the four well-known religious orators whose statues adorn it, facing the four cardinal points of the compass – Bossuet, Fénelon, Fléchier and Massillon – were all bishops (it is also known as the Fountain of the Four Bishops) but never cardinals. The **Café de la Mairie** is a good spot to soak up the sunshine while you sip a drink or munch a sandwich before visiting the 17th- and 18th-century church of Saint-Sulpice. You may also like to have a look at the elegant windows of the **Saint-Laurent Rive Gauche** ready-to-wear boutique.

Saint-Sulpice is a large and somewhat overwhelming church both inside and out, with its heavy squarish towers and the tall flights of steps leading up to the west front, consisting of a Doric colonnade surmounted by an Ionic. It is well known for its huge organ and has a number of interesting things to see inside, including frescoes by Delacroix (in the first chapel to the right) and two large shells given to François Ier by the Venetian Republic and used as holy water stoups; they are mounted on curious rock-like bases draped with seaweed by the sculptor Pigalle. The marble obelisk in the north transept is precisely positioned to be struck by a ray of sunshine passing through an aperture high up in the south transept at midday at the winter solstice; at other times of year it strikes the Meridian line represented by a marked brass strip running between the obelisk and a bronze plate in the south transept.

Leave the church by the north-east door, on the corner of the rue Garancière and the **rue Saint-Sulpice**, long known for its shops selling devotional objects; look out on the left for one devoted entirely to candles, though they are not all ecclesiastical these days. Continue eastwards to the **rue de Tournon**, look right for a good view of the Luxembourg Palace, then walk on beyond the rue de Condé and turn right into the **rue de l'Odéon**, which has several fashion boutiques and bookshops. Walk up to the **place de l'Odéon** and its well-known theatre, built to resemble a classical temple. No. 1 in the square was once the Café Voltaire, frequented by Voltaire himself and by many other literary figures, including Diderot and d'Alembert, who are said to have met here to discuss their idea for a major new encyclopaedia. No. 2 was the home of Camille Desmoulins, who helped to instigate the storming of the Bastille and ended his short life as yet another victim of the guillotine. *The Barber of Seville* was written by Beaumarchais at 26 rue de Condé and his sequel, *The Marriage of Figaro*, was first performed at the **Théâtre de l'Odéon**. The theatre was opened in 1782 to house the Comédie française and in our own time became famous as the home of the company headed by Jean-Louis Barrault and Madeleine Renaud until their sympathy for the student rioting in 1968 led to their expulsion. The theatre now acts as an overspill for the Comédie française and stages seasons by visiting foreign companies.

The square has a seafood restaurant, **La Méditerranée**, with an interesting past (Cocteau was a regular customer) and is filled with paintings by its famous patrons. The restaurant guides shun it and it is certainly over-priced, but I have a soft spot for its attractive setting, with the **Luxembourg Gardens** beckoning enticingly for a post-lunch stroll.

The **rue Corneille**, with **Le Moniteur**, a good art and design bookshop, on the corner, brings you to the **rue de Vaugirard**. Cross it and you have reached one of the pleasantest places in Paris for a relaxing wander. The gardens are full of flower beds and statues, mainly of writers and French queens (look out for Mary, Queen of Scots), a highly romantic fountain, the **Fontaine Médicis**, and an ornamental pond where children sail their boats, frowning with concentration, before being whisked off by their parents to visit the puppet and Punch and Judy shows. There are plenty of the spindly metal chairs familiar from Peynet's drawings of Parisian lovers – you'll probably have to pay a franc or two if your sitting on one happens to coincide with the round of the stern attendant. When everyone has left the chairs remain companionably grouped together, as though a ghostly conversation were still taking place. The view is slightly spoiled by the upwards-thrusting mass of the Tour Montparnasse, but otherwise this is a peaceful haven in which to dawdle under the lime trees, rest or picnic.

The **Luxembourg Palace** was built after Henri IV's assassination, by his widow Marie de Médicis, who apparently found the Louvre too gloomy. She instructed

91

her architect, Salomon de Brosse, to model it on the Palazzo Pitti in Florence, where she had spent her childhood. Among its decorations was a series of scenes from her life specially commissioned from Rubens (now in the Galerie Médicis in the Louvre). The queen was banished only a few years after the palace was completed, but it remained a royal domain until the Revolution, when it was used as a prison. It is now the seat of the Senate, France's upper house, and is not open to the public, though visits to the library, with decorations by Delacroix, are occasionally permitted, usually on Sundays. Temporary art exhibitions are held in the adjoining **Petit Luxembourg** (entrance in the rue de Vaugirard).

Montparnasse

A gate in the gilt-decorated railings in the south-eastern corner of the gardens takes you to the **rue Auguste-Comte** and into the garden in the middle of the **avenue de l'Observatoire**. On the right are various university buildings: the arcaded courtyard of the **Faculté de Pharmacie**, decorated with portraits of well-known scientists set in medallions, and the red-brick **Institut d'Art et d'Archéologie** with bas-reliefs of Egyptian figures. At the end of the garden the bronze **Fontaine de l'Observatoire**, designed by Davioud, is a magnificent sight with its trembling, rearing horses with fishtails, its leaping dolphins and turtles, and its four naked ladies at the top holding aloft a globe to represent the four corners of the earth. The sculpture is by Carpeaux and the setting superb: behind it stretch the Luxembourg Gardens leading to the palace and on clear days the **Sacré Coeur** is visible in the far distance.

The **Observatoire** (Observatory), whose white dome has become steadily more visible, was designed by Claude Perrault, the architect of the colonnade on the east side of the Louvre (and the brother of the fairytale-inventor *par excellence* who wrote of Cinderella and her slipper). It can be visited, but only once a month, on written application – and there is a waiting list. More accessible is the church attached to the former abbey of **Val-de-Grâce**, which you can reach by turning left into the **boulevard du Port-Royal**. (Ⓜ Port-Royal) It was built by Anne of Austria in thanksgiving for the birth in 1638 of a child who was to grow up to be Louis XIV. After 23 years of childless marriage to Louis XIII, a far from satisfactory husband, the event seemed like a miracle both to the queen and to her people. (I have always thought it a good joke that the building opposite is one of Paris's best-known maternity hospitals.) The Jesuit-style church is famous for its baroque decorations, especially the canopy over the altar with its twisted marble columns and the painting in the dome by Pierre Mignard depicting hundreds of huge figures, mostly saints and martyrs, plus Saint Louis leading Anne of Austria towards God to show Him a model of her intended church. The abbey buildings were turned into a military hospital during the Revolution. The cloisters and a small museum can be visited.

The romantic-looking Fontaine Médicis in the Luxembourg Gardens in fact depicts the jealous Cyclops Polyphemus poised to crush to death Galatea the Nereid and her lover Acis

Now retrace your steps and cross back over the avenue de l'Observatoire to the **Closerie des Lilas***, a well-known literary meeting place guarded by a statue of Marshal Ney, the 'bravest of the brave', who refused to arrest Napoleon and instead fought for him at Waterloo. He was shot for treason in 1815 not far away from here, where no. 43 in the avenue now stands. The Closerie really was surrounded by a thousand lilac trees once, in its early days as a *guingette*, a cross between a restaurant and a popular open-air dancing place. It was frequented by the Parnassian poets, by Baudelaire and Verlaine, the Surrealists, and by Ernest Hemingway, who is alleged to have written at least one of his novels propped up at the bar (a brass plaque marks the very spot). It is still fashionable today, and though the restaurant is over-priced, you can spend a pleasant evening in the atmospheric bar or the downstairs brasserie without spending a fortune.

A little way beyond the Closerie, turn left into the **rue d'Assas**, where you can visit the little **Musée Zadkine**. The Russian sculptor Ossip Zadkine came to Paris in 1909, at the age of 19. In 1928 he moved into a house with a tiny garden set in a courtyard at no. 100bis, and spent the rest of his life there. His studio, two other rooms and the garden are full of his often tormented-looking sculptures in a variety of materials, his tools are still hanging up in a row where he left them, and pieces of furniture he carved himself are dotted about. The whole place is an enchantment, especially in the spring when the garden is full of daffodils. Opposite the courtyard entrance, the botanical garden behind the Faculté de Pharmacie is a good place for a few minutes' stroll.

The **rue Joseph-Bara** on the left will bring you to the **rue Notre-Dame-des-Champs**, from where the little **rue Paul-Séjourné** leads to the **boulevard du Montparnasse**. Turn right and continue to the **place Pablo-Picasso**, usually referred to as the **carrefour Vavin**. (Ⓜ Vavin) To the right on the **boulevard Raspail** is a powerful **statue of Balzac** by Rodin (a copy on the platform at Vavin métro station is an impressive sight as you travel through). The crossroads marks the beginning of the Montparnasse that long enjoyed the reputation of being a centre of bohemian and artistic life, though it has changed drastically since the seventies.

The name was first used ironically in the 17th century, when students from the Latin Quarter made a habit of declaiming their poetry on what was then a rubble-strewn mound made of blocks of stone from some disused quarries. The 'mount' was flattened in about 1725, and by the 19th century the whole area had been built on. But as it was just outside the Tax-Collectors' Wall, the lively bars and restaurants that had already sprung up there did a roaring trade by serving wine at duty-free prices. The local cabarets were famous, especially the **Grande Chaumière** (in the street of the same name just north of the carrefour Vavin), which is now an art school.

Then, in the early years of this century, came one of those sudden switches of fashion from Right to Left Bank (or vice versa) that often occur in Paris and the painters and writers who had once congregated in Montmartre abandoned the northern heights for this southern district, which soon became one of Europe's liveliest centres of modern art. Modigliani, Fernand Léger and Chagall lived and worked in La Rûche (see Beyond the Centre), the sculptor Constantin Brâncuşi had a studio in the impasse Ronsin and Picasso lived for a while in the boulevard Raspail. *Le Douanier* Rousseau and Kies Van Dongen, Braque and Matisse, Kandinsky and Klee were all Montparnassiens (or 'Montparnos' as the inhabitants were popularly known), and the district's lively reputation soon attracted poets like Max Jacob and Apollinaire, Cocteau, Blaise Cendrars and André Breton. And the animated discussions that took place at the café tables often switched to politics, as a large number of political refugees from eastern Europe settled in the district, including both Lenin and Trotsky. (You can visit Lenin's flat at 4 rue Marie-Rose, but only by appointment.) In the thirties a new wave of 'refugees' descended on Montparnasse, as a colony of expatriate American writers made Paris their home. Hemingway was one, Ford Madox Ford another, Gertrude Stein yet another. And Henry James was often to be seen in the Closerie des Lilas.

What is left of all this bohemian living that made Montparnasse's reputation (Murger's *Scènes de la vie de bohème* was actually set in Montparnasse)? The best-known cafés and brasseries are still there. **La Coupole***, at 102 boulevard du Montparnasse, was renovated from head to toe in 1988 but, to the relief of its regular patrons, looks much the same and still attracts artists and intellectuals and beautiful people as it has done for decades. It's large, noisy and fun. And if you cannot hear what your companion is saying, you can enjoy yourself instead guessing which now-famous artists painted which pillar in return for a few square meals. Here are some clues: they include Sonia Delaunay, Juan Gris and Chagall. The **Dôme** at no. 108 is another café with a lively past, now well known for its seafood, and on the other side of the boulevard are two more landmarks, the **Sélect** and **La Rotonde**.

Opposite the rather uninteresting church of Notre-Dame-des-Champs the **rue de la Gaîté** is still the entertainment centre of Montparnasse, lined with theatres, dance halls and cabarets as it has been for well over 200 years (hence the name). But since the disappearance of Bobino's, much of the life seems to have gone out of it. With the growth of sex shops this area can be rather sleazy at night, and the cafés and brasseries on the boulevard are often taken over at the weekends by noisy revellers up from the suburbs. But if lively Parisian nightlife is what you're after, as opposed to the sort of Paris-by-Night show put on on the Champs-Elysées or in Montmartre solely for tourists, you'll get a varied slice of it here.

Cemetery-lovers should take the **boulevard Edgar-Quinet** eastwards to the main entrance of the **Cimetière du Montparnasse** (Ⓜ Edgar-Quinet), to pay homage to a bevy of distinguished writers – Baudelaire, Sainte-Beuve and Maupassant, say, or Jean-Paul Sartre and Simone de Beauvoir – and a rather smaller number of artists and musicians, such as Zadkine and César Franck. Other inmates are Alfred Dreyfus, the victim of the 'Dreyfus Affair', and Jean Seberg and her diplomat and novelist husband Romain Gary. Don't miss Brâncuşi's sculpture **The Kiss** in the north-eastern corner, or the distinctly odd tomb of a gentleman called Pigeon, whose lifesize bronze effigy is sitting up in bed reading by the light of his claim to fame – a little lamp still known in French as a *lampe Pigeon* – with his wife sleeping peacefully at his side.

By now you will have had several glimpses of the structure that symbolises the transformation of much of Montparnasse into a sleek business district. (Ⓜ Montparnasse-Bienvenüe) The **Tour Maine-Montparnasse**, to give it its full name, is huge, dominating large portions of Paris with its 57 storeys towering 200 metres into the air. Europe's tallest office block, it was built in the early seventies on the site of the old Gare Montparnasse, where the German garrison surrendered in 1944. But the name of the square in front of it, **place du 18 juin 1940**, commemorates an earlier event: General de Gaulle's famous radio broadcast from London after the Fall of France. The tower was designed as the focal point in a scheme to bring new vitality to a rather run-down part of the city by creating a large new business sector, and is just one feature, albeit the most spectacular, of a vast rebuilding programme that involved pulling down whole streets of working-class flats and houses. It has never been popular with Parisians and the whole scheme, like many such projects undertaken in the sixties and early seventies, is severely criticised in an age when more user-friendly architecture is preferred even by professional planners.

For a glimpse of eighties solutions to the problems of modernising a whole district, a walk in what was once the village of Plaisance, in southern Montparnasse, is instructive. Beyond the new **Gare Montparnasse**, the **place de Catalogne** is the first large square to be built from scratch in Paris since Haussmann's day. To reach it you should take the **rue du Départ**, on the eastern side of the tower, then the **rue du Maine** in front of the station and the **rue du Commandant-Mouchotte**, dominated by the Méridien Hotel. The square is adorned with a modern fountain called 'The Crucible of Time' and flanked by two striking buildings by the Spanish architect Ricardo Bofill, one in stone ('The Amphitheatre') and one in glass ('The Columns'), the two linked by a neo-classical structure. Bofill's work is always interesting and these buildings certainly have a strong personality. To see what Plaisance was like before the developers moved in, stroll round the streets on either side of the rue d'Alésia, many of which still have artisans' cottages and bars frequented by the locals that have changed remarkably little over the years. (If you are short of time, Ⓜ Plaisance is on a direct line from Ⓜ Montparnasse-Bienvenüe.)

After this detour you should return to the Montparnasse Tower via the station. As part of the renovation scheme, the sprawl of railway lines is being roofed over with a large slab with pink Breton granite much in evidence – the district has always had many connections with Brittany, many of whose sons and daughters, emigrating to Paris, had their first taste of the capital at the Gare Montparnasse, which is still surrounded by Breton restaurants. In these environment-conscious days this 'roof' will be topped by gardens and sports facilities, and a 12-kilometre 'green corridor', with a cycle path and a track for hikers, will stretch beside the new high-speed railway line.

The large shopping centre at the foot of the tower houses a branch of the department store **Galeries Lafayette** and any number of smaller shops. A lift shoots you up in a few seconds to the 56th floor for the spectacular view from the top. It's certainly worth going up if the weather is good, though it's harder than you might think to get your bearings and work out which famous landmark is which, even with the help of the panoramic table. There's a cafeteria on this floor and a rather expensive restaurant below.

There are two specialist museums near the tower. To reach the **Musée Bourdelle**, walk up the rue de l'Arrivée on the west side of the tower, turn right into the **avenue du Maine** and then left into the **rue Antoine-Bourdelle**. As with the Zadkine Museum, this is an opportunity to see the work of the sculptor Antoine Bourdelle, who started his career as assistant to Rodin, in his own home and studio; it also gives you a glimpse into Montparnasse as it once was, with its hotch-potch of wooden buildings and little gardens. From here, walk to the end of the street, turn sharp left into the **rue Armand-Moisant** and continue to the **boulevard de Vaugirard**. The **Musée de la Poste et de la Philatélie** (Post and Stamp-collecting Museum) is on the right at no. 34. This is a good place to take children, with its exhibits illustrating the history of the postal services and a work-shop where you can see stamps being printed.

If you have any stamina left, the **Catacombs** (box, Walk 4) and **La Rûche** (Beyond the Centre) can easily be visited from Montparnasse. Otherwise there are plenty of opportunities for a meal or a drink, or an evening of entertainment in a cinema, theatre or nightclub. Alternatively, a short bus ride down the rue de Rennes will bring you back to Saint-Germain-des-Prés and its countless restaurants.

Hotels and Restaurants

For general advice on choosing where to stay and where to eat, see Practical Information; prices are moderate unless otherwise stated.

Hotels

Abbaye Saint-Germain 10 rue Cassette, 6e (45-44-38-11). Rather expensive, but worth it for the pretty rooms, some of them on two floors, and the quiet setting in a converted abbey close to the church of Saint-Sulpice and the Luxembourg Gardens.

Angleterre 44 rue Jacob, 6e (42-60-34-72, fax: 42-60-16-93). Once the British Embassy (hence the name), this rather expensive hotel is one of the most delightful in Saint-Germain, with its comfortable and spacious rooms, its pretty paved courtyard and its ideal situation in a street full of antique shops in the heart of the *quartier*.

Deux-Continents 25 rue Jacob, 6e (43-26-72-46). An elegant little *salon* overlooking the street and small but mostly attractive rooms.

Fleurie 32 rue Grégoire-de-Tours, 6e (43-29-59-81). Redecorated and generally renovated at the end of the 1980s; some of the attractive rooms are now rather expensive, but the position, just off the boulevard Saint-Germain, is very convenient, the staff are friendly and the façade, with statues set in little niches, is a joy.

Left Bank 9 rue de l'Ancienne-Comédie, 6e (43-54-01-70, fax: 43-26-17-14). Opened in 1989 right next to the newly glamorous Café Procope just by the Odéon crossroads. Expensive and chic, with air conditioning (a rarity in Saint-Germain), antique furniture and tapestries, and 17th-century beams in most rooms.

Marronniers 21 rue Jacob, 6e (43-25-30-60). Rooms and bathrooms can seem inconveniently small, but this is easily outweighed by the delights of the well-kept little garden overshadowed, as the name suggests, by two tall chestnut trees. Bookings are very hard to come by, so plan well ahead.

Perreyve 63 rue Madame, 6e (45-48-35-01). Fairly low prices in this hotel close to the Luxembourg Gardens; tiny bathrooms but plenty of charm.

Racine 23 rue Racine, 6e (43-26-00-60). Prices are relatively low by Saint-Germain standards for this quiet and modest little hotel close to the Odéon theatre and the Luxembourg Gardens.

Régent 61 rue Dauphine, 6e (46-34-59-80). Pleasant atmosphere, friendly service and well-planned, though mostly smallish, rooms in one of the streets running up from the Seine to the Odéon; the most popular, right at the top, have their own tiny balconies.

Saints-Pères 65 rue des Saints-Pères, 6e (45-44-50-00). A 17th-century mansion built by one of Louis XIV's architects, converted into a very attractive hotel with a courtyard garden, elegant furniture and decoration — even frescoed ceilings in some rooms — and well placed just off the boulevard Saint-Germain and close to the good shopping in the rue de Sèvres. Prices vary widely.

Seine 52 rue de Seine, 6e (46-34-22-80). Now under the same management as the Marronniers and the Welcome and completely renovated; just a few steps from the excellent Buci street market.

Vieux-Paris 9 rue Gît-le-Coeur, 6e (43-54-41-66). Modest but full of atmosphere: a 15th-century building in a narrow street. The wiring and plumbing have seen better days, but Hemingway and Dos Passos stayed here, the service is friendly and you're right in the heart of things just by the lively place Saint-Michel. Fairly low prices.

Welcome 66 rue de Seine, 6e (46-34-24-80). Under the same management as the Marronniers but more modest. Rooms overlooking the boulevard are noisy (double glazing helps in winter), but the atmosphere is pleasant, and the Buci street market is on the doorstep.

Restaurants

Assiette au Beurre 11 rue Saint-Benoît, 6e (42-60-87-41). Art nouveau décor and fairly expensive cuisine, specialising in seafood, in the heart of Saint-Germain-des-Prés. Inexpensive lunchtime *menu*.

Assiette au Boeuf 22 rue Guillaume-Apollinaire, 6e (42-60-88-44). Confusingly similar name to the more expensive restaurant next door, but this is a cheerful member of a small chain of good-value places offering 'formula' meals in art-nouveau style décor by trendy designer Slavik; a bit noisy, but fun.

Bistro de la Gare 59 blvd du Montparnasse, 6e (45-48-38-01). The famous Rougeot with its superb (and genuine) art nouveau décor was converted some time ago into a member of another chain of 'formula' restaurants. Lively, good-value, with fast service if you're in a hurry, and particularly good puddings. Opposite the Tour Montparnasse.

Aux Charpentiers 10 rue Mabillon, 6e (43-26-30-05); closed Sun. Once the headquarters of the Carpenters Guild — hence the name, and the faded sepia photos on the walls of groups of masters and journeymen with their elaborate 'master pieces'. Straightforward home cooking, famous for its regular *plats du jour*.

Chez Bébert 71 blvd du Montparnasse, 6e (no telephone bookings). Good North African cuisine in Montparnasse.

La Chope d'Alsace 4 carrefour de l'Odéon, 6e (43-26-67-76). Helpfully open seven days a week, year-round, from midday to 2 a.m. Filling Alsatian specialities, traditional *plats du jour* and seafood platters.

La Closerie des Lilas 171 blvd du Montparnasse, 6e (43-26-70-50). Frequented more for its atmosphere than its food – it's probably better to eat in the brasserie section than in the expensive restaurant. One of *the* meeting places for writers and intellectuals for decades ('Hemingway-drank-here' plaque in the bar). If you decide on the restaurant, try to get a table on the pretty terrace.

La Coupole 102 blvd du Montparnasse, 14e (43-20-14-20). This huge (600 seats) and famous brasserie, rightly referred to as an 'institution', changed hands in 1988, and was done up from top to toe, but it still attracts a lively throng of artists, showbiz stars and aspiring starlets, politicians, plus hordes of less glittering Saturday-nighters. Very noisy but great fun.

A la Cour de Rohan See box in Food and Drink.

La Cour Saint-Germain 156 blvd Saint-Germain, 6e (43-26-85-49). Almost on the corner of the rue de Buci and a useful inexpensive spot for 'formula' meals in the wooden-partitioned dining room upstairs overlooking the boulevard.

L'Echaudé Saint-Germain 21 rue de l'Echaudé, 6e (43-54-79-02). Small and attractive, on a corner site between the Seine/Buci market and the place Fürstemberg. Good-value *menu*, more expensive lunchtime *carte*; lively local clientele, plus some tourists; open to 2 a.m.

Le Gregory 6 rue Grégoire-de-Tours, 6e (43-54-90-06). Most of the restaurants lining this lively street just off the boulevard Saint-Germain are tourist traps, but the unpretentious Gregory usually gives fair value.

L'Heure Gourmande See box in Food and Drink.

La Lozère 4 rue Hautefeuille, 6e (43-54-26-64); closed Sun, Mon and Aug. If you're tired of *le tout Paris* you'll enjoy being transported to a rustic village in the remote Lozère region by the filling regional specialities, the unpretentious décor and the friendly service.

La Petite Cour 8 rue Mabillon, 6e (43-26-52-26). The geranium-filled courtyard below street level is a delight for a summer meal, but the inside is attractive too, with elegant décor and comfortable armchairs. Light and subtle cuisine.

Le Petit Saint-Benoît 4 rue Saint-Benoît, 6e (no telephone bookings). Popular for its cheap but satisfactory meals made up of timeless dishes like *blanquette de veau*, its lively clientele and its long history: it has been going strong since 1860 and was much frequented by horse-drawn-cab drivers. Get there early to be sure of a table, especially on summer evenings when the pavement tables make a good vantage point.

Le Petit Zinc 25 rue de Buci, 6e (46-33-51-66). Again very popular, always crowded until it closes at 3 a.m. Straightforward cuisine, with some specialities from the Massif Central, and deliciously fresh seafood.

Polidor 41 rue Monsieur-le-Prince, 6e (43-26-95-34). Famous for its low prices, its literary associations (André Gide, James Joyce, Paul Verlaine and Paul Valéry were all habitués), its classic bistrot décor, complete with chest of numbered drawers for regulars' napkins – and a chunk of the medieval city wall in the cellars.

Le Procope 14 rue de l'Ancienne-Comédie, 6e (43-26-99-20). Probably France's first coffee house (opened in 1686), completely redesigned for the bicentenary of the French Revolution: fair enough, as the key revolutionaries used to meet here. Expensive *carte* but good, if limited, lunchtime *menu*.

Museums and Places of Interest

Musée de la Monnaie (Coin and Medals Museum) 11 quai de Conti, 6e. Closed Mon and mornings, late opening Wed; workshops can be visited on Tue and Fri afternoons. Ⓜ Odéon, Pont-Neuf

Ecole Nationale Supérieure des Beaux-Arts (Fine Arts Academy) Exhibition entrance 17 quai Malaquais, 6e; courtyard entrance in rue Bonaparte, 6e. Special exhibitions only, no permanent collection. Ⓜ Saint-Germain-des-Prés

Musée Delacroix (Delacroix's home and studio) 6 pl de Fürstemberg, 6e. Closed Tue. Ⓜ Saint-Germain-des-Prés

Jardin du Luxembourg (Luxembourg Gardens) Puppet and Punch and Judy shows: usually Wed, Sat and Sun afternoons. Ⓜ Notre-Dame-des-Champs, Saint-Placide

Palais du Luxembourg rue de Vaugirard, 6e. Visits sometimes possible on Sun but check locally; temporary exhibitions are held in the adjoining **Petit Luxembourg**. Ⓜ Odéon, Ⓡ Luxembourg

Observatoire (Observatory) 61 av de l'Observatoire, 14e. Open only first Sat in the month, and you must write in first to the Secrétariat (enclose an international reply coupon). Ⓜ Denfert-Rochereau, Ⓡ Port-Royal

Eglise de Val-de-Grâce pl Alphonse-Laveran, 5e. Ⓡ Port-Royal

Musée Zadkine 100bis rue d'Assas, 6e. Closed Mon. Ⓜ Notre-Dame-des-Champs, Vavin

Musée Bourdelle 16 rue Antoine-Bourdelle, 15e. Closed Mon. Ⓜ Montparnasse-Bienvenüe

Musée de la Poste et de la Philatélie (Post and Stamp-collecting Museum) 34 blvd de Vaugirard, 15e. Closed Sun. Ⓜ Montparnasse-Bienvenüe

Walk 4
The Faubourg Saint-Germain, Invalides, Champ de Mars

Starting point: carrefour Croix-Rouge, 6e; Ⓜ Sèvres-Babylone. This Left Bank walk starts on the borders of the sixth and seventh *arrondissements* and covers the whole of the seventh, including several major sights: the new Musée d'Orsay, the Invalides and Napoleon's Tomb, the Rodin Museum and the Eiffel Tower.

The walk starts with the Faubourg Saint-Germain, the aristocratic district that lies between Saint-Germain-des-Prés and the Invalides. The Faubourg became *the* fashionable place to live from about the 1680s, when France's top families began to desert the Marais and built splendid *hôtels particuliers* (mansions or town houses) on open ground in what was then the sparsely populated Grenelle plain (the rue de Grenelle still runs right through the district). Virtually all these great houses were built during a fifty-year span, which explains the all-of-a-piece impression that strikes you as you walk through the streets where Madame Récamier once held her famous *salon*, and where, for almost a century, from the 1830s to the First World War, the great hostesses of the type that people the pages of Proust gave splendid receptions and balls.

About 150 of these fine late 17th- and 18th-century houses have survived. Until quite recently they were still lived in for much of the year by the aristocracy — in the summer they decamped, with bag and baggage and retinue of servants, to their ancestral châteaux. But they are now mostly ministries and other official buildings. This has the advantage of having ensured their survival — the prestige of France requires that they be beautifully kept up — but the disadvantage, in these security-conscious times, of making them largely forbidden territory. The façades overlooking the street are often interesting, but as the roads are fairly narrow it is hard to get far enough away to see them in perspective, and they are rarely as lovely as those overlooking the gardens, which are hidden well out of sight of those without special passes.

A word here about the typical structure of these *hôtels*. The building visible from the street, with its huge double doors, tall and wide enough to allow a carriage to drive in (the term *porte cochère*, carriage doorway, is still used in modern French for such entrances), is just one side of a complex of buildings grouped round a large paved courtyard, the *cour d'honneur*. You may be lucky enough to catch a glimpse of one or two of these on weekdays, when the great doors swing open to allow official limousines in. The parallel structure on the far side, with tall windows overlooking the *cour d'honneur* on one side and lovely formal gardens on the other, housed the suites of apartments where the aristocratic families lived. To say that you lived *entre cour et jardin*, between the courtyard and the garden, made it clear to your listeners that you belonged to the privileged few.

The whole of the seventh *arrondissement* is still very much a *beau quartier*, a discreet and expensive residential district stretching right to the pleasant avenues surrounding the Champ de Mars, on either side of the Eiffel Tower. But from the tourist point of view it has the disadvantage of being dead at night and, to a large extent, at weekends. It has some excellent restaurants, but they chiefly cater for politicians and diplomats (the National Assembly and the Foreign Ministry are in this part of Paris), for media people and publishers working in the area and for the posh local residents, none of whom is around during the weekend.

The walk starts at the **Croix-Rouge crossroads** in the heart of an upmarket shopping district. In the side streets leading from here to the boulevard Saint-Germain are some expensive fashion boutiques, including **Sonia Rykiel** in the rue de Grenelle, and the **rue de Sèvres** has several cheaper and larger fashion places such as **Tiffany's** or **Carroll**. All these side streets are worth exploring. One, the **rue des Saints-Pères**, has a small museum, the **Musée-Bibliothèque du Protestantisme Français**, with some interesting material from the period when Protestant preachers led a clandestine life, setting up folding pulpits in the 'Wilderness', a remote area near Nîmes in southern France that is still largely Protestant. Before starting on the walk proper, you might like to order a coffee at the café on the crossroads or have a glass of wine at **Au Sauvignon***, on the corner of the rue des Saints-Pères.

The Red Cross that gave this little corner of Paris its name was allegedly a large crucifix painted bright red and placed here in the 16th century to ward off pagan emanations surviving from the temple dedicated to Isis that once stood here. It has been replaced today by an equally bold sight: a modern statue of a centaur by the provocative sculptor César, who has produced work made out of bits of old cars compressed together, and, in the heady days of performance art, out of foam squeezed out of a giant tube. This piece is a homage to Picasso.

The rue de Sèvres leads westwards to the **Sèvres-Babylone crossroads**, dominated by the **Lutétia Concorde hotel**, which has recently been done up in chic art déco style by fashion designer and neighbour Sonia Rykiel. The rooms are expensive but the ground-floor brasserie* won't break the bank. On the far side of the triangular **square Boucicault**, with its garden and children's playground, is Paris's oldest department store, **Au Bon Marché**, built on a metal frame designed by Gustave Eiffel fifteen years before he embarked on the plans for his tower. It is considerably less crowded than its competitors near the Opéra (see Walk 7) and is famous for its food section (called *L'Epicerie*, but it covers much more than mere groceries) and its antiques department.

A little way along the **rue de Babylone** running along the north side of the store a curious sight greets you: **La Pagode** at no. 57 is an art cinema in the form of a pagoda, with a little tea room attached. It was built in 1896 by the wife of the enterprising founder of Au Bon Marché, who gave elegant receptions there, and became a cinema in the thirties (tea room open from 4 p.m. on weekdays, from 2 p.m. on Sundays).

Now walk northwards down the **boulevard Raspail** and take the first turning on the right, the **rue de la Chaise**, which once housed Madame Récamier's *salon*, in a wing of what had been an abbey. Nos 5 and 7 form an elegant house which Napoleon bought for his sister Pauline Borghese and her family. There are more 18th-century mansions in the **rue de Grenelle**. Turn right to look at nos 15 and 20, then retrace your steps and walk westwards. Nos 27 and 29 are less decorative examples of the architecture of the Faubourg and at no. 36 is what purports to be the oldest restaurant in Paris, **La Petite Chaise***. Just after you've crossed the boulevard Raspail, you come to the elaborate **Fontaine des Quatre-Saisons**, designed by the sculptor Bouchardon in the 1740s to fulfil the practical function of providing water for the wealthy new inhabitants of the Faubourg. Next door at no. 59, the **Hôtel Bouchardon**, where Alfred de Musset lived and wrote several of his plays, including *Lorenzaccio*, is being turned into a new museum of modern painting, the **Musée Dina-Vierny**.

Beyond here nos 73, 75, 81, 85, 87 and 102 are all interesting 18th-century houses. Turn left into the rue de Bellechasse, then left again into the **rue de Varenne** for a short detour to see the **Hôtel Matignon**, the official residence of the prime minister (no. 2). Both this large hôtel, where Talleyrand once entertained in style, and the Italian embassy at no. 3 overlook a large garden, but sadly nothing is visible from the street. When you have had your fill of the lovely mansions in this street, return to the rue de Bellechasse, turn right and walk towards the Seine. Cross over the **boulevard Saint-Germain** and the **rue de l'Université**, a sought-after residential street, and continue until you reach the **rue de Lille**. (ⓜ Musée d'Orsay) The rest of the rue de Bellechasse is now a traffic-free zone, attractively paved with granite slabs and often thronged with tourists, as this has become one of the cultural highspots of Paris.

To your right towers the façade of the railway station-turned-museum, the **Musée d'Orsay**, controversial up to its opening at the end of 1986, now happily accepted as a major European museum. To your left is another museum, somewhat upstaged by its new neighbour, but still interesting: the **Musée de la Légion d'Honneur**, housed in the **Hôtel de Salm**. This was one of the last grand mansions to be built in the Faubourg, in 1782, for a German count who died on the guillotine twelve years later. It was then won in a lottery by a picaresque figure who had started life as a wig-maker's apprentice and later bought the pretty Bagatelle château in the Bois de Boulogne (see Beyond the Centre). But he was soon clapped into jail for forgery and the mansion was bought by the Swedish embassy. One of the ambassadors was married to Madame de Staël, so it was here that she

held her famous political *salon* before going into exile. The *hôtel* was bought for Napoleon in 1804 by the Grand Chancellor of the Légion d'honneur, a military and civil decoration he had founded a couple of years earlier, which entitles its holders to wear the discreet little red rosette you will soon spot in the buttonhole of distinguished-looking gentlemen as you travel round Paris. The building was burnt down during the Commune and had to be heavily restored. Before going in, it is worth walking round to the **quai Anatole-France** for a glimpse beyond the garden of the elegant rotunda on the river side.

The museum covers the history of the orders of chivalry under the *ancien régime*, and of various foreign decorations, as well as the Légion d'honneur itself and the men and women who have been awarded this most prized of all French decorations.

Now walk up the steps to the **Musée d'Orsay**, admiring a large bronze rhinoceros, a horse, even a trapped elephant — open-air exhibits as an appetiser for the riches inside. The building dates from the end of the 19th century, the height of the Railway Age, and was designed by Victor Laloux to house the terminus for trains from Orléans and the south-west of France. The site had previously been occupied by the Palais d'Orsay, the seat of the Cour des Comptes (audit office) and the Conseil d'Etat (council of state), but that had been burnt to the ground during the Commune. Laloux's grandiose Gare d'Orsay, exuding the confidence of the times, was built on a glass-roofed iron frame typical of the period, but this utilitarian structure was embellished with a monumental façade worthy of its riverside site almost opposite the Louvre, and a coffered ceiling with elaborate stucco decoration.

It was ceremonially opened on Bastille Day 1900, only a fortnight after the first line of the brand-new *Métropolitain* or underground railway had started operating, to the admiration of visitors who flocked to Paris from all over the world for the Exposition Universelle. A luxury hotel was added later, and proved popular, even though the station had only a forty-year life span: by the outbreak of the Second World War it had been rendered obsolete by the new long trains plying up and down the newly electrified lines — too long for its platforms. So the proud station was downgraded to a terminus for an unimportant suburban network and the mainline trains travelled to the Gare d'Austerlitz further east.

Yet the majestic building never lost its appeal, even in the years when nostalgia for a more leisurely era and its architecture seemed eccentric. General de Gaulle cleverly stage-managed his return to power with a dramatic speech in the hotel ballroom during the Algerian crisis in 1958, Orson Welles chose the deserted station as the setting for his film of Kafka's *The Trial* in the early sixties, and a few years later various scenes in Bertolucci's *The Conformist*, based on a Moravia novel, were shot in and around the hotel. Jean-Louis Barrault and Madeleine Renaud found a splendid home for their theatre company there in the seventies and another part of the building formed a temporary home for the Drouot auction house while its new premises were under construction on the Grands Boulevards (Walk 7).

Previous pages: The stylish design of the Musée d'Orsay incorporates the old station clock

But a permanent use for Laloux's building still hadn't been found. A demolition permit had been issued in 1970 and it was very nearly replaced by a huge hotel. But in 1973 an enlightened arts minister declared it a listed building and four years later agreement had been reached on turning it into a museum of 19th-century art. The dates eventually fixed on were 1848 to 1914, the idea being that its collections would take over where the Louvre left off, and would in turn be continued by the National Museum of Modern Art in the Pompidou/Beaubourg Centre. It would therefore include the superb Impressionist collection then in rather cramped quarters in the Jeu de Paume in the Tuileries Gardens, the Post-Impressionists in the Palais de Tokyo near the Trocadéro, and some paintings and sculpture from the Louvre, such as late work by Delacroix or Ingres. This was the period when Paris was transformed by Haussmann's rebuilding, and was embellished with elaborate new buildings like Charles Garnier's opera house, the department stores and the stations; when it staged a series of ambitious World's Exhibitions and acquired its reputation as a centre of fashionable nightlife; when the Impressionists created a whole new way of looking at painting. Remember all this as you join the long queues and shuffle slowly in (if you've had the fore-sight to buy a museum pass – see box in Practical Information – you can avoid queuing).

The architects didn't have an easy task, not least because the express métro line running beneath the building sets up vibrations. Costs escalated, and the opening was postponed so often that the ever-sceptical Parisians were soon ridi-culing the whole scheme. But when it did eventually open at the end of 1986 and they saw the superbly restored building and the stylish interior and fittings by the Italian designer Gae Aulenti, they were impressed, along with the rest of the world, at the way the station architecture (even the traditional clock for meeting under) had been preserved, yet adapted to its new role as a display case for paint-ings, sculpture and decorative art. One criticism voiced in the early days was that visitors were so overwhelmed by the architecture that they paid too little attention to the exhibits. That view is heard less often now, though there is perhaps some-thing to be said for a brief initial visit to admire the sweep of the vast 'nave' and walk through the sculpture-lined concourse on the ground floor, followed up by a later visit concentrating on the rest of the collections.

I should perhaps declare an interest here: I was a Friend of Orsay long before the museum eventually opened, years late, and have loved everything about it from the moment I was shown a scale model of the planned museum and was allowed to peer over a parapet to see the work on restoring the ceiling and the huge arching struts of the roof. I admit that the architecture mesmerises you, but it is an archetypal example of the station and department store design carried out bang in the middle of the museum's 66-year time span, and as such a fitting setting for the art of the period. My only slight disappointment is with the Impressionists in their long gallery on the upper level, often thought to be the jewel in the crown of the M'O (that's what those who work there like it to be called, but the abbrevia-tion doesn't really seem to have caught on). Perhaps because they always seem to be uncomfortably crowded with visitors, but also because there are so many paintings crammed into rooms that seem rather small and a bit dark, I rather preferred these lovely canvases in the Jeu de Paume and wish they could have been displayed in the larger rooms overlooking the Seine on the lower floors.

There is no space here to describe the collections in detail, so I shall simply mention a few things I'd hate you to miss and recommend that you take one of the colour-coded leaflets at the information desk just inside the entrance (the ones in English have a Union Jack on them), pick out the rooms that appeal to you most and then see what is on in the way of temporary exhibitions. Bear in mind that if you want to see everything you'll need to set aside a whole day. The 'invitation to history' display on the lowest level is a useful brief introduction to the museum and the major landmarks in the period it covers. One tip: you'll save time by avoiding the crowded escalators and using the lifts instead when you're ready to visit the upper floors, but they are tucked away at the entrance end, so keep your eyes open.

You will probably want to admire the Ingres and Delacroix and the early Manets on the ground floor, the Bonnards and Vuillards on the middle floor as well as the Impressionists, but I hope you won't turn your nose up, as many French visitors do, at the late 19th-century Establishment painters whose work was snapped up by the Salon judges while the Impressionists were rejected. They weren't all very good painters, but they help you to understand what the Impressionists were up against, and they are superbly displayed in the ballroom on the middle floor (marked S on the plan). The art nouveau collections on the same floor are a bit of a curate's egg: good on the Ecole de Nancy (wonderful inlaid furniture by Emile Gallé) and some interesting decorative details by Guimard, designer of the métro entrances, but rather a hotchpotch in the 'International art nouveau' section. On the ground floor, behind the sculpture concourse, don't miss the scale model of the Opéra, opened up like a doll's house so you can see inside, and the model of the whole of the Opéra district beneath your feet, seen through a pane of glass.

The museum restaurant is in the gilded and painted hotel dining room on the first floor and worth it for the décor alone, though the food is good value too. On the top floor, the **Café des Hauteurs** will do for a quick snack beside the terrace offering lovely views over the Seine and the Tuileries up to the Sacré-Coeur in Montmartre. The museum also has an excellent bookshop, and a card shop (accessible from the *quai*).

After your visit you may like to stroll through some of the streets stretching east towards Saint-Germain-des-Prés and down to the river, beyond the rue du Bac. This is antique dealer country, known as the **Carré Rive Gauche**, a name invented by the many dealers who have smart little shops in the square bounded by the **rue du Bac**, the **rue de l'Université**, the **rue des Saints-Pères** and the **quai Voltaire**. In the **rue de Verneuil**, the 18th-century **Hôtel d'Avejan** at no. 53 has been restored and now houses the Maison des Ecrivains and the Centre National des Lettres, a writers' centre run by the arts ministry which stages interesting lectures and readings, most of them open to the public. It also has a small restaurant overlooking the street, the **Café des Lettres***.

Museum Boutiques

Where once they sold nothing more exotic than postcards and guide books, Paris's museums have now latched on to the commercial potential of opening well-designed shops offering a wide range of gifts, often including reproductions of exhibits. Some have excellent modern bookshops too. Opening times are generally the same as those of the museum itself.

Musée des Arts Décoratifs (Walk 6) To the left of the main entrance, expensive but very beautiful pieces, ranging from designer scarves and china to eye-catching stationery and office accessories. At least one new design is commissioned each time an exhibition is staged, fitting in with its theme. To the right, a good art bookshop, also stocking postcards and posters.

Musée des Arts de la Mode (Walk 6) Small boutique on the fifth floor, whose wares include re-creations of famous scents in replicas of the original bottles, and copies of accessories by designers like Schiaparelli; a note on the article's history is included.

Bagatelle (Beyond the Centre) Pretty boutique in the mini-château sells rather expensive items, most of them with a garden theme. Among the cheapest are very Parisian artificial flowers and bunches of fruit to pin to your hat or lapel. Also attractive notebooks, sketchbooks and artists' portfolios with a reproduction of the château.

Centre Beaubourg/Pompidou (Walk 8) Stylish shop specialising in contemporary design plus toys. Two art bookshops.

Forum des Halles (Walk 8) A boutique called *Paris Musées* stocks replicas of exhibits from all the City of Paris museums, plus upmarket souvenirs, many of them genuinely inventive.

Muséum d'Histoire Naturelle (Walk 2) As well as the official museum bookshop (in the south-east corner of the Jardin des Plantes), there is a good 'unofficial' natural history bookshop in the rue Buffon. Between them they cover the whole field of natural history. Wall posters with paintings of fungi, shells, birds, wild flowers and so on make good presents to encourage nature-minded children to widen their French vocabulary. Also charming postcard reproductions of early engravings of the menagerie.

Institut du Monde Arabe (Walk 2) Bookshop-cum-gift shop with a wide range of jewellery and craft items from the twenty-odd Arab countries.

Louvre (Walk 6) Right beneath the Pyramid is a very stylish art bookshop whose upper floor sells replicas of objects in the museum and attractive stationery and accessories with architectural motifs. There are plans to extend the range, and a specially created scent is to be launched in 1991 or thereabouts.

Musée de la Monnaie (Walk 3) Medals designed by contemporary artists.

Musée d'Orsay (Walk 4) Excellent art bookshop covering the museum's period (1848–1914); separate *carterie* selling postcards and posters is accessible from the quai Anatole-France even if you're not visiting the museum.

Return to the junction of the rue de Lille and the rue de Bellechasse. From here you can walk towards the river and take one of the boats that sets out from below the **quai Anatole-France** beside the **Piscine Deligny**, a floating swimming pool liable to be packed with topless sunbathers (and ogling admirers) on hot summer afternoons. The boats ply up and down the Seine to the Canal Saint-Martin and along it to the new La Villette park (Beyond the Centre), but trips last about three hours, so you must plan accordingly.

Continue along the rue de Lille past the **Hôtel de Beauharnais** at no. 78, which was lived in at one stage by Eugène de Beauharnais, the son of the Empress Joséphine. He spent fabulous sums on redesigning and decorating it, adding an Egyptian peristyle, and his elaborate decorative schemes have survived in what is now the German ambassador's residence. You can see the lovely garden façade from the quai Anatole-France and imagine the receptions given there by Eugène and by his sister Queen Hortense of Holland, wife of Louis Bonaparte and mother of Napoleon III, who also lived there for a time, before the house was sold to the King of Prussia.

When you reach the boulevard Saint-Germain you get a good view of the neo-classical façade of the **Palais Bourbon**, where the French Parliament, the Assemblée Nationale, holds its sittings. Most of the building is 18th century, but this is a pompous early 19th-century addition, impressive when lit up at night, and best seen from the **Pont de la Concorde** just opposite, or from the **place de la Concorde**. It has some well-known frescoes by Delacroix in the library but little else of interest as it has been drastically altered since it was two separate mansions, the Hôtel de Bourbon and the Hôtel de Lassay. It has been the seat of the lower house of France's Parliament since the end of the Napoleonic era and its original name of Chambre des députés (*députés* being constituency members) is still often used. Since the end of the Second World War it has officially been called the Assemblée Nationale.

The police on duty probably won't let you get very near, and the next building along, the foreign ministry (generally referred to as the **Quai d'Orsay** from the name of the quayside along this stretch of the river) is also heavily guarded. Turn left down the **rue Aristide Briand** and walk past the Palais Bourbon to the **place du Palais-Bourbon**. The brasserie on the corner is a useful place for a quick meal or snack. When Parliament is sitting it is fun to sit here and watch the *députés* and journalists and secretaries and security men bustling in and out. Every now and then a posse of motorcycle outriders will come screeching to a halt as the limousine bearing some political high-up sweeps into the courtyard opposite.

The **rue de Bourgogne** has elegant houses and several peaceful hotels, but you should continue along the **rue de l'Université** to the **esplanade des Invalides**, recently grassed over and planted with trees to create a pleasant sweep of ground towards the Seine. From here you get a good view of the imposing **Hôtel des Invalides**, which you can reach by turning left and walking along the **rue de Constantine**, past the **Canadian Cultural Centre** and the **British Council** and **British Institute**, in adjoining buildings. At the river end of the esplanade is the air terminal for Orly airport and a station on the express métro line that runs westwards to Versailles. (Ⓜ and ⓇⒺⓇ Invalides)

Les Invalides was commissioned by Louis XIV as a military hospital and a rest home to house the wounded, elderly or infirm ex-soldiers (*invalides* in French) who fought in his various campaigns. It wasn't entirely a philanthropic gesture, of course, as he also saw it as a way of encouraging recruitment to his armies — before then a potential soldier had had good reason to be apprehensive about what would happen to him in old age or if he was wounded. Plans for a complex of buildings, including a church, were drawn up by Libéral Bruant and the foundation stone was laid in 1671. Six years later work started on a second church, designed this time by Jules Hardouin-Mansart, who surmounted it with a dome that seems to be part of the façade as you gaze at its huge length from the esplanade, though it is in fact set well back from it. The original six or seven thousand old soldiers have dwindled to less than a hundred and Les Invalides is now known chiefly as the home of the Military Museum and several other smaller collections, and of Napoleon's Tomb, housed in the Eglise du Dôme.

The **Musée de l'Armée** (Military Museum) spreads over several buildings grouped round the *cour d'honneur* and covers a huge range of weapons, from primitive stone axes to jewel-encrusted sabres, plus uniforms and armour, flags and standards, military decorations, Napoleana of course, a collection of First and Second World War memorabilia, and a model illustrating the D-Day landings. The same ticket entitles you to visit the **Galerie des Plans-Reliefs** (up under the roof on the west side), a collection of scale models of key fortresses, with accompanying plans and maps. It was undergoing restoration and reorganisation when this book was written and by the time you read this should include a video presentation of how and why the models were made (some date from as early as the mid-17th century).

The west side of the *cour d'honneur* includes the façade of one of the Invalides' two churches, **Saint-Louis-des-Invalides.** Before going in, don't miss a sight that still plays a part in the folk memory of Parisians: to the right of the entrance is one of the legendary fleet of taxis that transported soldiers to the Battle of the Marne in 1914. Also known as 'the Soldiers' Church', the rather bare building makes a telling prelude to the opulence of Napoleon's tomb in its twin church (they are literally joined together, a glass panel enabling you to glimpse the **Eglise du Dôme** at the far end). Apart from its large organ, on which Berlioz's *Requiem* was first performed, Saint-Louis is adorned with little but the threadbare flags and standards captured from various enemies, hanging affectingly from the cornice way above your head. The crypt and vaults are full of tombs, but they are open only when special masses are said for the high-ranking military heroes laid to rest there. Before visiting the Eglise du Dôme and its famous tomb, walk out into the courtyard to admire the tiered classical façade, whose regilded dome is dazzling against a sunny sky.

Napoleon's Tomb is vastly impressive. The colours come as something of a shock: a shiny dark-red sarcophagus made of porphyry, resting on a green granite pedestal. The way the tomb seems to be sunk down is unexpected. But nothing can detract from the almost tangible sense of *La Gloire* that is so dear to the hearts of Frenchmen (and women, though perhaps less so). They flock here in their thousands, just as their ancestors followed the Little Corporal on to the battlefields of Europe and Egypt, and in December 1840, 19 years after his death in exile on St Helena, braved thick snow to trudge behind the coffin carrying his remains beneath the Arc de Triomphe, down the Champs-Elysées and over the Seine to lie in state in this very church. A *son-et-lumière* performance of this high point in the history of Paris, *Le Retour des Cendres*, is given in the courtyard in both French and English on summer evenings. In case you're puzzled by the use of the word *cendres*, ashes, it doesn't mean that the ex-Emperor was cremated, the term is a figurative one for his mortal remains. It had taken many years of patient negotiations to persuade the British to part with them. And another long period elapsed before the elaborate tomb, designed by Visconti, was ready. It was eventually revealed to a waiting world by Napoleon III 21 years later, in 1861.

The tombs of some of his highest-ranking soldiers surround their chief, and also in the crypt is the tomb of his sad son, the Duke of Reichstadt, or King of Rome, or the Eaglet, as he was variously known, who died in Vienna in 1832 at the age of 21. His remains, too, were transferred to Les Invalides long after his death. Oddly enough, they were brought to Paris on the centenary of the return of his father's remains, in a sentimental gesture dreamed up by none other than Adolf Hitler. Another moving moment: when you read the inscription immortalising Napoleon's own words, 'I should like my last resting place to be on the banks of the Seine, among the French people I loved so much.'

Beside the Eglise du Dôme, the **Jardin de l'Intendant** was originally a *jardin à la française* surrounding an ornamental lake, with an avenue of lime trees on the western side. The lake was filled in at the beginning of this century, but has now been reinstated; the gardens have recently been restored and make a delightful place to rest and gaze up at the shiny dome above you, or at the statue of its designer Jules Hardouin-Mansart.

Opposite the north wing of Les Invalides is another much larger garden, surrounding the **Hôtel Biron**, a mansion built in 1728 for another former wig-maker (wig-making was clearly a lucrative profession in those days). It was later turned into a convent but is of interest today because Auguste Rodin lived and worked there from 1907 until his death in 1917. In return for the use of a studio and flat (a privilege also enjoyed at various times by Rilke and by Cocteau), he agreed to leave his collection of his own work to the State, which had bought the *hôtel* in 1910. This collection forms the basis of the **Musée Rodin**, which spills over into the lovely garden: you can admire famous sculptures like *The Burghers of Calais* and *The Thinker* in a pleasantly leafy setting before you go into the house. Built by Jacques Gabriel, the father of the architect of the Ecole Militaire, which you will come to shortly, it makes a fine setting, with its panelled *salons*, for the milky whiteness of marble pieces such as *The Cathedral* (a pair of hands arching together) or *The Kiss*. The museum also has a good selection of sketches and drawings, and some work by Rodin's tormented mistress Camille Claudel. Temporary exhibitions by contemporary sculptors are held in the rose garden, an ideal spot for an interlude of quiet contemplation. With a bit of luck the little *buvette* (refreshment kiosk) will be open and you can relax with a drink or snack.

After leaving the museum, turn left and walk across the esplanade, past the Invalides, and continue along the **rue de Grenelle**. (Ⓜ Latour-Maubourg) You are now in the residential heart of the discreet seventh *arrondissement*, inhabited by *bon chic bon genre* (often abbreviated to *BCBG*) families – the French equivalent of Sloane Rangers or Preppies – identifiable by their green loden overcoats, their neat navy skirts and cardigans, their well-behaved children with carefully trimmed hair and alice bands. There are some good and not too expensive fashion boutiques, stylish but less avant-garde than those in Saint-Germain-des-Prés or Les Halles, both in the rue de Grenelle and in the parallel **rue Saint-Dominique**, a busy shopping street which you can reach by turning right into the **rue de l'Exposition**, just after crossing the **avenue Bosquet**. Before doing so you may like to stroll through the food market in the **rue Cler** (the stretch to the left, leading to the **avenue de la Motte-Picquet**). You could perhaps buy picnic ingredients here, for eating in the gardens near the Eiffel Tower. Or you could have a coffee and a snack in one of the cafés surrounding the **place de l'Ecole-Militaire** at the far end of the rue Cler. (Ⓜ Ecole-Militaire)

The rue de l'Exposition has an important place on the culinary map of Paris because not so long ago it was the home of a tiny restaurant called **L'Archestrate**, run by one of the high priests of the *nouvelle cuisine*, Alain Senderens. Senderens has now moved on to higher things, presiding over the extremely expensive **Lucas-Carton** in the place de la Madeleine (Walk 6), but it's interesting to think that he started his Paris career in this modest street. Turn left at the end into the **rue Saint-Dominique** and you will come to a little restaurant that has remained modest – and is none the worse for that. The **Fontaine de Mars*** is on the corner of a small arcaded square adorned with the large fountain that gives it its name. Sculpted figures depict the Goddess of Health, Hygiea, ministering unto Mars, the God of War, a choice of subject that makes sense when you know that it was originally at the entrance to a military hospital. Cars have now been banished from the square, the arcades have been cleaned up and an alfresco meal at one of the red-and-white-checked tablecloths is a pleasantly relaxing prelude to a visit to the Eiffel Tower.

The rue Saint-Dominique ends at the **avenue Rapp**. Art nouveau lovers should make a brief detour to the right to no. 29, a splendid example of the style. Beyond the **place du Général-Gouraud** lies the **Champ de Mars**, a very French public garden to your left, with sandy paths and neat flower beds and fenced-in strips of lawn stretching to the Ecole Militaire (military academy), a less formal series of gardens to your right, swarming with tourists and overshadowed by the huge legs of the Eiffel Tower, which seems unexpectedly large and overpowering close to, very different from the spindly structure glimpsed from a distance as you travel round Paris.

The Champ de Mars was once, as its name (meaning the Field of Mars) suggests, a vast parade ground, designed by the 18th-century architect of the Ecole Militaire Jacques-Anges Gabriel, *Premier Architecte du Roi*, whose later masterpieces included the twin buildings on the north of the place de la Concorde (Walk 6) and the Petit Trianon at Versailles. The cadets who practised manoeuvres there included an ambitious young Corsican called Napoleone Buonaparte, whose passing-out certificate cautiously commented that he might go far, if circumstances proved to be on his side – a famous example of understatement. The Champ de Mars was soon being used for non-military events, such as the Celebration of the Federation, staged before 300,000 spectators on the first anniversary of the storming of the Bastille, or the Celebration of the Supreme Being four years later. This elaborate ritual culminated in Robespierre setting alight a gigantic cardboard effigy of Atheism, which crumpled to a heap of ashes, revealing to the astonished gaze of the multitude the figure of Wisdom. A hundred years later the gardens were the setting for a whole series of World's Exhibitions, for one of which Gustave Eiffel designed what was intended to be a temporary structure to commemorate the centenary of the French Revolution.

Before walking down to his tower, walk a little way to the left towards the **Ecole Militaire** to admire its sober classical façade surmounted by a dome and to muse on the curious fact that it was funded by a tax on playing cards – a scheme dreamt up by the playwright Beaumarchais, author of *The Barber of Seville* and *The Marriage of Figaro*. The building is still used as a barracks and staff college and is not open to the public. You might like at this point to make a short detour to the **Village Suisse**, on the far side of the **avenue de Suffren**. I used to enjoy looking for bargains there when it was a collection of small junk shops, but it has now gone upmarket and has been taken over by chic antique dealers, so prices are inevitably high.

As you walk through the gardens towards the river, the peaceful scenes of local children playing, queuing for donkey rides or watching Punch and Judy shows give way to serried ranks of sellers of souvenirs and postcards, ice creams and T-shirts. Queues snake round the **Eiffel Tower**'s huge struts for much of the year and you should be prepared for a long wait if you are determined to see the views from the second and third floors. They are certainly superb in clear weather, though as with the Montparnasse Tower, it's not so easy to find your bearings. Before you join the queue, have a quick look at the curious grotto between the south and east struts. It was designed in the thirties and has recently been restored. Not many people know of its existence, so you may have a few quiet moments to yourself before plunging into the crowds.

The tower was built for the Exposition Universelle of 1889, to designs by a couple of engineers working in the office run by Gustave Eiffel, rather than by the great man himself. Their scheme won a competition that attracted more than 700 entries for a temporary reminder to the people of Paris of the heady days of the French Revolution a hundred years earlier. But when the celebrations were over and the exhibition pavilions were pulled down the tower, ridiculed at first by intellectuals, had become so famous that it stayed put. Ever since the official opening ceremony, performed by the Prince of Wales, later King Edward VII of England, it had become a symbol of national pride at a time when French morale was still low after the humiliations of the Franco-Prussian War.

And in June 1989, as Paris geared itself up for the bicentenary celebrations of the storming of the Bastille, 400,000 people gathered on the Champ de Mars to watch a spectacular hundredth birthday party for the Iron Lady. Fireworks crackled in the darkening sky, laser beams created special effects, Placido Domingo sang

La Marseillaise and 6,000 performers did their bit to join in the fun, accompanied by recordings of that most Parisian of all voices – Edith Piaf. This elaborate happening was the culmination of several years of work to make the structure lighter and generally spruce it up. And although, at just over 300 metres high, it isn't any longer the tallest building in the world, it certainly looks as if it is when the new lighting system makes it glow from within and snake upwards into the night sky.

The facilities have also been modernised. The tower now has a post office and (in the summer months) a branch of the Paris Tourist Office, various restaurants and snack bars, including the extremely expensive **Jules Verne**, for which you need to book weeks in advance, and a free video show on its history. And you can stay up there till midnight every night in July and August and on Fridays and Saturdays in April, May and June. If you've had enough of the crowds you can round off the walk with a meal in one of the quiet side streets near the Champ de Mars or stroll across the Seine for good views of the tower from the **Trocadéro**, which is where the next walk begins.

While you are in this part of Paris you may like to plan a visit to the city's famous sewers (see box). The entrance in the **place de la Résistance** is easily reached by taking the avenue Rapp from the place du Général Gouraud just before you reach the Champ de Mars, or you can walk along the quai Branly eastwards from the tower.

Overleaf: *The twin wings of the Palais de Chaillot, built for the 1937 Exhibition, seen through the struts of the Eiffel Tower on the other side of the Seine*

Underground Paris: Catacombs and Sewers

It sometimes seems odd that with so many beautiful places to visit in Paris, two of the most popular tourist attractions involve leaving the City of Light for a dank plunge into its depths. But the Catacombs do undoubtedly have a macabre fascination, and even the city's sewers can provide a pleasurable *frisson* if you've temporarily had your fill of paintings and architecture and vistas. Children usually adore both visits. Make sure both they and you are warmly dressed, and do make sure to take a torch.

Catacombs

The **Catacombs** were originally stone quarries, first used in the Gallo-Roman period. Lying disused, they provided the ideal solution to a problem that had been worrying the 18th-century city fathers for decades and was starting to be a real danger to public health. Until then Paris had only one cemetery, the Cimetière des Innocents, in the Les Halles market district right in the centre of the city, where the Fontaine des Innocents now stands (Walk 8). Bodies were simply flung in there, quicklime was poured on top, and they were left to rot. Matters were getting out of hand, the stench was becoming unbearable, and on one occasion after a bad storm people living nearby were appalled to find their cellars full of decomposing corpses. Something clearly had to be done, and in 1786 a decision was taken to consecrate the quarries on the south-eastern edge of the city and transfer the contents of the cemetery there. For nights on end, huge carts could be seen trundling over the cobbled streets and dirt tracks, accompanied by chanting priests and piled high with a mass of skulls and bones and rotting bits of flesh. No question of sorting them out or keeping families and social classes together — the remains of millions of Parisians, buried over a period of about 1,400 years, were unceremoniously carted off to their new resting place. Other similar transfers took place, from the cemetery of Saint-Jacques-du-Haut-Pas for instance, in the 19th century. Altogether the mortal

---

Hotels and Restaurants

For general advice on choosing where to stay and where to eat, see Practical Information; prices are moderate unless otherwise stated.

Hotels

Bellechasse 8 rue de Bellechasse, 7e (45-51-52-36). Smallish but pleasant rooms, some on the top floors with old beams, though furnishings are modern. Try for once for a room overlooking the street, as you'll have a lovely view over the leafy garden hidden behind a wall opposite the hotel. (May be closed in 1991 for renovation.)

Elysées-Maubourg 35 blvd de Latour-Maubourg, 7e (45-56-10-78). Modern and well run, with some fairly expensive rooms. Very close to the Invalides.

Les Jardins d'Eiffel 8 rue Amélie, 7e (47-05-46-21). In a quiet side street close to the Eiffel Tower and the Invalides — and to the rue Cler street market. Smallish modern rooms; friendly atmosphere.

remains of some 8 million souls await you in the catacombs. Most of the 2,500-odd victims of Madame Guillotine must be among them.

If you can stomach it, the visit does certainly give you a vivid sense of the passing of the centuries, as you clamber down a steep stone staircase, and about 400 metres below street level reach an iron door with a dramatic inscription carved in the stone surround: 'Stop! Here is the Empire of Death!' Behind it are twilit corridors lined with bones, an incredible number of them, stacked neatly from floor to ceiling, the skulls horribly visible, sometimes grotesquely arranged into patterns. A ghoulish commentary by the guide greatly adds to the effect. The Catacombs, he tells you, have been a draw for VIPs visiting Paris ever since they acquired their new inhabitants. He also tells you that during the Second World War these eerie corridors became the headquarters of the Resistance Movement to the German occupying forces, who apparently never discovered what was going on beneath their feet.

The Catacombs (Catacombes) 1 pl Denfert-Rochereau, 14e. Closed Mon and weekday mornings. (Ⓜ Denfert-Rochereau)

Sewers

Not as macabre but still requiring a strong stomach is a visit to the Egouts or Sewers built in the 19th century by the ubiquitous Baron Haussmann. Before his time many Paris streets seem to have been pretty well open sewers. Visits can be cancelled if rain has flooded some of the tunnels — always check before turning up. The network covers 2,000 kilometres and serves several other purposes nowadays: telephone lines and traffic light cables snake through them, and — not a very nice thought — so do the city's clean water pipes.

The Sewers (Egouts) pl de la Résistance, 7e (entrance at the Left Bank end of the Pont de l'Alma, on the corner of the quai d'Orsay). Closed Thur and Fri. (Ⓜ Alma-Marceau, ⓇⒺⓇ Champ-de-Mars)

Lenox 9 rue de l'Université, 7e (42-96-10-95). Beautifully decorated rooms, the most expensive on two floors and with their own balcony. Chic bar and welcoming atmosphere.

Pavillon 54 rue Saint-Dominique, 7e (45-51-42-87). Some rooms are not all that comfortable, but there's lots of charm in this little hotel set back beyond a narrow entrance courtyard from a very Parisian shopping street running between the esplanade des Invalides and the Champ de Mars.

Solférino 91 rue de Lille, 7e (47-05-85-54). Small hotel near the Musée d'Orsay, popular with the British for its pretty rooms and pleasant atmosphere.

Varenne 44 rue de Bourgogne, 7e (45-51-45-55). Quiet rooms overlooking a leafy courtyard where breakfast is served in fine weather, in the heart of the Faubourg near the Rodin Museum and the Invalides.

Verneuil Saint-Germain 8 rue de Verneuil, 7e (42-60-82-14). Attractive small rooms near the Musée d'Orsay, in the posh antique dealers' district; a quiet street, yet only a short walk from the lively restaurants and cafés in Saint-Germain-des-Prés.

Restaurants

Brasserie Lutétia 23 rue de Sèvres, 6e (45-44-38-10). The old Lutétia Hotel, redecorated in chic, mainly thirties, style by fashion designer Sonia Rykiel, has both an expensive restaurant and this relaxed brasserie overlooking the Sèvres-Babylone crossroads. Inexpensive *menu*.

Café des Lettres 53 rue de Verneuil, 7e (42-22-52-17). Restful place for a light lunch or supper, very close to the Musée d'Orsay, attached to an elegant *hôtel* converted into a centre for writers. Summer meals in the courtyard are a particular delight – and you can browse through literary magazines in various languages while you are waiting for your meal.

Le Champ de Mars 17 av de La Motte-Picquet, 7e (47-05-57-99); closed Mon, Tue for dinner, and about mid-July to mid-Aug. Reliable, traditional cuisine at reasonable prices between the Invalides and the Ecole Militaire.

La Chaumière 35 rue de Beaune, 7e (42-61-26-09). Old-established restaurant in the heart of the antique dealers' district and one of the few in the area open at weekends. Countrified décor, as you would guess from the name (which means 'The Cottage'), traditional cuisine.

Chez Marius 5 rue de Bourgogne, 7e (45-51-79-42); closed Sat for lunch, Sun and Aug. Good, expensive classical cuisine in an old-established restaurant near the Musée Rodin favoured by members of parliament (the National Assembly is just down the road).

Le Crik 8 rue de Bellechasse, 7e (47-05-98-66); closed Mon. This useful annexe to the rather expensive *Sologne* restaurant (whose own cuisine can be disappointing) serves light meals all day to about 8 p.m. – convenient if you are visiting the Musée d'Orsay and want to stagger your lunchtime.

La Ferme Saint-Simon 6 rue Saint-Simon, 7e (45-48-35-74); closed Sat for lunch, Sun and Aug. Chic but not stuffy (showbiz clientele in the evening); inventive cuisine and good-value lunch *menu*, but the *carte* is expensive. In a little street in the Faubourg, not far from the Musée d'Orsay.

La Fontaine de Mars 129 rue Saint-Dominique, 7e (47-05-46-44); closed Sat evening, Sun and Aug. I've known this restaurant for twenty-odd years and I'm glad to say it's barely changed, except that the square outside and the fountain that gives it its name have been spruced up. Unpretentious home cooking, traditional red-checked tablecloths, smiling service and lunch *menu* at amazingly low price – and near the Eiffel Tower too.

Maison de l'Amérique Latine 217 blvd Saint-Germain, 7e (45-49-33-23); closed weekends and Aug. The food can be variable but now that most of the Faubourg mansions are inaccessible, it does give you a rare chance to see an archetypal early 18th-century *hôtel* with a large garden – where you can eat out on summer evenings.

La Marlotte 55 rue du Cherche-Midi, 6e (45-48-86-79); closed weekends and Aug. Traditional home-style dishes cooked with a light touch are popular with the chic local residents plus a sprinkling of well-known politicians. Near Sèvres-Babylone crossroads.

La Petite Chaise 36 rue de Grenelle, 7e (42-22-13-35). Claims to be Paris's oldest restaurant (opened 1680) and full of lively atmosphere. Set *menu* only.

Le Petit Niçois 10 rue Amélie, 7e (45-51-83-65); closed Sun, for lunch Mon and Aug. Friendly little place, specialising in Mediterranean fish and tasty dishes from Nice.

Aux Petits Oignons 20 rue de Bellechasse, 7e (47-05-48-77); closed Sun. Tiny restaurant close to the Musée d'Orsay. Flowery décor, unpretentious cuisine and lively atmosphere.

Thoumieux 79 rue Saint-Dominique, 7e (47-05-49-75). Filling cuisine from south-west France, bustling atmosphere, excellent-value *menu*.

Museums and Places of Interest

Musée de la Légion d'Honneur 2 rue de Bellechasse, 7e. Afternoons only, closed Mon. Ⓜ Solférino, Ⓡ Quai d'Orsay

Musée d'Orsay 1 rue de Bellechasse, 7e. Closed Mon, late opening Thur. Ⓜ Solférino, Ⓡ Quai d'Orsay

Canal trips from Musée d'Orsay to La Villette: departure from quai Anatole-France, 7e, beside Piscine Deligny (floating swimming pool). Ⓜ Solférino, Ⓡ Quai d'Orsay

Palais Bourbon entrance for guided visits and for attending a sitting of Parliament: quai d'Orsay (inquire locally about times). Ⓜ Assemblée Nationale, Invalides

Invalides: *Musée de l'Armée* (Army Museum) esplanade des Invalides, 7e. Open daily. *Galerie des Plans-Reliefs* Open daily. *Eglise Saint-Louis-des-Invalides* Open daily. *Eglise du Dôme* (housing *Napoleon's Tomb*) Main entrance in pl Vauban, 7e. Open daily. *Son-et-lumière – Le Retour des Cendres* (*Napoleon's remains are returned to France*): performances are held in the *Cour d'honneur* from about Easter to Oct, in French and English, but may be cancelled at short notice, so check locally. Ⓜ Latour-Maubourg, Varenne

Musée Rodin 77 rue de Varenne, 7e. Closed Mon. On Sat and Sun afternoons from May to Sept coaches ply back and forth between the rue de Varenne and the Rodin Museum at Meudon in the southern suburbs. Ⓜ Varenne

Eiffel Tower Champ de Mars, 7e. All three floors are open daily, but be prepared for long queues. *Cinémax* (video presentation of tower's history) on first floor. Ⓜ Bir-Hakeim, Ⓡ Tour Eiffel–Champ de Mars

Egouts (Sewers) See box.

Boat trips on the Seine *Bateaux Parisiens–Tour Eiffel* start from Left Bank end of the Pont d'Iéna every day about every 30 mins; trips last about an hour. Ⓜ Trocadéro, Ⓡ Tour Eiffel–Champ de Mars

Walk 5
The Champs-Elysées District

Starting point: the terrace of the Palais de Chaillot, pl du Trocadéro, 16e; Ⓜ Trocadéro, overlooking the Jardins du Trocadéro. As well as the avenue des Champs-Elysées itself, this Right Bank walk includes the City of Paris Museum of Modern Art, a large number of specialist museums and the Grand Palais, which stages major art exhibitions. It starts in the 16th *arrondissement* and moves on to cover much of the 8th.

This is upmarket country, including many of Paris's poshest addresses, and nowadays often seems more international than Parisian. It houses the top embassies, a whole string of European headquarters of multinationals, international advertising agencies, luxury hotels and very expensive restaurants, and cinemas where the films are often showing in English, with French subtitles. The cafés and shops on the Champs-Elysées attract more foreign and provincial visitors than Parisians and the many museums create an influx of tourists to the area all year round. As a result, the charm of Paris is perhaps less evident here than in most other districts. But the Champs-Elysées do have a magic of their own, in spite of the continuous flow of traffic, and it is hard not to sense the significance of 'Les Champs' to Parisians, who traditionally throng here on great occasions. An evening out at one of the busy restaurants in the area — not all are beyond the pocket of ordinary tourists — followed by a stroll along the broad pavements among the crowds and the bright lights, does give you some inkling of Paris as a great cosmopolitan city, one of the world's major centres of entertainment and nightlife, and as such is not to be missed.

The walk starts on the top of the Chaillot Hill (**Colline de Chaillot**) with an impressive panorama from the terrace between the curving wings of the **Palais de Chaillot**, built in 1937 more or less on the spot where Catherine de Médicis once had a small country château. A few generations later the house was bought by Queen Henrietta Maria of England, who turned it into a convent which soon appealed to well-born widows as a pleasant place in which to withdraw from the world. But in the early 19th century the height of the hill was reduced and the

122

whole area was redeveloped in readiness for the huge palace that Napoleon had decided to build for his son the King of Rome. Grandiose plans were drawn up by Charles Percier and Pierre Fontaine, the leading architects of the period, who were largely responsible for the *Empire* style in decoration (they worked for Napoleon and Josephine at Malmaison). But the emperor's enforced exile spelled the end of the dream and in 1827 the hill was rechristened to commemorate the capture of the Trocadéro fortress in the Bay of Cadiz four years earlier by the Duc d'Angoulême's troops.

A large square was laid out in the middle of the century, but the planned replica of the fortress was never built either, and the site was taken up instead with a Moorish-style structure designed for the 1878 World's Exhibition. This was eventually replaced by what you see today – yet another building designed for an international exhibition.

The monumental palace is very thirties in style, with its neo-classical colonnades, vast doorways, lofty inscriptions (written by Paul Valéry) and huge scale. It is big enough to house four museums, plus a theatre, a film library offering frequent showings and a restaurant. Before choosing which ones to visit (to take in all of them would mean abandoning the rest of this walk), I recommend spending a little time enjoying the view – this is the best vantage point for admiring the structure of the Eiffel Tower – and perhaps strolling in the gardens beneath the terrace, with their ornamental ponds and fountains and curious, almost horizontal, jets of water, and their many statues.

Then run the gauntlet of the guard of honour formed by the gilded bronze statues on the terrace itself and walk out into the **place du Trocadéro**. It centres round an equestrian statue of Maréchal Foch, generalissimo of the Allied armies at the end of the First World War, and a whole series of broad avenues radiates out from it. For a good view of the whole complex of Chaillot buildings, cross over to one of the cafés between the avenue du Président-Wilson and the avenue Raymond-Poincaré on the east side. From their tables you can read Valéry's words: the 'rare and beautiful things' he speaks of in the right-hand pavilion are displayed in an anthropological museum and a museum devoted to seafaring, the 'works created by the miracle-working hand of the artist' refer to the superb copies of ecclesiastical art and architecture in the left-hand wing.

The **Musée de l'Homme** (Museum of Mankind) displays well-known anthropology and ethnology collections and puts on a full programme of films, especially during the school holidays in February, at Easter, in the first half of November and over Christmas and New Year (there is less on in the summer). It has some interesting prehistoric exhibits and particularly good departments on the development of musical instruments down the centuries in various cultures, on African art and on South American art and artefacts. In the entrance hall are a small bookshop and a restaurant called **Le Totem**, whose main attraction is its big picture windows overlooking the Eiffel Tower.

The **Musée de la Marine** (Maritime Museum) is popular with children for its scale models of ships of various kinds, its submarines and its eclectic range of actual craft, from a pleasure boat used by Marie-Antoinette for outings at Versailles or a stunningly elaborate rowing boat built for Napoleon, down to a pathetically fragile-looking vessel that landed in Thailand in 1987 with many hundreds of 'boat people' on board and was subsequently brought to Le Havre in a container ship. The labelling is often sketchy, or even non-existent, but the exhibits are well-displayed and there are some fine paintings, including a detailed series by Joseph Vernet depicting most of France's harbours and a model of the obelisk in the place de la Concorde (Walk 6) being transported from Luxor. The gift shop in the entrance hall includes model ships and compasses and a wide variety of seafaring items.

I am always surprised to see how few visitors to Paris venture into the **Musée des Monuments Français** in the other wing of the Palais de Chaillot. Perhaps the name is offputting – and hard to translate – or the idea of seeing copies has little appeal in a city where there are so many lovely *real* buildings to visit. But there are copies and copies, and these lifesize plaster replicas of some of France's most important sculpture and architectural features are in a class of their own. The idea was dreamed up by the energetic Viollet-le-Duc, who referred to it as the 'Comparative Sculpture Museum'. If you are at all interested in art and architecture don't miss the opportunity to study in close up, say, a Romanesque portal from Saintes or another from the abbey of Saint-Pierre-de-Moissac, or a lovely little Flight into Egypt from Autun Cathedral, with Mary looking pensive and Joseph straining as he pulls the ass jerkily along. The copies help you to grasp the huge scale of many of these buildings and to appreciate the wealth of decorative details in a way that is virtually impossible *in situ*, where you are so often having to dodge passing cars or crane your neck to see carved scenes way above your head. There are some useful painted wall maps, too, pinpointing France's cathedrals, past (demolished), present and ex- (demoted to mere churches).

Quite apart from being instructive, the museum should whet your appetite for exploring the rest of France – I defy anyone not to feel compelled to plan a trip to Bourges after seeing the interlaced foliage from the north portal of the cathedral and the cheeky figures peering out of windows in Jacques Coeur's house. And there is more to come: the upper floors are devoted to reproductions of some of the finest examples of Romanesque and Gothic wall painting, again copied down to the tiniest detail, plus some good stained glass.

If some of the portals and arches seem a bit like stage sets, the **Musée du Cinéma** (Cinema Museum) in the basement is full of real sets, including a street scene from *Les Enfants du Paradis*. This can be a frustrating place to visit – the guided tours (compulsory) are liable to be cancelled without warning – but please do persist if you are at all likely to be carried away by the magic of the cinema. The first of the rabbit warren of little rooms concentrate on the fore-runners – Edward Muybridge's attempts to break down movement, magic lanterns, shadow puppets – and the early history of the medium. But the museum branches out from here into an eclectic collection of items such as costumes worn by Garbo or Rudolf Valentino, photos of the beautiful Alida Valli, Eisenstein's annotated script of *Ivan the Terrible* or sketches for scenes from *Last Year in Marienbad*. There's even a model of the Pathé studios in Montreuil. The arrangement is higgledy-piggledy, and all the more charming for that. And the guides are knowledgeable and enthusiastic, very good at letting children – under supervision – work some of the early equipment.

Also down in the basement is one of Paris's two **cinémathèques** or film libraries (the other is in the Beaubourg Centre, Walk 8), which puts on several screenings a day (except Monday) of classics from all over the world. Programmes are printed in the weekly 'What's On' publications and in some of the national dailies, or you may be able to pick up a leaflet in the Palais de Chaillot. This same wing also houses the entrance to the large **Théâtre National de Chaillot**, the current version of what was once the famous TNP or Théâtre National Populaire, run by the great Jean Vilar, where Gérard Philipe became a popular idol in parts such as Kleist's Prince of Homburg or Musset's Lorenzaccio or Corneille's Le Cid. In recent years the theatre has changed direction (and directors) rather too often – after restoring its reputation with a series of much-acclaimed productions Antoine Vitez, now sadly dead, was enticed away to run the Comédie française. But if you are a theatre-goer it is certainly worth seeing what is on during your visit.

Until 1985 the Palais de Chaillot had one final attraction, an **aquarium**. But it is now being restored, and there seems to be some doubt about whether it will ever reopen, though the official date given is 1992.

After a restoring drink or coffee at one of the cafés round the *place*, walk east down the **avenue du Président-Wilson** until you come to the **place d'Iéna** (the French version of Jena, where Napoleon's troops scored a notable victory over the Prussian army in 1806). On the far side of this road junction at the heart of an expensive but rather dull residential district is the **Musée Guimet**, housing an important collection of Far Eastern art. Originally a private collection – though it has been much added to – it includes huge Khmer sculptures from Cambodia, some very early Chinese archaeological exhibits, Mongolian art from the steppes and work from Vietnam, Tibet, Thailand, Burma, Afghanistan and the Indian sub-continent. Although this is primarily a museum for specialists, the exhibits are now beautifully displayed, after a long period of restoration stretching over twelve years, and it offers much to interest the lay visitor. (I found it instructive, on a recent visit, to study late 12th-century Buddhas immediately after admiring Romanesque sculpture up the road in the Palais de Chaillot.)

Continue down the avenue, passing, if it happens to be a Tuesday or a Saturday, a little open-air market, where you might like to buy some fruit to eat in the gardens of the **Palais Galliéra**, a late 19th-century building in Italian Renaissance style. This now houses the **Musée de la Mode et du Costume** (Fashion and Costume Museum), where you can visit temporary exhibitions – there is no permanent collection on display – on specific themes or periods, generally including items from the museum's rich collection of accessories. Even if it is in between shows, spare a few moments for a quiet sit-down in the gardens, where local children love playing, before crossing the road to the **Palais de Tokyo**, another monumental building which owes its existence to the 1937 Exhibition.

This again has two wings, the eastern one taken up with the **Musée d'Art Moderne de la Ville de Paris** (the City of Paris Museum of Modern Art). Although the vast rooms seem rather chilly and the steep staircases make a visit tiring, the museum has some very interesting paintings, including work by Picasso and Modigliani, Matisse, Léger and Chagall, a good collection by Robert and Sonia

Delaunay and a room full of Rouaults. Dufy's gigantic *La Fée Electricité* once again dates back to the 1937 Exhibition – it adorned the Electricity Pavilion.

The second wing stages temporary exhibitions organised by the **National Photography Centre**, which is now based there. Photography is a fashionable art form in France at the moment and these shows are usually crowded. The museum's cafeteria is a useful place for a quick meal, or you may prefer to wait until you reach the cafés and brasseries at the bottom of the hill in the **place de l'Alma**, which commemorates another military victory, when the French and British, under Lord Raglan, defeated the Russians during the Crimean War. The square also has a couple of expensive restaurants, **Chez Francis** and, round the corner in the **avenue Marceau**, **Marius et Janette**. Alternatively, you may like to break off your walk to enjoy lunch on one of the sightseeing boats which set off from the landing stage alongside the **Pont de l'Alma**. Spare a moment to look at the figure of the Zouave soldier beneath the bridge, which has assumed mythical proportions for Parisians: they traditionally come to see how much of him is under water when the level of the Seine is rising. (Ⓜ Alma-Marceau)

A little way along the **avenue Montaigne** you come to the **Comédie des Champs-Elysées**, one of the city's most fashionable theatres. It is also used for ballet performances during the winter dance season, a tradition dating back to the days when Diaghilev's Ballets Russes shocked Paris with Stravinsky's *Rite of Spring*, and has a more experimental annexe next door, the **Studio des Champs-Elysées**. On the other side of the street the **Bar des Théâtres*** is a lively place for a meal or a drink, often thronged with models from the top fashion houses that line this avenue and the surrounding streets. Until the late 19th century this was no more than a poorly lit path running through allotments dotted with fairly sordid *guinguettes* and bars, but it is now one of the chic-est avenues in Paris. On the left is the deluxe **Plaza-Athénée Hotel** with its fashionable **Relais-Plaza** restaurant and **Régence-Plaza** bar, and several of the world's top *couturiers* have their headquarters here, including Dior and Nina Ricci. If you're visiting Paris in December or January you'll find the trees lit with tiny white lights and the *couturiers'* windows a fairyland of colours and glitter.

Continue beyond the elegant **rue François-Ier** to the **Rond-Point des Champs-Elysées**, a busy junction, adorned with flowerbeds and fountains, about a third of the way up what is generally referred to as 'the best-known avenue in the world'. The translucent glass pigeons by Lalique which once adorned the fountains have disappeared, but the Rond-Point is still attractive, and a good place, in spite of the traffic, from which to compare the two contrasting sections of the **avenue des Champs-Elysées**. (Ⓜ Franklin-D.-Roosevelt)

To your right, gardens and avenues of trees stretch slightly downhill to the place de la Concorde. To your left, the avenue climbs up towards the Arc de Triomphe, seeming more like a six-lane highway, thronged with traffic at most times of day and night, than the glamorous international mecca you may have imagined.

The avenue was commissioned by Louis XIV's minister Colbert from master gardener André Le Nôtre (see box, Walk 6), who designed it as a continuation of the central avenue of the Tuileries Gardens (Walk 6), the whole conceived as a 'triumphal way' leading westwards out of Paris to Versailles, and a splendid vista to be admired from the terrace of the Tuileries Palace. The road he carved through marshland and brushwood and a few market gardens in 1670 was first called Le Grand-Cours, to distinguish it from the **Cours-la-Reine**, the name still borne by the tree-lined ride beside the Seine planted by Marie de Médicis over half a century earlier. After various very French changes of name it was rechristened 'the Elysian Fields' during the Revolution: its leaders had a penchant for classical mythology. The name has stuck, though even at the time the area was a great deal less idyllic than the label. The gardens were somewhat unsalubrious waste ground, dotted with flimsy wooden huts surrounded by a few tables, selling drinks and snacks. One of them was run by a gentleman called Le Doyen, who also offered his customers a skittle alley – humble beginnings for what is today the very expensive and elegant **Restaurant Ledoyen**, half-hidden by trees on the southern side of the Champs-Elysées, and recently bought by the glamorous Régine. There were a few open-air dancing places too, some of them doubling as brothels.

In 1815 the Cossack army bivouacked here, chopped down the chestnut trees for firewood and left behind a sea of mud. It wasn't until the Second Empire that the avenue really came into its own. The gardens were replanted and laid out in trim walks and rides, and by the end of the 19th century the lower half of the Champs-Elysées was lined with theatres. The **Théâtre des Ambassadeurs**, once a café frequented by foreign diplomats – hence the name – is still there, though now called the Espace Cardin, but the legendary Alcazar d'Eté, where Mistinguett drew huge audiences, has sadly vanished. On the southern side, a popular 'panorama' was converted into the even more popular Palais de Glace skating rink in 1894 – Colette wrote of enjoying skating there. And once again a big Paris Exhibition, this time the 1900 Exposition Universelle, produced new buildings: the **Grand Palais** and the **Petit Palais**, still standing to your right. A grand mansion in the rue du faubourg Saint-Honoré, with long gardens backing on to the Champs-Elysées gardens, was turned into the presidential palace.

Try to imagine the gardens as they were when Proust was a child, playing in the snow with the model for 'Gilberte', surrounded by nursemaids in ribboned bonnets wheeling their charges in prams like miniature carriages, while full-scale carriages swept along on their way to the Bois de Boulogne, their smartly dressed female occupants often escorted by dashing horsemen.

The upper section of the avenue, to your left as you stand at the Rond-Point, has never been lined with gardens. When Napoleon had the Arc de Triomphe built in the early years of the 19th century there were a mere six houses. During the Second Empire the district became fashionable and handsome mansions sprang up, only one of which has survived, no. 25, built for the famous courtesan 'La Païva' (see box), though the Hôtel de Massa, once at nos 52–60, was dismantled in the twenties and rebuilt near the Observatoire. This part of the avenue is therefore a modern street, filled with airline offices, banks, office blocks, cinemas, car showrooms, cafés and restaurants, and its main interest lies in the crowds that parade up and down and in the shopping arcades leading off it, mostly taken up with expensive boutiques that are cosmopolitan rather than Parisian.

127

L'Hôtel de la Païva (25 avenue des Champs-Elysées, 8e)

The dazzlingly beautiful Marquise de Païva, one of the best-known courtesans in Paris during the Second Empire, was born plain Theresa Lachmann, the daughter of Polish Jews who had fled to Russia to escape one of the many pogroms. She married young, in 1836, but soon grew bored with her husband, a French tailor, and aspired to higher things. She left him and became the mistress of various men-about-town, then in 1851 married one of her lovers, a Portuguese aristocrat called Francisco da Païva-Araujo, whose fortune she was soon busy spending to bolster her social ambitions.

She made up her mind that they would live in the most luxurious house in Paris and bought a plot of land on what was then more or less waste ground just beyond the Rond-Point. She commissioned the architect Pierre Mangain to design an opulent mansion, whose main rooms are adorned with ceiling paintings by Paul Baudry, who was later to decorate the Grand Foyer in the Opéra. (The beautiful but rather muscular nude in the ceiling painting in the *salon* is thought to be the only surviving portrait of the Marquise.) The house is decorated with carved oak panelling, vast chandeliers and bronze statues, and the curving onyx and marble staircase leading up to Madame la Marquise's bedroom soon became the talk of Paris.

The bedroom itself has a carved wooden ceiling adorned with a marchioness's crown and the taps in the *ensuite* bathroom, allegedly inspired by a palace in Constantinople, are encrusted with rubies.

In this palatial house, completed in 1866, the Marquise entertained in style, swallowing up the fortune of many a lover with her extravagant receptions attended by artists and intellectuals – Delacroix and the Goncourt brothers are among those who have left accounts of evenings spent there – as well as the aristocratic *beau monde*. Legend has it that she was also a spy, in the Mata Hari mould.

After twenty years of marriage she cast her husband aside, had their union annulled by the Pope and took as her third husband a much younger lover, an extremely rich 25-year-old cousin of Bismarck, Fürst Henckel von Donnersmarck. The rejected Marquis shot himself a couple of years later – a very public suicide after the pudding course at a dinner he had been hosting at a restaurant on the Grands Boulevards. Not long after, the Paris career of his ex-wife came to an end when Bismarck appointed his dashing young cousin governor of Alsace-Lorraine, which had been annexed by Germany during the Franco-Prussian War. She vanished with him into provincial exile and died in 1884. The Count sold the Paris mansion soon afterwards.

In 1895 it again became a centre of fashionable Paris society when it was turned into a luxury restaurant by a former chef to the Czar of Russia, one Pyotr Cubart. But after a few years of glory the expense of running these huge premises led to near-bankruptcy and Cubart went back to Russia and the Czar's service. The Travellers' Club took over the house at the beginning of this century, but occasional guided tours are arranged, often on Sunday mornings (check in one of the 'What's On' publications).

The Champs-Elysées are gradually being smartened up, with flowerbeds and stylish street furniture designed to restore some of their former glamour, so strolling there should become more pleasant. But walking the whole length of the avenue is tiring – the Arc de Triomphe seems nearer than it really is, because of its huge size – so I recommend walking first down through the gardens, then taking a bus (or the métro on Sundays) up to near the top.

Before you do so, walk a little way to the left to see **L'Hôtel de la Païva**, then cross over for a quick look at the **Galerie Elysées-Rond-Point**, which is typical of the modern shopping arcades leading off the avenue, but has an extra attraction in the shape of a huge piece of animated sculpture illustrating the principle of perpetual motion. Walk out at the far end, then circle the Rond-Point, passing the **Drugstore Publicis-Matignon**, with various places to eat or drink. If it is a Thursday, Saturday or Sunday, you may like to stop off for a look at the open-air stamp and postcard market that has been held in and between the **avenue Matignon** and the **avenue de Marigny** for decades. Otherwise cross back after admiring the gardens to the southern side of the Champs-Elysées. Straight ahead is the former Palais de Glace, now the **Théâtre Renaud-Barrault**: the company headed by Jean-Louis Barrault and his wife Madeleine Renaud puts on generally excellent productions in the main theatre and in the more experimental **Petite Salle**, and the theatre has a particularly pleasant restaurant*.

Beyond the theatre you come to the huge **Grand Palais**, pompous but splendid with its glass roof and its lively sculptures of flying horses and chariots on the four corners. It looks its best at night, when the roof seems to glow from within and the horses race against the darkening sky. The entrance at the top of the flight of steps beyond the garden in the avenue du Général Eisenhower leads to the **Galeries du Grand Palais**, where major temporary art exhibitions are held. They attract large crowds in the daytime, so try to visit them between 6 p.m. and 8 p.m., or up to 10 p.m. on Wednesdays. The entrance on the corner of the **avenue Churchill** also leads to exhibition space, and the one right on the avenue Churchill is used for the trade shows and other events held in the vast hall with its art nouveau iron and steel pillars and staircases. This section is due for refurbishment in the near future and may one day house a concert hall.

Yet another entrance, this time in the **avenue Franklin-D.-Roosevelt**, takes you into the **Palais de la Découverte**, a science museum which seems old-fashioned beside the modern presentation in the new Science City at La Villette (Beyond the Centre). But there is plenty to see in the rooms leading off the domed entrance, devoted to topics as varied as thermodynamics and nutrition. Demonstrations are held at frequent intervals, there are enough things to pull and push to satisfy any child and the **Planetarium** is extremely popular, especially during the school half-term holidays, when you must book early for the three or four sessions held every day except Monday (sometimes more at the weekend).

Continue along the avenue Franklin-D.-Roosevelt after admiring at no. 17 the pretty house, dwarfed nowadays by tall blocks of flats, that in 1945 was bought by a restaurateur called René Lasserre, who had started learning his craft at the age of eleven, as a washer-up in a Paris café. He soon turned it into one of Paris's best-known and most elegant restaurants, as **Lasserre** still is today – but you have to

The decorative Pont Alexandre III leads to the Grand Palais with its flying chariots and four

be very rich to eat there. Turn left and walk through the garden behind the Grand Palais for a good view of the **Pont Alexandre-III**, which was also built for the 1900 Exhibition. It is the prettiest of all Paris bridges with its cherubs and lamps and its winged horses atop pillars at either end. The regilded dome of the Invalides on the Left Bank looks superb from here too.

Then turn round and get a good look at the Grand Palais from the bridge before crossing over to the **Petit Palais**. Its galleries, built round a colonnaded courtyard which makes a good place for a rest, interrupted only by the splashing of the fountain, display works from the City of Paris's art collections. The museum is gradually being restored – the **Grande Galerie Nord**, one of the two sculpture galleries, has recently been reopened – and unfortunately you are liable to find that substantial parts of it are shut. This is a pity, as it has 19th- and early 20th-century French paintings, including several Cézannes, Courbets and Bonnards, the rich Dutuit Collection of 16th- and 17th-century Dutch and Flemish paintings, Greek ceramics, Roman bronzes, tapestries, ivories and much more besides, the Edward Tuck Collection of 18th-century furniture and tapestries and Chinese porcelain, and a good Dutch painting collection.

Opposite: The gilded gateway to the Petit Palais, adorned with the Ship of Paris

Now continue down the Champs-Elysées Gardens to the **place de la Concorde**, for a sweeping view of the whole avenue framed by the **Chevaux de Marly**. These marble sculptures of trembling, neighing horses being captured were carved by Guillaume Coustou in the 1740s for the ornamental drinking trough and fountain at the royal château of Marly outside Paris. They are echoed on the far side of the square by a pair of winged horses by Coustou's uncle Antoine Coysevox, chief sculptor to Louis XIV. But do not risk life and limb by trying to cross the square, one of the busiest in Paris, at this point. It is best visited from the Tuileries Gardens, which are included in the next walk.

The sight of the Champs-Elysées stretching up to the Arc de Triomphe, with the skyscrapers of the Défense and its new arch (Beyond the Centre) visible in the far distance, makes it clear why so many ceremonial events have been staged here. One of the first came on a bleak and wintry day in December 1840, when hundreds of thousands of Parisians turned out to pay their last respects to Napoleon. Forty-five years later another huge crowd followed the funeral procession for Victor Hugo, and the victory processions after the two world wars were held here too. Mass demonstrations tend to take place on the Champs-Elysées – the pro- and anti-de Gaulle marches in 1968, a march in favour of retaining church schools more recently. And as well as the traditional Bastille Day military parade on 14 July, the final stage of the Tour de France cycling marathon also ends on the avenue.

But instead of marching, you should now aim for the bus stop at the bottom end of the gardens and catch a 73 bus to the avenue George-V towards the top of the Champs-Elysées. If you are doing this walk on a Sunday, when the 73 doesn't operate, you will have to walk up as far as Ⓜ Champs-Elysées-Clémenceau and travel to Ⓜ George-V on the Vincennes–Neuilly line. While waiting for the bus you can peer through the trees to see the **American Embassy** in the **avenue Gabriel**, a once-fashionable place for walking that is now heavily patrolled by security officers guarding both the American and British Embassies and the presidential Elysée Palace.

Once arrived at the **avenue George-V**, you may feel like a drink or a coffee at **Le Fouquet's** (it is fashionable to pronounce the 't's', *à l'anglaise*), on the south-east corner. It has recently been rescued from closure or conversion into something very different by arts minister Jack Lang, who declared it not quite a 'national monument' but a *lieu de mémoire*, a piece of folk memory which deserved to survive. If you prefer somewhere less fashionable, you have plenty of choice, especially on the north side, whose pavements are packed with café tables in fine weather. Almost opposite the avenue George-V is another landmark, the **Lido**, which stages the most lavish revues in Paris and is surrounded every night of the year by the coaches that transport tourists from all over the world for a spot of very expensive 'Paris by Night'. A tourist mecca of a different kind can be found a little higher up on the other side: the **Paris Tourist Office** at no. 127, a useful source of information; French Rail have a tourist office in the same building. Just beyond here is the **Drugstore-Publicis**, popular with young people for a drink or a meal, and a handy place for foreign newspapers. A small museum devoted to

President Eisenhower has been opened here, on the site of his wartime head-quarters. (Ⓜ Charles-de-Gaulle-Etoile)

You have now reached the **Etoile**, or the **place Charles-de-Gaulle**, as it is officially known nowadays, though Parisians still use the old name, an abbreviation of place de l'Etoile, laid out by Baron Haussmann with twelve broad avenues radiating from it. At its centre is the **Arc de Triomphe**, which you should reach via the tunnel leading from the north side of the Champs-Elysées (only the truly foolhardy try to slip through the traffic). The arch was given a thorough clean-up in 1989 in readiness for the bicentenary celebrations and is now creamy white, its sculptures standing out in sharp relief. It looks majestically solid amid the swirling traffic, perched high up on its hill and creating a feeling of huge mass (it is over 50 metres high and almost as wide), especially when you come across a glimpse of it from one of the radiating avenues.

Ever one with an eye for the grand gesture, Napoleon commissioned the arch in 1806, just after his victory at the Battle of Austerlitz, as a permanent monument to his armies. Although it was not completed until thirty years later, long after his fall from grace, it seems only fitting that the first major ceremonial event to feature this Roman-style triumphal arch should have been the transfer of the former emperor's remains on the imperial hearse drawn by 16 caparisoned horses. The original commission had gone to Jean Chalgrin, who also designed the church of Saint-Philippe-du-Roule close to the Champs-Elysées, and the arch is adorned with colossal groups of sculptures, carved in high relief by various artists. The finest are those by the Burgundian sculptor François Rude, especially the stirring scene on the right-hand pillar facing the Champs-Elysées. It depicts the departure of Napoleon's volunteers in 1792, inspired by the spirit of patriotism embodied in the winged figure of *La Patrie*, the Motherland, and is generally known as 'La Marseillaise' (see frontispiece).

Inscribed on the inside of the arch are the names of hundreds of French generals (those who died in action are underlined), and towards the top you can make out a long list of victories won by the 'glorious armies' Napoleon had wanted to commemorate. Beneath the arch is the Tomb of the Unknown Soldier, its eternal flame ceremonially rekindled every evening by a different regiment. On great state occasions and national holidays a huge French flag is unfurled from the top of the arch, red, white and blue floodlights pierce the sky and, on 14 July, a thrilling fly-past is staged, the fighter planes leaving behind a trail of red, white and blue vapours.

There is a little museum in the arch, displaying items connected with the long building programme and with the ceremonies held there. It is something of an anticlimax after the grandeur of the arch itself − though there is a video show in French and English these days too − and you will probably find it more interesting to continue to the platform at the top to enjoy the views over Paris and beyond the city boundaries to the modern Défense district with its much bigger arch.

You may well feel that this is an appropriate note on which to end this long walk, proceeding perhaps to a café table on the Champs-Elysées for a drink and a spot of people-watching. You may also be ready now for a meal, but you will already have noticed that rather than the chic restaurants many people fondly imagine finding all along the avenue, such places — they did once exist, but now only Le Fouquet's is left — have been squeezed out by the fast-food chains. But there are still some good and reasonably priced places in side streets like the rue Marbeuf.

If you have enough energy left to press on, walk down the Champs-Elysées and turn off to the left along one of the roads leading to the **place Chassaigne-Goyon**, where you can have a look at Chalgrin's church of **Saint-Philippe-du-Roule**, built to look like a Graeco-Roman basilica, before turning right into the **rue du faubourg Saint-Honoré** and walking along to the **rue Royale**. I also recommend this as an after-dinner stroll (take the **rue La Boétie** or the **avenue Franklin-D.-Roosevelt**, depending on where you have had dinner). This elegant district is pleasanter in the evening, when you can window-shop in leisurely fashion, undisturbed by the heavy daytime traffic.

Continue along the rue du faubourg Saint-Honoré, past the **avenue Matignon**, which has some well-known art galleries, and an interesting bookshop, **Jullien-Cornic** at no. 29 on the corner of the faubourg, specialising in fashion and costume titles. The beautiful gates on the northern side of the **place Beauvau** lead into the Interior Ministry, in an elegant mansion built for the Marquis of Beauvau, a marshal in the French army. On the other side of the faubourg is the **Palais de l'Elysée**, the presidential palace since 1873 but once the home of Madame de Pompadour, Caroline Murat (Napoleon's sister) and the Empress Josephine; it was even turned into a sort of pleasure palace at one time, with an ice-cream parlour, gaming tables, restaurants, ballrooms and a children's playground. Security is so tight nowadays that you will have to peer into the courtyard from the other side of the street.

Further along on the same side, at no. 35, you come to the **British Embassy**, which, like the Elysée Palace, has a long garden running right down to the Jardins des Champs-Elysées. The British ambassador's residence, a few doors away at no. 39, shares with the Elysée the distinction of having been lived in by one of Napoleon's sisters, but this time, as readers of Nancy Mitford's *Don't tell Alfred* will remember, the occupant was the beautiful Pauline, Princesse Borghese. In the **rue d'Aguessau** opposite the embassy is the **embassy church of St Michael**.

From now on the main interest of the faubourg Saint-Honoré is its window displays: many of the world's top *couturiers* have showrooms or ready-to-wear boutiques here, at no. 24 the one-time saddler **Hermès** sells a quarter of a million of its status-symbol silk headsquares every year, and perfumiers, jewellers and luxury shops of all kinds follow one after the other. Even if you're not interested in fashion, it's worth having a glimpse of a district that has been a byword for *le luxe parisien* for decades. The faubourg ends at the **rue Royale**. (Ⓜ Madeleine)

A side trip can be made from this walk to the **Parc Monceau**, a delightful public garden in a residential district which also contains two museums. From here you can walk to another museum, the **Musée Jacquemart-André**, then continue to the **church of Saint-Philippe-du-Roule**, and walk along the rue du Faubourg-Saint-Honoré to the rue Royale, as at the end of the main walk. Alternatively, you can visit the Jacquemart-André Museum from the church — if it happens not to be a Monday or Tuesday or in August – and then walk on to the park and its museums and take the métro back to the Etoile.

The **Parc Monceau** (Ⓜ Monceau) lies at the heart of what was once a village surrounded by woods where from the 14th century onwards the aristocracy came to hunt game and wildfowl. Nowadays this part of the 8th *arrondissement* is the natural habitat of the *haute bourgeoisie*, whose offspring may be observed in their prams in the park, wheeled by uniformed nannies. It dates from the end of the 18th century, when the Duc de Chartres, father of King Louis-Philippe, decided to create a *jardin à l'anglaise*, a little piece of mock pastoral landscape, very different from the formal shapes and lines of a *jardin à la française*. The result is charming, with little lakes and waterfalls, picturesque ruins, pagodas and pyramids and statues. The entrance gates, in wrought-iron decorated with gilt, are particularly beautiful. Beside the métro is the **Pavillon de Chartres**, also referred to as the **Rotonde** (rotunda), one of the few surviving toll gates designed by Nicolas Ledoux for the Tax-Collectors' Wall (see box, History).

Leave the park by the **avenue Velasquez** exit. One of the mansions on the avenue is now the **Musée Cernuschi**, famous for its collections of Chinese art assembled by the house's owner, an Italian banker. Just behind the museum (entrance in the **rue de Monceau**) is another former private mansion, now the **Musée Nissim-de-Camondo**. Like Cernuschi, the Comte de Camondo bequeathed his collections to the nation, but his consist of very beautiful 18th-century furniture and tapestries and *objets* of all kinds. This elegant house is not at all like a museum: you feel that you are the guest of an 18th-century family of taste and discernment as you wander through the flower-filled rooms.

When you leave the museum, turn right and walk down the rue de Monceau, then right into the **avenue Ruysdaël**, left into the **rue Murillo** and left into the **rue Rembrandt**. This little detour will give you a chance to see some Second Empire houses, very typical of this part of Paris, and eventually bring you to the **place du Pérou**. A short walk beyond here and you have reached the **boulevard Haussmann**. Turn left and you soon come to the **Musée Jacquemart-André**, another museum that feels pleasantly like a private mansion.

It is well worth visiting both for its neo-classical architecture, with a curving exterior staircase and a colonnade, and for its collections of 18th-century and Italian Renaissance art. It also has some beautiful furniture. Don't miss the Tiepolo frescoes adorning the staircase or the little Uccello painting of St George killing the dragon, as well as paintings by Botticelli and Tintoretto and Titian, and by Boucher and Watteau among the French school on the ground floor.

Walk back to the rue de Courcelles and continue to the **avenue Myron-T.-Herrick**, which brings you to the church of Saint-Philippe-du-Roule. From here you can continue to the rue Royale as above, or walk back to the Champs-Elysées, or simply take the métro (Ⓜ Saint-Philippe-du-Roule).

Hotels and Restaurants

For general advice on choosing where to stay and where to eat, see Practical Information; prices are moderate unless otherwise stated.

Hotels

Atala 10 rue Chateaubriand, 8e (45-62-01-62, fax: 42-25-66-38). Quite expensive, but worth it for the pretty garden, mostly charming rooms (a few have their own terrace, with lovely views) and the quiet setting near the Champs-Elysées; has its own restaurant too.

Banville 166 blvd Berthier, 17e (42-67-70-16). Not very central, but lots of charm: pretty rooms with good-sized bathrooms, friendly service and peaceful atmosphere.

Bradford 10 rue Saint-Philippe-du-Roule, 8e (43-59-24-20). Quiet and elegant, yet not too expensive, even though it is near the Faubourg Saint-Honoré; the rooms are spacious too, with good modern bathrooms.

Colisée 6 rue du Colisée, 8e (43-59-95-25). Small rooms, but quite comfortable, and reasonably priced for this very expensive area just off the Champs-Elysées.

Etoile-Park 10 av Mac-Mahon, 17e (42-67-69-63). Stylish modern décor and well-planned rooms are the plus points of this pleasant hotel in one of the broad avenues leading off the Etoile.

Regent's Garden 6 rue Pierre-Demours, 17e (45-74-07-30). A comfortable mid-19th-century house, a gift from Napoleon III to his doctor, has been turned into a delightful and fairly expensive hotel, sought after for its garden dotted with statues and a fountain, its spacious and well-furnished rooms. Book well in advance if you fancy being woken by birdsong only a stone's throw from the Etoile.

Résidence Lord Byron 5 rue Chateaubriand, 8e (43-59-89-98). Quiet and discreet, yet very near the Champs-Elysées. Some rooms are expensive, others quite reasonably priced; the pleasantest overlook an inner courtyard.

Restaurants

L'Alsace 39 av des Champs-Elysées, 8e (43-59-44-24). Busy brasserie, open round the clock, is well known for its Alsace specialities (especially *choucroutes* and open fruit tarts) and its deliciously fresh seafood, which is even more delicious when accompanied by a fruity Alsace wine. If you are tempted to find out more about the region and its many delights, don't miss the information office and small boutique next door.

L'Assiette au Boeuf 123 av des Champs-Elysées, 8e (no telephone bookings). One of a chain of lively restaurants serving good-value 'formula' meals against a background of fashionable art nouveau-ish décor.

Bar des Théâtres 6 av Montaigne, 8e (47-23-34-63). An entertaining place for a late supper (open to 2 a.m.); popular with a colourful theatre crowd in the evenings, and at lunchtime often full of glamorous models from the nearby fashion houses.

Bateaux-Mouches (see under Museums and Places of Interest) Even if it sounds corny, a meal on one of the glass-roofed riverboats is not to be despised: traffic-free sightseeing combined with unexpectedly good classical cuisine.

Baumann Marbeuf 15 rue Marbeuf, 8e (47-20-11-11); closed part of Aug. Run by a well-known Alsace restaurateur, so good for *choucroutes*, but also top-quality grilled meat; open late and always busy.

Le Bistrot d'à Côté 10 rue Gustave-Flaubert, 17e (42-67-05-81); closed Sat for lunch, Sun and part of Aug. This outpost of the burgeoning empire of well-known chef-restaurateur Michel Rostang is a copy of an old-style bistrot in what was once a bakery. It's more like a private room, with shelves full of knick-knacks, marble-topped tables, blackboard menu, café curtains on brass rods. *Cuisine bourgeoise* at its best, with a slight bias towards Lyonnaise specialities.

Bistrot de l'Etoile 13 rue Troyon, 17e (42-67-25-95); closed Sat for lunch, Sun. Another example of a top chef opening up a cheaper bistrot 'annexe': this one is run by Guy Savoy opposite his expensive eponymous restaurant. Modern décor with the emphasis on pale wood, rather chic, and *cuisine bourgeoise*.

Le Boeuf sur le Toit 34 rue du Colisée, 8e (43-59-83-80). Large and lively brasserie once frequented by Cocteau, with twenties décor, friendly and efficient service, excellent seafood and long opening hours (closes at about 2 a.m.).

Boutique à Sandwiches 12 rue du Colisée, 8e (43-59-56-69); closed Sun and Aug. Probably the best-known and certainly the most fashionable sandwich place in Paris, to eat there or take away right through to 1 a.m.

Chez André 12 rue Marbeuf, 8e (no bookings taken). Definitely an 'institution': the menu's still written in purple ink, the waitresses never seem to change, though the ownership has changed after half a century. Traditional *cuisine bourgeoise* and good wine list at reasonable prices.

Chez Tante Louise 41 rue Boissy-d'Anglas, 8e (42-65-06-85); closed weekends. Another long-standing bistrot; this one has recently been done up but still has an almost provincial feel about it, although it is only a few steps away from the plush shops in the Faubourg Saint-Honoré and the place de la Madeleine.

La Fermette Marbeuf 1900 5 rue Marbeuf, 8e (47-20-63-53). For once the turn-of-the-century tag is genuine, not just a nod to a lasting fashion in interior decorating: during building work in the seventies the workmen stumbled on superb art nouveau décor hidden behind false walls and ceiling. It is now visible for all to admire, but the food is good and reasonably priced too, and the atmosphere lively.

Grand Palais Cafeteria Adequate food at low prices and pleasant views over the gardens lining the Champs-Elysées.

Musée d'Art Moderne Cafeteria Another museum cafeteria, useful for a quick lunch during a round of museum visits; a few tables outside in fine weather.

Restaurant du Rond-Point Théâtre Renaud-Barrault, av Franklin-D.-Roosevelt, 8e (42-56-22-01); closed Sun for dinner. Relaxed restaurant in the theatre run by the great Jean-Louis Barrault and his equally great wife Madeleine Renaud (who often pop in here themselves). Bits of scenery adorn the walls and the clientele is lively.

Savy 23 rue Bayard, 8e (47-23-46-98); closed weekends and Aug. Old-established bistrot with a regular clientele; reasonably priced dishes, including some with a regional flavour.

Le Vigneron Fromager 48 rue du Colisée, 8e (42-25-01-46); closed Sat for lunch and Sun. As the name suggests, specialises in wine and cheese, at pleasantly low prices.

137

Museums and Places of Interest

Palais de Chaillot pl du Trocadéro, 16e. Houses four museums: *Musée de l'Homme* (anthropology and ethnology museum) Closed Tue. *Musée de la Marine* (Naval Museum) Closed Tue. *Musée des Monuments Français* (sculpture and architectural details) Closed Tue. *Musée du Cinéma* (cinema museum) Guided tours only, closed Tue; tours are often cancelled at short notice, so check just beforehand. Ⓜ Trocadéro

Musée Guimet (Far Eastern art) 6 pl d'Iéna, 16e. Closed Tue. Ⓜ Iéna, Alma-Marceau

Palais Galliéra (Costume Museum) av du Président-Wilson. Special exhibitions only. Ⓜ Iéna, Alma-Marceau

Musée d'Art Moderne de la Ville de Paris (modern art) 11 av du Président-Wilson, 16e. Closed Mon, late opening Wed. Ⓜ Iéna, Alma-Marceau

Boat trips on the Seine: *Bateaux-Mouches* leave from Right Bank end of the Pont de l'Alma, 8e, every day at intervals of about 30 mins; trips last about 1hr 15 mins; *lunch trips* (daily except Mon) last about 1hr 45 mins, *evening trips with dinner* (daily, casual clothes not accepted) about 2½ hrs, *afternoon trips with musical accompaniment* (weekends only) about 1½ hrs. For all these special trips it is advisable to book. Ⓜ Alma-Marceau, ⓇⒺⓇ Pont de l'Alma

Grand Palais Entrances in av Winston-Churchill, pl Clemenceau and av du Général-Eisenhower, all 8e. Special exhibitions only (no permanent collections). Closed Tue, late opening Wed. Ⓜ Champs-Elysées-Clemenceau

Palais de la Découverte av Franklin-D.-Roosevelt, 8e. Closed Mon. Ⓜ Franklin-D.-Roosevelt, Champs-Elysées-Clemenceau

Petit Palais av Winston-Churchill, 8e. Closed Mon. Ⓜ Champs-Elysées-Clemenceau

Musée Cernuschi (Oriental art) 7 av Velasquez, 8e. Closed Mon. Ⓜ Villiers

Musée Nissim-de-Camondo (18th-century furniture) 63 rue de Monceau, 8e. Closed Mon, Tue. Ⓜ Villiers

Musée Jacquemart-André (18th-century French art, Italian Renaissance) 158 blvd Haussmann, 8e. Usually afternoons only, closed Mon, Tue and Aug, but opening times vary during special exhibitions. Ⓜ Saint-Philippe-du-Roule, Miromesnil

Walk 6
From the Madeleine to the Louvre and the Palais Royal

Starting point: the east side of the place de la Concorde, 8e, in front of the gates leading to the Tuileries Gardens; Ⓜ Concorde. This Right Bank walk covers much of 'Royal Paris', including the former royal palace of the Louvre, the Tuileries Gardens and the Palais Royal. It starts on the edge of the eighth *arrondissement*, then takes in two-thirds of the first.

This is a walk that leaves you in no doubt about the French predilection for grand vistas. The sweeping views up the Champs-Elysées from the place de la Concorde, and through the Tuileries to the Louvre, the place de la Concorde itself, often referred to as France's most beautiful public square, framed at either end by the Palais Bourbon beyond the Seine and the church of the Madeleine at the far end of the rue Royale, the avenue de l'Opéra leading to the glittering opera house, the harmonious place Vendôme and the rhythmic sweep of the arcades of the rue de Rivoli opposite the Tuileries, all create an impression of the elegance and grandeur of French town planning over the centuries. And the newly created 'landscape' of the Cour Napoléon of the Louvre, centring on its stylish modern Pyramid, provides the example *par excellence* of the new French determination to create the appropriate setting for Paris's major buildings and thus make them more attractive to visitors and Parisians alike.

This is a key area for museum-goers: a few minutes' walk from the Louvre itself, now much more accessible and easy to explore, you can visit the Musée des Arts Décoratifs (applied and decorative art) and the new Musée des Arts de la Mode (fashion and costume). Then there are plenty of opportunities for window-shopping in the place de la Madeleine, the rue de Rivoli and the rue Saint-Honoré, and for peaceful strolling in the Tuileries and the Palais Royal gardens. Church-lovers can explore the Madeleine, Saint-Germain-l'Auxerrois and Saint-Roch and the walk includes France's best-known theatre, the Comédie française.

A well-heeled area of smart shops and elegant flats, it includes the Ritz and several other top hotels, plus a good range of restaurants and tea rooms. Apart from the short rue Royale and the place de la Concorde, traffic congestion is not a major hazard, and the arcades of the rue de Rivoli and the Palais Royal are ideal for wet-weather wandering.

The walk starts in the octagonal **place de la Concorde**, so large that its majesty is somehow undimmed by the constant ebb and flow of traffic racing round and across it from all directions. It was designed in the middle of the 18th century by Jacques-Anges Gabriel, the architect of much of Versailles and of the Ecole Militaire, as a fitting setting for a statue of Louis XV commissioned from Edmé Bouchardon by the merchants of Paris to celebrate the king's recovery from a serious illness. The place Louis-XV, as it was originally christened, was then on the outskirts of the city but gradually acquired a pivotal importance with the building of the **pont de la Concorde**, linking it to the Left Bank, and, early in the next century, of the **rue de Rivoli**.

But by then the royal statue had been toppled and replaced by a huge figure of Liberty. The square's name had been changed to the 'place de la Révolution' and it had become the site of the dreaded guillotine, on which well over a thousand people were executed between 1793 and 1795. Its first important victim was Louis XVI, in January 1793, followed later by Marie-Antoinette, and in due course by the leaders of the Revolution, Danton and Robespierre and their associates. Napoleon had the statue of Liberty removed and eventually the commonsense 'bourgeois king' Louis-Philippe swept aside plans to replace it with Charlemagne, or possibly one of the recent French monarchs, and instead seized gratefully on an earlier gift to the French people from Egypt of a pink granite **Obelisk** dating from the reign of Ramses III. No one, he felt, could be inspired to knock down a monument over 3,000 years old as a symbol of absolute monarchy or anything else. The obelisk was hoisted into place in 1836 and at about the same time the eight pavilions in the corners of the *place* were adorned with statues of female figures representing major French cities. Have a good look at the one to your right as you face the obelisk: it personifies Strasbourg and the sitter was Victor Hugo's long-time mistress, the actress Juliette Drouet.

On either side of the Tuileries gates are figures astride winged horses by the classical sculptor Antoine Coysevox — Fame to the right and Mercury to the left. With the usual Parisian love of symmetry, they are mirrored on the far side of the square by the '**Chevaux de Marly**' guarding the entrance to the Champs-Elysées (see previous walk). From this vantage point you enjoy a superb view up the **Champs-Elysées** to the **Arc de Triomphe** and on to the **Défense** with its new giant arch. When you have had your fill of it, walk cautiously over to the platform surrounding the obelisk — Parisian motorists are not known for their considerateness to pedestrians — and turn right for another famous view, this time of the twin arcaded *hôtels* built by Gabriel round courtyards on the north side of the square, and on to the **church of the Madeleine**. The **Hôtel de la Marine**, on the right, is the headquarters of the French navy; its twin now houses the deluxe **Hôtel Crillon**, with a well-known bar, and the French Automobile Club. Turn 180° to

Beyond the ornamental pool in the Tuileries Gardens, a glimpse of the Sacré-Coeur in Montmartre

face the south and the Madeleine is mirrored in the classical façade of the **Palais Bourbon** beyond the Seine (Walk 4). Then turn east for a leafy vista through the **Tuileries Gardens** to the **Arc de Triomphe du Carrousel** and, lightened by its shiny new pyramid, the huge bulk of the **Louvre**.

Now cross back to the Tuileries gates and walk through them for a brief stroll in the formal gardens laid out in the reign of Louis XIV by that great landscape gardener André Le Nôtre (see box). To the north of the octagonal miniature lake, on which Parisians young and old love sailing their model boats, don't miss a copy of his bust by Coysevox. The mid-19th century building behind it, the **Jeu de Paume**, was until recently the home of Paris's famous Impressionist collection. Now that those beautiful canvases have been moved to the Musée d'Orsay (Walk 4) it is to be restored and will one day reopen as a centre for temporary art exhibitions. Its twin on the south side, the **Musée de l'Orangerie**, is famous for its series of *Waterlilies* by Monet, grouped round oval rooms on the ground floor. On the first floor is an excellent former private collection of late 19th- and early 20th-century paintings, by artists ranging from Cézanne to Matisse, Utrillo to *Le Douanier* Rousseau.

The gardens were planned as a formal approach to the Palais des Tuileries, designed by Philibert Delorme for Catherine de Médicis in the 16th century, on the site of what had once been tile kilns (*tuileries* in French). The palace was a

141

André Le Nôtre – Gardener Extraordinaire

André Le Nôtre was born in a little house near the Louvre in 1613, the son and grandson of royal gardeners. He learnt about garden design from his father, taking over from him as gardener of the Tuileries Palace and its grounds in 1637. But he also read widely in the subject, as well as studying architecture and painting. The true creator of the formal *jardin à la française*, he was one of the trio of artists with articled names working under Colbert to glorify Louis XIV through the grandeur and beauty of the buildings put up during his reign. Le Nôtre himself was appointed *premier jardinier du roi* (chief royal gardener), while Louis Le Vau, the son of a master mason, became *premier architecte du roi* (chief royal architect) and Charles Le Brun was *premier peintre du roi* (chief royal painter).

The three worked together at Vaux-le-Vicomte, where Le Nôtre experimented with the ideas that were eventually to come to fruition in his masterpiece, the formal gardens and grounds of the palace of Versailles. But he also designed a large number of other important gardens in and around Paris, including the Jardin des Tuileries, Chantilly, Saint-Germain-en-Laye, Saint-Cloud, Meudon, Dampierre and Sceaux. He advised Madame de Maintenon on the plans for her pretty château at Maintenon and, more surprisingly, even had a hand in designing St James's Park in London.

He was the first gardener to become famous in his own right, as the inventor of a style of landscape gardening based on geometry where nothing is left to chance, where nature is invariably subdued and restrained. Man's absolute mastery over nature, best exemplified in the terraces at Versailles adorned with statues and vases,

parterres and fountains, ornamental pools and gravel paths bounded by neatly trimmed hedges, was seen as the symbol of absolute monarchy. And according to Professor Pevsner, Le Nôtre was also indirectly responsible for the informal grounds surrounding Palladian country houses in Britain, planned as a reaction to the rigidity and 'tampering with nature' brought to a peak of perfection in his grand gardens.

In the Tuileries Gardens, which he began to lay out in 1664, he abandoned the traditional medieval schema of neat squares, delicately worked as in embroidery, in favour of a central axis round which the whole garden is designed. His plan, based on a broad avenue sweeping westwards beyond the Tuileries across open fields that were to become the Champs-Elysées, and originally conceived as extending as far as Saint-Germain-en-Laye, had a strong impact on the development of Paris, whose *beaux quartiers* gradually moved westwards too.

Over three centuries later his influence is still being felt. I.M. Pei, the Chinese-American architect who designed the controversial Pyramid in the Cour Napoléon of the Louvre, has said that he made a careful study of the royal gardener's work and that he sees his Pyramid as a landscape solution in the Le Nôtre tradition, in which reflected sky and water are the essential elements of the composition, rather than a purely architectural solution.

Le Nôtre lived to see the new century, dying at what was then the great age of 87. He was buried near the Tuileries in the church of Saint-Roch, where you can visit his tomb, with its bust by the classical sculptor Antoine Coysevox. There is a copy of the bust at the western end of the gardens themselves.

long building just east of what is now the avenue du Général-Lemonnier and parallel to it. Later building joined it to the Louvre by means of long wings stretching beside the Seine and along the rue de Rivoli. It became the residence of France's sovereigns and was enlarged and rebuilt several times over the years until Louis XIV transferred the court to Versailles. It was the scene of one of the bloodiest episodes during the Revolution, when Louis XVI's Swiss guards were massacred in 1792. After the Revolution it was the seat of the government, then a royal residence again during the Restoration. But it was badly damaged by fire during the Commune in 1871 and eventually demolished in the 1880s, though you can still admire a few little bits of it beneath the terrace to the east of the Jeu de Paume – an arcade of Ionic columns and a couple of columns with plinth and entablature. The site of the palace was converted into another formal garden which is due to be restored to its former glory by the time the redevelopment of the whole of the Louvre area is completed towards the end of the nineties.

With its tree-lined avenues to the west and its neat flowerbeds and tiny box hedges and ornamental pools and statues to the east, the **Jardin des Tuileries** is a delightful place for strolling. In fine weather there are donkey rides and roundabouts for children and little kiosks beneath the trees sell drinks and snacks.

Leave the gardens by the Jeu de Paume exit and cross over the **rue de Rivoli**, once an elegant shopping street but now mainly a centre for tourist souvenirs, with some rather dowdy dress shops, though it still has several smart hotels. At this end of the street **W.H. Smith**'s Paris bookshop, at no. 248, on the corner of the **rue Cambon**, has been a handy source of maps, guidebooks and newspapers and magazines in English since 1903, though its celebrated 'English tea rooms' closed in 1989 to make way for more book departments. Turn left and walk past the Hôtel de la Marine, then turn right into the **rue Royale**. On the left-hand side at no. 3, **Maxim's**, now owned by the *couturier* Pierre Cardin, is still a fashionable and very expensive restaurant, and this is also a street for well-heeled present buyers: elegant jewellery at **Fred** at no. 6 (the name oddly has a chic ring to the French), stylish china at **Villeroy & Boch**, glass at **Lalique. Christofle**, at no. 9, has a small museum devoted to the art of the gold- and silversmith, and if you're feeling peckish, **Ladurée** at no. 16 is a turn-of-the-century tea room selling elegantly tiny sandwiches, mouthwatering *pâtisseries* and light lunch dishes.

At the far end of the street the **church of Sainte-Marie-Madeleine**, invariably referred to simply as 'la Madeleine', looks for all the world like an ancient Greek temple with its massive Corinthian columns raised above a broad flight of steps. It started life as a medieval village church dedicated to Mary Magdalen just east of the **place de la Madeleine** at what is now 8 boulevard Malesherbes: Proustians should note that Proust was born in the 19th-century block of flats on this site, but the famous cork-lined room was a little way away in the boulevard Haussmann. As Paris expanded westwards and this area became increasingly chic, its boulevards and avenues lined with elegant mansions, a bigger church was needed and the present site was chosen in the 18th century.

The new church was designed on a similar plan to Saint-Louis-des-Invalides (Walk 4), but was constantly modified, and it was still unfinished when the

143

Revolution put an end to church building. At various times it narrowly escaped being converted into a bank, a court house, a community hall, even a railway station. Eventually Napoleon decreed that it was to be a temple dedicated to his 'Grande Armée'. The half-finished church was pulled down and the building you see today was completed in 1842, by which time both Napoleon and his architect Vignon were dead and Louis XVIII had announced that it would be a church after all. It is now one of the most fashionable in Paris, popular for society weddings and often staging concerts. The inside is dark and rather forbidding, but it has some good sculpture, including Rude's *Baptism of Christ* to the left of the entrance.

To the west of the church is another temple: **Lucas-Carton**, with superb art nouveau décor and fittings designed by Louis Majorelle, now presided over by one of the high priests of *nouvelle cuisine*. Alain Senderens certainly deserves the French accolade of 'temple of gastronomy', even down to the hushed cathedral-like atmosphere, but only those with fat wallets should attempt to worship there. Gourmet eating is a major preoccupation in this part of Paris, for the place de la Madeleine also boasts the most luxurious food emporium in Paris. To reach **Fauchon**'s three shops in the north-east corner of the square, walk past the open-air **flower market** on the east side of the church; here too is one of the tourist offices of the Paris Transport Authority (RATP) – you can buy coach excursion tickets there.

Fauchon's windows are as mouthwatering an example of conspicuous consumption as you're ever likely to encounter. Only those who object on principle to the French love of food and wine should miss a visit to this Aladdin's cave of edible and drinkable goodies, both to goggle at the food displays and to observe the shop's regular patrons intent on choosing their purchases. **Hédiard** on the other side of the square is another supremely upmarket grocer's, but it cannot quite compete in luxury with Fauchon. If looking at all that food has made you hungry, Fauchon has a self-service room where you can treat yourself to a superior snack. On the Hédiard side is a kiosk selling half-price theatre and opera tickets for that day's performances only (open from about 12.45 p.m. to 7 p.m.).

Don't eat too much or you'll feel miserable looking at the beautifully cut but skimpy swimwear and sportswear in **Erès** on the corner of the **rue Tronchet**, a detour recommended to keen shoppers, with its good accessory shops (**Carel** on the right for shoes, **La Bagagerie** just beyond for leather goods) and stylish outfits at **Cacharel**. The **rue Vignon** between the two Fauchon shops has several interesting restaurants, including **La Ferme des Mathurins*** at no. 17 and **Le Roi du Pot-au-Feu** at no. 34. At no. 21, one of the city's best cheesemonger's, **La Ferme Saint-Hubert***, also serves light cheese dishes, while **La Maison du Miel** at no. 24 specialises in an amazing range of honeys, some of them a deep chestnut-brown. At the south-eastern end of the square the elegant but rather staid department store **Aux Trois Quartiers** was being rebuilt in 1990 and may have reopened as a shopping centre, with a big menswear section, by the time you read this.

Now walk past the store eastwards along the **boulevard de la Madeleine**, pausing at no. 11 to remember Alphonsine Duplessis, who lived and died there and was immortalised as Alexandre Dumas *fils*'s consumptive heroine, *La Dame aux Camélias*, and thus as Verdi's *La Traviata*. This is the westernmost of the 'Grands

Boulevards', which are the subject of the next walk. Turn right into the rue Cambon and walk down to the **place Maurice-Barrès** with the **Eglise de l'Assomption**, now a centre of the Polish community in Paris. Then turn left into the **rue Saint-Honoré**, a country lane which became one of Paris's major east–west thoroughfares serving the Louvre and the Palais Royal. Its elegant shops are frequented mainly by wealthy tourists and fairly elderly *Parisiennes*, who love to buy hand-embroidered gloves or ivory-handled umbrellas here, while their daughters and grand-daughters prefer the trendier boutiques in Saint-Germain-des-Prés or Passy or round Les Halles.

Window-shop on to the **rue de Castiglione**, then turn left to admire the harmonious proportions of the octagonal **place Vendôme**. Its 17th-century façades, designed by Jules Hardouin-Mansart, face towards a statue of Napoleon perched on top of a tall bronze-faced column inspired by Trajan's Column in Rome and carved with spiralling friezes in low relief depicting scenes from the Battle of Austerlitz. The **Colonne Vendôme**, and indeed the whole square, looks particularly lovely at night. And it is at its best in December, when it becomes a rich treasure house of lights and fir branches and huge red and gold bows and garlands as some of the world's top jewellers – Boucheron and Van Cleef & Arpels and Chaumet – tempt customers with dazzling displays, and on a couple of evenings before Christmas throw open their shops to invited guests and ply them with champagne and canapés. Even without an invitation you can enjoy the sight, and for the rest of the year the **Ritz Hotel** on the west side, beside the **Justice Ministry**, provides an entertaining parade of guests in smart cars. You might even feel like splashing out on a drink in the famous bar, frequented by Proust, Scott Fitzgerald and Hemingway.

Some of the elegant mansions in the place Louis-le-Grand, as it was originally called, were built by the Scottish financier John Law, before his spectacular crash (see Walk 8), others by various wealthy bankers. In the centre at that time stood an equestrian statue of Louis XIV, in Roman dress. This suffered the usual fate of being toppled during the Revolution – and in crashing to the ground ironically killed a loyal Republican *citoyenne* called Rose Viollet who was selling copies of Marat's revolutionary paper *L'Ami du peuple*. It was replaced by a column with a statue of Napoleon, again in Roman dress, but this too was melted down during the emperor's exile and superseded by a huge fleur de lis. That went when Louis-Philippe commissioned a statue of Napoleon as the 'Little Corporal', complete with great coat and corporal's hat, but it in turn was replaced by the figure you can just make out today, perched high up on its column – a copy of the original Napoleon.

Now walk back down the rue de Castiglione, past, on the left-hand side, the excellent but very expensive **Carré des Feuillants** restaurant (the name comes from the monastery of strict Bernardines – *Feuillants* – that once stood here). On the right is the **Intercontinental Hotel**, whose inner courtyard complete with splashing fountain is a good place for a drink on hot summer days. In colder weather you may prefer tea and cakes at **Angélina***, an elegant tea room-cum-restaurant just round the corner at 226 rue de Rivoli. It used to be the well-known **Rumpelmayer**, first opened in 1903, and still sells superb chocolates and other confectionery if you have sweet-toothed friends to take presents to.

Walk east beneath the rue de Rivoli arcades. During the Second World War the deluxe **Hôtel Meurice** at no. 228 was the headquarters of the German commandant Dietrich von Choltitz, who fortunately decided to turn a deaf ear to an order from Hitler to destroy central Paris. **Galignani**, at no. 224, is an old-established traditional bookshop. It boasts of having been 'the first English bookshop established on the Continent' and has a big department of art books in both French and English, plus fiction and non-fiction in English. **Maréchal**, at no. 232, has Limoges china thimbles, scent bottles and other pretty objects, while **Fleurmay**, at no. 204, is good for stylish modern silver jewellery. If you feel like a quick meal or a snack, there are several café-brasseries beneath the arcades, such as the **Rivoli-Park** at no. 216; they are not cheap – this is an expensive area – but service is generally fast, simple dishes such as *onglet aux échalotes* or *crème caramel* are reliable, and at the window or pavement tables you can enjoy people-watching too. There are also several restaurants in the rue du Mont-Thabor, running parallel to the rue de Rivoli and well away from traffic noise.

Continue to the **place des Pyramides**, with its gilded statue of Joan of Arc, who was wounded in 1429, during the English army's occupation of Paris, when she launched an attack against the gate that then stood here. Now walk across the rue de Rivoli and into the Tuileries Gardens again. At this end they are adorned with plump female sculptures by Aristide Maillol and offer good views of the **Arc de Triomphe du Carrousel**, now beautifully restored. It is modelled on the arch of Septimus Severus in Rome and looks magical at night, when the pink marble columns glow under the floodlights and the gilded chariot and four glitter on the top of the arch. Open-air concerts here are a treat worth planning for.

This is also a good vantage point for your first reasonably close-up view of the shiny glass and steel **Pyramid** in the **Cour Napoléon** of the Louvre, designed by the Chinese-American architect I.M. Pei and offering glimpses of the heavily decorated architecture of the main wings of the **Louvre Palace**. Opinions are still divided on this new and controversial 'monument', but many of those who initially opposed it tooth and nail have been won over by the purity of the lines and by the magnificence of the views from the underground entrance area it is its main function to light. But before visiting the Louvre via the Pyramid you should walk back along the **avenue du Général-Lemonnier** to the rue de Rivoli, then turn right past the **Pavillon de Marsan**, the westernmost tip of the long north wing of the Louvre, which houses the **Musée des Arts Décoratifs** (Applied and Decorative Arts Museum, entrance at no. 107).

The 'Arts Déco' was closed for several years in the early eighties for drastic refurbishment, during which its collections were completely reorganised. Exhibits are now grouped by theme – drawings, glass, wallpaper, toys and so on – as well as by period. The 20th century is properly represented for the first time, with some beautiful art nouveau and art déco exhibits, including Lalique jewellery and Gallé glass, in the 1900–25 section, along with a reconstruction of Jeanne Lanvin's Paris flat, with marble floors and 'Lanvin blue' shantung wall coverings embroidered with marguerites. A large new **Galerie Contemporaine** made up of

The Arc de Triomphe du Carrousel, modelled on the arch of Septimus Severus in Rome

six rooms covers the period from the end of the Second World War to the late eighties.

Instead of a series of small, rather dark rooms, the museum's rich collections, starting with the Middle Ages, are now housed in light and airy spaces. The glass roof has been stripped of its paint and nearly 2,000 square metres of exhibition space have been added. Young architects were commissioned to design the new areas, such as the **Galerie d'Actualité**, the work of the fashionable Philippe Starck, famous for his stylish designs for Paris restaurants and cafés, including **Le Café Costes** in the square des Innocents (Walk 8). The museum's toy collection spreads over four rooms and children are also well catered for with workshops and special events. On either side of the main entrance area are a good art bookshop, which also sells postcards, and a boutique full of desirable modern pieces ranging from designer scarves and jewellery to stationery and tableware. And on Thursday afternoons experts in the various departments are available to talk about their speciality to visitors, who are also free to consult reference books in the library.

Next door in the Pavillon de Marsan, reached via the Arts Déco Museum or from a separate entrance at no. 109, is the new **Musée des Arts de la Mode** (Fashion Arts Museum), opened in 1985 and housing costumes and *couture* outfits from the older museum's stores. Temporary exhibitions are regularly staged here too, and the museum again has a little boutique with scarves and scent bottles, books on fashion and costume and some attractive gift items. The museum is on the top five floors of the newly restored building, reached by an irritatingly slow lift or a long climb up the stairs, but don't give up, as the display is stylish and the exhibits interesting.

After these two museums, continue along the rue de Rivoli to the **passage Richelieu**, which gives you an interesting view of the Louvre Pyramid, at its best when the glass panels are gleaming in the sunlight or beneath floodlights, the pools and fountains shimmering. In the passageway, stop to study the plan of the whole scheme to create 'Le Grand Louvre', as you'll find it will make it easier to grasp the layout once you're beneath the Pyramid. You will probably have to queue to reach the entrance and the large courtyard may be marred by ugly metal crush barriers to contain the crowds. But console yourself with the thought that things were much worse before the scheme got under way and use the queuing time to ponder the history of the palace and absorb the thinking behind its latest transformation. You might also like to conjure up an image of Henri IV, 'Good King Henry', sowing and tending his own asparagus beds in the north-east corner of the adjoining courtyard, the **Cour Carrée**.

The Louvre was originally a medieval fortress with keep and towers forming part of Philippe Auguste's 12th-century wall. It was designed to protect what was then the westernmost limit of the city. When Charles V built fortifications further west, the Louvre became a royal castle within the city walls, but was not transformed into a palace until 300 years later, under François Ier, who brought some of the finest Italian Renaissance artists to work on Pierre Lescot's designs. Parts of the old fortress were demolished, including the vast keep, and work started on the south-west corner of what is now the Cour Carrée.

From then on virtually all French monarchs and emperors had a hand in redesigning or adding to the Louvre, right down to the end of the 19th century, when the western end of the north wing was embellished under the Third Republic with the Pavillon de Marsan. The courtyard on the site of the original 'Vieux Louvre' was not completed until the 17th century, during the reigns of Louis XIII and Louis XIV, but before then Henri II's widow Catherine de Médicis had commissioned Philibert Delorme to build the Tuileries Palace to the west of the Louvre, and had started building the **Petite Galerie**, designed as the first link in a chain of buildings joining the two palaces. This leads south towards the river and the scheme was taken a stage further when Henri IV added the **Galerie du Bord de l'Eau** on the south side. The western half of this long south wing was rebuilt during the Second Empire, and substantially added to on the north side, but Catherine's scheme of extending the Louvre westwards has remained intact.

The Cour Carrée had been completed by the time Louis XIV decided to move the court out of Paris to Versailles in 1678. But for the next 125 years or so all building work stopped and the palace was gradually taken over by artists and craftsmen and assorted writers and teachers who set up workshops and academies in the royal apartments and in various ramshackle buildings grafted on to the main wings. The arrival of Napoleon brought an end to this shambles: once he was settled into the Tuileries he had the clutter of makeshift buildings removed

I.M. Pei's Pyramid in the Cour Napoléon harks back to Le Nôtre's landscape gardening

and drove out the colonies of artists who were now little more than squatters. He widened the **place du Carrousel** and decorated it with its triumphal arch, then commissioned his architects Percier and Fontaine to design a north wing running alongside the rue de Rivoli. This was completed under Napoleon III, who also added the south façade of the Cour Napoléon. But the vast complex of buildings that had grown up over the years was opened up again in 1871, when most of the Tuileries Palace was destroyed. Its eventual razing a decade later created the basic outline that you see today – a vast letter 'A', with the west façade of the Cour Carrée forming the bar, and the place du Carrousel no longer an inner courtyard, but a huge open space adorned with formal gardens.

By this time the Louvre had been a museum and art gallery for almost a century. Like so many institutions in France, it owes its existence to the Revolution: in 1793 the Convention had the royal art collections, originally started by François

Ier, moved to the Grande Galerie and opened them to the public. A few years later they were swelled by the works of art seized by Napoleon's armies from all over Europe – the museum even became the Musée Napoléon for a while. But after his downfall most of the war booty was returned to its rightful owners and the painting collections are still based on the masterpieces amassed by François Ier and Louis XIV, on Louis XVI's collection of works by the great Dutch and Flemish painters, plus a whole series of bequests from rich benefactors.

Although the big Impressionist collection was moved out in the 1940s and the Musée d'Orsay was to take over much of the work of late 19th- and early 20th-century artists, by the 1970s the Louvre was severely overcrowded. In spite of its important collections of Oriental and Egyptian, Greek and Roman antiquities, its prints and drawings and its furniture and *objets d'art*, surveys showed that the average visitor felt intimidated and overwhelmed by the vast and rambling maze of rooms and stayed a remarkably short time. The museum had a dingy look both inside and out and public facilities left a great deal to be desired. Something clearly needed to be done to make one of the world's leading museums more appealing to visitors. Shortly after he became president in 1981 François Mitterrand took the bull by the horns and announced plans for 'Le Grand Louvre' that would prepare the palace-turned-museum for the 21st century by restoring and cleaning the fabric, totally refurbishing and modernising the exhibition rooms and galleries, rehanging many of the pictures, creating a completely new entrance in the Cour Napoléon designed to reduce queuing, redesigning all public facilities, banning tourist coaches to an underground car park, and allowing more exhibits to go on show by enabling the museum to take over the large areas of the north wing occupied by the Finance Ministry since 1871.

The first stage of the new Louvre was eventually unveiled in 1989, with attendants in chic uniforms designed by Yves Saint-Laurent. A few months later the Finance Ministry officials reluctantly moved out. But the new Richelieu Wing that is to replace them will not open until the museum's bicentenary in 1993 and the whole grandiose scheme will not be complete until 1996 or 1997. By then at least 85 per cent of the exhibits will have been moved, the exhibition space will have doubled to over 70,000 square metres, and vast numbers of paintings and other objects will have been brought out of store. So what you see now is an interim phase, but one that even the most prejudiced observer must surely agree is an improvement.

The most important innovation, and the biggest area of controversy, is the famous Pyramid. Forget all you have heard and read about it and decide for yourself whether there could have been a more practical and more stylish solution to the major space and light problems facing the Louvre. I.M. Pei has said that he chose a pyramid because it takes up less space than a cylinder or a cube and because its steeply sloping transparent sides, divided by narrow steel struts into diamond shapes, both reflect and refract daylight and floodlighting and allow visitors to see through them to enjoy the architecture of the 19th-century façades, the sculpted decoration standing out sharply against the newly restored stonework. The Cour Napoléon, until recently dusty and neglected-looking, with a few fenced-in shrubs and wispy trees in the middle, is now bright and light, enlivened by the reflections in the main Pyramid and its little offspring, and by the play of light in the fountains and ornamental pools surrounding it. And riding proudly in front of it is Louis XIV, a lead cast of a marble equestrian figure carved by Bernini, who submitted one of the original plans for the Cour Carrée.

Once you get to the head of the queue and step into the Pyramid, pause before walking down the spiral staircase, or taking the shiny cylinder of a lift, to peer down at the marble-faced entrance hall below. Its detractors say that it looks more like the entrance to a métro station than to a major museum, but there is no denying its efficiency as a way of channelling visitors and the views upwards through the Pyramid are not to be missed. Once you are down below, start by picking up a leaflet in French or English from the central information desk. These have clear ground plans explaining how the collections have been divided up into three main 'regions', Richelieu (the north wing), Denon (the south wing) and Sully (the buildings round the Cour Carrée to the east). Each 'region' is then sub-divided, like Paris itself, into numbered 'arrondissements', and a complex system of colour coding will – in theory at any rate – make it easy to find your way around and pick out what you want to see. Until the final transformation is com-pleted some rooms are liable to be shut in rotation, but the big notice boards in the entrance area should list any closures, along with details of guided tours, lectures (the museum now has a well-equipped auditorium), slide shows and special exhibitions.

Now buy a ticket from one of the ticket windows and decide where you want to go first. Escalators take you up to the three regions. In 1990 Oriental and Egyp-tian antiquities, French paintings from the 14th to the 17th centuries and *objets d'art* were all reached via the 'SULLY' escalator, while the rest of the painting collections were in 'DENON', along with sculpture, prints and drawings, and Greek, Roman and Etruscan antiquities. But please do not take this as Gospel: study the leaflets available during your visit.

The Sully area also includes the interesting rooms on the history of the Louvre and the palace's medieval foundations. Ideally, you should start your visit there, but as both the history rooms and the foundations can be visited up to 10 p.m., you may prefer to concentrate first on the art collections, which close at 6 p.m. most of the week. But do please find time to visit them at some point, as they help you to understand how this whole area of Paris has developed over the centuries. I particularly like the ten scale models displayed vertically in glass cases, which illustrate how public buildings (painted blue-grey) have gradually squeezed out ordinary dwellings (painted terracotta) and show the sequence in which the gardens were laid out and the bridges built over the Seine.

The circular area leading into the history rooms, adorned with marble reliefs from the Tuileries Palace by the 16th-century sculptor Jean Goujon, also brings you into the impressive medieval section, first discovered in 1866, rediscovered in 1977 when work was being carried out in the Cour Carrée but not properly ex-cavated until 1984. Here you can walk round what was once the moat surrounding the turreted medieval fortress familiar from the 'October' miniature in the *Très riches heures du Duc de Berry*, and see the bases of the huge central keep, the drawbridge leading to the East Gate, Charles V's Library Tower and various walls and embankments. Good plans with keys in English and French are available. A visit to these awesomely large remains is both an enjoyable history lesson, very popular with children, and a good corrective to the view of the Louvre as purely a museum.

What you choose to visit in the main collections must be decided by your own preferences — to see everything would take weeks. I have no space here to do justice to the wealth of exhibits on display and recommend that you visit the elegant bookshop beneath the Pyramid to buy a guide to all or part of the collections. It also sells copies of some of the best-known exhibits and stylish stationery and other gifts printed with a 'Louvre' motif. Postcards are on sale in the little shop next door and prints can be bought a little way down the corridor.

First-time visitors should know that most people's list of 'musts' is headed by Leonardo's *Mona Lisa*, known in French as *La Joconde* and one of the twelve Italian paintings assembled by François Ier that formed the nucleus of the royal collection. If the crowds round it are too forbidding — it is surprisingly small, and encased in a glass box to protect it from vandals — the Italian section includes five other Leonardos, among them the beautiful *La belle Ferronnière* and the *Virgin of the Rocks*, plus fine examples of Renaissance painting by Titian and Raphael among many others. The large French painting department seems more logical in its new arrangement, with canvases by individual artists mostly grouped together: for instance twenty major works by Poussin can be seen in a single room. The collections end with Delacroix, who painted the ceiling in the glittering Galerie d'Apollon in the *Objets d'art* department, now displaying the French crown jewels; its main decoration is mid-17th-century.

The pride of the sculpture department is Michelangelo's figures of captive slaves from Pope Julius II's tomb, and the *Venus de Milo* and the *Winged Victory* are clear 'musts' in the Greek and Roman antiquities department. Highlights in the Egyptian antiquities section include a large sandstone bust of Amenophis IV and a little *Seated Scribe*; children usually like the Crypt of Osiris, which recreates the atmosphere of an embalmer's workshop. And do try to fit in the Roman sculpture department, started by Napoleon in 1800 when he bought the Borghese Collection: since 1983 it has been displayed in the beautiful ground-floor rooms used by Anne of Austria as her summer residence, decorated with stucco and marble and wonderful painted ceilings and frescoes by the 17th-century Italian artist Romanelli.

If you need some sustenance before, during or after your visit to the Louvre, there are a self-service restaurant and a café leading off the entrance area beneath the Pyramid, and **Le Grand Louvre***, a full-scale restaurant continuing to serve meals after the museum closes. Further restaurants and food shops, plus a 'regional centre' offering specialities from various parts of France, are planned for the **Galerie du Carrousel**, leading from the entrance area beneath the place du Carrousel.

Leave the Louvre via the **Cour Carrée**, where you can admire the newly cleaned decoration by Jean Goujon on the façade designed by Pierre Lescot between the **Pavillon de l'Horloge** and the southern wing. The friezes and allegorical scenes stand out in sharp relief, graceful and full of life, and in the sunlight the whole courtyard takes on a warm honey tone. You are now standing above the medieval foundations, with the keep in the south-west corner.

The gateway in the east wing brings you out to the **rue de l'Amiral-de-Coligny**, from where you get a good view of the colonnade on the east front of the Louvre, one of the masterpieces of French classical architecture. It was designed by Claude Perrault, brother of the fairytale author *par excellence* Charles Perrault – he invented Cinderella and her ugly sisters, as well as being chief buildings assistant to Louis's minister Colbert. Claude was a doctor by profession but a respected amateur architect who also drew up the plans for the Observatoire (Walk 3). Opposite the Louvre is the **church of Saint-Germain-l'Auxerrois**, from whose belfry the signal was given for the Massacre of St Bartholomew in 1572. One of the first victims of this wholesale slaughter of Protestants was the admiral who gave the street its name. The church originally dated from as early as the 6th century, but was burnt down during the Norman invasions and substantially rebuilt from the 12th century onwards for some 400 years, then severely damaged again during rioting in the early 19th century. As a result it has a Romanesque belfry, a Gothic chancel and ambulatory, a Late Gothic porch and some Renaissance details. It is well known for its concert programme and for the elegance of its west front, which looks particularly delicate under floodlighting.

Walk from the church towards the Seine for a good view of the Ile de la Cité and the Left Bank. At night the scene is spectacular: the silhouette of Henri IV on the Pont Neuf illuminated against the background of the Panthéon, the Institut de France dome opposite gleaming brightly and the Eiffel Tower in the distance to the right. In the daytime, I recommend a pause for tea or coffee and cakes at **Cador**, a tea room on the corner of the **rue des Prêtres-Saint-Germain-l'Auxerrois**, which has some of the most delicious *pâtisseries* in Paris plus a pretty listed interior of pinky-brown marble. Now walk back past the church to the rue de Rivoli (Ⓜ Louvre) and cross over, then turn left to walk past a statue of the unfortunate admiral and beyond it, at the end of the first set of arcades, to the **Louvre des Antiquaires**, an expensive antiques emporium on several floors, with a restaurant and bar in the same building; art and/or history exhibitions are often held here.

One side of it faces on to the **place du Palais-Royal** (Ⓜ Palais-Royal), which you should cross diagonally to reach the **place Colette**. On the corner with the rue Saint-Honoré the narrow **Café de Nemours** is as busy today as it was in the 18th century, seeming more like an Italian coffee house than a Parisian café. Before walking through the archway into the Palais Royal courtyard and gardens, continue round the place Colette to the entrance to the Théâtre français in the **place André-Malraux**.

Better known as the **Comédie française**, it is one of the world's most famous theatres, specialising in the great 17th-century dramatists Corneille, Racine and Molière, but increasingly widening its repertoire to include many contemporary plays. In the foyer you can study the programme for the week (though it is shut for part of the summer) and perhaps buy some tickets for a performance. Many of the seats are regularly booked by season-ticket holders so it is not always easy, and it's no good trying to plan ahead, as booking starts only a week in advance, in person at the theatre. But if you are at all interested in the theatre, do persist, bearing in mind Lord Chesterfield's comment to his son: 'The tragedies of Corneille and Racine, well attended to, are admirable lessons, both for the heart and the head. There is not, nor ever was, any theatre comparable to the French.' And quite apart from the generally high standard of acting and staging these days – the uncomfortably declamatory style that used to be favoured until recently has now all but vanished – the theatre has many historical associations.

It was founded in 1680 by royal command of Louis XIV, who ordered a merger between two troupes of actors, one of them headed by Molière until his death a few years earlier. (The theatre is still often referred to as 'La Maison de Molière'.) They performed in various playhouses on the Left Bank, then for a while in the Tuileries, before moving into the theatre built alongside the Palais Royal. In one corner of the mirror-lined gallery on the first floor, you can see the high-backed chair in which Molière collapsed on stage during the fourth performance of his play Le Malade imaginaire in 1673, dying shortly afterwards.

As you leave the theatre, turn right to admire the view up the **avenue de l'Opéra** to the huge opera house (see next walk). On the far side of the *place*, in the rue Saint-Honoré, the **Moroccan Tourist Office** has taken over the famous **Café de la Régence**, which moved there in 1854 from its previous premises in the place du Palais-Royal, where Napoleon played chess and Voltaire and Diderot and Rousseau congregated to talk philosophy, drink coffee, and again play chess, later followed by Alfred de Musset, Baudelaire and all the capital's literary luminaries. Now walk back to the place Colette and turn left into the *cour d'honneur* of the **Palais Royal**.

The palace was not originally royal but was the private residence of Cardinal Richelieu, chief minister to Louis XIII, who left it to the king in his will. But Louis himself died a few months later and his widow Anne of Austria moved in with the new boy king Louis XIV. It remained in the hands of the royal family, mainly the Orléans branch, one of whom, nicknamed 'Philippe Egalité' for his democratic views, commissioned the elegant terraced houses round the gardens behind the palace. He had them built as a speculation, and let out the ground floors as shops, cafés and restaurants. The Palais Royal soon became a fashionable place to shop and stroll and by the end of the 18th century most of the city's best-known restaurants had opened here – the Café des Mille Colonnes, of whose very beautiful *patronne* Sir Walter Scott was an ardent admirer, and the Café de Foy on the **Galerie de Montpensier** on the west side, the Grand Véfour, Véry and the Trois Frères Provençaux on the **Galerie de Beaujolais** at the far end, and the Café Février and Beauvilliers on the **Galerie de Valois** on the east side. The whole Palais Royal area was for decades both a mecca for high society and, before and during the Revolution, a meeting place for political activists. The impetus for the storming of the Bastille is said to have been given by a fiery speech from Camille Desmoulins standing on one of the café chairs. It also became a centre for low as well as high life, with prostitutes touting for business beneath the arcades and gambling dens seemingly in every other building.

Little of this activity can be sensed now as you stroll in the peaceful gravelly garden beneath the trees, where local residents sit and chat in fine weather and children play round the ornamental pool and fountain. The palace has become the home of the Council of State and is not open to the public, but you can wander in the main courtyard and decide whether you are shocked or stimulated by '**Les Colonnes de Buren**', a series of rows of black-and-white-striped columns of differing heights by the contemporary sculptor Daniel Buren, commissioned by the arts minister, whose headquarters are in the rue de Valois wing of the palace. They aroused a lot of fury among Parisians, many of whom thought them quite unsuitable in this setting, but the rhythm they set up is undoubtedly interesting, and they can look positively beautiful at night, when tiny rows of lights pick out the main lines.

Of all the famous restaurants grouped round the gardens, only the **Grand Véfour*** has survived, its 18th-century décor of gilded mirrors and carved panelling and painted silk wall coverings still intact and officially listed as a 'historic monument'. It is very expensive (though the lunchtime *menu* is more affordable) but worth considering for a special meal, not least because its beautiful décor and perfect setting are matched by its historical and literary associations. Colette, who lived almost next door at 9 rue de Beaujolais, with windows overlooking the gardens, and Jean Cocteau, another Palais Royal resident, were regulars, and in previous centuries it had been a meeting place for Paris's literati: it was here that the Romantics dined after the celebrated 'battle' with the Classicists over Victor Hugo's play *Hernani* at the Comédie française. But there are several other adequate restaurants beneath the arcades, and in fine weather lunch or dinner beneath a parasol overlooking the fountain at **La Gaudriole*** or **Muscade*** is a delight.

The shops in the arcades are not as busy as in the days when a young woman from Normandy called Charlotte Corday came here to buy the knife with which she killed Marat. But they are still popular with collectors — stamps and medals, dolls and musical boxes are the stock in trade of many of those in the left-hand gallery, while on the right you'll find a good bookshop, the **Librairie de Valois**, an engraver's, **Guillaumot**, dating back to 1784, antique shops and several art galleries, including one with a little room devoted to Colette, a charming spot with photographs and vases of flowers and pretty furniture. Her Palais Royal flat is to be reconstructed as part of the new Colette Museum due to open at her birthplace, Saint-Sauveur-en-Puisaye in Burgundy. You may even feel inspired to join the Association Arcade Colette and make a donation to help the embryo museum on its way.

Leave the gardens by the **Peristyle de Beaujolais**, turn left and walk along the **rue de Beaujolais**. On the right-hand side is the pretty façade, adorned with cherubs and window boxes, of the **Mercure Galant** restaurant*. Also here is **Willi's Wine Bar**, a British-run establishment popular with Parisian yuppies. At the far end, opposite the elaborate façade of the **Théâtre du Palais-Royal**, a plush-and-gilt theatre built, like the Comédie française, by Philippe Egalité, you can cut through to the **rue de Richelieu** (climb the steps beside 47 rue de Montpensier).

Turn left, and walk past no. 50, where Madame de Pompadour lived when she was plain Antoinette Poisson, and no. 40, where Molière died at home shortly after his collapse on stage that February night 300-odd years ago, to admire the

Fontaine Molière, set diagonally across the junction with the **rue Molière**. The fountain was designed by the 19th-century sculptor Louis Visconti, who also built Napoleon's Tomb and the Four Seasons Fountain in the Faubourg Saint-Germain (Walk 4), and has sculptures by James Pradier. **Au Bec Fin**, a few steps away in the **rue Thérèse**, is a long-standing café-theatre which often puts on interesting performances and can usually be relied on to supply a reasonable dinner before, after or between the shows.

Now walk down the rue Molière, across the avenue de l'Opéra and along the rue de l'Echelle. Turn right into the rue Saint-Honoré and walk to the **church of Saint-Roch**, whose foundation stone was laid by Louis XIV in 1653. Much of the later building was funded by the ubiquitous John Law (Walk 8), who had just been converted to Catholicism. Here you can pay homage to another major *Grand Siècle* playwright, Pierre Corneille, who lived nearby and was buried in the church, and to that great gardener André Le Nôtre, whose tomb has a bust by Coysevox. The church, with three organs, is well known for its concerts, and you might like to plan to round off your walk by attending one of them. If a meal seems the most pressing requirement, you can have a snack at **Eden Tartes**, at 21 rue Saint-Roch, or a full-scale meal at one of the restaurants in the **place du Marché-Saint-Honoré**, the last stopping point on this walk. Reach it by continuing a little way along the rue Saint-Honoré, then turning right into the **rue du Marché-Saint-Honoré**, where at no. 10 **Le Rubis*** is another popular wine bar.

The square was the site of the famous Jacobins monastery that gave its name to the political club that used to meet in the library under the leadership of Robespierre and was to play an important part in the Revolution. In 1794 the '9 Thermidor' revolt that overthrew Robespierre led to the monastery being turned into a market and in 1806 the building was pulled down. The centre of the square is now filled with an ugly building of flats, a garage, and a covered market, the **Marché-Saint-Honoré**. Plans have been announced for it to be replaced with a more attractive structure surrounded by a pedestrian precinct, which will make dining at one of the open-air terraces, **L'Absinthe***, say, or **Le Bistrot d'H** or **La Grille Saint-Honoré***, even more pleasant. But this part of Paris has a good choice of restaurants, and is also within easy reach of the Left Bank, if you prefer to dine across the river in Saint-Germain-des-Prés, and of Les Halles.

Hotels and Restaurants

For general advice on choosing where to stay and where to eat, see Practical Information; prices are moderate unless otherwise stated.

Hotels

Duminy-Vendôme 3–5 rue du Mont-Thabor, 1er (42-60-32-80). Room prices vary greatly in this pleasant and comfortable hotel in a quiet street near the Tuileries Gardens, so check carefully before booking.

Family 35 rue Cambon, 1er (42-61-54-84). This small and good-value hotel near the place de la Concorde, once a private mansion lived in by Louis XVI's finance minister, really is family run and is understandably popular, so you must book early.

Montana-Tuileries 12 rue Saint-Roch, 1er (42-60-35-10). Just off the rue Saint-Honoré, pleasantly small and very comfortable; fairly expensive.

Place du Louvre 21 rue des Prêtres-Saint-Germain-l'Auxerrois, 1er (42-33-78-68). Fairly expensive but very well situated opposite the church of Saint-Germain-l'Auxerrois, a few minutes' walk from the Louvre, from the Pont Neuf (leading to the Ile de la Cité and the Left Bank) and from Les Halles and the Beaubourg Centre. Rooms (some on two floors) have been entirely refurbished, with mostly modern furnishings, and there's a vaulted cellar for romantic breakfasts.

Royal Saint-Honoré 13 rue d'Alger, 1er (42-60-32-79). Some rooms are expensive (the nicest have their own balcony), but this is a convenient place to be, the décor is attractive and you may find it handy to have a restaurant on the premises (though it is closed at weekends).

Tuileries 10 rue Saint-Hyacinthe, 1er (42-61-04-17). Small hotel in an 18th-century building in a quiet street near the Marché-Saint-Honoré with its pleasant restaurants; well-modernised, with air conditioning.

Restaurants

L'Absinthe 24 pl du Marché-Saint-Honoré, 1er (42-60-02-45); closed Sat and Sun for lunch. Attractive dining room adorned with art nouveau bits and bobs and plenty of pictures, friendly service and lively clientele make this a pleasant spot for dinner or for an open-air lunch. Fairly expensive.

Angélina See box in Food and Drink.

Armand au Palais Royal 2 rue de Beaujolais, 1er (42-60-05-11); closed Sat for lunch and Sun. Once the Palais Royal stables, now an elegant restaurant with views of the palace arcades. Excellent-value lunch *menu*, otherwise expensive; specialises in modern (which means deliciously light) variants on classical cuisine dishes.

La Ferme des Mathurins 17 rue Vignon, 8e (42-66-46-39); closed Sun. Small restaurant near the Madeleine offering moderately priced home-style cooking, excellent value, pleasantly French atmosphere.

La Ferme Saint-Hubert 21 rue Vignon, 8e (47-42-79-20); closed Sun and for dinner on Mon, Tue and Wed. Attached to what many insist is the finest cheese shop in Paris, and naturally enough specialising in cheese dishes, hot and cold.

La Gaudriole 30 rue Montpensier, 1er (42-97-55-49); closed Sun for dinner. The main attraction here is the view of the Palais Royal Gardens and the breath of air provided by the fountain on hot summer days when you can eat outside. The cuisine is based on filling dishes from the south-west.

Le Grand Louvre Beneath the Pyramid entrance to the Louvre Museum (40-20-53-41); closed Tue. Run by well-known restaurateur from south-west France; reasonably priced *menus*, plus salads with a glass of wine throughout the afternoon.

Le Grand Véfour 17 rue de Beaujolais, 1er (42-96-56-27); closed Sat for lunch, Sun and Aug. One of the best-known restaurants in Paris, ideally set at the far end of the Palais Royal

Gardens, becomes affordable at lunchtime if you stick to the remarkable-value *menu*. It started life towards the end of the 18th century, became very fashionable in the 19th (Napoleon was a regular), then declined, but was revived in the fifties under Raymond Oliver, one of the first of the superstar chefs who travelled the world promoting French cuisine. He recently sold it to the Taittinger champagne family who have beautifully restored the original décor.

La Grille Saint-Honoré 15 pl du Marché-Saint-Honoré, 1er (42-61-00-93); closed Sun, Mon for lunch and most of Aug. Good classical cuisine restaurant with a regular clientele.

Lescure 7 rue de Mondovi, 1er (42-60-18-91); closed Sat for dinner, Sun and Aug. Tucked away behind the place de la Concorde in a quiet street, with surprisingly reasonable prices for this expensive area, which explains why it is always busy. Traditional dishes and friendly service. A few tables outside in summer.

Le Mercure Galant 15 rue des Petits-Champs, 1er (42-97-53-85); closed Sat for lunch and Sun. The best time for this pretty restaurant, in a quiet street behind the Palais Royal gardens, is the evening, when you can enjoy its discreet elegance without spending a fortune: it is one of the few restaurants in the area that offers a reasonably priced dinner *menu*.

Muscade 36 rue de Montpensier and 67 Galerie de Montpensier, 1er (42-97-51-36). Over-priced but attractive, with a sought-after terrace in the Palais Royal gardens; also a tea room.

Poquelin 17 rue Molière, 1er (42-96-22-19); closed Sat for lunch, Sun, part of Aug and part of Sept. Jean-Baptiste Poquelin was Molière's real name, so this pleasant restaurant a few steps away from the great man's statue-fountain is a good place to pay homage to him after admiring the Comédie française. The *menu* is good value too.

Ruc'Univers 159 rue Saint-Honoré, 1er (42-60-31-57); closed Aug. Busy brasserie close to the Louvre and the Comédie française, popular for late suppers; good seafood.

Le Soufflé 36 rue du Mont-Thabor, 1er (42-60-27-19); closed Sun. As you would expect, the star dishes here are soufflés, both savoury and sweet. There are usually more foreign tourists than French people, but it's a useful place to know about for a fairly quick and reasonably priced meal in this expensive area behind the Tuileries Gardens.

Museums and Places of Interest

Jeu de Paume Tuileries Gardens, pl de la Concorde, 8e. Closed for renovation at time of writing; due to be used for temporary exhibitions. Ⓜ Concorde

Orangerie Tuileries Gardens, pl de la Concorde, 8e. Closed Tue. Ⓜ Concorde

Musée des Arts Décoratifs (applied arts) 107 rue de Rivoli, 1er. Closed Mon, Tue; open from 12.30 p.m. only (from 11 a.m. Sun). Ⓜ Palais-Royal, Tuileries

Musée des Arts de la Mode (fashion arts) 109–11 rue de Rivoli, 1er. Closed Mon, Tue; open from 12.30 p.m. only (from 11 a.m. Sun). Ⓜ Palais-Royal, Tuileries

Palais du Louvre Entrance to all collections through the Pyramid in the Cour Napoléon, 1er. Closed Tue, late opening Mon and Wed. The permanent 'History of the Louvre' exhibition, the excavated medieval sections, the bookshop and the temporary exhibitions are open till 10 p.m. but all except the bookshop and the temporary exhibitions do not open till midday. Cassettes in English can be hired. Ⓜ Palais-Royal

Walk 7
The Opéra and the Grands Boulevards

Starting point: place de l'Opéra, 9e, in front of the opera house; Ⓜ Opéra, Ⓡ Auber. This Right Bank walk roughly follows the string of boulevards running eastwards from the Opéra to the place de la République, covering parts of the second, ninth and tenth *arrondissements*, plus a little of the third.

To enjoy this walk to the full a little effort of the imagination is required. The broad boulevards running eastwards from the Opéra are noisy and thronged with people and traffic, and they get progressively seedier as they reach into the working-class eastern districts. But they have played an important part in the history of Paris, and especially its entertainment, and they still exercise a powerful attraction for Parisians, who smile nostalgically when they hear Yves Montand singing: '*J'aime flâner sur les grands boulevards*', even if they rarely venture there themselves. And although much of the area is now given over to fast-food outfits, cinemas, seedy bars and discos, plus the occasional sex shop, the memory of the legendary actors and actresses who once drew huge crowds to the famous theatres lining the boulevards is still green – *théâtre du boulevard* is the term used today for variety and undemanding light-entertainment plays. And the reputation of the fashionable cafés with their cosmopolitan clientele – the Café Tortoni, Frascati, the Café Riche and the Café Anglais – still lingers on, long after they have disappeared for ever.

The streets on either side of the boulevards are well worth exploring. Very busy and often choked with traffic on weekdays, they are almost uncannily quiet at weekends and in the evenings, and in high summer, when many of the small businesses that flourish there – mainly connected with the rag trade to the south, with the antique and collectors' trades to the north – close down for a month or so. This is an area where you must keep looking upwards: above many a faceless ground floor, disfigured by ugly shop fronts, you will spot fine architectural details, elegant balconies, medallions and garlands, swathes of fruit and cornucopias carved in stone. And as so often in Paris, peering through doorways can be rewarding – an elegant, mirror-lined passage leading to a colonnaded courtyard there, a villagey house decorated with fretwork and overgrown with creeper there. The last part of the walk takes you into more affluent territory round the Bourse (stock exchange) and the Bibliothèque Nationale (national library), which is in the throes of a major upheaval as plans are finalised for a new library in eastern Paris.

Before you set out, a word on how the boulevards appeared. They can be said to have originated in 1660, when Louis XIV decided that the ring of ramparts put up three centuries earlier by Charles V and later extended westwards (see History) was no longer necessary and had it demolished. The defensive ditches on either side were filled in and the wide strip of land that resulted was turned into a ring of broad roads, planted with trees and adorned with triumphal arches instead of the old gateways in the fortifications. With memories of the original function still fresh in people's minds, it became known as 'the *boulevard*', a military term meaning bulwark or rampart. By the middle of the next century the Parisians had adopted their new road as a place to take the air and it became increasingly fashionable, especially at the western end, where smart hotels and private mansions, restaurants and shops started to spring up. At the other end it was more like a fairground, with open-air entertainers of all kinds, later accompanied by permanent theatres, delighting the inhabitants of the more popular eastern districts. *Boulevardier* became a synonym for 'man-about-town' in the 19th century, when the '*Grands Boulevards*' as they were now known, were one of the centres of European fashion. Their decline did not set in till the First World War and although they are no longer fashionable, they are still one of Paris's main entertainment districts, busy until late at night.

The walk starts at the **Opéra**, the magnificently opulent 19th-century opera house designed by Charles Garnier, then a completely unknown architect whose plans won him a competition organised by the arts minister in 1860. The green-tinted domed roof and elaborately decorated façade look best against the backdrop of a bright blue sky or lit up at night. Then, as the glittering building draws your gaze away from the traffic swirling round the square's central island, Haussmann's scheme to emphasise this symbol of Paris as the cultural centre of Europe by creating wide avenues leading up to the **place de l'Opéra** comes into its own.

The full launch of the new 'people's opera house' at the Bastille in eastern Paris is expected eventually to lead to the Palais Garnier, to give the Opéra its official name, staging mostly ballet — or at least that's the theory. But if precedent is anything to go by, this strategy may well change over the years. At the time of writing it is still staging grand opera, with seat prices very high, as well as housing the national ballet company. You can enjoy the building without spending time and money acquiring tickets by visiting the little **Opera Museum**, which also entitles you to climb up the elaborate staircase in the foyer, built from various shades of marble, stroll in the splendid gallery running along the main façade and view the ceiling that Chagall painted over the tiered auditorium in the sixties. The ceiling doesn't really go with the red plush and gilt and chandeliers of the rest of the decoration, but is still very pretty. The auditorium seems oddly small — almost cosy — inside that vast building.

The main façade is raised above the place de l'Opéra by steps running the whole width of the building. A series of pillared arcades are adorned with groups of sculptures. The best known of these, Carpeaux's *La Danse* (which so shocked a Second Empire worthy that he threw a bottle of ink at it), is a copy, as the weather-beaten original, carefully restored, is now on display in the sculpture gallery in the Musée d'Orsay (Walk 4). The theatrical effect is enhanced as you walk round the building by the large lamps held aloft by caryatid-like figures. On the western side of the square the **Café de la Paix**, an elegant vantage point traditionally frequented more by wealthy foreigners than Parisians, is a good but expensive restaurant as well as a café. It opened in 1863 and the decoration in the dining rooms was designed by Charles Garnier himself, to put opera-goers in the right mood before they walked across the road to attend a performance.

The Grands Boulevards run to your left and right as you face the Opéra, while behind you the **avenue de l'Opéra** sweeps down to the Comédie française and the Louvre (Walk 6). Before exploring the boulevards, walk via the **rue Scribe** to the left of the opera house, or the **rue Halévy** and the **rue Gluck** on the right-hand side, to the busy department stores on the **boulevard Haussmann**. **Au Printemps** and **Galeries Lafayette**, the best known of Paris's *grands magasins*, were built in 1864 and 1894 respectively and still exude the confidence of the age when commerce was king, though their superb central staircases have sadly been demolished. They seem fairly similar nowadays, with the emphasis on fashion — men's, women's and children's — accessories and cosmetics. The current formula on the fashion floors consists mainly of a series of franchises — shops within shops — for the main ready-to-wear fashion houses. Both have large bookshops, toy departments, hairdressers, travel agents and restaurants. They operate well-organised systems if you want to take advantage of the duty-free shopping available to non-residents, and lay on fashion parades, British weeks, Italian fortnights and the like. On the other side of the boulevard are **C & A** and **Marks & Spencer** (a haven for expatriates as well as tea- and scone-loving French Anglophiles) and beyond this little nucleus of 'big stores' is a large shopping area ranging from the upmarket shops in the rue Tronchet behind the Madeleine (Walk 6) to the much cheaper boutiques in the **rue du Havre** leading to the **Gare Saint-Lazare** (the station for various suburban lines, for mainline trains to Normandy and for the boat train linking with the Dieppe–Newhaven Channel crossing) and the streets east of 'Les Galeries', as Galeries Lafayette is generally known.

From Au Printemps, cross over the boulevard and walk down the rue Auber, then turn right into the rue Boudreau and left for a stroll via the **square de l'Opéra-Louis-Jouvet** and the arcaded place Edouard VII (named after the former Prince of Wales, a very popular figure in France) to the **boulevard des Capucines**. In this haven of peace, remote from the bustle of the boulevards, are two theatres, the **Athénée-Louis Jouvet** and the **Edouard VII**, and **Le Square***, a lively restaurant popular with a theatrical crowd. To your right once you reach the boulevard, on the corner of the **rue Caumartin**, is the famous **Olympia music hall**, which once echoed to the powerful voice of Edith Piaf, a frail little figure in black, dwarfed by the huge stage. It is still a sign that a popular singer has arrived if he or she tops the bill at the Olympia, which started life in 1889 as 'Les Montagnes Russes' (the French for switchback or roller-coaster).

161

Turn left along the boulevard towards the place de l'Opéra and pause at **no. 14**, another landmark in the history of entertainment: it was in the basement of this building that the Lumière brothers staged, in 1895, the first public showing of what proved to be the forerunner of the modern cinema. On the other side of the boulevard the garish **rue Daunou** is famous as the home of **Harry's Bar**, haunted by Hemingway and still a landmark for visiting and expatriate Americans. A little further along on the same site, at no. 25, the Musée Cognacq-Jay, filled with beautiful 18th-century *objets d'art* and paintings, closed at the end of 1988. It will eventually be transferred to the Hôtel Donon in the Marais (Walk 9).

When you reach the place de l'Opéra you may like to spend a few moments window-shopping in the **rue de la Paix**, lined with expensive jewellers' (Cartier *et al*) and leading to the place Vendôme (Walk 6). The **avenue de l'Opéra**, once ultra-fashionable, is now rather dull – travel agents and airline offices outnumber the shops, though at no. 37 **Brentano's** is a well-known English-language bookshop dating back to 1895. Make your way round the square and continue along the boulevard des Capucines. Beyond the rue de la Chaussée-d'Antin, the **boulevard des Italiens** takes over. The name comes from the Théâtre des Italiens, where a half-Italian and half-French troupe of actors based their performances on the Commedia dell'Arte repertoire in the 18th and early 19th centuries. The theatre was on the site of what is now the Opéra Comique or Salle Favart (see below).

As you walk along the boulevard des Italiens, try to forget the traffic and the nondescript passers-by and imagine that you are back in an age when it was the heart of fashionable Europe, peopled with *Muscadins*, or *Merveilleuses*, or *Dandies*, or whatever the current in term was for the ardent followers of fashion who paraded here, or gossiped in the cafés and restaurants that lined the boulevard. *Tournedos Rossini* was allegedly invented at the Café Anglais at no. 17, whose famous wine cellar was bought by the owner of the Tour d'Argent restaurant in the Latin Quarter (Walk 2) when the building was demolished during the First World War. Equally chic were the Café de Paris at no. 24, the Café Hardy at no. 20 and its neighbour the Café Riche at no. 16. Then there was Tortoni at no. 22, founded by a Neapolitan who employed a waiter called Tortoni; he later became the owner and turned it into the most famous meeting place on the boulevard, remaining fashionable long after Frascati and its terraced gardens (at 23 boulevard Montmartre) had to close. All these legendary places have vanished, but at least the enlightened heads of the **Banque Nationale de Paris** decided to keep the façade of the **Maison Dorée**, which took over from the Café Hardy at no. 20 and is described in glowing terms by Balzac.

Continue along the boulevard on the right-hand side, past the palatial **Crédit Lyonnais** building, whose iron frame was designed by Gustave Eiffel, and the **Café Gramont**, one of the many café-brasseries that is typical of the boulevards today – not at all glamorous, as its illustrious predecessors were, but a useful place for a quick meal, cheerfully and professionally served. The streets behind the north side of the boulevard are a newspaper stronghold (*Le Monde* was until recently in the rue des Italiens) but you should turn off to the right down the rue Marivaux to the **place Boïeldieu** to see the entrance façade, supported by caryatids, of the **Opéra Comique**, as most Parisians still call what is now technically the **Salle**

Favart. It is constantly changing its name, but remains the home of light opera and operetta. The inside is worth visiting, but you'll have to attend a performance (ballet is often staged here in the winter months, if you're not an operetta fan) to see the elaborately decorated walls and ceiling in the upstairs foyer, florid in the late 19th-century manner, but very appealing.

Opposite the entrance is the house into which Alexandre Dumas *père* moved in 1823 and where his son and namesake was born a year later. To the right, a pretty little flower garden has recently been laid out. Walk past it along the **rue Saint-Marc**. (Ⓜ Richelieu-Drouot)

At no. 32 **Les Lyonnais** was once a cabbies' rest but in the fifties became a restaurant famous for its *lyonnaise* cuisine. Walk a few steps to the right down the **rue Richelieu** to see the **Fontaine Saint-Marc** in front of a modern block – a dandelion scattering its fluffy seeds on the wind. The **Bistrot du Boursier** opposite will provide an adequate meal at reasonable prices. Continue along the rue Saint-Marc to the **rue Vivienne**. At no. 33 **Au Duc de Praslin** sells pretty tin boxes filled with pralines and other traditional sweets.

Beyond the rue Vivienne, turn off to the left (no. 10) into the **Passage des Panoramas**, one of the most interesting of the glass-roofed shopping arcades that were a feature of this part of Paris in the 19th century (see box). It was opened as early as 1800 by an American engineer, Robert Fulton, who invented the steamship and an early version of the submarine and was soon attracting crowds of

Exploring the *Passages* and *Galeries*

Nineteenth-century Paris was the golden age of the glass-roofed shopping arcade, usually linking two main thoroughfares and adorned with elaborate light fittings, mock-marble pillars and the like. The *passages* or *galeries*, as they are known, came into fashion in about the 1820s and fell virtually into disuse half a century later, when Baron Haussmann's planning schemes changed Paris so dramatically and the new department stores took over something of their role. But they are coming back into their own now that modern pedestrian precincts have created a liking for quiet and traffic-free shopping and window-shopping.

The Grands Boulevards area has the lion's share of the city's most attractive arcades, many of them recently restored and now lined with restaurants and tea rooms, small specialist shops and old-established businesses such as printers'

and engravers', pipe-makers or musical instrument builders. Most of them have wrought-iron gates at either end, which may well be closed at about 8.30 or 9 p.m., and on Sundays and public holidays, though as more restaurants are attracted to them the tendency is to open longer hours.

Among the most interesting to visit are the **Passage des Panoramas** (11 blvd Montmartre, 2e) and, facing it on the other side of the boulevard, the **Passage Jouffroy** leading into the **Passage Verdeau** (see overleaf). The **Passage des Princes** (5 blvd des Italiens) was being restored in 1990. The **Passage du Caire**, in the heart of a rather seedy area, is for aficionados only, but the elegant **Galerie Vivienne** and **Galerie Colbert** beside the Bibliothèque Nationale and the **Galerie Véro-Dodat** close to Les Halles (Walk 8) are all enjoying a new lease of life.

paying customers to the *passage* to see his revolving painted 'panoramas' with views of Paris, Rome, the island of St Helena and so on. Both it and the **Galerie des Variétés** with which it intersects have been restored and are full of delights, with their ochre pillars painted to look like marble and their old shop fronts.

Stern, at no. 47, is a well-known engraver's, dating back to 1840, and at no. 57 the original early 19th-century façade and décor of Marquis, one of France's most famous chocolate makers, has been preserved by the owners of **L'Arbre à Cannelle***, a pretty tea room, all pillars and cinnamon-coloured cushions (*cannelle* means cinnamon) and painted panels and marble patterned floor. This is an excellent spot for a light lunch or a Saturday brunch (closed on Sundays), but the arcade has several other eating places: a couple of cheerful *trattorie* (you'll often hear Italian spoken in this part of Paris), **Croquenote**, where you can spend an evening listening to old French (and other) songs, and **Perry Brothers**, founded in 1870 – in Wales! Its Paris branch, decorated in pale leek green, opened here in 1986. On the same side, **Trompe l'Oeil** sells marble objects and realistic artificial fruit.

Walk out at the far end into the **boulevard Montmartre** (Ⓜ Montmartre) and cross over to the **Passage Jouffroy** right opposite. The arcade is a pleasing jumble of shops, selling everything from oriental kitsch (**Le Palais oriental**) to toys and games. **Pain d'Epices** on the left specialises in pretty children's clothes, friezes, mobiles, with a second shop next door full of attractively wrapped soaps and other decorative gifts. On the right are windows displaying exhibits from the **Musée Grévin**, Paris's famous waxworks, opened in 1882 by a well-known cartoonist; another branch is now open in the Forum des Halles (Walk 8). The entrance to the waxworks, a good place to take children, is on the boulevard itself, right next to the arcade at no. 10.

At the far end of the arcade is the modest but quiet **Hôtel Chopin***. Beside it, steps lead down to the **Galerie des Livres**, with a row of second-hand bookshops and a shop selling cinema posters. Walk through it, cross over the rue Grange-Batelière at the end and continue into a third arcade, the **Passage Verdeau**, which boasts a nice old-fashioned haberdasher's, **Au Bonheur des Dames**, a narrow shop selling old postcards, **Le Ruagué**, a small restaurant, and picturesque old lamps.

Walk back to the rue Grange-Batelière and turn right towards the **rue Drouot** to see the **Nouvel Hôtel Drouot**, a striking modern building opened in 1980 to house the Drouot auction rooms, whose former building, dating back to 1852, was demolished in 1976. After an interlude in the Palais d'Orsay on the Left Bank (Walk 4), the auctioneers returned to their old haunts, filling the streets and the many bars, restaurants and cafés with noise and bustle for much of the year. The new building, faced with grey and off-white marble and surrounded by paving stones in the same colours, offers a stylish variation on the typical 19th-century theme of a tall, purpose-built block, with round porthole-like windows up at the top instead of the traditional *oeil-de-boeuf*. Various pieces of sculpture, plus plants and trees in tubs, adorn the square in front of the main entrance.

The streets round about are full of antique dealers, autograph experts and stamp dealers. Keep an eye open here for decorative flourishes on the upper storeys, and don't miss the art déco detail on the post office in the rue Chauchat. The street also offers a good view up to the wedding-cake silhouette of the **Sacré Coeur** in Montmartre (Walk 10).

North of here lies the **Nouvelle Athènes**, an interesting area that was once a major intellectual centre and still has some fine buildings. It is described at the beginning of Walk 10, but if you prefer you could visit it from here by walking to the top of the rue Drouot and along the rue du Faubourg Montmartre to the **church of Notre-Dame-de-Lorette** (or take the no. 42 bus).

Another side trip that can be made from here is to the **rue de Paradis**, famous as the centre of the high-class glass and china trade and also housing the Musée de la Publicité. If you decide to do this, you can rejoin the boulevards further east and will not have missed any major landmarks. In fact you will have chalked up an extra landmark by passing the famous **Folies-Bergère cabaret**, which you reach by turning east off the rue Drouot into the rue de Provence, which soon becomes the rue Richer. The Folies, where the great Mistinguett once performed, but now rather tawdry, are at no. 32. The continuation of the street, the **rue des Petites-Ecuries** (where the royal stables once stood), brings you close to a well-known brasserie, **Flo***, in the **cour des Petites-Ecuries**, where Ninon de Lenclos, a dazzling blend of *femme de lettres* and leader of fashionable society, had her country house in the 17th century – no doubt entertaining there her many lovers, including the Duc de La Rochefoucauld and the Grand Condé. The rue d'Hauteville or the rue Martel on the left bring you up to the rue de Paradis, with its china and glass showrooms and the **Musée du Cristal** run by the house of Baccarat at no. 30bis (you can also buy pieces here). At no. 18, a warehouse and showroom for a faïence manufacturer has been turned into the **Musée de la Publicité**, originally devoted only to posters but now including other types of advertising material too. The museum is to be moved to the rue de Rivoli (check locally). But the building itself is a museum piece, with its iron and glass frame and beautiful ceramic panels.

If you have made this detour, return to the boulevards via the rue d'Hauteville or the brashly commercial rue du faubourg Saint-Denis (Ⓜ Strasbourg Saint-Denis). Otherwise walk down the rue Drouot (Ⓜ Richelieu-Drouot) and turn left back into the boulevard. Walk past the Musée Grévin, beyond which is the **rue du Faubourg Montmartre**, famous as the home of **Le Palace** (at no. 8), a trendy nightspot popular with a young crowd who flock to its rock evenings. Equally famous is the amazing **Chartier** restaurant* at no. 7. The **boulevard Poissonnière**, which comes next, was called after the fishmongers and fish wholesalers who congregated here on the way to the central market (Walk 8). It has a famous cinema, the suitably majestic **Rex**, and the **Théâtre des Variétés**, while in its sequel, the **boulevard Bonne-Nouvelle**, is the **Théâtre du Gymnase**.

Once again you must shut your eyes to the more glaring manifestations of 20th-century urban living, forget the fast-food outfits and the sleazy cafés with their pintables and juke boxes, and think yourself into the time when the eastern end of the boulevards in general and the drastically truncated boulevard du Temple in particular were a byword for a popular evening out.

The boulevard du Temple was named after the Knights Templar, who had been associated with this part of Paris until the 14th century. By the 18th century it was a tree-lined thoroughfare and was fast becoming Paris's main centre of popular entertainment, lined with stalls selling confectionery and drinks, and booths in which acrobats, mimes, puppet masters, contortionists, fortune tellers and their ilk performed. In 1791 French theatre was freed from state controls and dozens of new theatres sprang up along the eastern boulevards. Many of the city's most famous 19th-century playhouses were here: the Gaîté and the Ambigu-Comique, the Théâtre de la Renaissance and the Théâtre de la Porte Saint-Martin. And the best-loved actors of the time, especially the incomparable Frédérick Lemaître (see box), became a magnet for huge crowds of theatre-goers. When Dumas *père's* new Théâtre Historique opened with a performance of his own play *La Reine Margot*, people queued for two whole days to get seats. And as so many of the theatres specialised in melodramas full of blood and corpses, the boulevard was soon nicknamed the 'Boulevard du Crime' (Crime Boulevard).

Frédérick Lemaître

The undoubted star of the 'Boulevard du Crime' was the larger-than-lifesize actor Frédérick Lemaître, who was immortalised by Pierre Brasseur in Marcel Carné's brilliant film *Les Enfants du Paradis*. Lemaître, who started his stage career on all fours as a pantomime lion, became the idol of a popular audience perched high up in the gods (*le paradis* in French) at the top of the pretty theatres, decorated in a riot of gilt and plush, that lined the Boulevard du Temple.

Born in 1800, he first attracted huge audiences with his ebullient parody of the part of Robert Macaire at the Théâtre de l'Ambigu, in *L'Auberge des Adrets*, a run-of-the-mill melodrama by three gentlemen who were at first horrified by his sending up of the part, but soon gratified by the crowds he drew. Lemaître scored triumph after triumph, in plays such as *La Tour de Nesle*, specially written for him by Alexandre Dumas *fils*, in whose *Kean* (about the great British actor Edmund Kean) he also starred. He soon became known as the 'French Kean', but his best-known nickname was 'the Talma of the Boulevards', a reference to the tragedian François-Joseph Talma (1763–1826), who had been Napoleon's favourite actor. In the words

of Robert Baldick, whose biography of Lemaître is an excellent introduction to this part of Paris, his name 'calls to mind a picture of a theatrical giant rousing Parisian audiences to frenzy with rampageous, volcanic performances that would have crippled a score of lesser men'.

Although he was offered parts at the Comédie française, he remained faithful to the boulevard theatres that had made his name, especially the Théâtre de la Porte Saint-Martin. In return his public never forgot him, and though he died in poverty – largely thanks to his extravagant life style – the whole of Paris, or so it seemed, turned out for his funeral cortège in 1876.

There is a statue of Lemaître in the square named after him at the point where the Canal Saint-Martin re-emerges from the tunnel it enters at the Bastille. You can see it from the canal boats that ply between the quai de l'Arsenal or the Musée d'Orsay and the Bassin de la Villette, or you can make a brief detour from the place de la République at the far end of the boulevards (second turning on the left off the rue du faubourg du Temple, 10e). A third alternative is to enjoy a walk beside the canal after a pilgrimage to the Hôtel du Nord (see below).

Most of the Boulevard du Crime abruptly vanished during Haussmann's demolitions, but there are still a number of theatres in the surrounding streets. The Renaissance and the Porte Saint-Martin are still there, in the boulevard Saint-Martin. Both were virtually destroyed during the Commune, but were later rebuilt. The Renaissance was presided over in the 1890s by Sarah Bernhardt, who commissioned Alphonse Mucha to produce the superb posters of herself in leading roles that are collectors' items today – Musset's Lorenzaccio, for instance, or Dumas fils's La Dame aux Camélias. Another legendary actress, Marie Bell, was running the nearby Gymnase when I was a stage-struck student in Paris in the 1960s. I still have a vivid memory of peering down from the crowded gods, imagining I was back in the golden age of the Boulevard du Crime as I watched Marie Bell play Racine's Phèdre as a Scarlet Woman, draped in a tight-fitting crimson robe and with long red fingernails. Madame Bell was following in the tradition of the tragedian Rachel, a frail beauty with huge eyes and a powerful voice, who made her début at the Gymnase before becoming a star of the Comédie française.

Then at the Porte Saint-Martin audiences thrilled to Lemaître and Coquelin the Elder created the eponymous hero of Edmond Rostand's play Cyrano de Bergerac. At the Ambigu (originally in the Boulevard du Temple, later at 2 boulevard Saint-Martin, but knocked down in 1966 to make way for a block of flats), Dumas père's The Three Musketeers was first performed.

Keep all this firmly in mind as you walk along the now rather dull **boulevard Saint-Denis** and **boulevard Saint-Martin**. On your way you pass not one but two huge stone triumphal gateways. The **Porte Saint-Denis** comes first, at the junction with the rue Saint-Denis and the rue du Faubourg Saint-Denis (Ⓜ Strasbourg Saint-Denis). It was first in time too, placed there in 1672 to celebrate Louis XIV's highly successful military campaign on the Rhine. It looks like a small-scale version of the Arc de Triomphe with its huge inscription 'LUDOVICO MAGNO' and a lot of relief decoration depicting episodes from the campaign and allegorical scenes. The **rue Saint-Denis** to your right has been the city's main red light district for centuries and is distinctly sleazy, with prostitutes lolling against virtually every doorway and sex shows in abundance. The boulevards, too, get seedier as you progress eastwards, passing the second triumphal arch, the smaller **Porte Saint-Martin**, built to commemorate the capture of Besançon. It replaced a gateway in Charles V's fortifications, which had been pulled down a couple of decades earlier, in 1650. Its decoration again includes battle scenes and portrays the king as Hercules, oddly wearing a huge wig but otherwise stark naked.

On the other side of the boulevard **Le Louis XIV** is a well-known restaurant but is shut from the end of May to early September. The boulevard now starts climbing upwards, and you soon find yourself above the level of the road. Opposite you are first the **Théâtre de la Renaissance**, then the **Théâtre de la Porte Saint-Martin**, adorned with caryatids and a row of open-mouthed carved heads at the top. At **no. 29** on the right-hand side a plaque tells you that Georges Méliès, the magician (he really was a conjuror at one time) who produced the earliest

Previous page: *The Porte Saint-Denis, built to commemorate Louis XIV's campaign on the Rhine*

trick films, using dissolves and fades before anyone else, was born there in 1861. The inscription endearingly refers to him as 'inventor of countless illusions'.

If you are enough of a cinema enthusiast to be interested in Méliès you must make a short detour before reaching the end of the boulevards. And if you're just a sucker for the picturesque and feel like getting off the beaten track, this is for you too. Cross over the boulevard by the disconcertingly small bust of Brahms, and then walk up the **rue de Lancry**. This unexciting street housed towards the end of the 18th century a pleasure ground called the 'Vauxhall d'Eté' where patrons could amuse themselves with allegedly 'English' entertainments like climbing a greasy pole or jousting or Blackpool-style illuminations. But the object of your pilgrimage comes at the far end, where you reach the **quai de Valmy** running alongside the **Canal Saint-Martin**. Just before you get there, you pass the **Gigot Fin***, a modest little place with its twenties décor intact where you might feel like stopping off for lunch.

But the thirties are the decade to remember here, the golden age of French cinema, when Marcel Carné made the legendary *Hôtel du Nord* with Arletty and Louis Jouvet. For there ahead of you, on the other side of the canal, is the **Hôtel du Nord** immortalised on celluloid – though very nearly vanished in reality, as it was saved from the developers' bulldozers at the eleventh hour by a vigorous campaign by *cinéphiles*. It was to be turned into a cinema museum, but that plan has sadly been abandoned and it has been restored and divided into flats overlooking the footbridge on which one of the most famous scenes in the film took place (actually it was shot in the studio, with a replica – no location shooting in those days).

Walking along beside the canal is very pleasant, meandering over the footbridges, watching the barges and canal boats negotiating the locks and catching glimpses of ordinary working people leading their daily lives far from the tourist centres. Alternatively, you can enjoy all these delights by taking one of the half-day cruises along the canal (Beyond the Centre).

The boulevards end in the vast **place de la République**, a Haussmann creation that once formed part of the Boulevard du Crime. (Ⓜ République) It still houses the barracks the baron built for the troops who were to be on the alert to quell any signs of rioting in the working-class districts stretching to the east. The barracks replaced a 'Diorama', where Jacques Daguerre first showed his daguerrotypes, the precursors of modern photographs. Ironically, considering Haussmann's motives in building it, the square is traditionally a rallying point for trade union and other demonstrations, with the faithful assembling in front of the pompous '**Monument to the Republic**' in the middle, topped by an olive-branch-brandishing female, draped, like her sisters seated well below, in a Grecian-type garment. The bronze reliefs at the bottom depict scenes from the history of the French Republic, starting with the Tennis Court Oath. The demonstrators then march off down one of the wide avenues the baron cut through the potentially rebellious districts surrounding his new square. You should now do the same, taking the **rue de Turbigo** running south-west.

When you come to a fork, take the left-hand branch, the **rue du Temple**, which brings you into the heart of the district once ruled over – a state within a state – by the Knights Templar. (Ⓜ Temple) In 1140, 22 years after the order was founded in Palestine, the Templars came to France and had soon built a large tower in the middle of the land on which they settled outside the walls of Paris. Round it they erected a walled enclosure which housed several thousand people, including the craftsmen and tradesmen whose descendants still people the area today. But Philippe le Bel distrusted their huge power – they were one of the city's major landlords – and suppressed the order in 1307, accusing the Templars of heresy (many of them were subsequently burnt at the stake). Some of their possessions were granted to the Knights Hospitallers of St John of Jerusalem, whose modern French counterparts, the Chevaliers de Malte, still preside over the **church of Sainte-Elisabeth**, which is worth a visit just before you reach the **square du Temple** (the site of the enclosure), for its finely carved biblical scenes in the ambulatory.

The Revolution spelled the end of the luxurious lifestyle enjoyed by the Knights of St John, who were expelled. But the tower had one last role to play in the history of Paris: in 1792 it was selected as a prison for Louis XVI and Marie-Antoinette, their children Madame Royale and the little Dauphin, and the king's sister Madame Elisabeth. The new rooms in the Musée Carnavalet (Walk 9) include a touching reconstruction of the cell where they were held, which seems to draw more visitors than any other exhibit. The king was taken from the Temple to his death on the guillotine, but Marie-Antoinette was moved to the Conciergerie before she followed him to the scaffold (Walk 1). The Dauphin allegedly died in the Temple two years later, in 1795, but rumours persisted that he had somehow been spirited away and the body of another child substituted.

Most of the buildings were demolished in 1805 and a few years later the tower itself was pulled down. The site was used for an open-air second-hand clothes and fabric market, which has survived to today. Most of the clothes are new nowadays, and are sold in the conventional way from stalls inside a turn-of-the-century market building on the far side of the square, but it is still known as the '**Carreau du Temple**' from the days when the goods were laid out on the flagstones (*carreaux* in French). The Carreau is still very popular for cheap clothes and if you are brave enough to haggle – the traditional way of doing business here – you may come away with a bargain. Alternatively, you can have a quiet sit-down in the gardens before setting off along the **rue Réamur**, leading right off the rue du Temple.

Before turning left into the **rue Volta**, don't miss a splendid sight: a huge carved angel with outspread wings covering three storeys of no. 57 rue de Turbigo. The narrow rue Volta boasts what is allegedly the oldest house in Paris, at **no. 3**. It is believed to date from about 1300 and is fairly typical of the period with its half-timbering and what were once shops or workshops on the ground floor, whose shutters would be let down by means of a rope during the daytime to form a counter for displaying wares. The picturesque network of old streets round here has recently become a miniature Chinatown, crammed with restaurants and bars. They are well worth exploring: if you glance into the courtyards you will often see old wooden shutters, virginia creeper and clematis climbing up the walls, a rural little world behind the seedy houses. Turn right into the **rue au Maire** and cross the **rue Beaubourg** and the **rue de Turbigo** to the **rue Cunin-Gridaine**, which runs alongside the **church of Saint-Nicolas-des-Champs**. On this side you can enjoy the sight of a Renaissance doorway, an ancient porch and a tiny garden, with a cloisters feel about it. The church was built in the 15th century, on the site of a much earlier one, and has some interesting paintings.

Turn right out of the church, cross the **rue Réamur** and you come to the **Conservatoire National des Arts et Métiers**, which houses the **Musée National des Techniques**. (Ⓜ Arts-et-Métiers) The complex of buildings includes the former **church of Saint-Martin-des-Champs**, part Romanesque and part Gothic, and the refectory built in the 13th century by the architect of the Sainte-Chapelle, Pierre de Montreuil, now used as a library. The museum is a bit old-fashioned but charming, covering the whole field of craftsmanship and technology, with exhibits ranging from automata (the most famous, La Joueuse de Tympanon, once belonged to Marie-Antoinette) to model trains, early bicycles and cameras and (in the church) the little plane in which Blériot crossed the Channel. The museum is due for refurbishment during the nineties, so there seems to be some hope that it will not be pushed into oblivion by Paris's smart new 'Science City' (Beyond the Centre).

If you are feeling tired or are short of time, you can now travel two métro stops from Ⓜ Arts-et-Métiers to Ⓜ Bourse. But if you do you will miss a brief plunge into a rather seedy but very busy district known as the **Sentier**, which will give you a glimpse of how ordinary people live and work in this overcrowded city. To reach it, walk through the square Chautemps opposite the Conservatoire entrance, cross the **boulevard de Sébastopol**, walk along the **rue du Caire** to the rue Saint-Denis, cross over, and, a few steps to the right, turn left into the **Passage du Caire**, a long and forking shopping arcade given over mainly, like the rest of the district, to the rag trade and its attendant industries. The name of the passage, and of the surrounding streets (rue d'Aboukir, rue du Nil and so on), are a hangover from the Egyptian craze that was launched by Napoleon's victorious campaign in Egypt. At the far end the entrance to the arcade is surmounted by huge pharaohs' or sphinx's heads. The little square in front has been restored and adorned with a piece of modern sculpture. Thronged with people by day, it is peaceful and almost provincial at night and on Sundays, and at the height of summer when most of the shops are shut. (Ⓜ Sentier)

By venturing this far you have come upon the nucleus of narrow streets that once formed the heart of the notorious Cour des Miracles so vividly described by Victor Hugo in Notre-Dame de Paris. In this thieves' lair the blind and lame beggars who haunted the streets of Paris miraculously became whole again as they cast off their crutches and eye patches and handed over the days' takings to the bosses of the underworld. But have no fear, the area was cleaned up by the energetic chief of police in 1667 and is now perfectly safe, peopled by a hard-working petite bourgeoisie and an increasing number of immigrants.

Cross over the **rue des Petits-Carreaux** at the end of the rue du Caire and turn right, then left off the **rue Poissonnière** to the **rue des Jeûneurs**, which unexpectedly becomes winding and almost hilly as it goes down to the **rue du Sentier** and on to the **rue Notre-Dame-des-Victoires**, its rather gloomy buildings filled with a rabbit warren of courtyards at ground level. **Pile ou Face**, opposite the end of the rue des Jeûneurs, is a pleasant little restaurant but rather over-priced, no doubt because it is frequented by stockbrokers and others whose business brings them to the **Bourse** (stock exchange), just a few steps away. The entrance to the Bourse, a classical temple devoted to the god of Money since it was built in the early 19th century, is on the rue Vivienne side, and guided tours of the building can be made. (Ⓜ Bourse)

Now walk southwards down the **rue Vivienne**, turn right into the **rue Colbert** and left into the **rue de Richelieu** to visit the **Bibliothèque Nationale** (entrance at no. 58). The future of this famous copyright library is somewhat in doubt since the announcement in 1989 that the new Bibliothèque de France, to be built beside the Seine beyond the Gare d'Austerlitz, will house all the printed books now in the BN, as it is known to the academic world. The original plan had been to transfer all books published after 1945, and there are some fears that, without any books, the venerable institution will become nothing more than a museum. It was originally based on the royal collections, swelled in this case by those of Cardinal Mazarin, whose magnificent collection of paintings and *objets d'art* was housed in the Hôtel Tubeuf, the core of the present building, which was enlarged by Mansart and known as the Palais Mazarin. (A good view of the courtyard and façade can be seen through the railings in the **rue des Petits-Champs**: turn left from the rue de Richelieu.) You may be able to get a glimpse of the arching vault of the **reading room** from the vestibule, but you can't go in without a reader's pass. You can, however, visit the **Cabinet des Médailles et Antiques**, which has recently been restored and includes cameos and other treasures as well as coins and medals, and, when a special temporary exhibition is taking place, the superb **Galerie Mazarine**.

Recent restoration has also happily revived the splendours of two *galeries* running off the rue des Petits-Champs. The **Galerie Colbert** forms part of the 17th-century Hôtel Colbert on the other side of the rue Vivienne, now an annexe to the BN, and houses two little museums, the **Musée des Arts du Spectacle**, devoted to the theatre, and the **Musée Charles Cros**, whose self-explanatory subtitle is 'the Museum of Sound Reproduction'. It also has a little shop selling cards, books and various objects connected with the BN's collections. The **Galerie Vivienne** is the most beautiful of the city's covered arcades with its mosaic-patterned floor, its semi-circular windows above the shop fronts, its ochre paintwork adorned with flourishes of carved decoration, bathed in the creamy light that pours through the glass roof. It has a bookshop that has been there since it opened in the 1820s, and a tea room punningly called **A Priori-Thé***.

It is only fitting that this walk should end with one last arcade, the tiny **Passage des Pavillons**, which leads from the rue des Petits-Champs to the peaceful **rue de Beaujolais** behind the Palais-Royal gardens. Like so many of its fellows it has a bookshop: this one is called **Bel-Gazou**, the nickname used for her daughter by Colette, who lived and died a few steps away, overlooking the gardens. If you are ready for a meal, you might like to stroll back to the Bourse and the lively

The glass-roofed Galerie Vivienne, built in the 1820s, still has its original bookshop

Vaudeville brasserie* opposite, or eat in the Palais-Royal gardens (Walk 6) or in or around the **place des Victoires**, where the next walk starts.

Hotels and Restaurants

For general advice on choosing where to stay and where to eat, see Practical Information; prices are moderate unless otherwise stated.

Hotels

Chopin 46 passage Jouffroy, 9e (47-70-58-10). Small, modest, but quiet rooms in one of the 19th-century shopping arcades off the boulevard Montmartre (entrance next to the Musée Grévin waxworks, between 10 and 12 in the boulevard). It used to be called the 'Hôtel des Familles' and still has a friendly family atmosphere and low prices.

Corona 8 cité Bergère, 9e (47-70-52-96). Well placed if you want to explore the network of arcades and side streets off the boulevards. Comfortable, attractive rooms, some of them fairly expensive.

Gaillon-Opéra 9 rue Gaillon, 2e (47-42-47-74). Small, pleasant and central, just off the avenue de l'Opéra and within walking distance of most of the sights in the Madeleine, Grands Boulevards and Les Halles areas.

Riboutté-Lafayette 5 rue Riboutté, 9e (47-70-62-36). Slightly off the beaten track but quiet, friendly and quite cheap. The rooms are small but mostly pretty and there are plenty of restaurants nearby, as well as the china shops in the rue de Paradis.

Restaurants

L'Amanguier 110 rue de Richelieu, 2e (42-96-37-79). The first of this successful mini-chain to open and still very pleasant with its garden-style décor (tables outside, too, in fine weather), relaxed atmosphere and good-value *menu*.

L'Arbre à Cannelle See box in Food and Drink.

Chartier 7 rue du fbg Montmartre, 9e. No bookings taken, so get there early to enjoy to the full this amazing Paris institution. It's been going strong for over a hundred years and doesn't seem to have put its prices up for the last couple of decades. Good basic cooking, bustling atmosphere.

Drouant 18 rue Gaillon, 2e (42-65-15-16). If you're of a literary bent you should consider spending an evening in this hallowed spot which started life in 1880 as a wine merchant's and delicatessen, soon turned into an elegant restaurant frequented by well-known authors and has been the setting of the announcement of the famous Prix Goncourt for decades. But unless you're prepared to pay a lot for the privilege, make sure you're in '**le Café'** (previously known as '**le Grill'**), which serves a good *menu*.

Flo 7 cour des Petites-Ecuries, 10e (47-70-13-59). This well-known brasserie dating back well over a century has a real feel of Alsace about it with its wooden panelling, leather-covered seating and stained glass, its sturdy cuisine and its cheerful clientele. In a courtyard leading off the busy rue du fbg Saint-Denis that once housed the royal stables.

Au Gigot Fin 56 rue de Lancry, 10e (42-08-38-81); closed Sat for lunch, Sun and part of Aug. You can soak up a genuinely Parisian atmosphere and enjoy equally genuine unpretentious cuisine (the speciality is of course *gigot* or leg of lamb) when you're making a pilgrimage to the legendary Hôtel du Nord overlooking the Canal Saint-Martin. Modest and inexpensive, with a choice of several *menus*.

Le Grand Café 4 blvd des Capucines, 9e (47-42-75-77). A good place for getting an inkling of what the Grands Boulevards were like in their heyday: a bustling, cheerful and very professionally run brasserie, with elaborate new art nouveau-style décor and excellent seafood, where you can eat round the clock.

Julien 16 rue du fbg Saint-Denis, 10e (47-70-12-06). Original art nouveau décor and fun atmosphere are the main attractions of this lively brasserie, popular with tourists but also with a late-night theatre crowd. Even if you've booked, your table probably won't be ready, but the classic brasserie dishes and the generous seafood platters are worth waiting for, so relax and enjoy the bustle.

Oh! Poivrier! 2 blvd Haussmann, 9e (no telephone bookings). One of a chain of fast-food outlets with-a-difference: stylish hi-tech décor, low prices, good salads and light hot dishes, pretty puddings, colourful cocktails and wine by the glass. Just by the Drouot auction rooms.

Au Petit Riche 25 rue Le Peletier, 9e (47-70-68-68); closed Sun. Attractive original 19th-century décor and layout, with a series of small dining rooms; popular, especially at lunch-time, with auctioneers from the Hôtel Drouot. Traditional cuisine based on specialities from the Touraine (particularly good fish with wine sauces).

Le Square 6 sq de l'Opéra, 9e (47-42-78-50); closed Sat for lunch and Sun. This peaceful backwater close to the bustle of the place de l'Opéra boasts two theatres, so the restaurant attracts a chic theatre crowd in the evenings. Lively and stylish and good for an outdoor meal away from traffic noise and fumes. The 'piano bar' stays open till dawn most nights.

Le Vaudeville 29 rue Vivienne, 2e (42-33-39-31). The thirties décor and trimmings have been well restored in this fashionable brasserie opposite the Bourse. Open year-round and good for *al fresco* eating at weekends or in August when the traffic round the Bourse is stilled. Mixture of typical brasserie dishes and more inventive cuisine.

Museums and Places of Interest

Opéra pl de l'Opéra, 9e. The *Grand Escalier* (main staircase), *Grand Foyer* (foyer), little *museum* and (except when rehearsals are taking place) the theatre itself with its *Chagall ceiling* are open for a few hours every day except Sun. Ⓜ Opéra

Musée Grévin (waxworks) 10 blvd Montmartre, 9e. Open daily (afternoons only in term time). Ⓜ Montmartre

Musée du Cristal 30bis rue de Paradis, 10e. Closed weekends. Ⓜ Château-d'Eau, Gare de l'Est

Musée de la Publicité 18 rue de Paradis, 10e. Closed Tue. Ⓜ Château-d'Eau, Gare de l'Est. Due to move to the rue de Rivoli (check locally)

Musée National des Techniques 270 rue Saint-Martin, 3e. Closed Mon. Ⓜ Arts-et-Métiers

Bourse rue Vivienne, 2e. Visitors' gallery and video presentation open weekday mornings; security is tight (take your passport). Ⓜ Bourse

Bibliothèque Nationale 58 rue de Richelieu, 2e. *Cabinet des Médailles et Antiques* (coins and medals gallery): closed Sun, afternoons only; *Galerie Mazarine*: temporary exhibitions only; *Reading room*: open to ticket-holders only. Ⓜ Bourse

Galerie Colbert Hôtel Colbert, rue des Petits-Champs, 2e. Houses *Musée des Arts du Spectacle* (Theatre Museum) and *Musée Charles-Cros* (sound reproduction) whose opening times change frequently. Ⓜ Bourse

Walk 8
Les Halles, Beaubourg and the Hôtel de Ville

Starting point: place des Victoires, 1er; Ⓜ Bourse. This Right Bank walk covers the eastern half of the first *arrondissement* and the western end of the fourth.

Centuries of history came to an end when the old central food market, known simply as Les Halles, moved out to the suburbs in 1969, and the glass and wrought-iron market buildings were pulled down. Yet the many dire predictions that the loss of the vast and picturesque market – and of the colourful characters working there – would spell death to the whole of this area in the heart of Paris have proved largely unfounded. It is probably just as lively in its new guise, its historic 'Old Paris' flavour superseded by a youthful vitality centred on the Forum, the stylish glass and concrete shopping and leisure centre opened in 1979, the gardens round it that were finally completed a decade later, and the neighbouring place des Innocents. And many of the cafés and restaurants that played such a large part in the life of Paris have not only survived the market's departure, but have experienced a new lease of life – and have been joined by a whole host of interesting new places as it gradually became clear that Les Halles was still very much in business as a local and tourist attraction.

Much of the new vibrancy of the area stemmed from an earlier piece of urban development – the 'Plateau Beaubourg' surrounding the startlingly futuristic (or so it seemed at the time) Georges Pompidou Arts Centre, known to Parisians as Beaubourg, which opened in 1977. To the south of the district, the Hôtel de Ville has been spruced up, the square in front of it sparkling with fountains, but the medieval streets behind the town hall have changed little over the centuries, and make a peaceful end to a walk in which you will often be jostled as you make your way through the crowds who have made this one of the centres of youth culture. Apart from Beaubourg, the home of the National Museum of Modern Art, there is little to be visited, but it is an excellent area for getting a feel of Paris new-style, and for deciding for yourself whether the French have made a success of their solution to the problem of inner-city regeneration.

176

Les Halles — an Anatomical Portrait

Les Halles, the home of Paris's central food market for over 800 years, started life as an open-air market in the early 12th century. Its first *halles* (covered market buildings) date from about 75 years later and it spread rapidly until by the 19th century, when Emile Zola famously christened it 'the belly of Paris', it had become a vast, colourful and chaotic tangle of streets and alleyways badly in need of modernisation, even though the big wine and leather sections had by then been transferred to the Left Bank by Napoleon.

With his usual pioneering fervour, Napoleon III decided to tackle the problem by commissioning from Victor Baltard a series of pavilions in iron and glass, rather similar in structure to the huge railway termini then being built. During the opening ceremony the adjoining Fontaine des Innocents ran with wine and Les Halles embarked on a new and prosperous era. The whole district became a hive of activity round the clock, as it was soon the done thing to finish up a night on the town by heading for one of the hundreds of restaurants and bars fringing the market for a warming onion soup, a plate of pig's trotters or just a glass or two of wine. By this time the market had opened up for the day, so a tradition grew up of a 'democracy' in which well-dressed revellers shared tables and zinc counters with the rough market porters and raucous fishwives.

But just a century later, the endless traffic jams caused by the market, which could anyway no longer cope with the needs of the spreading Greater Paris area, and the stench of the rotting refuse, eventually led to its being transferred lock, stock and barrel to modern buildings out in the suburbs at Rungis near Orly Airport. Two years later, in 1971, the pavilions were pulled down — a decision now seen as vandalism. The chances of reviving the area seemed slim, as controversy raged over what was to be done with the *Trou* (hole) that was left. The cartoonists had a field day and the papers were full of photos of the church of Saint-Eustache marooned above a huge pit, its bottom filled with fetid water, while in the foreground a lonely lifebelt bravely defied would-be suicides. Although a busy underground transport junction was speedily put together (including two of the new express métro lines), the various plans for the site met huge opposition. Futuristic office schemes were abandoned by the incoming President Giscard in favour of an international trade centre. But that too was rejected by the site's new boss, Mayor Chirac, who eventually decreed that it was to be one big, ecologically sound, traffic-free public amenity. The *belly* of Paris, a bold advertising campaign announced, would become instead its *heart*.

At the end of 1988, two decades after the market moved out, the final stage of the transformation of Les Halles was completed. Ten years earlier had seen the opening of the Forum, a multi-storied, glass and concrete shopping and leisure centre curving downwards to a piazza well below ground level. After initial problems it is now very successful, its luxury boutiques booming and its leisure amenities, cultural and sporting, always packed. All round it are well-tended gardens crisscrossed by paths for strollers. Many of the old restaurants are still flourishing and new ones have sprung up, though the area has suffered the inevitable epidemic of fast food, often driving out the chic boutiques and art galleries that opened up in the surrounding streets in the early days. But it would be churlish to deny that visiting this lively area does give you a feeling of being in the heart of things — and that its soul hasn't been quite lost either.

The walk begins north-west of Les Halles, in the **place des Victoires**, an oval square adorned with an equestrian statue of the Sun King by the Monégasque sculptor François Joseph Bosio, who also sculpted the chariot-and-four on the Arc de Triomphe du Carrousel (Walk 6). The original statue on this site was in marble and was commissioned by an ardent admirer of the king, a valiant old soldier with a string of titles, including Duc de La Feuillade, Marshal of France. Determined that his gesture of homage should be seen to full effect, he bought up most of the surrounding houses, then had them demolished and replaced with an elegant square ringed by opulent mansions, in one of which he lived himself, enjoying a fine view of his hero. The statue shared the fate of most of its species during the Revolution – a contemporary engraving shows the mob heaving on ropes to bring it crashing to the ground the day after the fall of the monarchy on 10 August 1792. Napoleon had it replaced by a nude statue of General Desaix, a key figure in his Egyptian campaigns who was killed during the Battle of Marengo. But it caused such mirth among the irreverent Parisians that it was eventually removed. Then during the Restoration Louis XVIII returned his ancestor to his rightful place by commissioning a new statue, and there he rides to this day, looking particularly dramatic from the rue des Petits-Champs to the west of the square.

The square has recently become one of *the* fashion centres of Paris, with a series of chic boutiques (Kenzo, Victoire, Cacharel, Thierry Mugler are the best-known names), and the once dilapidated façades have been cleaned up. The restaurant on the south side, **Le Louis XIV***, specialises in the rather rich cuisine of the Lyon region.

Now make for the north-east corner and walk along the **rue Vide-Gousset**, consisting of only two houses and presumably once a pickpocket's or bandit's paradise (the name means 'pocket-emptier'), to the place des Petits-Pères. On the corner of the square and the rue du Mail, **Chez Georges*** is an old-established restaurant, and on the other side of the road **Le Rubis** is an old-style *bistrot à vin* rather than one of the sleek new breed of wine bars. The **rue du Mail** has some interesting 16th- and 17th-century houses, one of them (no. 12) lived in by Madame Récamier of *salon* fame. The **place des Petits-Pères**, dominated by the **basilica of Notre-Dame-des-Victoires**, seems more Italian or French provincial than Parisian, with its baker's, **Au Panetier**, first opened in 1902, and a sleepy-looking religious bookshop, **La Maison Bleue** (with a façade painted as blue as the name suggests), which also sells rosaries and other ecclesiastical items. The church is famous for the ex-voto crammed on to every available space on its walls – it has been the centre of a Marian pilgrimage for over 150 years – and for its paintings by Van Loo of scenes from the life of St Augustine (the Petits-Pères are Augustinian friars or hermits).

Return to the place des Victoires and walk round it to the **rue Catinat**, which brings you out opposite the imposing gateway of the **Banque de France**. It started life as a private mansion built by François Mansart for a *conseiller d'état* called La Vrillière. He had a fine painting collection, which Bernini visited in 1665, in a beautiful gallery whose walls were decorated with white and gilded stucco and niches displaying busts and statues from classical antiquity. But the whole building was drastically altered in the 19th century. **Au Pied de Biche*** on the corner of the rue de La Vrillière is a pretty restaurant, or if you want only a quick meal, the café-restaurant **La Tourelle**, on the corner with the **rue Croix-des-Petits-Champs**, is always packed at lunchtime with local office workers – a sure sign of value for money. Turn right when you get to it and walk down the rue Croix-des-Petits-Champs, fronted by the long façade of the Banque de France. On the other side are several interesting shops, such as **Chaise-Longue** at no. 30, which sells stylish but reasonably priced items that make good presents – tableware, bits and pieces for the office, well-designed corkscrews, kitchen implements and so on. **Robert Clergerie** at no. 46 is a fashionable shoe shop. The tiny blue and white front of **La Clef du Périgord** is particularly appealing.

The **rue du Colonel-Driant** on the left gives you a good view of the **Bourse du Commerce** on the edge of Les Halles, but I recommend a different approach – walk through the triangular square to no. 2 rue du Bouloi, the entrance to the **Galérie Véro-Dodat**, surmounted by statues nestling in niches. The **Café de l'Epoque** just inside is the sort of place where you can enjoy a quick and good-value meal in a genuinely French ambiance instead of having to opt for a faceless fast-food restaurant.

The arcade is one of my favourites, not only because it is very attractive with its slender fake marble pillars, brass-framed windows and mirrors, mahogany panels, painted ceiling and black and white tiled floor, but because of its historic associations. It was built by two gentlemen, Benoît Véro and François Dodat, who had made their fortune as *charcutiers* and bought the mansion which now sits astride it in 1819. In 1585 it had seen the birth of a baby who was destined to become Louis XIII's minister Richelieu, and half a century later belonged to the father of the infamous Marquise de Brinvilliers (see box, Walk 9). Véro and Dodat developed the whole site and opened up the arcade. It was an immediate success, as its shops – a jeweller's, a perfumier's and a *corsetière* among others – caught all the passing trade from those who used it as a handy short cut from the food market to the Palais Royal. In 1838 the tragedian Rachel lived in a flat above it, in walking distance of the Comédie française where she played so many leading roles. And in January 1855 the poet Gérard de Nerval had a last drink in one of the cafés here before he was found hanged near the Châtelet – probably a suicide, though foul play was suspected in some quarters.

The whole gallery has recently been restored and is ideal for some peaceful window-shopping. You might feel like buying one of the antique dolls displayed in **Capia** – or perhaps a lute from the lute-builder's? You can also eat in the **Restaurant Véro-Dodat**, all lace curtains and marble tables.

At the far end of the arcade, turn left and walk along the **rue Jean-Jacques Rousseau** – he lived here for a few years, at what is now no. 52 – then cross the **rue du Louvre**, a useful place to remember as it houses Paris's only all-night post office, further up on the right. The **Bourse du Commerce** (commodities exchange), a round building dating from 1889, replaced the city's corn exchange, but the site had two centuries earlier been that of the Hôtel de Soissons, a very grand mansion designed by Philibert Delorme and Bullant for Catherine de Médicis. The tall fluted pillar on the south-eastern side of the building, allegedly used as an observatory by the queen's astrologer Cosimo Ruggieri, is all that is left of it. Walk round

179

the colonnaded rue de Viarmes to the left, noticing the many restaurants straight ahead in the **rue Coquillière**, especially the famous **Au Pied de Cochon***, still thriving in spite of the disappearance of its former market clientele. **Le Pavillon Baltard** to your left is a lively brasserie, and on the corner of the rue Jean-Jacques Rousseau and the rue Coquillière **L'Alsace aux Halles** is a place for trying some filling Alsatian cuisine. The **church of Saint-Eustache** gradually comes into view and to your right stretches the new **Jardin des Halles** with, in the distance, the curving shapes of the **Forum**, referred to by the designers as 'Les Chanterelles', the name of the trumpet-shaped fungi that feature on many Parisian menus. For you are now about to discover what has replaced the famous market since the traders moved out in 1969 (see box), no doubt in lorries rather than trundling away their handcarts brimming over with vegetables, as they are depicted in a curious piece of plaster sculpture in their one-time parish church.

Walk into the gardens via the **allée Louis-Aragon** – all the paths criss-crossing them are named after poets. Then turn left across the little bridge towards the **place René-Cassin**, sloping down like an amphitheatre towards the church. Here you can enjoy the rare treat in France of sitting on the grass, tell the time by the modern sun-dial and admire the sculpture by Henri de Miller of a huge listening head propped on a hand. First have a look

The church of Saint-Eustache, seen through the struts of the Forum des Halles shopping and entertainment centre, curving over like trumpet-shaped fungi

into Saint-Eustache through the pane of glass imaginatively filling one wall facing the amphitheatre, then walk round to the left to the entrance in the **rue du Jour**. Opposite the west door, don't miss the charming narrow house with a balcony and garlanded decoration, one of several interesting houses in this street. This is also a boutique centre, with that of the couturier **Agnès B** almost opposite the church, next to the **James Joyce** pub.

The **church of Saint-Eustache** is one of the best known in Paris, with its Gothic ground plan and basic structure adorned with Renaissance decoration. It has certainly been one of the beneficiaries of the redevelopment of the area, as it is much more visible than in the days when it was crowded in by the market which had already been trading there for a good 75 years when the first chapel was built alongside Philippe Auguste's wall in the early 13th century. Most of the present building dates from the 16th and 17th centuries, though the façade was still unfinished in the mid-18th century and was replaced by a neo-classical one. The church was closely involved with the life of its parishioners working in the food market, its cool cellars even used as an overflow for storing fish and vegetables.

Its plan is similar to that of Notre Dame, with a tall nave flanked by double aisles, and the decoration on the vaulting of both the nave and the choir is particularly fine. The stained glass in the choir depicts scenes from the life of St Eustace, whose legend is similar to that of St Hubert — he was allegedly converted to Christianity when, during a hunting expedition, he came across a stag with a shining crucifix perched between its antlers. Its many works of art include Colbert's tomb, in the last chapel on the left-hand side, designed by Le Brun, an early painting by Rubens, *Les Pèlerins d'Emmaus*, in the previous chapel (his *Adoration of the Magi*, in the second chapel in the nave on the same side, is a copy) and Simon Vouet's *Martyre de Saint Eustache* on the tympanum of one of the west doors. The church has been the setting for some key moments in the lives of famous figures — Louis XIV's first communion, the christenings of Richelieu and Molière, whose funeral also took place here (clandestinely — the church frowned on the acting profession in those days), along with those of the poet and fabulist Jean La Fontaine, and the composer Jean-Philippe Rameau. Organ concerts have been held here for many years and the church has a long musical history which includes the first performance of Berlioz's *Te Deum*, in 1855.

The square behind the east end of the church, known as the **pointe Saint-Eustache**, where the rues Montmartre and Montorgueil meet the rue Rambuteau, has various cafés-brasseries that make a pleasant spot for sitting over a drink or a light lunch. **L'Esplanade**, for instance, has good salads. Then walk up the **rue Montorgueil**, once the centre of Paris's oyster trade with its own oyster park, and still a busy market street crammed with wholesale butchers and dairies and fishmongers and greengrocers. Along with the cafés and bars where their owners rest from their labours, they give you something of the flavour of the old Halles, especially very early in the morning. Above some of the shops you can spot pretty balconies and carved details (on no. 17, for instance) and on the right at no. 38 a large gilded snail perched above traditional dark-green shutters tells you that you're approaching **L'Escargot Montorgueil***, a well-known restaurant that dates back to 1832. Turn right into the rue Etienne-Marcel and walk to no. 20 for a look at the **Tour de Jean-sans-Peur**, in the courtyard of a school; it was built in the very early 15th century. Then walk a few steps up the rue Française to the **rue Tiquetonne** for another glimpse of the layout of medieval Paris – the street dates back to 1360 and still has a few houses with old beams. Don't miss the tree carved on no. 10. Return via the rue Marie-Stuart to the rue Montorgueil. (Ⓜ Etienne-Marcel)

At no. 51 on the left, you must pay a visit to the **Pâtisserie Stohrer**, one of the oldest in Paris. It was opened in 1730 by a Polish pastry cook who had followed Marie Leszczyńska to Versailles when she married Louis XV five years earlier. It still sells some 18th-century specialities, including the romantically named *Puits d'amour*, or 'Well of Love', a well-shaped pastry case filled with caramel-flavoured *crème pâtissière*. A tray of these delicacies is held aloft by La Renommée (Fame), a semi-nude lady in a flowing transparent garment, in one of the 19th-century wall paintings adorning the interior by Paul Baudry, who decorated the Grand Foyer in the Opéra. The pretty glass ceiling is over a century earlier, dating from the opening of the shop.

Walk past the **rue Saint-Sauveur**, another street offering glimpses of 'le Vieux Paris', at which point the rue Montorgueil changes its name and becomes the **rue des Petits-Carreaux**. At no. 10 on the right is another interesting shop, **Rödel**, a tea and coffee-merchant's subtitled 'Au Planteur'. The pretty shopfront is decorated with a scene in which a colonial gentleman in a cream three-piece suit and a broad-brimmed straw hat, smoking a long-handled pipe, is being served a steaming cup of coffee by a Negro servant in striped Bermuda shorts. The scene takes place against a background of tropical vegetation and a sign tells you that the shop has been 'specialising in quality coffees since 1845' – though sadly the inside has been stripped of its original décor and now sports faceless fifties design.

When you reach the rue Réamur a large green arch proudly marks the entrance to the 'Marché Montorgueil'. From here you can cross over, turn right into the rue du Nil and visit the **site of the 'Cour des Miracles'**, the notorious thieves' den, and the **Passage du Caire**, if you had to leave them out of the previous walk, then return to the rue Réamur via the rue Saint-Denis. Otherwise you should simply walk along the rue Réamur to the right as far as the rue Saint-Denis. On the corner, keep an eye open for the façade of **nos 61–3 rue Rambuteau**, a riot of medallions and mosaic insets and signs of the Zodiac, plus a clock. (Ⓜ Réamur-Sébastopol)

The **rue Saint-Denis** is sleazy, but it gives you some interesting glimpses of the secret life of Paris being played out behind the street façades. As you glance through open doorways you see what appear to be whole streets in miniature, plunging deep into courtyard upon courtyard, like the set for some creepy thriller (nos 177 and 191/3 are good examples on the right-hand side as you walk down the street). Return to the rue Montorgueil via one or more of the warren of old streets to your right, perhaps the **rue Saint-Sauveur** and the **rue Dussoubs** (Goldoni died at no. 21 at the great age of 86, in 1793). The **Passage du Grand-Cerf**, with decorative ironwork and old shopfronts, was being restored in 1990 but may be open again by the time you read this. Then return via the rue Montorgueil to the Pointe Saint-Eustache. (Ⓜ Etienne-Marcel, Halles)

Now walk back into the Jardin des Halles via the **Porte Saint-Eustache** and spend a little while strolling along the paths lined with flower beds surrounded by trim box hedges and lemon trees. From the **allée Saint-John Perse** you get a good view of the **Porte du Pont-Neuf**, a pavilion-like structure deliberately harking back to the market buildings designed by Baltard. The **allée Federico Garcia Lorca** leads to the **Jardin des Enfants** (children's garden) and **Jardin des Tout-Petits** (toddlers' garden), both of which are strictly out-of-bounds to both teenagers and adults.

Follow the signs to the **Forum**. There are good views of the gardens from the café terrace beside the **Pavillon des Arts**. Just beyond here escalators lead down into the bowels of the Forum and Ⓜ Halles, but first climb up the spiral staircase to the **Terrasse** for a bird's eye view. The entrance to exhibitions in the Pavillon des Arts is at the top of the staircase. A little further on you come to the **Maison de la Poésie**, with a round room for lectures or readings, surrounded by showcases for special exhibitions, and a little reference library if you feel like dipping into some French poetry or checking up on the details of the life of a poet you've come across in Paris.

Walk on round the terrace, enjoying the views of Saint-Eustache and the Bourse du Commerce, with the Eiffel Tower in the far distance. And glance over the parapet to the lively **rue Pierre-Lescot**, which is gradually being smartened up. Then go down the steps into the gardens, where with a bit of luck there will be an old merry-go-round whirling away, and take one of the escalators down into the **Forum**. Here you're on your own: remember there are four levels to contend with and keep an eye open for the plans dotted about at intervals. You may feel like a stroll round the chic boutiques, mostly on Niveau –1, or the bigger shops on Niveau –2, where you can browse in the vast bookshop in the **Fnac** store or join the crowds clustered in the record and video departments. Niveau –2 is also full of restaurants and cafés, while the floor below, Niveau –3, has an open-air piazza, the **place Basse**, where you can get some air if you're feeling claustrophobic, and goggle at a peculiar piece of pink marble sculpture, by an Argentinian artist, called **Pyègemalion**. This floor is also the way to get, via the place Carrée, to the swimming pool (or to watch others swimming through the glass wall!) and the gym, plus various cinemas, a huge auditorium for concerts and other cultural happenings, a **vidéothèque** where you can sit for hours viewing videos on the history of Paris (for a small fee), and a record library. There's even a tropical garden down here (you may have noticed the four glass pyramids at ground level that draw down the necessary light).

The Forum's museums and the new **Centre Océanique Cousteau** are on the top floor (Niveau –1), in the area labelled 'Grand Balcon'. The **Musée de l'Holographie** is great fun. It takes Dennis Gabor's forties invention of the technique of holograms and creates a magic world where ballerinas twirl round, rabbits suddenly appear out of nowhere and figures seem to wink at you. Then there's a branch of the **Musée Grévin** waxworks on the boulevard Montmartre (Walk 7), which concentrates on the legendary Belle Epoque with scenes featuring Gustave Eiffel, Victor Hugo, Sarah Bernhardt, Pasteur working in his laboratory and Jules Verne's submarine. The Cousteau Centre wasn't yet open when this book was written, but it should contain exhibits connected with submarine life and the work of Commander Cousteau.

When you've seen all you want to and done everything that takes your fancy (you can even play billiards), make your way up to ground level and head for the south-east corner of the gardens, where a boutique called **Paris-Musées** sells copies of exhibits from some of the city's best-known museums. Now walk into the **square des Innocents**, the site of a famous cemetery whose inhabitants were removed to the Catacombs at the end of the 18th century (Walk 4). The square is surrounded by fast-food restaurants and cafés, most of them not worth bothering with, but the stylish **Café Costes** on the north side, done up in stark fifties style, is fun and very fashionable with a young crowd. Otherwise if you are ready for a meal, you would do better to head for one of the many old-established restaurants or the wine bars springing up round here, often converted from a market traders' bar.

The **Fontaine des Innocents** in the middle of the square, designed by Pierre Lescot and decorated with sculptures by Jean Goujon, was described by Bernini as 'the most beautiful piece of France'. Its Renaissance detail is even lovelier now that the whole fountain has been restored, though for much of the year the steps are so crowded with groups of lively youngsters or tired tourists resting their legs that you may find it hard to get a good look at it. At its south-east corner the square meets the **rue de la Ferronnerie**, famous as the place where, in 1610, 'Good King Henry', Henri IV, was assassinated in his carriage by a fanatical schoolmaster called François Ravaillac. The crime took place outside no. 11, which by grim coincidence — or was it fate? — was a shop called Le Coeur couronné percé d'une flèche (The Crowned Heart pierced by an Arrow). On the corner with the rue Saint-Denis, the **Bistro de la Gare**, the first of a successful chain, is rather better than most of the eating places in this touristy area.

Leave the square by the **rue Berger** and walk eastwards, across the boulevard Sébastopol, to the crowded (beware pickpockets) **rue Aubry-le-Boucher**, where you are confronted with the odd but by now surely familiar sight of the **Centre National d'Art et de Culture Georges-Pompidou**. This multi-purpose cultural centre was the brainchild of President Pompidou. His aim was twofold: to find a good use for the Plateau Beaubourg, a run-down area that had been stripped of most of its slums in the thirties, but was now little more than a giant car park; and to restore France to what he believed to be its rightful place as the world's centre of contemporary art — a role it had lost to London and New York. The result of his scheme, designed by Enzo Piano and the then little-known Richard Rodgers, was the controversial building that now officially bears his name, though the iconoclastic Parisians invariably refer to it as the Centre Beaubourg, or more often simply Beaubourg.

So much has been written about Beaubourg since it opened in 1977 that you will probably be prepared for the primary colours, the funnels (it has often been likened to an ocean liner or oil refinery) and especially the 'inside-out' design with escalators, ventilation shafts, air-conditioning and heating ducts, air and water pipes all thrust to the outside to ensure the maximum space inside for the **Musée**

National d'Art Moderne (National Museum of Modern Art), transferred here from the Palais de Tokyo (Walk 5), a huge public library, an industrial design centre, temporary exhibitions rooms and so on. But try to imagine the shock it created when it first opened. Yet in spite of the horror expressed by conservatives, the building has proved a resounding success, attracting more visitors than any other museum or monument in Europe (though sceptics claim the statistics are falsified by the frequent comings and goings of the library users).

Whether or not you care for the architecture – and it certainly doesn't seem as outlandish now as it once did – you are bound to find something to interest you inside: the permanent collection of contemporary art is reckoned to be the finest in the world, the temporary exhibitions are often outstanding and it also has two art bookshops. Concerts and lectures are held in various auditoria, as well as in the **Institut de Recherche et Coordination Acoustique/Musique**, generally shortened to **IRCAM**, headed by Pierre Boulez (entrance from the place Igor-Stravinski beside the centre). There is also a **cinémathèque** showing film classics from all over the world. The **Piazza** in front of the building is an attraction in its own right, a passable imitation of a medieval fair with its fire eaters, conjurors, escapologists, impromptu musicians. The streets round about are packed with eating places, mostly pretty mediocre, but certainly lively, though you may prefer

The 'inside-out' design of the Georges Pompidou/Beaubourg Arts Centre thrusts ventilation shafts, air-conditioning ducts and escalators to the outside

to head for the restaurant on the top floor of Beaubourg itself, which will also give you a chance to enjoy glorious views over Paris. The centre is open till 10 p.m. every night except Tuesday and I recommend an evening visit, when the crowds have thinned (inside at any rate), the views are even lovelier, and the building itself, except in high summer, is a blaze of lights.

But I shall not attempt to recommend a way of visiting the centre, except to say that you should study the huge noticeboard on the left as you go in from the Piazza to see what exhibitions and other happenings are on that day; that a day pass (laissez-passer d'un jour) is good value, enabling you to visit not only the museum but all temporary exhibitions and all other parts of the centre; and that you should get hold of a leaflet describing what can be seen in the various rooms in the museum on the third and fourth floors, as the arrangement is constantly changing. One last piece of advice: this is a place for leaving your prejudices behind, forgetting about the clutter on the ground floor, usually thronged with backpackers, and enjoying the progressive spirit of the place which, for all its faults, has encouraged whole sectors of the population who had never previously been museum-goers to take an interest in modern art and culture.

The best way to reach the centre is via the rue Quincampoix. Before turning into it, admire the trompe-l'oeil on the corner of the rue Aubry-le-Boucher: a ventilation shaft has been concealed by what looks for all the world like a house with the inhabitants busily going about their daily lives. The **rue Quincampoix** is old and picturesque. Walk a little way south, then retrace your steps and continue in the other direction, admiring the 17th- and 18th-century façades.

This end of the street is strangely quiet in the daytime, only a few paces from the multilingual hubbub of the Piazza and the rue Aubry-le-Boucher, though in the evenings **Pacific Palisades***, a lively restaurant on the left, is humming with activity. Yet two and a half centuries ago this was briefly one of the busiest streets in Paris, thanks to the adventurous Scottish financier John Law, whose 'system' to restore France's tottering finances after the death of Louis XIV was eagerly embraced by the regent, Philippe d'Orléans. No. 65, now an innocuous wine merchant's, is the site of Law's bank, which set up a trading company with Louisiana known to the French as 'le Mississippi'. Speculation in the company's shares reached absurd heights, the rue Quincampoix was mobbed day and night for months on end and had to be sealed off by the police. Eventually the whole paper edifice crashed spectacularly in October 1720, causing – like the earlier South Sea Bubble – the ruin of thousands of humble and not-so-humble citizens (though others of course had made colossal fortunes by selling at the right moment).

Now retrace your steps and turn right into the narrow **rue de Venise**, a less hectic way of approaching the Piazza and one that enables you to enjoy a stone carving on the corner of the rue Saint-Martin portraying the Ship of Paris, which 'is tossed by the waves but does not sink' (fluctuat nec mergitur is the city's defiant device). Before plunging into the crowds on the Piazza, walk round to the left to the entrance to **L'Atelier de Brâncuşi**, a reconstruction of the studio of the Romanian sculptor Constantin Brâncuşi, complete with his tools and quite a few pieces of sculpture. The studio is open erratic hours and you must knock or ring for admittance, but do visit it if you can for a moving glimpse of the spartan life he led during his many years in Paris and for the opportunity to see his pure and abstract work in a peaceful setting, without crowds of museum-goers to disturb you. The studio is attached to Beaubourg and can sometimes be reached via a side door in the centre, but it is so often shut that I advise you to approach it from here.

Another visit that can be made before you go into Beaubourg is to the **Quartier de l'Horloge**, just north of the vast building. This complex of modern housing and shops is enlivened by a clock-sculpture in brass and steel called **Le Défenseur du Temps** (Man defending Time), in the **rue Bernard-de-Clairvaux** (you can get to it via the rue Brantôme, which leads north of the rue Rambuteau). The work of a sculptor called Jacques Monestier, it consists of an armed man surrounded by a bird, a crab and a dragon, symbolising respectively the elements of air, water and earth. As each hour strikes, he brandishes his sword and shield and valiantly fights off one of the three in turn, except that at midday, 6 p.m. and again at 10 p.m. he has to tackle all three at once. Time your visit accordingly.

Then walk along the **passage des Ménétriers** and out to the rue Beaubourg. If it is a weekend or public holiday afternoon, cross over to the **impasse Berthaud**, a cul-de-sac almost opposite; at the far end is the **Musée des Instruments de Musique Mécanique**, full of musical boxes, barrel organs, pianolas and the like. If you enjoy exploring old streets, continue north to the **rue de Montmorency**, where you can see a very early house (no. 51) that was built for the alchemist Nicolas Flamel in 1407. Madame de Sévigné and the hapless Nicolas Fouquet, Superintendent of Finances at the beginning of Louis XIV's reign, whose château of Vaux-le-Vicomte in the Ile de France was confiscated by his jealous master, both lived in this street. It also has a good restaurant, **L'Alisier***. Have a look at the backside of Beaubourg, which seems very blue, then return to the Piazza and the centre itself (or you can make a less frenetic entrance from the **rue du Renard**).

When you've had your fill of Beaubourg, leave by the rue du Renard exit, turn right and right again to reach the **place Igor-Stravinski**. Ahead of you looms the **church of Saint-Merri**, to the right Pierre Boulez's IRCAM, but the main attraction of this square is the miniature lake in the middle, a riot of crazily revolving, gaudily coloured sculptures by the husband-and-wife team of Niki de Saint-Phalle and Jean Tinguely. Snakes rear up, a skeleton turns it head, hearts whirl round, each object intended to represent a composition by Stravinsky (the Firebird, for instance). It's all very colourful (especially at night, seen by the light of giant projectors) and great fun – and guaranteed to win over the weariest child.

Now walk to the right along the **rue du Cloître-Saint-Merri** to the **rue Saint-Martin** to admire the façade of Saint-Merri, a Late Gothic church with some beautiful wood carving. This end of the rue Saint-Martin is full of little shops and cheap restaurants. The shops change frequently, but my favourite, **L'Ecritoire** at no. 6, is still there and still selling pretty writing materials. Turn left out of the church, have a look at the sculpture at the junction of the **rue de la Verrerie** and the rue Saint-Martin and the pleasantly old-fashioned bookshop on the corner, **La Vouivre**, specialising in the occult, plus some religious and political titles. Then turn right into the **rue des Lombards**: the name comes from the rich merchants

WALK 8: LES HALLES, BEAUBOURG, HOTEL DE VILLE

from Florence, Genoa and sometimes Venice who set up in business here in the Middle Ages as bankers and money-lenders. One of them was the father of Boccaccio, who was born here in 1313. On the right at no. 10 **Le Tintamarre** is a lively café-theatre. Opposite, at no. 7, **Le Pavé** is a friendly bistrot with traditional décor and plain but good-value food. But there are plenty of restaurants to choose from in this little network of streets, including, on the corner of the rue Saint-Martin and the rue Pernelle, **Chez Benoît***, a well-known and rather expensive place that has been in business since 1912.

Turn left off the rue des Lombards into the **rue Nicolas-Flamel** and walk down to the **Tour Saint-Jacques**. The tower stands on the site of a chapel dating back to 850, which was superseded in the mid-12th century by a larger church that was a rallying-point for pilgrims setting off on the long road to Santiago de Compostela. It was known as Saint-Jacques-de-la-Boucherie because it was surrounded by butchers' stalls. The tower itself was built at the height of the Renaissance, but in an earlier Late Gothic style. Pascal conducted experiments in it in the mid-17th century (which explains why there is a statue of him in the gardens). The church was pulled down just after the Revolution but the tower escaped and was rented out to a manufacturer of lead pellets, who found the tower ideal for dropping globules of lead from a great height to make sure they formed perfect spheres. Leave the square by the south-west corner, which brings you into a large square facing the Seine.

The **place du Châtelet** takes its name from the grim fortress-prison that once stood there, but since Haussmann's day it has been dominated by two large theatres, one on either side. The **Théâtre du Châtelet**, the most opulent of the large playhouses that sprang up in Paris during the Second Empire, dates from 1862 and was built by Gabriel Davioud for the Imperial Circus, after their theatre had disappeared with the demolition of the boulevard du Temple (see previous walk). Intended as a 'people's theatre' and staging mainly operettas, it could seat as many as 3,600 people and was even equipped with stables – the huge stage was wide enough for a cavalry charge in a dramatisation of Jules Verne's *Michel Strogoff*. But it was also here that Diaghilev's *Ballets Russes* staged their legendary seasons (Stravinsky's *Firebird* first took wing here). After a period of decline and a brief renaissance as the Théâtre Musical de Paris it reverted to its old name in 1988 and underwent a major facelift. It now puts on a mixture of musicals, classical concerts, opera, operetta and ballet, and recitals by popular singers like the venerable Charles Trenet, plus some 45-minute lunchtime concerts (tickets may include a light meal).

The **Théâtre de la Ville** opposite, also designed by Davioud, was for many years called the Théâtre Sarah Bernhardt. The great actress was its director from 1899. It was here that she played some of her most famous roles, such as Napoleon's young son 'the Eaglet' in Rostand's play *L'Aiglon* – a distinct *tour de force* as she was 56 at the time. The inside of the theatre is now very modern and it puts on a variety of foreign and French companies. The fountain in the middle of the square commemorates Napoleon's major victories on the battlefield. Beneath it is a huge rabbit warren of underground corridors forming Paris's largest métro junction. Once rather unsafe at night, they are now regularly patrolled by the police and are popular with young people for the busking steel bands that often play down there.

Before leaving the square, pause to admire the medieval silhouette of the **Conciergerie** on the Ile de la Cité (Walk 1), then stroll to the right along the **quai de la Mégisserie**. This brief detour will explain a mystery: above the traffic noise you may have been puzzled by the sound of a cock crowing. For the *quai* is one gigantic open-air pet shop, with shops and stalls selling rabbits and cockerels, canaries and doves, birdseed and dog collars and tropical fish. This is a good place for amusing recalcitrant children who are complaining of an overdose of culture.

Then turn round and walk back past the **Pont au Change**, once the main beat of the city's money-changers, and on along the **quai de Gesvres** to the **Hôtel de Ville** (town hall). The square in front of it has recently been cleaned up and is now rather attractive, with fountains playing and plenty of strollers. Though peaceful now, it has been the setting for many a dramatic event, including a whole string of grisly public executions, with plenty of hanging, drawing and quartering and ceremonial burnings at the stake. Among the victims were the Templars (Walk 7), Henri IV's assassin and the celebrated poisoner, the Marquise de Brinvilliers (see box, Walk 9). The Hôtel de Ville as an institution dates back to the 13th century, when Louis IX (Saint Louis) asked the Parisians to nominate a provost and a team of aldermen to look after the running of the city. The best known of the provosts was Etienne Marcel, a wealthy cloth merchant, who virtually ruled Paris for a brief period in the following century, did his best to restrict the powers of the monarchy and let the English army into the city, but was assassinated in 1358. His statue can be seen in the garden on the river side. The building was not started until 1535 and took nearly a century to complete. It was seized by the revolutionary mob after the storming of the Bastille, then during the 1848 revolution became temporarily the seat of the provisional government, and 23 years later of the Commune. Eventually it was virtually burned to the ground when the Versailles troops captured Paris and the Commune was overthrown. It was later rebuilt in neo-Renaissance style and is rather splendid, especially seen against a pearly evening sky, with its turrets and chimneys and rooftop figures.

A Little Etymology

The square in front of the Hôtel de Ville or City Hall, now called simply the place de l'Hôtel-de-Ville, was known until the 1830s as the place de Grève. The name comes from *la grève*, meaning 'strand' or 'shore', because in those days the square sloped gently down to the Seine, as the Strand in London once did to the Thames.

From the Middle Ages onwards it became common for the unemployed to congregate here, a tradition that gave rise to the expression *faire la Grève*, which came to mean 'to be out of work'. The term has survived in modern French (with a small 'g'), but *les grévistes* are now voluntarily out of work: *faire la grève* is the standard term for 'to go on strike' and *une grève des transports*, say, is a public transport strike, or a *grève des éboueurs*, a dustmen's strike.

You can visit some of the elaborate state rooms on Monday mornings and it is worth checking to see if there is an interesting temporary exhibition on. The entrance is in the rue de Rivoli, opposite the **Bazar de l'Hôtel-de-Ville**, known by its initials as **BHV**, a fairly downmarket department store famous for its DIY department in the basement (this is the place to head for if you need a plug or adaptor). It was opened in 1856 as the 'Bazar Napoléon', by a man called Xavier Ruel, who had chosen the site because whenever his team of street sellers traded there, they sold more than anywhere else in Paris — an astute piece of early market research.

Now walk along the **rue Lobau** behind the Hôtel de Ville to the **place Saint-Gervais** and the **church of Saint-Gervais-Saint-Protais**, with a three-tiered classical façade, the earliest of its kind in France. The church holds organ concerts and has a long musical history — the Couperins, a distinguished family of musicians including the composer François Couperin, were organists here for nearly two centuries from 1656. It has good Late Gothic vaulting, beautifully carved choir stalls, some 16th-century stained glass and a large number of paintings.

After visiting it, complete this walk by going down the **rue de Brosse**, turning left into the **rue de l'Hôtel-de-Ville**, then left into the **rue des Barres**. These attractively restored streets are full of medieval details and include the headquarters of the **Compagnons du Devoir du Tour de France***, where you can share your lunch table with 'journeymen' learning their craft as their forebears did in the Middle Ages. Or you might prefer a cup of tea or a light meal in **L'Ebouillanté***, a picturesque tea room with views of the flying buttresses of Saint-Gervais. On the corner with the rue du Pont-Louis-Philippe an old baker's, complete with traditional painted panels beneath glass, has been turned into an attractive but expensive restaurant. But you are now on the edge of Le Marais, the focus of the next walk, which is full of reasonably priced restaurants, and just a short walk, via the **Pont Marie**, from the restaurants on the Ile Saint-Louis (Walk 1).

Hotels and Restaurants

For general advice on choosing where to stay and where to eat, see Practical Information; prices are moderate unless otherwise stated.

Hotels

Agora 7 rue de la Cossonnerie, 1er (42-33-46-02). Pretty rooms in a medieval street in the heart of Les Halles; little traffic noise as this is a pedestrian area, but be prepared for late-night revellers, especially in summer.

Ducs d'Anjou 1 rue Sainte-Opportune, 1er (42-36-92-24). Noisy in summer and the rooms, though well modernised, are very small, but you're right in the heart of things, overlooking an attractive square a few steps from Les Halles and close to the Beaubourg and the Louvre.

Restaurants

L'Alisier 26 rue de Montmorency, 3e (42-72-31-04); closed Sat, Sun and Aug. Good newish cuisine and pleasant atmosphere in an old street north of the Beaubourg boasting one of the earliest surviving houses in Paris.

Batifol 14 rue Mondétour, 1er (42-36-85-50). An old Halles bar turned into a busy bistrot, with original décor intact; good value.

Les Bouchons 19 rue des Halles, 1er (42-33-28-73). Colonial-style turn-of-the-century décor in a large and lively brasserie on the site of a shop selling corks (*bouchons* in French). Live piano music sometimes and jazz in the cellar in the evenings.

Le Châtelet Gourmand 13 rue des Lavandières-Sainte-Opportune, 1er (40-26-45-00); closed Sun, Mon and most of Aug. Cheerful bistrot just west of the place du Châtelet converted from a wine bar, with marble counter and thirties décor, plus a whole range of *menus* with the emphasis on grilled meat (but some fish too) cooked in traditional style.

Chez Benoît 20 rue Saint-Martin, 4e (42-72-25-76); closed weekends and part of Aug. Well-known bistrot between Beaubourg and the Tour Saint-Jacques, run by the same family for 80-odd years. Rather expensive but very Parisian with its counter and traditional dishes like braised beef; tables outside in summer.

Chez Georges 1 rue du Mail, 2e (42-60-07-11); closed Sun. Long-standing bistrot beside the place des Petits-Pères, famous for its wine list and serving traditional dishes.

Au Chien qui Fume 33 rue du Pont-Neuf, 1er (42-36-07-42). One of the restaurants that has survived from the great days of the food market, on the southern edge of the new Halles by the Porte du Pont-Neuf. Old photos on the walls remind you of what has gone for ever, but it's still lively and serves good-value traditional dishes until the early hours, with two *menus* at the same price, one of them based on seafood.

Les Compagnons du Devoir du Tour de France 1 pl Saint-Gervais, 4e (48-87-38-69); open lunchtime only, closed weekends. Something a bit different: the canteen used by the craft apprentices who still do a 'journeymen's' period travelling round France as their predecessors did in the days of medieval guilds. You can share their very inexpensive meal in this quiet part of Paris behind the Hôtel de Ville and chat to them about the tricks of their trade.

Le Comptoir 37 rue Berger, 1er (40-26-26-66). A traditional Halles bar converted into a wine bar and offering *meze*-style snacks plus wine by the glass — Paris's stylish answer to the downmarket snackbar, and still at low prices.

A l'Escargot Montorgueil 38 rue Montorgueil, 1er (42-36-83-51); closed Mon. Early 19th-century décor, full of mirrors and painted and moulded ceilings (one bit of the ceiling once belonged to Sarah Bernhardt!), adorns this well-known restaurant in a busy market street just behind the church of Saint-Eustache. As well as the snails that give it its name, traditional *cuisine bourgeoise*. A good place for a special evening out, as the *menu* is affordable.

Le Louis XIV 1bis pl des Victoires, 1er (40-26-20-81); closed weekends and Aug. Busy bistrot well-known for its *lyonnaise* cuisine, which means tripe and good fat sausages, though it does also serve some rather elaborate dishes.

Pacific Palisades 51 rue Quincampoix, 4e (42-74-01-17). A place for seeing the *jeunesse dorée* who frequent this lively area, though the street itself, just minutes from the Beaubourg Piazza, is quiet. Mostly *nouvelle cuisine*, open late.

Au Pied de Biche 6 rue de La Vrillière, 1er (42-61-43-78); closed weekends. A few steps from the place des Victoires and opposite the Banque de France, a pretty bistrot with mirrors, lacy curtains and lots of charm.

Au Pied de Cochon 6 rue Coquillière, 1er (42-36-11-75). The best known of the traditional restaurants round the food market is still open all day and all night, year-round. Lively atmosphere, thoroughly professional service, stylish new art-nouveau-ish décor, excellent seafood platters.

Pharamond 24 rue de la Grande-Truanderie, 1er (42-33-06-72); closed for lunch on Mon, Sun and most of July. Grilled pigs' trotters and tripe are the specialities in this Norman restaurant with turn-of-the-century décor, another survivor from the old Halles.

La Potée 3 rue Etienne-Marcel, 2e (42-36-18-68); closed Sat lunch and Sun. Tiled art nouveau décor, and the filling Auvergnat stew that gives it its name, are the chief claims to fame of this café-restaurant near Les Halles and Beaubourg.

Le Trumilou 84 quai de l'Hôtel-de-Ville, 4e (42-77-63-98); closed Mon. Deservedly popular for its low prices, cheerful atmosphere and convenient setting beside the Seine.

Museums and Places of Interest

Musée de l'Holographie (Holography Museum) and **Musée Grévin-Forum** (waxworks with son-et-lumière) Forum des Halles, rue Pierre-Lescot, 1er (look for signs saying 'Grand Balcon'). Closed Sun mornings. Ⓜ Halles, Ⓡ Châtelet-Les Halles

Centre National d'Art et de Culture Georges-Pompidou (**Centre Beaubourg**) (20th-century art) entrances in Piazza/pl Georges-Pompidou (off rue Saint-Martin) and rue du Renard, sometimes also in rue Rambuteau, all 4e. Closed Tue and up to midday other weekdays, but open to 10 p.m. Houses *Musée National d'Art Moderne* (Modern Art Museum), a big library, the *Centre de Création Industrielle* (design centre) and *Brâncuşi's studio* (mornings only most days, entrance from Piazza); many temporary exhibitions. Day passes available. Ⓜ Rambuteau, Hôtel-de-Ville

'Man Defending Time' (clock sculpture) 8 rue Bernard-de-Clairvaux, 4e; strikes on the hour every hour between 9 a.m. and 10 p.m., with more elaborate displays at midday, 6 p.m. and 10 p.m. Ⓜ Rambuteau

Musée des Instruments de Musique Mécanique (musical boxes and barrel organs) impasse Berthaud, 4e. Weekend afternoons only. Ⓜ Rambuteau

193

Walk 9
The Marais

Starting point: on the corner of the rue du Pont-Louis-Philippe and the rue de l'Hôtel-de-Ville, 4e; Ⓜ Pont-Marie. This Right Bank walk covers three-quarters of the fourth *arrondissement* and a little of the third. It includes many restored mansions and palaces dating from the 17th and 18th centuries, some of them housing museums, and much of it is a smart residential area.

Marais is the French word for 'marsh' or 'swamp' and this area to the north of the Seine was originally inhospitable swampy ground crossed by an arm of the Seine. In the Middle Ages the Knights Templar and various orders of monks drained the land and turned it into market gardens but it was not inhabited until Charles V had extended Philippe Auguste's ramparts and thus given it some protection from potential invaders. He even moved there himself, and later kings made the Palais des Tournelles their main residence. But after Henri II had been killed in a tournament there, his widow Catherine de Médicis had the palace demolished. Eventually Henri IV decided to use the site to build an elegant square, which became known as the place Royale. Now renamed the place des Vosges, it is still the heart of the Marais today.

But the area has been through a curious cycle of supreme fashionableness followed by neglect and its rehabilitation as a chic residential area is quite recent. Its heyday began when the aristocracy and the rich and fashionable flocked to build magnificent mansions close to the place Royale. From the early 17th century to about the middle of the 18th, several hundred beautiful houses were built, many of them by the finest architects of the day. And the Marais was peopled by artists and intellectuals as well as the aristocracy and the *nouveaux-riches* aping their lifestyle. But fashions in Paris never last all that long and gradually the cream of society moved to the Faubourg Saint-Germain on the Left Bank. The district slowly sank into neglect and the elegant courtyards and beautifully proportioned rooms were taken over by small-scale businesses and craftsmen, who made no attempt to keep up the fabric of the buildings and grafted on all sorts of ugly workshops, ripped out the decorations and destroyed the gardens.

The whole area could easily have been sacrificed to the developers' bulldozers, but fortunately an enlightened decision by General de Gaulle's arts minister André Malraux made the Marais a protected area in the early sixties and since then it has gradually been restored. There has been some legitimate criticism of the way the ordinary people of the area have been driven out by high rents. And as many of the elegant new flats into which the restored mansions have been converted have been bought as pied-à-terre by prosperous provincials, the Marais is liable to seem lifeless in the evenings and at weekends. But no one interested in architecture or the history of Paris could regret the rescue of these lovely buildings, many of them with historical associations. And the streets are increasingly lined with interesting small shops – fashion and design boutiques, specialist bookshops, craft workshops – and a good range of unpretentious small restaurants and tea rooms, which make a visit there even more pleasant. A number of the *hôtels* have been turned into museums – the Picasso Museum is a recent arrival – and can therefore be visited. Sadly, the advent of the coded entry system means that many others can only be glimpsed through railings or doors left open by chance, though the summer Marais Festival does give you an opportunity to attend concerts or ballet or theatre performances in some of the courtyards.

On the eastern edge of the Marais is the place de la Bastille, a focus of interest since the celebrations of the bicentenary of the French Revolution in 1989. The surrounding streets are becoming increasingly fashionable in young and intellectual circles and are experiencing a mushroom growth of fashion boutiques, art galleries and stylish restaurants and cafés.

After admiring the view southwards beyond the Ile Saint-Louis to the Panthéon, walk up the **rue du Pont-Louis-Philippe**, which has some interesting antique and other shops: a lute builder's, **Caran**, a small shop with well-designed tableware and other items, and **Papier Plus**, for beautiful stationery. Turn right into the **rue du Grenier-sur-l'Eau**. Facing you at the far end, at 26 **rue Geoffroy-l'Asnier**, is the splendid carved doorway, surmounted by a roaring lion's head, of the **Hôtel de Chalons-Luxembourg**, an early 17th-century mansion with a brick and stone façade that is slowly being restored. Turn right to see the sober **Memorial to the Unknown Jewish Martyr**, a huge cylindrical drum set against a wall bearing a Star of David. It has a little reading room and study centre open to the public. Then walk in the other direction up to the **rue François-Miron**.

On the left-hand corner is a little group of *hôtels* with some interesting decorative details. No. 44 now houses the **Association pour la Sauvegarde et la Mise en Valeur de Paris Historique**, where you can buy booklets and plans of the Marais and visit Gothic cellars and a Renaissance courtyard. On the other side of the street, nos 11 and 13 are much older, half-timbered 14th-century houses bulging out picturesquely over the little rue Cloche-Perce. One is now a small restaurant, **Le Relais Saint-Gervais**, where you can dine by candlelight in the vaulted cellars and enjoy live jazz in the evenings.

Now walk to the right along the rue François-Miron. The grandly named baker's on the corner of the rue Tiron, **Au Petit Versailles du Marais**, has a good example of the paintings beneath glass panels that traditionally adorned the exterior of many a Paris *boulangerie-pâtisserie*. No. 68 on the other side is the **Hôtel de Beauvais**, one of the Marais's best-known mansions, built in the mid-17th century for Anne of Austria's first chambermaid, Catherine Bellier. A hundred years later the Bavarian ambassador entertained his guests here with recitals by an

Opposite the Musée Carnavalet, one of many a baker's turned into a fashion boutique

infant prodigy called Wolfgang Amadeus Mozart, then only seven. The *hôtel* is slowly being restored and you may be able to get a glimpse of the courtyard and the Doric rotunda of a vestibule and spot the many rams' heads in what is left of the decoration: the ex-maid's name sounds like *bélier*, ram. She is said, by the way, to have owed her fortune to the queen's generosity as a reward for her having made a man of the youthful Louis XIV – a great relief to Anne, whose husband Louis XIII had been impotent for much of their marriage.

Continue along this street, noticing the wrought-iron decoration on nos. 74–76 and the elegant façade with stone balcony supports of no. 82, the **Hôtel Hénault de Cantorbe**, built at the beginning of the 18th century. As you come to the junction where the **rue de Rivoli** turns into the **rue Saint-Antoine** (Ⓜ Saint-Paul), don't miss another elaborate balcony: at no. 133 on the right, fantastic chimaeras provide the support, above a restaurant called, appropriately enough, **Les Chimères**. This aristocratic detail above a modern brasserie, sandwiched between a nondescript hairdresser's and a supermarket, is very typical of parts of the Marais today. The **rue Saint-Antoine**, traditionally peopled by cabinet-makers, is the high street of the Marais. It was from this busy working street that the people of Paris set out in July 1789 to storm the Bastille and even today, in spite of the recent gentrification of the district, the cafés and many food shops here are a good place for seeing ordinary Parisians going about their daily lives.

Now cross over the main road by the métro station. If you have children in tow, there may well be a small merry-go-round here to gladden their hearts. Walk up

Some boulangeries − *and falafel houses* − *are still thriving in the Marais*

the **rue Pavée** on the other side and cross the **rue du Roi-de-Sicile,** which com-memorates Saint Louis's brother, proclaimed King of Sicily in 1266. On the right, at no. 10 rue Pavée, is a small **synagogue** designed by Hector Guimard, the creator of Paris's famous art nouveau métro entrances (see Introduction). You are now approaching the part of the Marais that has been the city's main Jewish district for centuries, its high street the **rue des Rosiers,** which you reach shortly on the left. When the French withdrew from North Africa in the early sixties, many Franco-Jewish families moved from there to Paris, changing the character of the Jewish district, which had been predominantly East European in atmosphere, many of its little shops and restaurants run by exiles from Poland or Russia. The ambiance often seems more North African these days, and some of the Ashkenazi synagogues are now Sephardic. Guided tours of the more interesting ones are arranged at frequent intervals: check the 'What's On' guides for dates and times.

First turn right into the rue des Rosiers to enjoy the sight of another attractive *boulangerie-pâtisserie,* on the corner of the rue Malher. But on closer inspection you can see that the intricate loaves and plump *brioches* have given way to stylish outfits and jaunty hats. **Lolita Lempicka,** with an annexe, **Lolita Bis,** opposite, is one of many lively fashion boutiques that have recently invaded this part of the Marais, often taking over old food shops (corner of the rues des Rosiers and Pavée). Just round the corner, at 18 rue Pavée, is one of my favourite Paris junk shops. And just beyond here is the **Hôtel Lamoignon,** housing the **Bibliothèque Historique de la Ville de Paris,** a large public library specialising in the history of

197

the city, with a well-known Revolution collection. It was built at the end of the 16th century for the Duchesse d'Angoulême, daughter of Henri II, and Alphonse Daudet, the author of *Letters from my Windmill*, was one of its many tenants in the 19th century. Walk into the spacious courtyard to admire the fine façade with Corinthian pilasters surmounted by a triangular pediment and check to see whether there is a temporary exhibition on.

Now walk back to the **rue des Rosiers** and turn right. On the right is the elaborate façade of the **Hammam Saint-Paul**, a well-known Turkish bath and swimming pool. On the left you soon come to **Goldenberg*** at no. 7, the city's best-known Jewish restaurant and takeaway. Continue along this colourful street, perhaps stopping for a *falafal* snack if you're feeling peckish, and keeping an eye open for interesting doorways (at no. 23 on the left, for instance). The shops are a lively mixture of delicatessens and new fashion boutiques.

Turn right into the **rue Hospitalières-Saint-Gervais** to look at the splendid bulls' heads adorning what was once a meat market. In the summer, the café tables here are inviting. Turn left opposite the market building into the little **rue du Marché-des-Blancs-Manteaux**. Facing you at the end is the huge gateway of the Hôtel Amelot de Bisseuil, better known as the **Hôtel des Ambassadeurs de Hollande**, built in the mid-17th century and one of the first mansions to be restored. The playwright Beaumarchais wrote most of *The Marriage of Figaro* in this elegant building, which he used as a base for his arms-supplying activities during the American Civil War. You may be able to get into the first courtyard but unfortunately the beautiful Galerie de Psyché and the Italianate main bedroom are not normally open to the public (as with other privately owned mansions, occasional guided tours are arranged).

Turn right and walk a few paces for a good view of the Late Gothic turret on the **Hôtel Hérouet**, on the corner with the **rue des Francs-Bourgeois**, then retrace your steps and continue down the **rue Vieille-du-Temple**, which is lined with restaurants, wine bars and tea rooms, one of them inside the curious boutique of an interior decorator at nos 37–9. Now turn right into the **rue Sainte-Croix-de-la-Bretonnerie**. On the left, at no. 7, is a lively café-theatre, **Point Virgule**, and a few steps further on the **rue du Bourg-Tibourg** has the splendid **Mariage Frères***, which has been selling superior blends of tea to connoisseurs since 1854. This is one of my favourite tea rooms and it is also a good place to buy presents: white china tea caddies or little boxes decorated with a reproduction of the firm's original label, neat interlocking tea sets, tea cosies, egg timers, and of course tea, in shiny black tins. Beyond here in the rue Sainte-Croix-de-la-Bretonnerie on the right is the attractive **Hôtel de la Bretonnerie*** and on the left, at no. 15, the cheap and cheerful **Le Petit Gavroche*** bistrot.

Turn right into the **rue Aubriot**, a good example of a Marais side street: no grand mansions, but still very attractive, lit by old lamps, its pleasant houses built round little courtyards. It brings you out to the **rue des Blancs-Manteaux** and **church of Notre-Dame-des-Blancs-Manteaux** (the name comes from the white habits worn by a mendicant order that was once based here). The same name has been taken by the lively café-theatre on the corner. The little garden beside the church, with a sandpit for children, is a convenient place for a rest in fine weather.

Leave the garden by the swing gate at the far end and go into the church by the side door (if it is shut, walk out to the rue des Francs-Bourgeois, turn left, and go through the narrow door leading off the street). The church is best known for its elaborate Rococo pulpit and its organ (concerts are often staged here).

Return to the **rue des Francs-Bourgeois**, whose name commemorates the 'free citizens' who were housed in alms houses here in the Middle Ages (they were so poor they were 'free of tax'). Turn left as you leave the church. **Le Dômarais*** at no. 53bis is a pleasant restaurant in the unusual setting of what used to be the municipal pawnbroker's. If you peer through the gateway at no. 57bis you can just make out a brick tower whose stone base is one of the few surviving fragments of Philippe Auguste's medieval wall. Opposite here, at no. 60, is the entrance to the early 18th-century **Palais Rohan-Soubise** (also called the **Hôtel de Soubise**), one of the grandest buildings in the Marais and now housing the **National Archives**. It was built in 1705–8 for the Prince de Soubise on the site of a medieval *hôtel*, of which a single turret has survived on the façade overlooking the rue des Archives. Beyond the huge courtyard with its Corinthian colonnade, the entrance in the centre of the sober façade takes you into the **Musée de l'Histoire de France (Museum of French History)**, a selection of exhibits from the archives.

You need to be fairly knowledgeable about French history to appreciate the importance of some of them, but no one could fail to be moved by the facsimile of a page from the parliamentary register dated 10 May 1429, with a doodle in the margin drawn by a court usher in an idle moment − it is the only known sketch from life of Joan of Arc. Here too is the document revoking the Edict of Nantes, and the famous entry in Louis XVI's diary for 14 July 1789: 'Nothing,' he wrote firmly. And don't miss the codicil to Napoleon's will requesting that his remains should be brought back to France. At the end of the corridor you can visit the superb apartments lived in by the Prince and Princesse de Soubise, with their elegant Rococo decoration. Particularly lovely is the oval *salon*, all white and gilt decoration, with tall mirrors, sky-blue ceiling and paintings by Van Loo and Boucher.

Turn right when you leave the palace. You may feel in need of a reviving cup of tea or a light meal: combine them with browsing in **Mille Feuilles**, a lively bookshop-cum-tea room on the other side of the **rue des Archives**. Then walk northwards up the rue des Archives. On the left, on the corner of the **rue des Haudriettes**, is an attractively restored fountain built by one of the Princes de Rohan. **Le Connétable***, facing it, is a lively restaurant, and opposite that is one of the Marais's most interesting specialist museums, the **Musée de la Chasse et de la Nature (Hunting Museum)**, housed in the beautiful **Hôtel Guénégaud**, designed by François Mansart in the mid-17th century. The garden (visible from the rue des Quatre-Fils), with its very French *trompe-l'oeil* trellising, is particularly attractive, and the museum is worth visiting even if you don't share the joys of the chase. As well as an important collection of shooting instruments of various kinds, it has paintings by Rubens and 'Velvet' Breughel, and by the animal painter Oudry.

Now walk along the **rue des Quatre-Fils**. The stylish concrete and smoked-glass building at nos 11–13 is the **Centre d'Accueil et de Recherche des Archives Nationales** or CARAN, a computerised research centre where members of the public can consult documents, on microfilm, connected with French history. When you come to the **rue Vieille-du-Temple**, turn right to see, at no. 87, the façade of the **Hôtel de Rohan**, separated by a garden (which may soon be open to the public) from the Palais Rohan-Soubise, and dating from the same period. The elegant apartments lived in by the Cardinals de Rohan, one of whom was involved in the notorious 'Affair of the Queen's Necklace' (see box), can be visited

The Affair of the Queen's Necklace

Napoleon liked to say that the true start of the French Revolution could be dated to the complex scandal, familiar to every French schoolchild, surrounding a diamond necklace allegedly bought for Queen Marie-Antoinette. The 'Affair of the Queen's Necklace' (French scandals, even today, are invariably referred to as *affaires*) broke in 1785, by which time the queen was already highly unpopular, thanks partly to the scurrilous rumours about her supposedly dissolute life spread by her many enemies at court.

In August that year, the Cardinal de Rohan was arrested on a charge of obtaining from the court jewellers a diamond necklace worth the huge sum of over 1½ million *livres*, on the false claim that it was for the queen, and then neglecting to pay for it. The cardinal, from one of the country's highest-ranking families, was also a duke and a peer of the realm. He had been French ambassador to the Viennese court, where he had earned the hearty dislike of the queen's mother, the Empress Maria Theresa, both because of his unseemly private life, ill fitting a man of the cloth, and because she saw him as an enemy of the alliance between Austria and France.

Desperate to wipe out the prejudice against him that had been passed on from mother to daughter, and be accepted at court, he allowed himself to be hoodwinked by an adventuress called the Comtesse de la Motte, an illegitimate descendant of Henri II. The countess had somehow managed to persuade him, by means of

some forged letters, that he would earn the queen's favour if he acquired the necklace for her, using his well-known name to obtain credit.

When the jewellers wrote to the queen over the unpaid bill and the story came to light, the whole affair was very clumsily handled. Though the cardinal was eventually found innocent, the trial badly damaged the queen's already tarnished reputation, as the general public was quite convinced that she had been selling her favours to the cardinal (and to various other shady characters) for the price of a diamond necklace. The countess was flogged and branded and received a life sentence – ever wily, she managed to escape from the Salpêtrière prison after less than a year and turned up in London – but her intriguing had shown the whole court up in such a poor light that she undoubtedly helped to bring about the collapse of the *ancien régime*.

Among the cardinal's many hereditary offices was that of Bishop of Strasbourg, which explains why the family's superb mansion in the rue Vieille-du-Temple was also known as the Hôtel de Strasbourg. He was the last of the line. During the Revolution the *hôtel* was the headquarters of a club set up by Tallien, a member of the National Convention and husband of the Marquise de Fontenay, later Princesse de Chimay, who was nicknamed 'Notre-Dame de Thermidor' after the part her husband played in the uprising during the revolutionary month of Thermidor that led to the fall of Robespierre.

only when special exhibitions are held. But you may be able to get into the courtyard to see the thrilling relief of 'The Horses of the Sun' carved by Robert Le
Lorrain over the stable doors.

Now retrace your steps and continue up the rue Vieille-du-Temple to admire
the garden façade, decorated with hunting dogs and lions, of the **Hôtel de Juigné**,
usually known as the **Hôtel Salé**. This beautiful *hôtel*, one of the loveliest in the
Marais, earned its prosaic nickname because it was built for the collector responsible for the *gabelle* or salt tax, one of the *ancien-régime* taxes most resented by
ordinary people. (A *note salée* still means a steep or exorbitant bill.) After years of
patient restoration, it was opened in 1985 as the **Musée Picasso**, housing 'Picasso's
Picassos', the huge collection of the artist's work accepted by the state from his
heirs in lieu of death duties, together with his personal collection of the work of
other major artists. The City of Paris, who bought the *hôtel* in 1964, originally
planned to turn it into a costume museum. But the Picasso windfall was clearly an
opportunity not to be missed. It seemed to many an unlikely combination: a
supremely elegant 17th-century mansion built for a prosperous bourgeois and the
iconoclastic work of the *enfant terrible* of modern art. And yet it undoubtedly
works very well indeed.

*'The Horses of the Sun', Robert Le Lorrain's superb relief over the stable doors
in the courtyard of the Hôtel de Rohan*

Before walking round to the museum entrance via the **rue des Coutures-Saint-Gervais**, a street now filled with art galleries that has otherwise changed little since the 17th century, you may like to stop for refreshments at one of the restaurants opposite the *hôtel's* garden. One is punningly called **Le Petit Salé** (a traditional dish of salt pork with lentils). Or in fine weather you can enjoy a drink or a snack in the museum's café in the garden. Corneille's great drama *Le Cid* was first performed in the theatre that used to stand at the end of the garden.

In the doorway opposite the entrance to the museum is a busy boutique selling expensive postcards of Picasso's work. The museum itself is liable to be very crowded and the attendants are notoriously bossy and bureaucratic, but you will forget all this once you have managed to get inside and seen the superb staircase with its wrought-iron balustrade and richly carved ceiling, then started visiting the many rooms and admiring Picasso's prolific output.

The display is roughly chronological and there are helpful explanatory panels accompanied by photographs showing him and his various wives and mistresses and children at different periods. The collection includes some well-known pictures like *Portrait of Olga in an Armchair* and sketches for *Les Demoiselles d'Avignon*, but many more with which you are probably not familiar, and a huge number of drawings, prints and engravings (the Vollard Suite of 100 engravings dates from the thirties). Right at the top of the museum are paintings by Marie Laurencin, Matisse, Modigliani, Renoir, Van Dongen and many more collected by Picasso. Don't miss, in the former chapel, the interesting display of before-and-after photographs, which gives you an idea of the terrible state of dilapidation of this and many other *hôtels* in the Marais.

Turn right when you leave the museum. Notice on the corner an example of the low-cost housing that has been put up in the Marais recently, then walk across the rue de la Perle to the **Hôtel de Libéral Bruant** (or Bruand), designed for his own residence by the architect of Les Invalides. It now houses the **Musée Bricard de la Serrure** (**Lock Museum**), an interesting collection of locks and the locksmith's art since Roman times. If you have no time to visit the museum, have a look at the graceful courtyard. It is smaller than many of the Marais mansions and you might even imagine living there. Then cross over the **rue Elzévir**. No. 8, the **Hôtel Donon** has now opened as the **Musée Cognacq-Jay**, previously in the boulevard des Capucines (Walk 7). **Callisto** on the corner is another baker's converted into a boutique. The ceiling, with a pretty design of swallows, flowers and sheaves of corn, has been carefully preserved, and you can buy attractive knitwear and accessories here. The **Royal Bar** next door, adorned with photographs, is a pleasant place for a drink. The friendly **Sévigné** café on the corner of the **rue Payenne** serves light meals and gives you a refreshing view of the pretty garden in the **square Léopold-Achille**. On the corner is a decorative map of the Marais, one of several dotted through the district.

Walk down the rue Payenne. The **square Georges-Caïn** on the left is a romantic little public garden with an orangery, scattered with bits of statuary and a 17th-century bronze of Flora (or possibly Aurora) with a chariot. It was once the private garden of the **Hôtel Le Peletier-de-Saint-Fargeau**, which you can see on the far side, housing an extension to the Musée Carnavalet. On the other side of the street the **Hôtel de Marle**, with a pretty leafy courtyard, is now the Swedish Cultural Centre. There may be a good art exhibition on here. On the corner with the rue des Francs-Bourgeois, **Marais Plus** is another lively bookshop-cum-tea room, overlooking a tiny wild garden. **L'Orée du Marais*** to the right is a good bet for a quick and inexpensive meal, cheerfully served.

Now turn left and walk along to the decorative gilded wrought-iron railings, set in a rounded arch, that allow you to enjoy the formal garden of the **Hôtel Carnavalet**, the home of the **Paris History Museum**. The mansion belongs to the City of Paris and in a fit of bicentenary fervour, the city's coat of arms on the railings, featuring a storm-tossed sailing ship, has been painted a photogenic red-white-and-blue. A little further on on the other side, have a look at the garden of the **Hôtel Lamoignon**, which has also been well restored. Then turn left into the **rue de Sévigné** for the entrance to the **Musée Carnavalet**. The original building was designed by Pierre Lescot in the mid-16th century, but substantially altered and added to a century later by François Mansart. Madame de Sévigné lived here for most of the last twenty years of her life and loved the house passionately. As you go through the entrance you are struck by a bronze statue of Louis XIV by Coysevox in the middle of the *cour d'honneur*, set against the Renaissance façade of the original building. Behind him are four sensuous bas-reliefs of the seasons by Jean Goujon.

For over a hundred years the museum was housed in the many rooms of this *hôtel*, but in 1989 a large new wing was opened in the **Hôtel Le Peletier-de-Saint-Fargeau**, a sober 17th-century mansion whose main entrance, surmounted by a garland of foliage, is at 29 rue de Sévigné. But you can reach the new rooms directly from the Hôtel Carnavalet. The whole museum covers the history of Paris from the earliest times to our own century and the collections have been reorganised so that the new wing starts with the Revolution and continues with the 19th and 20th centuries, while the original building covers the period from the Renaissance to the late 18th century. The rooms previously devoted to the later exhibits are being restored and will eventually be used to display the museum's pre-Renaissance collections.

The whole museum has a pleasantly cosy feel, with its many small rooms, and gives you a good idea of the life of Paris through the centuries, with its emphasis on details like inn signs, or arms and armour, or reconstructed rooms and shops. The sequence is roughly chronological, but the Hôtel Carnavalet also includes the rooms lived in by Madame de Sévigné, with some of her furniture and other mementoes, and some beautiful gilded *salons* on the ground floor. Beyond them is a little door leading into gardens, where you can rest before tackling the new section. You may also like to buy something from the boutique just inside the entrance or the book and card shop beside it.

The opening of the new wing was timed to coincide with the celebrations for the bicentenary of the French Revolution and the focus is on the Carnavalet's rich collection of items connected with the Revolution. But you can also see a selection of paintings depicting Paris in the 20th century, a 'portrait gallery' of celebrities associated with the city – the singer Juliette Greco, the couturier Paul

Poiret, the poet and society hostess Anna de Noailles among many others – and reconstructions of a number of rooms: Proust's bedroom, complete with cork-lined walls and pile of exercise books on the bedside table, Anna de Noailles's bedroom, and the amazing ballroom designed in the twenties by José-Maria Sert for the Hôtel de Wendel, its walls and ceiling covered in one continuous sweep with a scene featuring the Queen of Sheba surrounded by camels and elephants, painted with coloured varnishes on a gold leaf ground. And on this same floor you can admire the art nouveau façade and interior dreamed up by Alphonse Mucha for the jeweller Fouquet's in the rue Royale, a peacock the main motif.

Beyond a series of rooms filled with paintings of dramatic moments in Paris's history, a stiffish climb brings you up the main staircase to the revolutionary collections (you might like to seek out the lifts at the rear of the building). The small rooms, carpeted and curtained, seem more like a private house than a museum as you peer at models of the Bastille, Robespierre's shaving bowl, a miniature guillotine and a whole range of souvenirs – snuff boxes, china and the like – then come to a reconstruction of the prison in the Temple where Louis XVI and his family were held, with the dressing table used by Marie-Antoinette and the bed on which Madame Elisabeth, the king's sister, slept. The chronological sequence follows on the ground floor, with rooms devoted to Napoleon and to the Restoration – an interesting contrast in official portraits, Napoleon in cavalry uniform, Charles X in elaborate state robes – and to the July Monarchy and the Romantic era.

When you leave the museum, pause to admire the façade of the Hôtel Le Peletier-de-Saint-Fargeau. The gentleman in question was, by the way, an aristocrat who voted for the death of the king but was stabbed to death by Pâris, a member of the royal bodyguard, the evening before the king was guillotined, while he was dining at the famous Café Février in the Palais Royal. He was the great-grandson of the senior civil servant who commissioned the mansion in the 1680s from Pierre Bullet, best known for his design for the Porte Saint-Martin on the Grands Boulevards. Now walk back down the **rue de Sévigné** to the **rue des Francs-Bourgeois**. From here you have a good view of the façade of the Jesuit **church of Saint-Paul-Saint-Louis**. If you have time, you can spend a pleasant half hour or so strolling along the rue des Francs-Bourgeois looking at the stylish little shops, which sell anything from hand-painted furniture to designer stationery and thirties costume jewellery.

Then continue down the rue de Sévigné to the **rue de Jarente**. This brings you into a network of narrow streets with several good and informal restaurants, like the **Auberge de Jarente*** at no. 7. Walk on to the tiny cobbled **impasse de la Poissonnerie**, whose photogenic fountain has recently been restored. Then walk back a few paces to the **rue Caron** and turn left to enjoy a very Parisian square, the traffic-free **place du Marché Sainte-Catherine**, surrounded by restaurants and cafés. My favourite for a full-scale meal is **La Baie des Anges*** on the south-east corner, but if you are merely in search of a drink, **Le Double Fond** opposite is a lively bar-cum-café full of curious trick exhibits.

Continue down the rue Caron and turn left into the **rue Saint-Antoine**. At no. 62, beyond the **rue de Turenne**, the **Hôtel de Béthune-Sully** was built by Jean

Androuet du Cerceau in the early 17th century and bought soon after it was completed by the Duc de Sully, who had been Henri IV's chief minister. He added a smaller building behind the main mansion and the two have now been beautifully restored, together with the gardens. The *hôtel*, one of the loveliest in the Marais, houses the **Caisse Nationale des Monuments Historiques**, an association organising excellent guided tours of important buildings in Paris and elsewhere in France. Just inside the gateway is a new bookshop where you can buy plans of the Marais and books about the area and the history of France.

Not so long ago the imposing façade was disfigured by shop signs and the courtyards were crammed with no fewer than thirty small businesses, ranging from an umbrella merchant to a manufacturer of straw boaters. But it now looks as it did when it was completed in 1624, with particularly rich sculptural decoration, including curvaceous female figures in niches representing the four seasons and the elements, on both the *cour d'honneur* and garden façades. Guided tours of some of the rooms in the main building take place at least once a week (usually weekends), enabling you to see the painted and gilded panelling and decorated ceilings. But on other days you can still climb the steps from the first courtyard and walk through to the lovely gardens and the **Petit Sully**, the name usually given to the building beyond them, probably originally an orangery. Informal concerts by music students are an added bonus in the summer and art exhibitions are often held here too.

Leave the garden by the north-east corner, which brings you out into the Marais's best-known square, the **place des Vosges**, originally called the place Royale. (If the Hôtel de Sully is shut, you will have to make the more traditional approach via the **rue de Birague**, a little further along the rue Saint-Antoine.) Allow plenty of time to enjoy this beautiful square. The mellow pinkish brick and stone façades, so pleasingly proportioned, and the low arcades running round all four sides create a sense of harmony both by daylight and perhaps even more at night, when the fountains in the central gardens are illuminated. Purists claim that the trees are an anomaly, preventing you from seeing the square as a whole, but they provide welcome shade on dusty summer days and certainly add to the attractions of the square for the lay visitor.

The square was planned by Henri IV, who felt that his capital needed an arena suitable for parades and ceremonial events. In 1605 he chose this site, left vacant half a century earlier when Catherine de Médicis had the Palais des Tournelles demolished, and now being used as a horse market. His architects, probably Androuet du Cerceau and Claude Chastillon, came up with an elegant symmetrical square flanked by nine houses on each side, with brick façades bordered in white stone and surmounted by tall blueish-grey slate roofs. Each rests on four arches at ground level and has four windows on each floor. Henri was assassinated before his square was ready and the official opening ceremony was performed two years later, in 1612, by his son Louis XIII, who celebrated his wedding to Anne of Austria there with an elaborate display of 1,300 horsemen and hundreds of dancers and musicians. The first inhabitants were the highest-ranking courtiers, but the **Pavillon du Roi** (King's Pavilion), bestriding the rue de Birague in the centre of the south side, and the **Pavillon de la Reine** (Queen's Pavilion), opposite it on the north

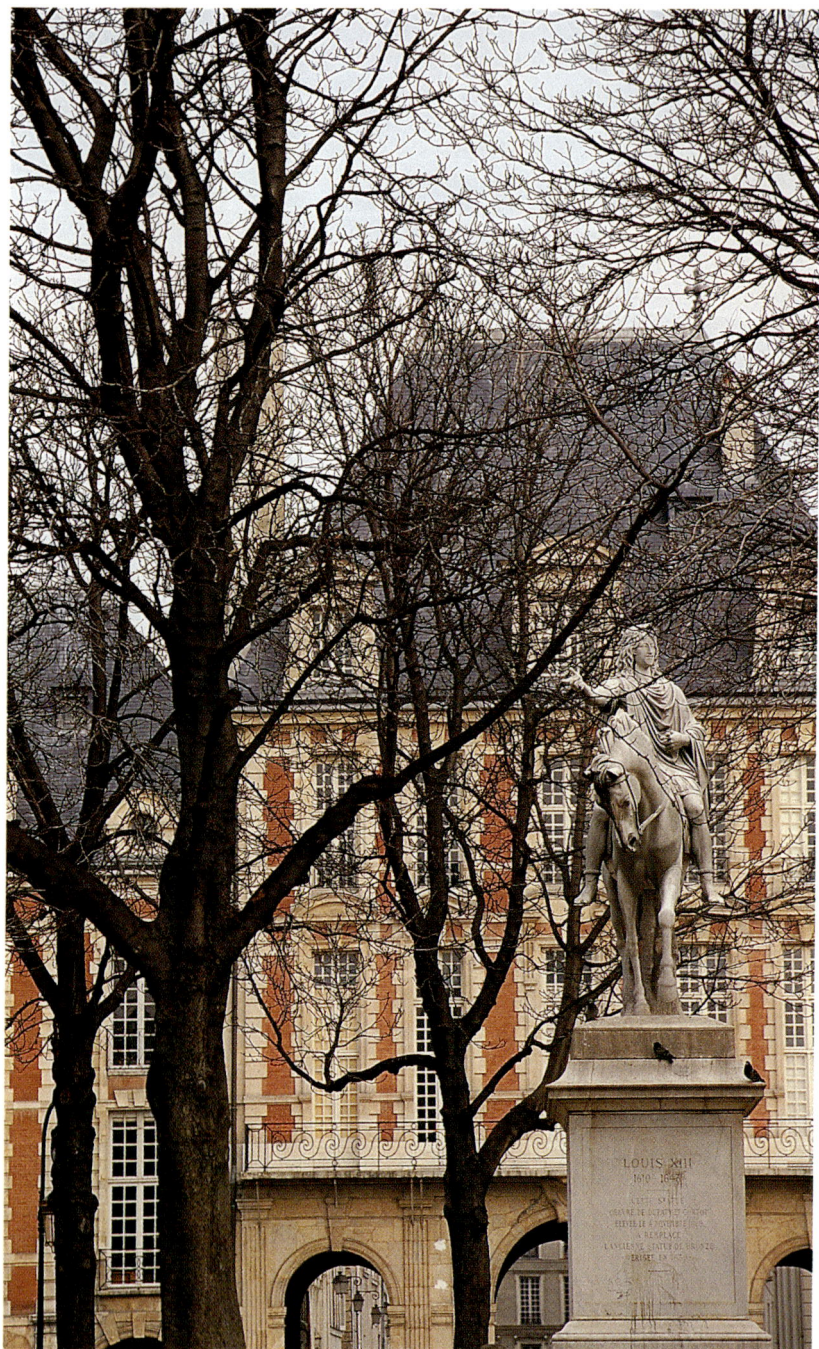

and now leading to a luxury hotel of the same name, were never lived in by the monarch or his consort.

The square was inhabited by many illustrious figures over the next 200 years. Madame de Sévigné was born at no. 1bis in 1626 and Cardinal Richelieu almost certainly lived for a while at no. 21, which belonged to his great-nephew the Duc de Plessis de Richelieu. Théophile Gautier occupied the second floor of no. 8 and was succeeded by Alphonse Daudet. And Victor Hugo lived in no. 6, the **Hôtel Rohan-Guéménée**, from 1833 until 1848. The **Maison de Victor Hugo** is now a museum of his life and work, including curious Gothicky pen-and-ink sketches by him, and the even more curious pieces of furniture he designed and decorated for himself and his family and for his mistress Juliette Drouet when she came to live near them in their exile at Hauteville House in Guernsey.

The museum was reorganised and redecorated for the centenary of Hugo's death in 1985 and now feels rather less like a private house, but it does still have enough of those miscellaneous mementoes that make you feel you're learning something about the man as well as his work – a horseshoe he picked up on the battlefield at Waterloo, say, or photos with his grandchildren (one apparently produced as a commercial postcard). And you get a good idea of Hugo as the Grand Old Man of French letters and politics, constantly caricatured but popular as a label for manufacturers selling 'Victor Hugo ink' or 'Victor Hugo calendars' or 'Victor Hugo watch cases'. On the ground floor you can buy playing cards featuring Esmeralda and her goat and Quasimodo from *Notre-Dame de Paris*, jigsaws, medals and reproductions of Hugo's drawings.

There are several places for tea or a drink beneath the arcades of the place des Vosges: a couple of health-food places on the east side just beyond the museum, **Vitamine** and **Nectarine**, the attractive **La Chope des Vosges** on the corner, on several levels, all with the 17th-century beams still in place, and **Ma Bourgogne*** on the north-west corner. You might like to plan a later meal at either of the last two, or at the more elegant **Coconnas*** on the south side or **La Guirlande de Julie*** on the north. To get a table at the fashionable and very expensive **L'Ambroisie** on the west side, you have to book weeks in advance. There are several antique shops on the north side, and just beyond the edge of the square, at 2 rue des Francs-Bourgeois, **Carnavalette** is a small second-hand bookshop with a good line in theatre programmes and ephemera from the thirties. Leave by the rue de Birague and turn left to walk along the rue Saint-Antoine to the **place de la Bastille**. Just before you come to it on the left, notice the **statue of Beaumarchais**, who owned a large mansion nearby that has since been demolished. (Ⓜ Bastille)

There hasn't of course been much to see at the Bastille since the notorious fortress-prison, dating from the 14th century, was stormed on 14 July 1789 and later demolished by an army of 800 workmen. (The stones were promptly turned into models of the fortress and other souvenirs by an enterprising French businessman, who even produced medals made from the chains worn by the prisoners.)

The place des Vosges centres on an equestrian statue of Louis XIII

But it would be a pity to miss a pilgrimage to this site that played such an important part in French history.

Stones in the square pick out the outline of this vast building which didn't really deserve its reputation – there were only seven prisoners when the furious mob arrived and none of them had been incarcerated for very long. But that didn't stop its being seen as *the* symbol of the despotic power of the *ancien régime*. And the act of destroying it is still a potent image to the French, who celebrate their 'National Day' on 14 July with dancing in the streets and fireworks – and commemorated its bicentenary in 1989 in grand style. It is certainly no coincidence that the Socialist President Mitterrand chose the place de la Bastille as the site of a new 'people's opera house', designed to bring an élite art within reach of the ordinary working people who inhabit the city's eastern *arrondissements*. You can see the striking curved building of the **Opéra de la Bastille**, by the Uruguyan architect Carlos Ott, on the far side of the square. It was ceremonially opened with a concert on the bicentenary, but regular opera performances are unlikely to start until well into the nineties.

On a fine day the curving surface reflects the newly regilded statue of the 'Genius of Liberty' perched on one leg on top of the **Colonne de Juillet** (July

Carlos Ott's Opéra de la Bastille, opened on 14 July 1989, the bicentenary of the French Revolution, in an increasingly chic area of eastern Paris

Column) in the centre of the square. This tall memorial commemorates those who died during the 'Trois Glorieuses', the three days of street fighting in July 1830 that stripped Charles X of his throne and replaced him with the 'bourgeois monarch' Louis-Philippe. It rests on a plinth originally designed for a large fountain in the shape of an elephant and beneath it was hollowed out a circular crypt faced with white marble in which were placed the remains of the 504 victims of the fighting, plus another 196 who died in the 1848 uprising – and an Egyptian mummy. If you're in a macabre mood you can reach it via an entrance in the plinth.

The whole of the Bastille district is going through its own peaceful revolution at the moment, gradually becoming a chic place to live for the young and lively. Some have been driven out of the Marais by rising rents, others are latching on to a trend as the limelight focuses on the new opera house and the local restaurants and cafés smarten themselves up to receive a new clientele. You might like to spend some time exploring the streets round about. You will mostly find a mixture of fairly run-down shops and bars and a growing number of fashion boutiques and small art galleries and bookshops, some of them catering to the smart crowd whose speedboats are berthed in the **Bassin de l'Arsenal**, a new marina at the beginning of the **Canal Saint-Martin**, which flows under the square. You can see the marina, bordered with trim lawns, from the railings at the south side of the square or through the windows on the eastbound platform of Ⓜ Bastille, or you might like to stroll beside the canal and enjoy a closer look.

Just east of the square, the **rue de Lappe**, leading off the **rue de la Roquette**, is a lively street with some picturesque old houses. It was once lined with dance halls – the famous **Le Balajo** is still there – and now has dozens of bars and restaurants, many of them Spanish, though it is still the headquarters of the Auvergnat population of Paris, with many places selling *charcuterie* and other specialities from the Auvergne. This is a good street for peering through into courtyards, where you will often find villagey houses and old pumps and scenes that seem very far removed from the trendy boutiques that are springing up all round. Many of the workshops are connected with the furniture trade that is centred on this part of Paris, but if you walk a short way up the **rue Amelot** running north of the square, parallel to the **boulevard Beaumarchais**, you may be able to visit at nos 17–19 a firm which has been specialising in making automata since 1865: **Decamps** often stages exhibitions of its extraordinary creations and demonstrations of how they are made.

All the streets on the eastern side, with their workshops and old houses, are worth exploring, and can be combined with a visit to the cemetery of Père-Lachaise (Beyond the Centre). But you should now walk round the west side of the square, past the **rue de la Bastille**, where **Bofinger*** at no. 7, a brasserie dating back to 1864, has riotous art nouveau décor and a lively atmosphere. Then walk down the **boulevard Henri-IV** towards the Seine.

At the bottom on the left-hand side the **Bibliothèque de l'Arsenal** was once the home of Henri IV's minister Sully, who commissioned Philibert Delorme to build a new arsenal or weapons store here. It has been a public library since the end of the 18th century, specialising in theatre history. It has a copy of every play written in French, as well as an important manuscript collection. Its librarian for twenty years from 1824 was the writer Charles Nodier, who held regular *salons* attended by the leading poets of the Romantic Movement – Lamartine, Vigny, Victor Hugo. Guided tours of the *hôtel*, including the beautiful panelled music room, are held only about once a month, but the library itself is worth a brief visit. Opposite it is the new **Pavillon de l'Arsenal** (see Walk 1). I make no apology for repeating my recommendation to visit this very interesting display of Paris town planning through the ages. (Ⓜ Sully-Morland)

Le Sully* on the corner of the boulevard is handy if you are in need of food or drink. Then cross over to the **quai des Célestins**. On the corner with the **rue du Petit-Musc** is the exuberantly decorated façade of the **Hôtel Fieubet**, a riot of cornucopias, swags of fruit and vegetables, lions' heads, caryatids with curly beards and bulging muscles – and lots more besides. Once abhorred by architectural purists for the way it concealed the late 17th-century design by Jules Hardouin-Mansart, it is now recognised by all but the stuffiest as a splendid example of 19th-century Baroque – and you may secretly find its vulgarity a welcome respite from the sober elegance of so much of the Marais. Walk up the rue du Petit-Musc and turn left into the **rue Charles-V**, a peaceful street with some elegant *hôtels* that are gradually being restored and turned into flats. No. 12 was the home of the notorious Marquise de Brinvilliers (see box). **L'Excuse***, on the corner of the **rue Saint-Paul**, is a pleasant and rather chic restaurant.

Opposite here, at nos 21 and 23–7, are entrances to the **Village Saint-Paul**, a series of courtyards that now house a charming enclave of antique and junk shops, second-hand bookshops, craft workshops and the odd tea room. Walk out on the far side into the **rue des Jardins-Saint-Paul**, where François Rabelais, creator of Gargantua and Pantagruel, died in 1553. A long stretch of **Philippe Auguste's medieval wall** has miraculously survived on the far side of the playground for pupils from the nearby Lycée Charlemagne.

Turn right, admire the cherubs and dolphins on the fountain at the end of the street and the close-up view of the dome of Saint-Paul-Saint-Louis, then walk right again along the winding **rue Charlemagne**. Turn left into the narrow **rue Eginhard** and follow it round to the rue Saint-Paul. Now turn left and left again beneath the archway into the **passage Saint-Paul**, a cobbled alleyway lined with stone bollards that has barely changed since the 17th century. The presbytery at no. 7 was once the Paris home of Le Grand Condé, that great military hero whose soldierly qualities mingled with a love of the arts – Molière and Racine were frequent guests during his retirement in the Château de Chantilly. The alleyway leads to the side entrance of the **church of Saint-Paul-Saint-Louis**, built for the Jesuits by Louis XIII in 1627. The interior is modelled on the Gesù church in Rome and its rich decoration includes a painting of *Christ in the Garden* by Delacroix and two shell-shaped stoups oddly donated to his parish church by the staunchly anti-clerical Victor Hugo.

The church still has the feeling of serving the local community, with whom you can mingle as you turn left into the busy rue Saint-Antoine and stroll past a row of tempting food shops. The **passage Charlemagne**, starting at no. 119, was being restored in 1990. If it is open again, you can walk through it, past the **Lycée Charlemagne**, once a Jesuit seminary, to the **rue Charlemagne** and turn right,

La Marquise de Brinvilliers
— France's Most Notorious Poisoner

The Marquise de Brinvilliers was born Marie-Madeleine d'Aubray on 22 July 1630. She was the daughter of the wealthy Antoine de Dreux d'Aubray, sire d'Offémont et de Villiers, who held a whole series of high-level public offices, including Counsellor of State. He was apparently too taken up with his public duties to keep an eye on his beautiful but wayward daughter, the eldest of five children, whose morals seem to have been highly lax even when she was a child — she boasted later of having committed incest with her brothers.

Her husband, a dashing young colonel called Antoine Gobelin, Marquis de Brinvilliers, whom she married when she was 21, seems to have led a pretty dissolute life — he too was rich, and was well known as a gambler and man about town. When they had been married eight years, Madame de Brinvilliers started a very public affair with one of her husband's friends, a cavalry captain called Godin, also known as Godin de Sainte-Croix. Her father was so incensed at her behaviour that he had the captain put behind bars in the Bastille where, according to one version of the story, he met a fellow-inmate, an Italian, who was an expert in poisons. Other authorities say the expert in question was Swiss, a perfectly respectable chemist called Christophe Glaser, whom Godin de Sainte-Croix met after being released from prison. It makes no odds, since the important thing was that his mistress, furious with her father and short of cash — she had already run through her large dowry — decided to put to good use the scraps of information she'd picked up from her lover.

Like many rich young women then and now, she did some good works, visiting the sick in the Hôtel-Dieu and other hospitals. She soon realised that this gave her an ideal opportunity for some experiments of her own and the little treats she took to the deserving poor were often laced with arsenic or vitriol. She even tried to perfect her technique on her own servants in the elegant mansion the couple lived in in the rue Charles-V, but they soon became suspicious of any unexpected gifts of cakes or jam pressed on them by their mistress.

In 1666 she put her newly acquired skills into practice and slowly poisoned her father, following the deed up four years later by killing her elder brother and, within a few months, her younger brother, thus getting her hands on the fortune they had inherited from their father. She also tried to poison her sister, a Carmelite nun, but never managed it. She would have done away with her husband too, but Godin apparently didn't fancy marrying her, no doubt suspecting that he might be next on the list of victims, and made sure that the marquis always had the necessary antidote in time. But at the end of July 1672 Godin himself died suddenly — of natural causes. Ironically it was this death, in which she had no hand, that brought about La Brinvilliers's downfall. The police were called in and found among the captain's possessions a locked casket containing details of her crimes and 'recipes', plus over twenty phials of poisonous substances.

She managed to avoid arrest by fleeing to England, then the Low Countries, where she was eventually discovered in a convent. Her trial lasted several months and she was found guilty and condemned to death exactly four years after the death of her lover. She conducted herself so bravely during the tortures that were then common before an execution that she became something of a popular heroine and the huge crowds who turned out to see her beheaded in the place de Grève (now the place de l'Hôtel-de-Ville), then watched her body being burnt, the ashes scattered on the wind, included many admirers.

then left into the **rue Figuier**. Otherwise continue to the attractive **rue du Prévôt** and walk down there instead.

At the bottom of the rue Figuier is one of only two surviving secular medieval buildings in the city, the turreted **Hôtel de Sens**, so called because it was for many years the residence of the archbishops of Sens. But its best-known inhabitant was the first wife of Henri IV, 'Queen Margot', who notoriously had one of her lovers beheaded in front of the *hôtel*. It dates back to 1475 (the Hôtel de Cluny in the Latin Quarter was started ten years later) and was completed in 1507, in a mixture of Gothic and Renaissance styles. It seems like a cross between a castle and a mansion, with its turrets and battlements overlooking the elegant formal garden. Since the sixties it has housed the **Bibliothèque Forney**, a fine and applied arts library which puts on temporary exhibitions in the building to the left just inside the courtyard. Admire this courtyard, climb up to the reading room (entrance on the far side) to enjoy the roaring dragons and griffons and scribes carved on the capitals, then walk round via the **rue de l'Ave-Maria** for a good view of the façade overlooking the garden, divided into neat squares in the medieval fashion. The whole effect is magical when lit up at night.

On the other side of the **rue des Nonnains-d'Hyères** is the **Hôtel d'Aumont**, the last of the Marais *hôtels* on this walk and one of the most majestic, although experts claim it has been over-restored. The sober garden façade on this side was designed in the mid-17th century by François Mansart, who worked with the painters Simon Vouet and Charles Le Brun to transform a more modest *hôtel*, the work of Le Vau and his architect Michel Villedo a decade earlier, into a sumptuous residence for the governor of Paris, Antoine d'Aumont, Marquis de Villequier. Further up this street, and almost opposite the Le Vau façade in the **rue de Jouy**, you can enjoy a glimpse of the old wooden balconies and staircases that have been preserved on the building beyond the courtyard.

If you prefer to end a long day's sightseeing in another part of the city, Ⓜ Pont-Marie is a few steps away on the **quai de l'Hôtel-de-Ville** and a short walk will bring you to Ⓜ Saint-Paul. But the Marais itself is full of pleasant restaurants and those on the Ile Saint-Louis are easily reached via the **Pont Marie**.

Hotels and Restaurants

For general advice on choosing where to stay and where to eat, see Practical Information; prices are moderate unless otherwise stated.

Hotels

Bretonnerie 22 rue Sainte-Croix-de-la-Bretonnerie, 4e (48-87-77-63). A 17th-century building converted into a pleasant hotel with original beams and a lounge-cum-breakfast room in the cellars. In a narrow street near the Archives Nationales.

Célestins 1 rue Charles-V, 4e (48-87-87-04). Small but prettily furnished rooms in a quiet street in the southern part of the Marais near the river — only 15 rooms, so book early.

Jeanne d'Arc 3 rue de Jarente, 4e (48-87-62-11). Small and well-run; modest but carefully renovated rooms, well situated near the restaurants in the pretty place du Marché Sainte-Catherine.

Place des Vosges 12 rue de Birague, 4e (42-72-60-46). A few steps away from the lovely place des Vosges yet reasonable prices, so its 16 rooms are inevitably very popular.

7e Art 20 rue Saint-Paul, 4e (42-77-04-03). You'll be in seventh heaven if you're a movie buff: stylish black-painted entrance brings you to a box-office-like reception desk surrounded by cinema posters – and bedrooms and other public areas (including a restaurant) are similarly adorned.

Vieux Marais 8 rue du Plâtre, 4e (42-78-47-22). Attractive rooms in a quiet street on the western edge of the Marais.

Restaurants

L'Auberge de Jarente 7 rue de Jarente, 4e (42-77-49-35); closed Sun, Mon and most of Aug. Delicious dishes from the south-west, popular for its *cassoulet*, served in a lively atmosphere just off the picturesque place du Marché Sainte-Catherine.

La Baie des Anges 2 pl du Marché-Sainte-Catherine, 4e (42-77-34-88). One of my favourite places for an outdoor lunch or dinner (it's a bit crowded if you have to eat inside), over-looking a pretty square in the heart of the Marais. Genuine Nice cuisine, which means *crudités* with anchovy dip, stuffed courgettes and aubergines, good fish, and friendly holiday atmosphere.

Bofinger 7 rue de la Bastille, 4e (42-72-87-82). One of the most breathtaking examples of Paris art nouveau, with lofty glass dome, stained glass, brass and mahogany and paintings by the popular Alsatian artist Hansi. Just off the place de la Bastille, so increasingly busy and lively. Good brasserie food too.

Ma Bourgogne 19 pl des Vosges, 4e (42-78-44-64); closed Mon. Bustling restaurant-cum-wine bar on the corner of the Marais's loveliest square, popular with foreign visitors and residents for Sunday lunch, but also pleasant in the evenings, when you can sit out under the arcades or squeeze into the cosy little dining rooms.

Coconnas 2bis pl des Vosges, 4e (42-78-58-16); closed Mon, Tue and mid-Dec to mid-Jan. Ideal setting a few doors away from the Victor Hugo Museum, with tables outside in summer. Particularly pleasant service and good-value *menu*. Rather chic.

Le Connétable 55 rue des Archives, 3e (42-77-41-40); closed Sat for lunch and Sun. Atmospheric place near the National Archives where you can eat in the old cellars. Lively, with old French songs in the evening.

Le Dômarais 53bis rue des Francs-Bourgeois, 4e (42-74-54-17); closed Sat, Sun and Mon for lunch. Almost opposite the National Archives, in what was once the showroom where the official pawnbrokers displayed unredeemed items before they were auctioned off – suitably elaborate décor of red velvet, statues and glass roof, plus good lunchtime *menu*.

L'Excuse 14 rue Charles-V, 4e (42-77-98-97); closed Sun. Small and rather elegant, in a quiet street in the south of the Marais just by the Village Saint-Paul antique and craft shops.

Goldenberg 7 rue des Rosiers, 4e (48-87-20-16). Well-known Jewish restaurant in the heart of the Marais's Jewish district. Bustling and friendly, with takeaway service too. Open late.

La Guirlande de Julie 25 pl des Vosges, 4e (48-87-94-07); closed Mon and Tue, mid-Dec to mid-Jan. Another restaurant under the arcades of the place des Vosges, with garden-style décor and fashionably light *menu*.

Mariage Frères see box in Food and Drink.

L'Orée du Marais 29 rue des Francs-Bourgeois, 4e (48-87-81-70). Modest and inexpensive, useful for a quick meal in the middle of sightseeing. Friendly service and good *plats du jour*.

Le Petit Gavroche 15 rue Sainte-Croix-de-la-Bretonnerie, 4e (48-87-74-26); closed for lunch on Sun. Tiny and always packed with locals, who love it for its friendly atmosphere and low prices.

Picasso Museum The museum has a little restaurant in the courtyard for light lunches, which moves into the garden on the other side in summer.

Le Sully 6 blvd Henri-IV, 4e (42-72-94-80). Nothing special, just a typical brasserie offering Paris's answer to the fast-food blight: good-value traditional dishes, fast and smiling service, a sprinkling of locals at lunchtime – and a convenient setting beside the Pavillon de l'Arsenal, near the Bastille and the *hôtels* in the south of the Marais.

Museums and Places of Interest

Memorial to the Unknown Jewish Martyr rue Geoffroy-l'Asnier, 4e. Closed Sat and on Sun morning from Sept to the end of June. Ⓜ Pont-Marie, Saint-Paul

Bibliothèque Historique de la Ville de Paris Hôtel Lamoignon, 24 rue Pavée, 4e. Special exhibitions only, but courtyard and library can be visited (except Sun and in Aug). Ⓜ Saint-Paul

Archives Nationales and **Musée de l'Histoire de France** (Museum of French History) Palais Soubise, 60 rue des Francs-Bourgeois, 3e. Afternoon only, closed Tue. Ⓜ Rambuteau

Musée de la Chasse et de la Nature (Hunting Museum) Hôtel Guénégaud, 60 rue des Archives, 3e. Closed Tue. Ⓜ Rambuteau

Centre d'Accueil et de Recherche des Archives Nationales (Archives reading room) 13 rue des Quatre-Fils, 3e. Closed Sat. Ⓜ Rambuteau

Musée Picasso (Picasso Museum) Hôtel Salé, 5 rue de Thorigny, 3e. Closed Tue; late opening Wed. Ⓜ Saint-Sébastien-Froissart, Saint-Paul

Musée Bricard de la Serrure (Locks Museum) Hôtel Libéral-Bruant, 1 rue de la Perle, 3e. Closed Sun, Mon and Aug. Ⓜ Saint Sébastien-Froissart, Saint-Paul

Musée Cognacq-Jay Hôtel Donon, 8 rue Elzévir, 3e. Closed Mon. Ⓜ Saint-Paul

Musée Carnavalet Hôtel Carnavalet and Hôtel Le Peletier-de-Saint-Fargeau, entrance 23 rue de Sévigné, 3e. Closed Mon. Ⓜ Saint-Paul

Hôtel de Béthune-Sully 62 rue Saint-Antoine, 4e. Guided tour on Sat or Sun afternoons, and sometimes on Wed afternoon; courtyards and gardens generally open to dusk; special exhibitions in Orangerie. Ⓜ Saint-Paul

Maison de Victor Hugo (Victor Hugo's House) Hôtel Rohan-Guéménée, 6 pl des Vosges, 4e. Closed Mon. Ⓜ Saint-Paul, Bréguet-Sabin

Colonne de Juillet (July Column) pl de la Bastille, 4e. Underground crypt generally open to dusk. Ⓜ Bastille

Bibliothèque de l'Arsenal blvd Morland, 4e. Guided tours about once a month, usually on Wed afternoon. Ⓜ Sully-Morland

Pavillon de l'Arsenal 21 blvd Morland, 4e. Closed Mon. Ⓜ Sully-Morland

Hôtel de Sens and **Bibliothèque Forney** 1 rue du Figuier, 4e. Special exhibitions only, but courtyard and library can be visited on Sat morning, and afternoons Tue–Sat up to 8 p.m. Closed Sun and Mon. Ⓜ Pont-Marie

Walk 10
Montmartre and Pigalle

Starting point: The place d'Estienne-d'Orves, 9e; Ⓜ Trinité. This last Right Bank walk introduces you to the hilly area, to the north of central Paris, that has long been associated with unconventional, often bohemian life. It starts in the ninth *arrondissement*, then climbs uphill to cover the south-eastern section of the eighteenth.

Montmartre has so many romantic associations, the name is so redolent of artists leading a picturesque bohemian existence — starving in a garret by day maybe, but living it up in bars and cabarets by night — that you're almost bound to be disappointed by it at first. Once you reach the top of the Butte Montmartre, the steep-sided hill crowned by the white wedding-cake silhouette of the Sacré-Coeur basilica, you find that many of the narrow streets are unpleasantly crowded with foreign tourists virtually all year round, though a sensible recent decision has banned the tourist coaches that used to cause monster traffic jams. The 'artists' jampacked with their easels into the place du Tertre produce little of interest and most of the many restaurants are both mediocre and over-priced.

And yet, and yet . . . If you move away from the little enclave round the Sacré-Coeur you can find street views that are still uncannily like an Utrillo canvas. If you explore the side streets you come across charming oases of peace with villagey houses and little gardens full of birdsong. And early on winter mornings you might be in a quiet provincial town as you join the little old ladies and young couples in the rue Lepic market, or sip a coffee as you watch the world go by. As is their wont, the tourist groups are sheep-like in sticking to the beaten track and even at the height of summer it is perfectly possible to enjoy a taste of 'Old Montmartre', whose highlights have been lovingly recreated in the Musée de Montmartre. The area also has one of the earliest churches in Paris, more interesting but far less crowded than the Sacré-Coeur.

Pigalle at the foot of the hill is frankly sleazy, but should be seen as one of the many facets of the city. And I have suggested approaching Montmartre via a district that is little known to tourists, the 'New Athens'. If you are short of time you can miss both this and Pigalle out and start this last walk at Ⓜ Abbesses. But you would be depriving yourself of a treat. And you would also miss two interesting and attractive museums, the Musées Gustave Moreau and Renan-Scheffer.

From the **place d'Estienne-d'Orves**, with its rather ugly 19th-century **church of La Trinité**, walk eastwards along the **rue Saint-Lazare** and take the first turning on the left, the **rue La Rochefoucauld**. You are now on the edge of a district known in the 18th and 19th centuries as 'La Nouvelle Athènes', the New Athens, mainly because of the neo-classical architecture of its houses. Although few foreign tourists have heard of it, it is full of interest, not only from the architectural point of view but because of its importance in the mid-19th century in the intellectual and artistic life of Paris. Even a brief list of some of the many writers, painters, musicians and actors who lived here reads like a roll call of *le tout Paris intellectuel* during the Romantic era – George Sand and Chopin, Delacroix and Berlioz, Viollet-le-Duc and Henri Murger were just some of them. It is pleasant to stroll in these quiet streets, admiring the architecture – many of the large *hôtels* now house prosperous insurance companies and have been well restored – and every now and then catching a glimpse of an elegant porticoed courtyard, a carved stone balustrade, a graceful Grecian urn silhouetted against a creeper-covered balcony.

But before leaving the rue La Rochefoucauld you can visit the delightful **Musée Gustave Moreau** at no. 14. Much of its charm stems from its having been created by the painter himself, at his own expense, above the house where he lived with his family at the end of the 19th century. He had parts of the house demolished and sacrificed a large chunk of the garden to make way for lofty studios specially designed for his large mystical canvases, peopled with unicorns and swans and beautiful female figures, and for a series of wooden display panels, neatly folding out from the walls, for some of the thousands of drawings and watercolours he left to the nation (only Picasso and Turner have left larger bequests). After a period of neglect, when he was remembered chiefly for his influence on his pupils Rouault, Matisse and Albert Marquet, Moreau's detailed canvases, and the mysterious symbolism underlying them, have come quietly back into fashion and the museum attracts far more visitors than it used to when I first started going there. But it still gives the feeling of being a private house with its spiral staircase to the upper studio, and even the lavatory allows you a glimpse of a typical 19th-century bourgeois home with its wooden seat with brass hinges, its wall 'fountain' (used as a wash-hand basin) and its huge gilt-framed mirror.

Continue up the rue La Rochefoucauld, then turn right into the **rue d'Aumale** and right again into the **rue Taitbout**. No. 80 is the entrance to the **square d'Orléans**, a little group of beautifully proportioned houses plus a couple of trees and a fountain. In this discreet square, one on either side, lived George Sand and Chopin when they were lovers. Walk back up to the rue d'Aumale and turn right. This brings you to the pretty **place Saint-Georges**, a peaceful square decorated with a memorial to the cartoonist Paul Gavarni, a regular contributor to the satirical revue *Le Charivari* and well known for his drawings of the local inhabitants, particularly the pretty girls of easy virtue nicknamed *Lorettes* from the **church of**

216

Notre-Dame-de-Lorette just down the hill and the street of the same name leading off the square.

On one side of the little *place* is the **Bibliothèque Thiers**, a history library (open to the public but you must apply in advance) in the house lived in by the statesman Adolphe Thiers. On the other side you can enjoy the attractive façade of a house frequented in the mid-19th century by fashionable writers and artists attending the *salons* held by the beautiful Polish hostess who became famous as the Marquise de Païva (see box, Walk 5). Statues in niches, garlands and swathes of carved decoration all add up to a charming whole, especially when the sunlight plays on the honey-coloured stone, and the square also boasts a provincial-looking house with a little garden, a theatre, and a junk shop in what looks like a conservatory, where you may be able to pick up a bargain (Ⓜ Saint-Georges).

Now walk northwards up the **rue Notre-Dame-de-Lorette**, past Delacroix's house (no. 58), cross over the rue Pigalle and walk along the **rue Chaptal** to no. 16, another delightful museum, again in what was once a private house. Set back from the street at the end of a leafy path, the **Musée Renan-Scheffer** is one of those secret places that transports you back to the pre-Haussmann era when Paris was not full of tall blocks of flats but of country-looking houses only one or two storeys high, with shutters and creeper-covered walls and surrounded by a little garden.

It was the home of the painter Ary Scheffer, who moved in with his mother in 1830 and every Friday held a reception for intellectual society. Delacroix and Liszt, Turgenev and Ingres, and especially George Sand were among his most assiduous guests and the house has been turned into a museum devoted to the artistic and literary circles who inhabited the New Athens. One room is full of mementoes of George Sand, including very personal items – little pieces of jewellery and pens and a couple of the ties she liked to wear. Don't miss the fan in which she is caricatured as a shepherdess while Liszt, every inch the Romantic hero, kneels at her feet, Chopin is portrayed as a parrot and Delacroix, nose well in the air, looks sardonically on. Scheffer's niece married the historian Ernest Renan, whose *Life of Jesus* created such a stir, which explains why another room in this pretty house is devoted to him. Leave the house through the conservatory, which has not just plants but a miniature grotto with splashing fountain, and if the weather is fine, pause for a few minutes in the tiny garden, enjoying the peace and greenery before you plunge into a district that is far from peaceful.

Return to the rue Pigalle, turn left and then right into the **rue Victor-Massé**. On the corner of the **rue Frochot** is a weird and wonderful art nouveau glassed-in verandah and, to the right of it, the entrance to another secret place, the **avenue Frochot**, an oasis of 19th-century houses in various styles with little gardens, on either side of a narrow cobbled street lit by graceful lamp standards. Victor Hugo lived for a while at no. 5 (and sallied forth to visit his mistress Juliette Drouet in her 18th-century house at 64 rue La Rochefoucauld) and Toulouse-Lautrec had his studio at no. 10. Sadly, a notice now proclaims that this is a private road, a coded entry system has been installed and, unless you're very lucky, you won't be able to walk through this haven to the **place Pigalle**. If your luck isn't in, walk instead along the **rue Frochot** to reach the seedy heart of Pigalle.

Just before you reach the *place,* pause for a quick glimpse of the inner world behind so many faceless Paris streets: walk discreetly through the entrance to 64 rue Pigalle and you feel as if you are in a little village, made up of a series of court-yards with small houses and tall blocks of flats, wooden shutters everywhere, some obviously smart dwellings, others with washing hanging at the windows. Nothing special, but it helps you to understand Paris and the traditional secrecy of Parisians. As you walk towards the place Pigalle, look upwards for a brief view of the Sacré-Coeur, still perched high above you. (Ⓜ Pigalle)

Pigalle has little to recommend it in the daytime, when even the prostitutes lurking in doorways seem despondent, the clubs and bars (many of them catering to a gay clientele) look distinctly tawdry and the funfair that operates for much of the year on the **boulevard de Rochechouart** seems as bedraggled as the sex shops and pornographic cinemas.

If you want to understand why Pigalle is still a name to conjure with, come at night, after visiting Montmartre, and you'll find it does have a certain seedy glamour, though don't expect to see many Parisians, and do keep a close hold on your wallet or handbag. The famous **Chat Noir** bar-cum-cabaret, presided over by the great Aristide Bruant, the *chansonnier* whose black-hatted and red-scarved silhouette is so familiar from Lautrec's poster, was at 84 in the boulevard. At no. 72

Montmartre Cabarets and Their Stars

Le Chat Noir at 84 boulevard de Roche-chouart was probably the best known of Montmartre's cabarets in the 19th century. It was here that the bourgeoisie came to be insulted by the famous *chansonnier* Aristide Bruant, one of the many Mont-martre characters immortalised in Toulouse-Lautrec's drawings and posters. He continued to wear his 'trademark' – a black hat and red scarf – when he took over the premises in 1885 and opened a new cabaret called **Le Mirliton.** An astute businessman, he ran it successfully for the next ten years, started up a magazine, also called *Le Mirliton,* for which Lautrec drew some of the covers, and which he used to advertise the many spin-off products that soon made him rich as well as famous – music scores and song sheets, records, booklets reproducing his famous mono-logues, filled with Parisian slang. At the age of 44 he started out on a series of very successful recital tours and later took on a couple of ghost writers and set himself up

as a novelist and playwright, producing 16 novels and six plays, all of which proved very popular. He died in 1925 but still seems to haunt Montmartre.

Another artiste who started out her career in Montmartre and was to be im-mortalised by Lautrec was the singer and *diseuse* Yvette Guilbert, she of the red hair and the long black gloves. She first ap-peared in public at the *café-concert* that was staged on winter evenings at the back of the **Moulin Rouge** dance hall, which opened in 1889 in the place Clichy. Among her co-performers there were stars whose names are familiar from Lautrec's work – the rubber-limbed Valentin le Désossé or Jane Avril and La Goulue.

Although the cabaret era is long over, the tradition still lingers on in Montmartre, and you can enjoy a lively evening at **Le Lapin Agile** (22 rue des Saules, see below), or at modest little restaurants-cum-cabarets like **Le Consulat** or **Chez ma Cousine,** at nos 18 and 12 rue Norvins.

you can still see the elaborate turn-of-the-century façade of the **Elysée-Montmartre**, a famous dance hall, and to your left the **boulevard de Clichy** leads to the **place Blanche** and the famous **Bal du Moulin Rouge**, again immortalised by Lautrec, and the **Théâtre des Deux-Anes**, one of only two surviving examples of that once very popular Parisian institution, the cabaret staging satirical songs written and performed by *chansonniers*, always witty, usually topical and often political.

But it is now time to cross the boulevard and climb up the **rue Houdon** to visit Montmartre. The name is probably a corruption of *Mons Martyrium*, 'Martyrs' Mount', allegedly arising when St Denis (or Dionysius) and a couple of priests were beheaded there in the year 272. (Legend has the saint calmly stooping to pick up his head, tucking it under his arm and striding off to a spot to the north where the town of Saint-Denis with its royal basilica now stands.) On the other hand it may be a version of *Mons Martis* or *Mons Mercurii*, as the Romans are known to have built temples to Mars and Mercury on top of the hill. Various settlements were built there over the centuries and by the 19th century Montmartre was a small village in a pleasant country district covered with vines and orchards and dotted with windmills – about thirty of them – used for grinding wheat and pressing grapes. The villagers mostly worked in the gypsum quarries that tunnelled under the hill.

But increasing industrialisation and Haussmann's demolitions made it seem a haven of peace conveniently close to the city and it was soon attracting a new population of artists and writers, plus modest families driven out of their homes as districts were razed to the ground. Although it officially became part of Paris in 1860, it kept a feeling of separateness and became popular as a place to escape from the treadmill of the city and enjoy an evening in one of the many cabarets and bars that soon sprang up. For a while Montmartre was the centre of Paris's bohemian intellectual life, inhabited by artists like Picasso and Braque, Modigliani and Utrillo, writers and poets too – Max Jacob and Gérard de Nerval among many others. Its heyday as an artists' colony lasted until the First World War, after which the genuine painters and sculptors migrated south to Montparnasse, leaving Montmartre to the pseudo variety whose descendants are still liable to try to paint your portrait in the more touristy spots today.

If you are ready for lunch, the small **Auberge Montmartroise*** at the top of the rue Houdon is a good place for a first taste of informal Montmartre, and much better value than most restaurants in the area. It is also a good example of a true Paris bistrot, with its mahogany counter surrounded by a brass rail, its red velvet curtains and *banquettes* covered in imitation leather, its big wooden bread board, and its talkative clientele. Turn left into the **rue des Abbesses** and walk along to the **place des Abbesses**, which boasts one of the only two surviving art nouveau métro entrances that still has its scalloped-edged glass roof (it was moved here from the place de l'Hôtel-de-Ville). (Ⓜ Abbesses)

On the left is the brick **church of Saint-Jean-de-Montmartre** and straight ahead the **square Louis XVI**, a little garden that was once part of the cemetery where Louis XVI and Marie-Antoinette were first buried after dying on the guillotine. When the cemetery was closed a chapel (now ruined) was built to their memory

219

by Louis XVIII but their remains were transferred to the royal basilica at Saint-Denis. At no. 9 in the narrow street to the right, the **rue Yvonne-le-Tac**, on the spot where St Denis was allegedly martyred, is a chapel where Ignatius Loyola and his followers took the vows that marked the first stage of the founding of the Society of Jesus. Walk past the **Hôtel Régyn's Montmartre*** and turn right into the **passage des Abbesses** for a glimpse of a modest Montmartre backwater, then climb up the steps at the end to the **rue des Trois-Frères** and turn left to visit one of the most picturesque squares in Paris, the sloping **place Emile-Goudeau**, perched above the street. The **Relais de la Butte*** on the corner has been serving unpretentious meals since 1672, the views over Paris are magical and the square itself, with its green-painted Wallace Fountain and its trees and railings and benches, is a delight.

But on top of all this, the square has an important place in the history of modern art. The modest low building on the left is a reconstruction of the **Bateau Lavoir**, a lopsided wooden structure housing a series of artists' studios lived in at various times by Kees van Dongen and Modigliani, Braque and Juan Gris, and especially Picasso, who painted his seminal *Les Demoiselles d'Avignon* here. Also living in the building at one time were the poets Max Jacob and Guillaume Apollinaire. Inside the window are a list of the famous inhabitants and photos of the ramshackle structure before it was destroyed by fire in 1970 – ironically just when the money had at last been raised to restore it and turn it into a museum. Instead it has been rebuilt in concrete, but it does still consist of 25 studios for up-and-coming artists.

Turn left into the **rue d'Orchampt** for an idea of what it once looked like: the wooden houses on the left are similar to the original Bateau Lavoir, christened by Picasso with the name for the floating laundries on the Seine. (There are various versions of the reason behind his choice, some saying that it swayed in the wind on top of the hill like the river laundries, others that with its shipboard cladding it looked a bit like a boat, and the 'laundry' part was a dig at the meagre washing facilities, with a single tap for the whole building.)

Admire the strange front door at 3bis rue d'Orchampt, then turn back and walk up the steps of the **rue de la Mire** to the top of the triangular **place Jean-Baptiste-Clément**, which commemorates the author of the romantic song *Le temps des cerises* and has a 19th-century fountain in vaguely Renaissance style.

The **rue Norvins** to the right leads straight to the heart of tourist Montmartre, but you should now take the **rue Lepic** to the left, which is still fairly peaceful, even though a short way down you are greeted by one of Paris's best-known sites, the **Moulin de la Galette**, painted by Renoir and Van Gogh and once housing a dance hall. At its foot is a little Italian restaurant, **Da Graziano**, and on the other side are several modest restaurants-cum-cabarets, including the **Piano de la Butte, La Petite Galette** and **Au Coin de Rue**, where you can often hear young singers being given their first chance to perform in front of an audience.

The area round the windmill is strictly out of bounds these days, with plenty of 'Keep Out' notices protecting the wealthy inhabitants of the spruced-up houses and flats, but to make up for this you can enjoy a little-known treat by climbing up the steps between nos 73 and 75 rue Lepic and walking through the **Hameau**

des Artistes, a peaceful haven of tiny houses and gardens, to the avenue Junot. Turn left, past the house lived in by Francisque Poulbot, who invented the kitsch 'Montmartre urchins' with cheerful grins you'll find on many a card and souvenir, and another built by Alfred Loos for the Dadaist Tristan Tzara. Continue to no. 25 for a stroll along the **Villa Léandre**, another charming row of little houses. Then, still on the same side, climb down the steps of the **rue Juste-Métivier** and turn left into the busy **rue Caulaincourt**, which will bring you downhill to the **Cimetière Montmartre**. If you're feeling tired, you could travel a couple of stops on one of the buses that pass here. And if a meal is what you need, **Le Clodenis*** on the right-hand side is a well-known restaurant, while **Le Cépage Montmartrois** is more modest.

Cross the railway bridge to the cemetery entrance and ask for a plan at the attendants' lodge to enable you to find your way around. Appropriately enough, in this centre of nightlife, the cemetery is particularly strong on entertainers of various kinds – the actors Sacha Guitry and Louis Jouvet, the playwright Georges Feydeau, the composer Hector Berlioz, and – a recent inhabitant – the *cinéaste* François Truffaut are all here, along with a bevy of well-known writers like Stendhal, Théophile Gautier, Dumas *fils* and Henri Murger.

After this detour, walk back up the rue Caulaincourt (or again wait for a bus). If you are ready for a taste of Montmartre ambiance, not too tainted by tourism, you could do worse than stop for a meal at **Les Copains d'abord** at no. 62. When you reach the **rue des Saules** you may like to turn left to visit the **Musée d'Art Juif**, on the third floor of a Jewish community centre. It is something of a jumble of cult objects and models of synagogues but it does include some lithographs by Chagall and a few other well-known artists. The museum is due to be moved to an *hôtel* in the Marais and you may prefer to wait until it has settled into its new and more spacious premises.

On the other side of the rue Caulaincourt the rue des Saules leads up to the prettiest part of Montmartre, very photogenic with its cottagey houses with pastel-painted shutters decorated with heart shapes cut out of them. On the left is the **Lapin Agile cabaret**, a bit crumbling but highly picturesque with its pink paint and green shutters. Picasso and Vlaminck and the other leading lights of the artists' colony used to spend their evenings here sitting on wooden benches and singing bawdy French songs and sipping the traditional tipple of cherries steeped in brandy, while the punning sign swung outside in the wind: *Lapin Agile* (Nimble Rabbit) is a play on the name of a cartoonist called André Gill, who was commissioned to paint the sign showing a rabbit escaping from a saucepan and is said to have slipped in the words '*Là peint A. Gill*' – 'A. Gill paints here'. You can still spend a pleasant and lively evening here, and the wooden benches and singing and cherries in brandy don't feel as if they have been laid on for tourists.

Opposite the Lapin Agile is the **Cimetière Saint-Vincent**, which includes the grave of Utrillo, the painter who is always associated with this little corner of Paris.

Previous page: *Picasso painted* Les Demoiselles d'Avignon *in a studio in the place Emile-Goudeau*

He lived for a while with his mother, the painter Suzanne Valadon, in one of the houses on the far side of Paris's one surviving **vineyard**, which still produces a rather thin white wine and is duly celebrated with a *Fête des Vendanges* (Grape Harvest Festival) each autumn. Before visiting the house, now a charming museum, continue up the rue des Saules and turn right into the **rue de l'Abreuvoir**, passing a pink house that appears in a canvas by Utrillo. It has been turned into a modest restaurant called, like the painting, **La Maison Rose**.

This quiet street brings you to the **allée des Brouillards**, a narrow path running alongside desirable-looking houses with front gardens (a rarity in Paris). Gérard de Nerval lived in the **Château des Brouillards**, a 'folly' at the entrance to the little avenue. At the far end steps take you down to the **place des Quatre-Frères-Casadesus**. From there, walk up the steps on the left to a little public garden, ideal for a short break with its fountain-statue depicting St Denis clutching his head in his hands, its lively children playing in a miniature adventure playground and its very French scene of elderly (and not-so-elderly) men playing *boules* and squabbling over who is winning.

When you are ready to leave, walk past the *boule*-players and out into the **rue Girardon**, which has long been the home of **L'Assommoir***, a picturesque if over-priced restaurant with red-checked tablecloths and good home cooking. Walk up to the right to the **rue Norvins**, which brings you almost on a level with the Moulin de la Galette. On the corner of the **rue Saint-Rustique**, a narrow and winding street that scarcely seems to have changed over the centuries, is an ex-cabaret called **A la Bonne Franquette**, which was painted by Van Gogh as *La Guingette*.

You are now just a few steps from the **place du Tertre**, the heart of tourist Montmartre, and are surrounded by old-established cabaret-restaurants like **Au Consulat** or **Le Tire-bouchon** (where Jacques Brel was first spotted) or **La Mère Catherine***. But before exploring this crowded area, walk down the rue des Saules and turn right into the **rue Cortot**, where at no. 12 you come to the **Musée de Montmartre**, which will introduce you to the delights of Montmartre before the days of mass tourism. This is the house where Utrillo and several other painters lived, but long before that it was the home in the 17th century — it is the earliest surviving house in Montmartre — of a well-known actor called Roze de Rosimond, who played Molière's roles in Molière's plays and even followed in his illustrious predecessor's footsteps to the extent of dying, like him, on stage during a perform-ance of *Le Malade imaginaire*.

You buy your ticket in the building overlooking the rue Cortot but then walk through a charming little garden to the house, perched above the vineyard with another garden leading downhill. Surprisingly few visitors to Montmartre come here, which makes it all the more pleasant to meander through the little rooms, soaking up the history of the 'Commune de Montmartre' and learning about the people who lived there. You can see the original of the *Lapin Agile* sign and admire a genuine zinc counter, complete with bottles and glasses, from a bar that once stood in the rue de l'Abreuvoir. A theatre room, with posters and photos and cuttings, includes pictures of the Gaumont Palace, 'the world's largest cinema', and elsewhere you can see a reconstruction of the study of the composer Gustave

Charpentier and a superb bust of 'Marianne', the symbol of republican France, from the *mairie* of the eighteenth *arrondissement*. There are no great works of art (though local artists sometimes exhibit in the restored attics), but if, like me, you love museums crammed with mementoes and exhibits with historical associations, allow plenty of time to enjoy this one.

Continue along the rue Cortot to the **rue du Mont-Cenis**, turn right and you soon reach the **church of Saint-Pierre-de-Montmartre**, one of the earliest in Paris, which has been the parish church since 1147 but has long been overshadowed, literally and metaphorically, by the huge bulk of the Sacré-Coeur. Walk through the bronze doors and you enter a quiet world, far from the crowds, with Roman-esque capitals carved with curious scenes (one depicts a man with a pig's head lifting a goat's tail, apparently symbolising lust), and decorated with acanthus leaves and stylised flowers. The last bay of the nave is probably all that remains of the huge Benedictine abbey that once crowned the hill, its abbesses com-memorated in the square where you first set off on your climb to the top. But this early church has even earlier relics: four marble columns, two of them just inside the entrance, against the west wall, the others in the chancel. They formed part of the chapel that stood on this site in the 6th century, but were probably originally carved for one of the Roman temples dedicated to Mars or Mercury.

The little cemetery beside the church (open only on 1 November, the Feast of All Saints, when the French traditionally visit their family graves) is on the site of a much larger cemetery dating from the Merovingian period and some Merovingian tombs have been found during excavations.

A noisy contrast to this quiet and holy place greets you as you walk across to the **place du Tertre**, crowded virtually all year round (winter mornings may be more peaceful) with so-called 'artists' busy at their easels and foreign tourists — the French rarely venture here — peering over their shoulders and buying post-cards and garish souvenirs. It's not at all Parisian, but it's all harmless fun and you can spend an entertaining half hour or so watching the crowds from a café table and perhaps even having your silhouette drawn — some of the results are sur-prisingly good likenesses. The many restaurants are inevitably over-priced, but adequate if you stick to plain grilled dishes, and some of the older ones, like **La Mère Catherine*** at no. 6, or **Au Cadet de Gascogne** at no. 4, do still have some-thing of the atmosphere of a village café-restaurant such as you can find all over France. In the evenings, most have live accordion music and plenty of *ambiance* to go with it. **La Crémaillière 1900*** at no. 15 is better than most, with a terrace-garden behind, and the square now has a rather chic tea room, **Patachou**, at no. 9, with big windows offering wonderful views over Paris, delicious *pâtisseries* and some light lunch dishes.

Leading off the square is the tiny **place du Calvaire**, famous for its views. A short way beyond it, in the **rue Poulbot**, children will enjoy **L'Historial de Montmartre**, a small waxworks with tableaux depicting scenes from the history and artistic life of the district.

Now walk back across the place du Tertre and turn right in front of Saint-Pierre. Follow the road round and you come to Montmartre's best-known sight, the huge **basilica of the Sacré-Coeur**, which you will certainly have glimpsed from a

Le Consulat is one of many lively cabaret-restaurants on top of the Butte Montmartre

distance as you walked round Paris. Close up it doesn't seem quite so white, and it is really rather hideous, but it is so much a part of the landscape of Paris that aesthetic considerations seem irrelevant. You need only know that it was built by public subscription in a neo-Romanesque-cum-Byzantine style as an expiation and a symbol of faith in the future of the Church after the disastrous Franco-Prussian War of 1870–1, and that it is one of the country's most important Roman Catholic buildings, included in Pope John Paul's itinerary when he visited France in 1980. The interior is again huge, and impressive with its forest of candles, its tall cupola and its vast mosaic of Christ with arms outstretched. For over a century, worshippers have kept up, night and day, even through the world wars, a 'perpetual adoration' at the high altar.

Many flights of steps lead down through the gardens from the Sacré-Coeur to the **place Saint-Pierre**. It makes a pleasant walk in good weather, with plenty of benches if you feel like resting your legs and watching the local children playing in the sandpits, oblivious of the coach parties climbing up and down. In bad weather, or if your legs are protesting after the cobbled streets on top of the hill, you can take the funicular (open to midnight), or walk back to get the little *Mont-martrobus*, which runs up to about 8 p.m. between the *mairie* of the eighteenth *arrondissement* and the place Clichy, with stops outside Saint-Pierre and at various strategic points on the way up the Butte, such as the rue Lepic, opposite the Moulin de la Galette.

At the foot of the flights of steps is the **Halle Saint-Pierre**, a 19th-century wrought-iron structure, once part of a well-known fabric market and now housing two new museums. One is the **Musée d'Art Naïf Max Fourny**, with a permanent collection of naïve art from all over the world and occasional temporary exhibitions when work can be bought. The other, the **Musée en Herbe**, is a children's museum with a fashionable 'green' or conservation bias, with a full programme of exhibitions, workshops, film shows and the like.

If you fancy spending the evening at the theatre, the **Théâtre de l'Atelier**, in the pretty **place Charles-Dullin**, is one of the most attractive in Paris. To reach it, take the **rue de Steinkerque** at the bottom of the gardens, then turn right into the **rue d'Orsel**. Otherwise continue down the rue de Steinkerque to the **boulevard Rochechouart**, admire the façade of the **Elysée-Montmartre** on the corner, and either stroll along the boulevard to the right to see Pigalle at night, or travel from Ⓜ Anvers to Ⓜ Blanche, have a look at the Moulin Rouge and walk a little further west to the **place Clichy**. From here the 95 bus, one of the few that runs until late in the evening, will take you on an interesting ride to wherever you feel like ending the evening in central Paris: it goes down the rue d'Amsterdam, famous for its magnificent cheesemonger's **Androuët** (where you could always stop off for a cheesey meal), past the Gare Saint-Lazare with its curious 'sculpture' made up of clocks and watches, on to the Opéra and the Palais-Royal, past the Louvre and its Pyramid, across the Seine to Saint-Germain-des-Prés and eventually ends its run in Montparnasse.

Hotels and Restaurants

For general advice on choosing where to stay and where to eat, see Practical Information; prices are moderate unless otherwise stated.

Hotels

Moulin Rouge 39 rue Fontaine, 9e (42-81-93-25). A good base for exploring the 'New Athens' area and Montmartre. Quite large rooms, some grouped round an inner patio; a few have their own terrace.

Hôtel Régyn's Montmartre 18 pl des Abbesses, 18e (42-54-45-21). Small but attractive rooms in a little hotel well situated at the foot of the prettiest part of Montmartre, right next to Ⓜ Abbesses. The quietest rooms (some with a view of the Sacré-Coeur) overlook a little garden square, but all were well modernised in the mid-eighties.

Résidence Montmartre 10 rue Burq, 18e (46-06-51-91, fax: 42-52-82-59). A quiet street leading off the rue des Abbesses, comfortable rooms and reasonable prices.

Terrass' Hôtel 12–14 rue Joseph-de-Maistre, 18e (46-06-72-85, fax: 42-52-29-11). Large, old-established and fairly expensive, on the edge of tourist Montmartre near the Montmartre Cemetery and the place de Clichy. Very comfortable rooms, restaurant and coffee shop, terrace for sunny breakfasts and drinks, panoramic views, though little Montmartre atmosphere.

226

Timhôtel Montmartre 11 rue Ravignan, 18e (42-55-74-79, fax: 40-20-96-98). The very modest Hôtel du Paradis, where Henry Miller used to stay, was modernised in the early eighties and became a member of the small Timhôtel chain. The site, overlooking the place Emile Godeau, where Picasso *et al* lived and worked, is still pretty heavenly, and the rooms, if a bit impersonal, are well planned.

Montmartre also has one of the few places in Paris offering short-term self-catering lets, the **Résidence Charles-Dullin** (see Practical Information).

Restaurants

L'Assommoir 12 rue Girardon, 18e (42-64-55-01); closed Sun for dinner, Mon, about mid-July to mid-Aug. Fairly expensive but reliable *cuisine bourgeoise* and a very convenient site in the heart of Montmartre yet slightly away from the tourist hordes.

L'Auberge Montmartroise 6 rue des Abbesses, 18e (46-06-81-48); closed Mon, Tue and Aug. Friendly inn that is also one of the few examples left of a genuine local bistrot. Good range of *menus*, with specially good-value *formule rapide* at lunchtime. Open late.

Le Bateau Lavoir 8 rue Garreau, 18e (46-06-02-00); closed mid-May to mid-June. A modest little place, which really is close to the Bateau Lavoir; a good bet for inexpensive meals, properly cooked.

Le Clodenis 57 rue Caulaincourt, 18e (46-06-20-26); closed Sun and Mon. Quite expensive (less so at lunchtime) but very pretty and with interesting specialities from the South of France.

La Crémaillère 1900 15 pl du Tertre, 18e (46-06-58-59). Surprisingly good value, considering its setting in the heart of tourist Montmartre, and attractive too, with a little garden done up to look like a typical Paris square, complete with Wallace Fountain, and dining room with art nouveau-style décor. Good for seafood.

Le Grandgousier 17 av Rachel, 18e (43-87-66-12); closed weekends (may open for Sat dinner) and part of Aug. Small and delightful, seeming far away from the garish place Blanche and place Clichy nearby. Convenient before or after a visit to Montmartre Cemetery.

La Mère Catherine 6 pl du Tertre, 18e (46-06-32-69). The food is no more than adequate but there's plenty of atmosphere in this villagey house, once the local presbytery, turned into a restaurant in 1793 by a lady called Catherine Lemoine. Oak-beamed dining rooms, red-checked tablecloths, tables on the pavement and in the little garden in fine weather, live music in the evening.

La Pomponnette 42 rue Lepic, 18e (46-06-08-36); closed for Sun dinner, Mon and Aug. Lively and old-established bistrot with old photos and posters, sketches and watercolours crammed on to the walls, often boisterous locals and good basic cooking.

Le Relais de la Butte 12 rue Ravignan, 18e (42-23-94-64); closed Mon and for lunch on Tue from Oct to Easter (no closure the rest of the year). Unpretentious, in a low 17th-century house a few paces from the Bateau Lavoir; village inn atmosphere, straightforward country-style dishes.

Wepler 14 pl Clichy, 18e (45-22-53-24). Large and bustling brasserie famous for its seafood; open late.

Museums and Places of Interest

Musée Gustave-Moreau 14 rue de La Rochefoucauld, 9e. Closed Tue. Ⓜ Trinité

Musée Renan-Scheffer 16 rue Chaptal, 9e. Closed Mon. Ⓜ Pigalle, Blanche

Cimetière Montmartre (Montmartre Cemetery) rue Caulaincourt/av Rachel, 18e. Ⓜ Clichy, Blanche

Musée d'Art Juif (Museum of Jewish Art) 42 rue des Saules, 18e. Afternoons only, closed Fri and Sat. Ⓜ Lamarck-Caulaincourt *This museum is due to move to the Marais in the early 1990s; check locally*

Musée de Montmartre (Museum of Old Montmartre) 12 rue Cortot, 18e. Closed Mon, open afternoons only (but from 11 a.m. on Sun). Ⓜ Lamarck-Caulaincourt, Abbesses

Historial de Montmartre (waxworks) rue Poulbot, 18e. Open daily. Ⓜ Abbesses

Halle Saint-Pierre 2 rue Ronsard, 18e. Temporary exhibitions only (*Musée en Herbe*), but also houses *Musée d'Art Naïf Max Fourny* (naïve painters). Open daily. Ⓜ Anvers

Beyond the Centre

Once you move outside the central districts of Paris described in the walks in this book, the number of sights to be seen naturally diminishes, but there is still much of interest on the city's fringes and you will probably feel the need, in summer at any rate, to head for one of the parks and woods on the outskirts for a refreshing break from time to time. By venturing further afield you will also get a better feel of life in Paris than in the tourist-frequented centre.

The western side of the city – the area round the Bois de Boulogne – has the greater concentration of museums and other sights and is traditionally the smartest residential district. Although the villages that once lay beyond Paris's eastern boundary have had their periods of prosperity, the east side of the city has long been the most 'disadvantaged', primarily a series of working-class districts with virtually no museums or places of interest, except for Père-Lachaise cemetery and, just outside the city limits, the Château de Vincennes. But recent moves to right the imbalance between east and west have resulted in some interesting large-scale development projects, including the huge new La Villette complex in the north-east, a business centre on either side of the Seine, a multi-purpose sports centre and a striking design for a new national library. And while much of the wholesale redevelopment of the seventies has little to recommend it, more recent rebuilding and smartening up of run-down streets has generally been more sensitive, making the eastern *arrondissements* well worth visiting for anyone interested in architecture and town planning. There are also plans for a 'green corridor', planted with trees and lawns, stretching from Vincennes through to central Paris. The Parc Georges-Brassens is a new attraction in the south, while the industrial north boasts the cathedral of Saint-Denis with the tombs of most of France's kings and queens. This chapter, divided into four geographical sections, gives brief descriptions of the most interesting places to visit, including some outside Paris proper, such as Vincennes and Saint-Denis. It tells you how to reach them by public transport, and suggests a few restaurants or cafés that are suitable for a meal before or after your visit.

West

Bagatelle

Ⓜ *Pont-de-Neuilly; then 15 minutes' walk or 43 bus to the place de Bagatelle plus 5 minutes' walk.*

Lunch beneath the tall chestnut trees in the delightful Bagatelle Gardens on the edge of the Bois de Boulogne is one of the most civilised treats Paris has to offer. The occasional hoarse cry of a peacock punctuates your meal, sparrows peck cheekily at the *petits-fours* that come with your coffee and after a leisurely pause you can stroll past the lawns dotted with daffodils and hyacinths and overhung by magnolias in spring, or in summer enjoy the favourite sport of the well-heeled Parisians who live within shouting distance of the Bois by exclaiming over the aberrations of the judging in the competition for the year's finest roses, in the very pretty rose garden adorned with a pagoda-like structure known as the **Kiosque de l'Impératrice**. The lilies and clematis are famous, the **Orangerie**, sometimes used for art exhibitions, is a graceful creamy-white building where orange trees really are grown, and the gardens are dotted with romantic ruins and waterfalls and miniature lakes full of ducks and moorhens.

To the left of the entrance is the **Petit Château**, built in just 64 days in 1777 by 900 workmen – for a wager. The Comte d'Artois, Louis XVI's brother, bet Marie-Antoinette 100,000 *livres* that he could have it built in time to hold a splendid party there to enliven her journey from Choisy to Versailles. To the amazement of the court, the queen lost and the pretty little château, recently restored and gleaming white, with sphinxes guarding the entrance, is still standing. The doors are rarely open, but you can peer in from the peaceful garden behind it. The estate was bought in 1835 by the Marquis of Hertford, who died there in 1870, leaving it to his illegitimate son Sir Richard Wallace, a great benefactor to Paris (Introduction), who also died there, in the same bed in the Comte d'Artois's bedroom, 20 years later. Both men left quite a mark on Bagatelle, turning the château into a comfortable mansion rather than an aristocratic folly and extending the gardens. Sir Richard built the **Trianon**, at right angles to the château, which is now used for exhibitions and has a little gift boutique selling charming items on a garden theme.

The restaurant (**Les Jardins de Bagatelle**, 40-67-98-29) is over-priced, but delightful for an alfresco lunch or a romantic dinner after the gardens have shut and only the peacocks can occasionally be heard (entrance from the route de Sèvres à Neuilly after dusk).

Bois de Boulogne

Ⓜ *Porte Maillot, Les Sablons, Pont-de-Neuilly (north side); Porte Dauphine, Porte d'Auteuil (east side); bus 73 and Petite Ceinture.*

The Bois de Boulogne, long known to Parisians as simply 'le Bois', is the city's best-known lung and offers a good escape from the sultry heat of summer. But it is beautiful in autumn too and in spite of the many roads that crisscross it, carrying heavy traffic during the morning and evening rush hours, it does give you a feeling of being out in the country (I have even seen a pheasant skulking in the undergrowth). Although it is very popular with families for weekend outings and with walkers and sports enthusiasts all week, its dicey reputation at night is well deserved and you would be most unwise to wander in it after dark.

Racing in the Paris Area

Going to the races in Paris and the Ile de France is as much a social event as a sporting one. Go to one of the major races at the **Longchamp** or **Auteuil** racecourses in their lovely leafy setting in the Bois de Boulogne – the **Prix du Président de la République**, say, on Palm Sunday at Auteuil, or the **Prix de l'Arc de Triomphe** at Longchamp on the first Sunday in October – and you'll be treated to a dazzling display of Paris fashions as well as an exciting race. Elegant, aristocratic-looking men and ultra-chic women in the latest fashions soon transport you back to the Proustian era when the Bois de Boulogne was a year-round place to see and be seen.

If your interests are purely sporting, bear in mind that Auteuil specialises in steeple-chasing, whereas Longchamp is the home of flat racing. **Vincennes**, at the opposite, eastern, end of Paris in the Bois de Vincennes, is the place for the popular sport of trotting.

But the prettiest racecourse is undoubtedly at **Chantilly** in the Ile de France, in a magical setting overlooking the château. You might like to time your visit to coincide with one of the key races in Chantilly's **Semaine hippique** in June – the **Prix du Jockey Club** on the second Sunday in the month, the **Prix de Diane** on the third Sunday.

Racing is also held at **Fontainebleau, Maisons-Laffitte** and **Saint-Cloud**, in the Ile de France round Paris. The Paris Tourist Office can supply dates and times.

Once a royal hunting forest, the Bois is still well wooded, but was laid out as a park during the reign of Napoleon III, who was much taken with London's parks. In the late 19th and early 20th centuries it was highly fashionable with the *beau monde*, who came here to take the air in their carriages or to cut a dash on their latest mounts – a scene familiar from the pages of Proust – or to attend race meetings at the **Auteuil and Longchamp racecourses**, which still attract an elegant and cosmopolitan crowd (see box).

Sporting opportunities are legion nowadays: you can go boating on the **Lac Inférieur** with its two central islands (one of which has a small restaurant, the **Châlet des Iles**, to which you can be ferried for a pleasant if over-priced meal or a peaceful drink); you can join the army of joggers or cycle along one of the many cycle tracks; you might like to go bowling near the attractive **Mare Saint-James**, a duck-inhabited lake on the Neuilly side, with its own island, or on the Passy side near the **Lac Supérieur**; you might even try riding, but the posh riding clubs are closed societies and you will probably need a suitably well-bred French friend to effect an *entrée*. If spectator sports are more in your line you can watch tennis at the famous **Roland-Garros stadium** in the south or polo beyond the lovely **Bagatelle Gardens** (see above).

The Bois's restaurants are mostly expensive, though **La Grande Cascade** near Longchamp (45-27-33-51) does offer a lunch *menu* (weekdays only) that makes a meal in this delightful 19th-century pavilion just about affordable – or you could join racegoers for tea and cakes on the terrace. Food for the mind is supplied by the interesting **Musée des Arts et Traditions Populaires**, devoted to folk art and

231

culture down the ages, and popular with children because, long before the word became common currency, it was offering plenty of 'interactive' displays. Shakespeare plays and concerts are also occasionally performed in the **Jardin Shakespeare**, whose romantic open-air theatre is full of natural pieces of scenery – a miniature waterfall and a lake (ideal for Ophelia), a carpet of heather (for *Macbeth*'s blasted heath), a lavender-filled terrace backed by cypresses (Prospero's island), a scented bower of roses, thyme and honeysuckle (*A Midsummer Night's Dream*).

Children will also love the **Jardin d'Acclimatation**, a cross between a small zoo and an amusement park, including a miniature farm with hens and geese, rabbits and sheep, and the **Musée en Herbe**, a children's museum with workshops and temporary displays that will keep them amused for many hours. Complete the treat by taking them there on the miniature train from the Porte Maillot corner of the Bois.

La Défense

(ⓜ) *La Défense or bus 73; the métro will also reach La Défense in 1991 or 1992.*

The first part of this high-rise business and residential district beyond the Pont de Neuilly was built in the sixties. Its skyscrapers can be seen from the Tuileries Gardens, towering over the Arc de Triomphe, which is now mirrored by **La Grande Arche**, a gigantic cube-shaped archway, opened in 1989 and vast enough for Notre Dame to fit inside it. The arch was used for the international summit held at the time of the bicentenary of the storming of the Bastille and six weeks later a new international foundation for the rights of man and the humanities, topically called the Fondation Arche de la Fraternité, was opened there on the 200th anniversary of the Declaration of the Rights of Man. The vast roof area, the **Belvédère**, is open to the public and offers stunning views across Paris (your entrance fee will help to fund the research and education programmes undertaken by the Foundation). The building will also be the home of the Housing Ministry and various private companies and institutes. With its shiny white marble surface and its huge size, the arch is highly visible, and is one of those places you either love or hate – certainly worth having a look at anyway.

The rest of the Défense district – the name comes from a bronze monument to those who died defending the city during the Franco-Prussian War – is dominated by the tall office blocks you can see from far away and softened by the occasional piece of sculpture or ornamental fountain. The long podium ('**La Dalle**') is a good place for getting a feel of the whole complex and the 73 bus will give you some curious glimpses of the few remaining little houses in Puteaux and Courbevoie, dwarfed by the surrounding towers. But on the whole the architecture is undistinguished and the new developments in the east of the city offer more of interest.

Neuilly

Neuilly has long had the reputation of being an upmarket residential area, but so many of its beautiful houses have been pulled down and replaced by luxury blocks of flats and offices that the main impression you get is of a busy business district

'Villas', 'Hamlets' and 'Cities'

The term **villa** has a special meaning in Paris. In the suburbs and in provincial towns it refers to a detached house, not very different from English 'villa', though without the seaside connotations. But Paris *villas*, mainly found in the prosperous western districts of Passy, Auteuil and Neuilly, are cul de sacs (a term not used, incidentally, in French, which has *impasse* instead), lined with low houses and often delightful oases of peace and greenery, with tiny gardens in front. Just the sort of place that makes you think: 'It must be lovely to live here', and particularly sought after in Paris, where both peace and greenery are at a premium.

The term **hameau** or 'hamlet' has a similar meaning and is inherited from the days when the outlying villages of Paris (many of them not absorbed into the city proper until 1860) were surrounded by little clusters of houses: *hameau* is still an administrative term in rural France for a place that is too small to be classified as a village.

Cités are clusters or rows of little houses, often including artists' studios (as in the **Cité des Artistes** in Montmartre), and the term has recently been taken up by estate agents and developers, in much the same way that London estate agents refer lyrically to 'villages', implying a sense of community. The most attractive example is the **Cité Floréale** near the Parc de Montsouris in south-eastern Paris, with its villagey streets all named after flowers: Iris Road, Mimosa Square, Wistaria Street, Convolvulus Place and so on (see South).

Passages may also be delightful, as in

the **passage Saint-Ferdinand** in Neuilly, a villagey enclave just off the six-lane highway of the avenue Charles-de-Gaulle.

Many of these peaceful places are officially private roads, but if you behave discreetly you can often wander in and savour their delights — on foot, no cars allowed. This may be more difficult at weekends and in the evenings, as the recent advent of the entryphone or 'coded' automatic entrance mechanism has been eagerly embraced by the lovers of privacy who live in such places. And a word of warning: some *villas* are dull, urban cul de sacs, though there will generally be some redeeming feature such as an ornamental wrought-iron sign over the entrance, or details left over from an earlier era — elaborately decorated pumps or pretty glass and iron canopies. But don't assume that all the *villas* and *cités* you spot on the map are worth visiting.

Here are some that are:

Villa Dietz-Monnin, Villa Molitor and **Villa Montmorency**, all in Auteuil (16e)
Villa Madrid in Neuilly
Villa Seurat, 14e, near the Parc de Montsouris (see South)
Villa Godin, 20e, backing on to the Père-Lachaise cemetery (see East)
Cité des Fleurs, 17e, off the avenue de Clichy
Cité Floréale, 13e, near the Parc de Montsouris (see South)
Cité des Artistes, 18e, in Montmartre (see Walk 10)
Villa Léandre, 18e, also in Montmartre (see Walk 10)

sandwiched between the **Porte Maillot**, with its conference centre, huge modern hotels and theatre (used for lavish stage productions and pop concerts), and the skyscrapers of **La Défense** further west. The old avenue de Neuilly, now called the **avenue Charles-de-Gaulle**, continues Le Nôtre's planned 'triumphal way' from the Louvre to Saint-Germain-en-Laye. But it is now a faceless artery cutting Neuilly in two.

One of the best open-air food markets in the Paris area is held in the **place du Marché** (Ⓜ Les Sablons) on Wednesday, Friday and Sunday mornings: you might like to cater for a picnic here, then walk across the main avenue and along the rue Paul-Déroulède into the **Bois de Boulogne**. Further west (Ⓜ Pont-de-Neuilly) the **rue de Longchamp**, with some good small food shops, or the **avenue de Madrid**, with the well-known restaurant **La Rascasse** at no. 10 (46-24-05-30, expensive) and a few doors away at no. 12 the cheerful **L'Amanguier** (47-45-79-73, much lower prices), again lead to the Bois, and to **Bagatelle**.

Neuilly has a number of good restaurants, and is certainly your best bet before or after a walk in the Bois, as the 16th *arrondissement* on the east side is rather thin on eating places. The **Drugstore** in the place du Marché is handy for a quick lunch or supper, and unexpectedly has a peaceful little courtyard-garden for summer meals; **Sébillon** (20 av Charles-de-Gaulle, 46-24-71-31) has been specialising in seafood and leg of lamb for decades, served by highly professional waiters in an art nouveau décor; and **Jenny Jacquet**, in the pretty place Parmentier near the Porte Maillot (46-24-94-14, closed Sat for lunch, part of Aug), offers deliciously light cuisine.

Neuilly itself has few sights, but there is a little **Musée de la Femme** on the way to the Bois (12 rue du Centre, afternoons only, closed Tue), which also has a collection of automata, and you can admire the pretty pink-painted house on the edge of the **Parc de la Folie Saint-James**, now a small public garden. Both were once part of an estate including an elaborate pleasure garden and the **Folie Saint-James**, an elegant 18th-century mansion built by a rich financier who became involved in the 'Affair of the Queen's Necklace' (box, Walk 9) and was soon ruined.

Passy and Auteuil

Once villages on the outskirts of Paris, now smart residential areas with modern luxury blocks of flats plus some elegant *hôtels* surrounded by gardens. Here you will find art nouveau buildings (see box, Introduction) and secluded private roads called *villas* or *hameaux* (see box), with the occasional villagey square to remind you of the area's past.

Maison de Balzac (*9 rue Raynouard, 16e;* Ⓜ *Passy; closed Mon*)
In this charming countrified house with a little garden, dwarfed by modern blocks, Honoré de Balzac wrote several of the novels in his great *Comédie humaine* sequence — and hid from his creditors. It is now a museum and reference library filled with manuscripts and mementoes, including the coffee pot in which he made the strong brew that kept him going for long stints of writing through the night. A back entrance enabled him to escape from unwelcome callers into the cobbled

The rue Berton has scarcely changed since Balzac used to creep down it to escape his creditors

rue Berton, which has remained virtually unchanged to this day: don't miss a walk down this peaceful lamplit backwater before or after visiting the museum.

Musée Marmottan (*2 rue Louis-Boilly, 16e;* Ⓜ *Muette, Ranelagh, bus Petite Ceinture; closed Mon*)

Former private collection displayed in the lovely 19th-century mansion of the art historian who amassed it beside the **Jardin du Ranelagh**, landscaped by Haussmann on the site of a popular open-air dance hall and 'pleasure palace' modelled on Lord Ranelagh's in London. You have the pleasant feeling of visiting a private house as you admire M. Marmottan's Renaissance furniture, tapestries and *objets d'art* and the bequests that have been added later, including some beautiful medieval miniatures and the superb collection of 65 Monet canvases donated by his son. This included the famous *Impression, Sunrise*, painted in 1872, that gave rise to the (originally sarcastic) 'Impressionist' label. Thankfully, that landmark painting and a number of others, stolen in 1985, were eventually recovered at the end of 1990. This museum, which is surprisingly little known to foreign tourists, now has one of the finest collections of Impressionists you'll see anywhere, with a whole series of glorious views of Monet's garden at Giverny in the lower gallery.

235

Musée du Vin (*rue des Eaux, 16e;* Ⓜ *Passy; open from midday, closed Mon*)
Small museum in vaulted medieval cellars with waxwork tableaux illustrating the
wine-making process (which was carried out in the old village of Passy by monks);
you can even do some gentle tasting here.

The **Brasserie Stella** (133 av Victor-Hugo, 16e, 47-27-60-54, closed Aug) is a lively
place to observe the chic inhabitants of this prosperous area but restaurants in the
seizième are mostly very expensive, so you may prefer to eat in Neuilly or in the
Bois de Boulogne (see above).

South

Parc Georges-Brassens

bus 89 or Petite Ceinture.

Large park opened in 1983 on the site of the old Vaugirard slaughterhouses (you
can still see splendid sturdy bronze bulls over the main gateposts, tails proudly
arched). This untouristy area is a good place for watching ordinary Parisians taking
the air or listening to music from the bandstand. Children will enjoy the adventure
playground while adults sit in the sun or admire the gardens or visit the second-
hand bookstalls in the old meat market buildings beside the park. Good for a
stroll before or after visiting *La Rûche* (see below).

Parc de Montsouris

Ⓡ *Cité Universitaire, bus 21, Petite Ceinture.*

A charming hilly park laid out by Baron Haussmann in the 1860s and again little
known to tourists. Complete with lake, a small-scale version of the Bey of Tunis's
Bardo Palace, winding paths and a particularly pleasant conservatory-style restaurant (**Le Pavillon Montsouris**, 45-88-38-52), it makes a good start to a visit to
the **Cité Universitaire**, a series of student halls of residence, mostly dating from
the twenties, set in leafy grounds just south of the park. Each building is set aside
for a different nationality and reflects its traditional architecture, creating some
interesting contrasts, and the Brazilian and Swiss *pavillons* attract many visitors
because both were designed by Le Corbusier.

East of the Parc de Montsouris is the **Cité Floréale**, a series of enchanting little
streets and squares, each named after a flower or tree (square des Mimosas, rue
des Iris, rue des Glycines . . .) and lined with tiny houses fronted by pocket-
handkerchief gardens. Behind this little enclave tower the brutish blocks that have
transformed much of the 13th *arrondissement* but Wistaria Street and Mimosa
Square are as charmingly peaceful and villagey as ever.

If you enjoy exploring areas well off the beaten tourist track you can walk from
the Cité Floréale to the **Butte-aux-Cailles**, another villagey district that has miraculously escaped the developers' attentions (aim for the place Paul-Verlaine, 13e). But

nearer at hand is a little group of peaceful old streets that again seem far removed from the bustle of modern Paris: stroll along the rue Saint-Yves to the north-west of the Parc de Montsouris, turn right into the rue de la Tombe-Issoire, then right again into the **Villa Seurat**, where Salvador Dalí and several other artists have lived. Return to the rue Saint-Yves via the rue de l'Aude and the rue des Artistes.

La Rûche

2 passage de Dantzig, 15e; bus 89 or Petite Ceinture.

Montparnasse's answer to the Bateau-Lavoir in Montmartre (Walk 10): the circular wine pavilion from the 1900 World Exhibition, bought by Alfred Boucher, a philanthropist and patron of artists (and something of a sculptor himself) who had the generous and practical idea of turning it into a place where artists could live and work in return for a nominal rent. He called it 'The Beehive' (*La Rûche* in French), imagining it as a series of 'cells' in which his protégés could work away like busy bees, untrammelled by daily cares. It sounds ludicrous, and the pomp and circumstance that surrounded the opening ceremony had its comical side, but M. Boucher's beehive soon became home and workplace to Chagall and Léger, Modigliani and Ossip Zadkine, among many others. It was very nearly demolished in the sixties but Chagall and a committee of sympathisers managed to save it (much of the funds raised came from the sums promised for the restoration of the Bateau-Lavoir before it burnt down) and it has now been restored and is again lived in by a community of artists. Stone caryatids surround the doorway and if you behave discreetly you may be able to walk round to see the charming cottagey garden adorned with sculptures.

Convenient for both La Rûche and the Parc Georges-Brassens is **Le Clos Morillons** (50 rue des Morillons, 15e, 48-28-04-37, closed Sat for lunch, Sun), a bistrot-turned-restaurant, elegant but cosy, with inventive cuisine and good-value lunch and dinner *menus*.

East

Père-Lachaise cemetery (also known as the Cimetière de l'Est)

main entrance in blvd de Ménilmontant, other entrances off the rue des Rondeaux (Porte de la Dhuya) and the rue de la Réunion (Porte de la Réunion), all 20e; Ⓜ Philippe-Auguste, Père-Lachaise, Gambetta; bus 61, 69, 76.

Paris's best-known cemetery (and also its largest open space) is named after Father François d'Aix de La Chaise, a Jesuit and former science and philosophy teacher who was Louis XIV's confessor from 1674 to his death in 1709 and carried out various political assignments for the king. He often stayed at Mont-Louis, the rest home and retreat the Jesuits had built on this spot, and helped to redesign it, hence the use of his name for the cemetery that was laid out here in the early 19th century, forty or so years after the Jesuits had been expelled from France.

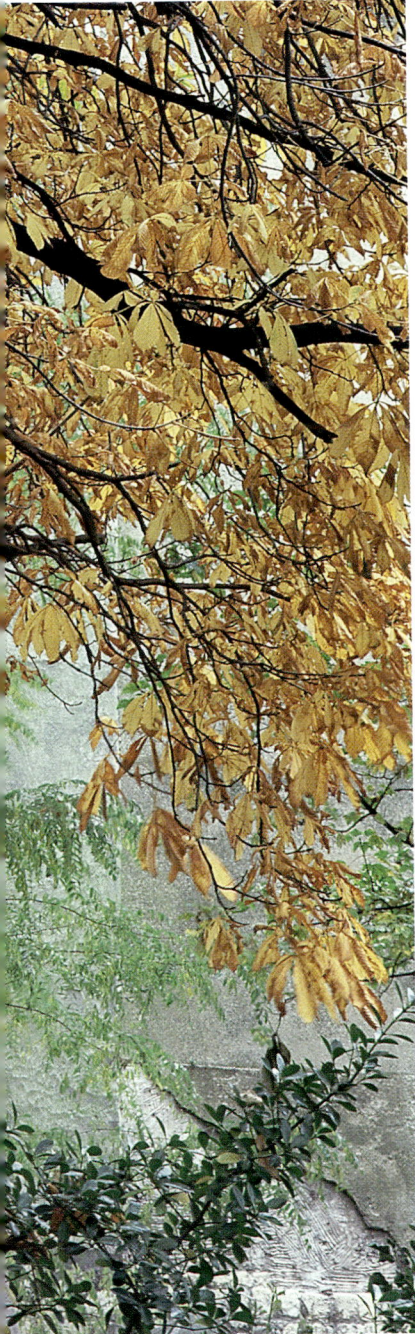

The cemetery is a romantic place, leafy and hilly, many of its tombs (built like little houses in the French style) adorned with sculptures. But it's hard to find your way around, so I recommend spending a few francs on a plan with the graves of celebrities pinpointed, or a bit more on one of the booklets by Vincent de Langlade, an expert on the cemetery, garrulous and bearded, who will take you on guided tours focusing on specific themes (buy plans and booklets from the porter's lodge by the main entrance, where you can also find out times of visits — or check in one of the What's On publications — or the bookshop near the Porte de la Dhuya entrance).

Among the most-visited tombs are those of the poet and playwright Alfred de Musset, romantically overhung by the weeping willow (regularly replanted) he wanted to watch over him, Edith Piaf and her young husband (always covered in flowers), the medieval lovers Abélard and Héloïse, in a suitably Gothicky tomb near the old Jewish cemetery that predates Père-Lachaise (see Walk 1) — and Oscar Wilde, adorned with a rather solid-looking sphinx designed by Jacob Epstein. But you can also pay homage to a host of writers and painters — Proust and Hugo, say, or Balzac, Molière and Alphonse Daudet, and Modigliani, Géricault and David among many others — and spare a few minutes for the splendidly named Fulgence Bienvenüe, to whom any visitor to Paris should be profoundly grateful (he masterminded the building of the métro system and his tomb boasts a bronze

The romantic, leafy cemetery of Père-Lachaise in eastern Paris, its house-like tombs adorned with sculptures

palm branch donated by an appreciative City of Paris). In the south-east corner is the tragic **Mur des Fédérés**, in front of which the last 147 of the rebels who set up the Paris Commune and were cornered in the cemetery were executed in 1871.

The pleasantest restaurant near Père-Lachaise is **Aux Becs Fins** (44 blvd de Ménilmontant, 20e, 47-97-51-52, closed Sun), but **Le Bistrot du 20e** is fairly near the Porte de la Dhuya entrance and is handy if you're also visiting Ménilmontant and Belleville (44 rue du Surmelin, 20e, 48-97-20-30, closed weekends and Aug) as well as being excellent value. You may be able to get a snack or a drink at the striking new **Théâtre de la Colline** (15 rue Malte-Brun) just off the place Gambetta and there are plenty of modest cafés in the side streets.

Belleville and Ménilmontant

Ⓜ *Ménilmontant, Père-Lachaise, Gambetta, bus 61, 69, 96.*

Once rustic villages on the vine-clad slopes north-east of Paris, popular with holidaying Parisians, then incorporated into the city in 1860, these two districts in the 20th *arrondissement* were until recently run-down working-class areas with a large immigrant population. In the seventies many of the picturesque but seedy old streets were pulled down and replaced by ugly tower blocks, but over the last few years there have been some more sensitive developments, and the whole area offers interesting contrasts between old and new. Only the most incurably romantic can truly believe that the inhabitants were better off in the little houses with no modern sanitation that used to line the steep and winding streets, but it's still a relief to know that in the **rue des Cascades**, say, or the **rue de la Mare**, you can find a few traces of the working-class Paris pictured in the songs of Edith Piaf or Maurice Chevalier, both of whom were born here.

Just off the winding **rue des Amandiers**, with a lively theatre of the same name, is the **Conservatoire Georges-Bizet** in the rue des Cendriers, an attractive new music academy with a miniature amphitheatre beside it for open-air concerts and surrounded by a mixture of faceless blocks of flats and some more imaginative developments. Just east of here the streets perched high up beyond Père-Lachaise cemetery (all named after the fruit trees that once grew here) offer some extraordinary views over the new developments and the **rue Orfila** takes you into a provincial-seeming world where you can still see a few trees and gardens and join the locals for an unpretentious meal at **Mère-Grand** at no. 20 (closed weekends).

You can combine a brief exploration of this area with **Père-Lachaise** (leave the cemetery by the Porte de la Dhuya) and with **Charonne** (see below).

Palais Omnisports de Paris-Bercy

Ⓜ *Bercy, bus 24.*

Huge multi-purpose sports centre beside the Seine, on the Right Bank east of the Gare de Lyon, near the new **Finance Ministry** buildings and opposite the site of the futuristic **Bibliothèque de France** (library) at Tolbiac. Worth a visit for some glimpses of the way eastern Paris is being revitalised.

Saint-Germain-de-Charonne

bus 76 from the Louvre, the Pont Neuf or the Marais.

A tiny late medieval church with some Romanesque portions and its own little cemetery, in an area on the eastern fringe of Paris that is being developed in a much more sympathetic way than the high-rise schemes perpetrated further north. The village of Charonne, which once had several monasteries and convents, an elegant château and an aristocratic population, was annexed to Paris in 1860. There are some attractive little houses in the **rue Saint-Blaise** and the square in front of the church still has a villagey feel, though the café on the corner has been converted into an upmarket grocer's. At the bottom of the rue Saint-Blaise is the charming little **place des Grès**, where you can enjoy a modest lunch or supper at **L'Auberge du Village** (3 pl des Grès, 20e, 43-73-46-39) before exploring the renovated houses just behind the square, with a little public garden beyond them. In the rue Saint-Blaise itself is the lively **Le Courtil** (15 rue Saint-Blaise, 20e, 43-70-09-32).

You might like to walk a little way east along the rue de Bagnolet to see some pretty 18th-century houses, especially the **Ermitage** on the corner of the rue des Balkans, built by the Duchesse d'Orléans (the daughter of Louis XIV and Madame de Montespan), who owned a large château here surrounded by grounds.

The steps beside the church will take you up to the rue Stendhal and on to the place Gambetta, from where you can visit both **Père-Lachaise** and **Ménilmontant** and **Belleville**. Alternatively, you can enjoy a little treat by walking west along the rue de Bagnolet towards the south entrance to Père-Lachaise and stopping off for a discreet visit to the delightful **Villa Godin**, a little row of houses with tiny gardens backing on to the cemetery.

Vincennes

Château de Vincennes

entrance in avenue de Paris, Vincennes; Ⓜ *Château-de-Vincennes,* Ⓡ *Vincennes, bus 56, 86.*

This royal castle just outside Paris proper has had an interesting history but can be disappointing and frustrating to visit: the approach is dusty and unkempt, much of the buildings seems neglected, in spite of recent restoration, and official opening times are often ignored, with scheduled guided tours cancelled. The atmosphere seems rather grim too, perhaps because it was often used as a prison (Nicolas Fouquet, whose château at Vaux-le-Vicomte brought down on him the envious wrath of Louis XIV, was incarcerated here, his gaoler the Comte d'Artagnan, one of Dumas's Three Musketeers).

The castle dates from the 14th century but the severity of the main building with its **Keep (Donjon)** and turrets is lightened by the classical **Royal Pavilions** at the far end of the courtyard, built by Mazarin (who died in the Pavillon du Roi) to designs by Le Vau three centuries later, and the Gothic **Royal Chapel** on the east

241

side. Henry V of England died on the second floor of the keep, which now houses a small museum illustrating the castle's history.

Bois de Vincennes

Ⓜ *Porte de Charenton, Porte Dorée, Château de Vincennes, bus 46, 86.*

Right the other side of Paris from the Bois de Boulogne and frequented by a rather different type of Parisian – mainly families from the working-class eastern *arrondissements*. Even its racecourse is known for its trotting races, rather than the more aristocratic steeple-chasing and flat racing at Auteuil and Longchamp.

But the Bois de Vincennes, in spite of its much less fashionable reputation, has as much to see and do as its western counterpart: a couple of lakes where you can hire rowing boats and canoes (each with a restaurant); a beautiful flower garden, known as the **Parc Floral de Paris**; a popular zoo; a Tibetan Buddhist temple; an excellent theatre converted from a cartridge factory (**La Cartoucherie**); a cycle track and athletics stadium; and the **Musée des Arts Africains et Océaniens**, housing magnificent collections of African (including North African) and Australasian art and crafts, plus a tropical aquarium (293 av de Daumesnil, 12e, closed Tue. Ⓜ Porte Dorée).

North

Canal Saint-Martin Cruises

The pleasantest way of visiting La Villette (see below) is to travel there by canal boat – a delightfully leisurely three-hour cruise along the Canal Saint-Martin from the Bassin de l'Arsenal (Walk 9) or, better still, from the Musée d'Orsay (Walk 4), which enables you to enjoy views of some of the city's best-known sights (the Musée d'Orsay itself, the Louvre, Notre-Dame and so on) from a different angle and without the more touristy atmosphere of the *bateaux-mouches*. The commentary (in French, but English too on request) is intelligent and informed, full of lively anecdotes, and the mood relaxed as the boat meanders through locks and alongside quays bordered with chestnut trees and old street lamps. Iron footbridges arch overhead, dotted with locals clutching *baguettes* as they peer down at the ever-fascinating sight of revolving bridges swinging into place, lock gates opening and shutting and the water climbing up inside the locks. The boat trip gives you a good view of the legendary **Hôtel du Nord** (Walk 7) and some interesting glimpses of the stylish architecture that is going up in many once-neglected districts, with big windows overlooking the canal, attractive balconies and decorative details, often fitting in surprisingly well with the traditional 19th-century blocks.

Two firms organise cruises: **Canauxrama** (13 quai de la Loire, 19e, 42-39-15-00) and **Paris Canal** (11 quai de la Loire, 19e, 42-40-96-97), generally leaving about 9.30 and again in the early afternoon. Check times locally and book in advance if possible, as the boats are quite small.

Marché aux Puces (flea market)

Ⓜ *Porte-de-Clignancourt.*

The days are long gone when you could count on picking up a bargain from one of the ramshackle stalls that made up Paris's famous flea market on the site of the old fortifications on the northern outskirts. The stalls are more like little shops now and the prices come into the antique (rather than junk) bracket. But it's still fun to stroll round and perhaps stop for a snack at one of the cafés. And you might just find something to take home in the way of a copper pan or a pewter jug (metalwork tends not to be as over-priced as most items) or a second-hand book.

Parc des Buttes-Chaumont

entrances in rue Manin, rue Botzaris, both 19e; Ⓜ *Buttes-Chaumont, Botzaris, bus 75 from the Pont-Neuf or the Marais.*

A delightful and romantic park, rather surprisingly a legacy of Baron Haussmann's era, as it is very different in spirit from most of his town-planning schemes: steep paths climb up grassy mounds (the park was landscaped from disused quarries), a tiny temple is perched on top of a rocky island in the middle of a lake, reached by a suspension bridge, and there are virtually no straight lines or vistas. A good place for taking the air if you are feeling stifled in central Paris, enjoying fine views and allowing children space to relax and play – there are various playgrounds and walking or sunbathing on the grass is allowed for once. There's a fairly grand restaurant (**Av Pavillon Puebla**, 42-08-92-62, closed Sun and Mon) in an elegant 19th-century building with lovely views and a much more modest one for light meals and drinks.

The Buttes-Chaumont can easily be combined with the **Canal Saint-Martin** and **La Villette** (see below).

Saint-Denis

Ⓜ *Saint-Denis-Basilique.*

Saint-Denis, a dreary-looking industrial town on the northern outskirts of Paris, has a fairly vibrant cultural life – the lively **Théâtre Gérard-Philipe** is here and an annual music festival is staged – but is best known for its cathedral, the first of the great Gothic cathedrals and the burial place of most of France's monarchs. The royal tombs have recently been restored and relit and you can now study their often superb sculpture at close quarters: an enlightened recent decision means that they are no longer chained off and instead of a guided tour you can wander at will, listening to a mostly excellent commentary in French or English from headphones.

A number of early kings, starting with Dagobert in the 6th century, were buried on this spot, revered as the place where the martyred St Denis is said to have collapsed after walking from Montmartre with his head clutched in his hands (Walk 10). But the cathedral (officially a basilica until the 1960s, hence the name of the

243

métro station) dates from the first half of the 12th century, when Abbot Suger built one of the first examples of the pure Gothic style, which inspired many of the later Gothic cathedrals. It was partly rebuilt by Pierre de Montreuil (the architect of the Sainte-Chapelle, Walk 1) in the 13th century and has been altered and restored many times over the centuries.

Its chief interest lies in the tombs, several of them designed by major architects and sculptors: Philibert Delorme and Primaticcio worked on the beautiful monument to François Ier and Claude de France, for instance, and Germain Pilon on François II's. Although the remains of the royal occupants were dispersed during the Revolution, as you move from tomb to tomb you experience a powerful feeling of the history of France unfolding before you, and the sculptures of the monarchs themselves, many of them carved during their lifetime, help you to retain a picture in your mind of the kings and queens whose palaces you have been visiting during your stay in Paris – children, too, find the tombs fascinating and learn some history in the process.

Saint-Denis also has an interesting museum, the **Musée Municipal d'Art et d'Histoire**, housed since the early eighties in a restored Carmelite monastery dating from the 17th century (22bis rue Gabriel-Péri, closed Sun morning and all day Tue). Appropriately for this fairly working-class town, it has a rich collection of items connected with the history of ordinary working people and with the Paris Commune. But you can also admire the work of Henri Daumier (over 4,000 engravings and lithographs), a modern art collection and rooms devoted to the life and work of the poet Paul Eluard, who was born in Saint-Denis.

La Villette

Cité des Sciences et de l'Industrie *Parc de la Villette, 30 av Corentin-Cariou, 19e, closed Mon;* Ⓜ *Porte de la Villette, Porte de Pantin, bus 75 from Pont-Neuf or the Marais.*

The slaughterhouses and meat market at La Villette in the north-east of Paris, originally built in the time of Napoleon III but modernised at vast expense in the sixties, were closed down in 1974 and subsequently partly demolished. At the beginning of the eighties a decision was taken to turn what was by then little more than waste ground beside the Canal de l'Ourcq and the Canal Saint-Denis into a vast park dominated by a futuristic science and technology museum and various other cultural and leisure facilities, the idea being to transform a dingy area, full of run-down industrial buildings, into a centre of youth culture. 'Science City' opened in 1986 and has proved very popular, especially with children, who spend happy hours working computers and becoming involved in projects ranging from astronomy to plant propagation and a series of displays connected with environmental

Saint-Denis: the magnificent Renaissance tomb of Louis XII and Anne de Bretagne

topics. Walks and demonstrations take place at frequent intervals, the centre also includes a big public library, a planetarium, an 'invention area', a cinema, and 'Explora', the permanent collection, is complemented by a whole host of temporary shows.

Just outside the building is **La Géode**, a shiny spherical cinema with a screen forming a 1,000-metre hemisphere, which has become one of the sights of Paris. And the Parc de la Villette also includes **La Grande Halle**, the old cattle market, built in 1867 in iron and steel and now used for exhibitions, trade fairs and events of various kinds; **Le Zénith**, a huge rock concert venue; the **Cité de la Musique**, a music academy and concert hall (due to open in 1991, probably with a small musical instrument museum), **Le Dragon**, a huge and brightly coloured toboggan beside the canal, the **Paris-Villette Theatre** and **Arletty Cinema**, the **Maison de la Villette**, an exhibition centre devoted to the history of the area in the **Rotonde des Vétérinaires**, and a series of bright red '**Folies**' dotted about the park, all of them variations on the theme of a cube and housing children's workshops and video areas, a café, an information centre, even an accident and emergency centre.

It's all great fun and though it can seem tiring, as everything is so spread out, the signposting is mainly excellent and you can pick up good explanatory leaflets in English or French from the information centre or the Cité des Sciences. You're bound to need refreshments at some point: **Croixement** (rond-point des Canaux, 42-41-82-00) is a casual but quite stylish brasserie-cum-bar inside the park, with a few tables outside in fine weather; or you might like to pay homage to the butchers and slaughterhouse men who once gave the district its character by walking out beyond the Grande Halle and the splendid **Lion Fountain** to the avenue Jean-Jaurès, where you can enjoy a hearty meat dish in one of the long-famous restaurants like **Au Boeuf Couronné** at no. 188 (42-39-44-44, closed Sun) or **Dagorno** at no. 190 (40-40-09-39), or even **Au Cochon d'Or** at no. 192 if you're feeling rich (42-45-46-46).

You can reach La Villette by boat along the **Canal Saint-Martin** (see above), followed by a short trip on a launch at weekends and during school holidays right into the Parc de la Villette, or a pleasant walk along the canal. Alternatively you can enjoy this walk by taking the métro to Ⓜ Jean-Jaurès, stopping to admire Ledoux's **Rotonde de la Villette**, one of the two surviving toll houses from the Tax-Collectors' Wall (box, History), then walking beside the **Bassin de la Villette**, perhaps stopping off for lunch at **Le Cargo** (41bis quai de la Loire, 19e), a rather trendy restaurant with a few sought-after tables overlooking the marina, or at one of the modest cafés-bistrots, traditionally frequented by bargees and lock-keepers, that are gradually being smartened up as the Stalingrad–Villette area takes on a new lease of life: **Le Bistrot du Port**, perhaps (50 quai de la Loire, 19e, closed Sat and for dinner on Sun). Then continue past some old warehouses converted into artists' studios along the **quai de la Marne**, cross the footbridge (which may be raised to let a barge through) and walk on beside the Canal de l'Ourcq into the Parc de la Villette.

Index

Churches, *hôtels* and museums are listed under their name, with the letters (C), (H) or (M) as appropriate.

INDEX